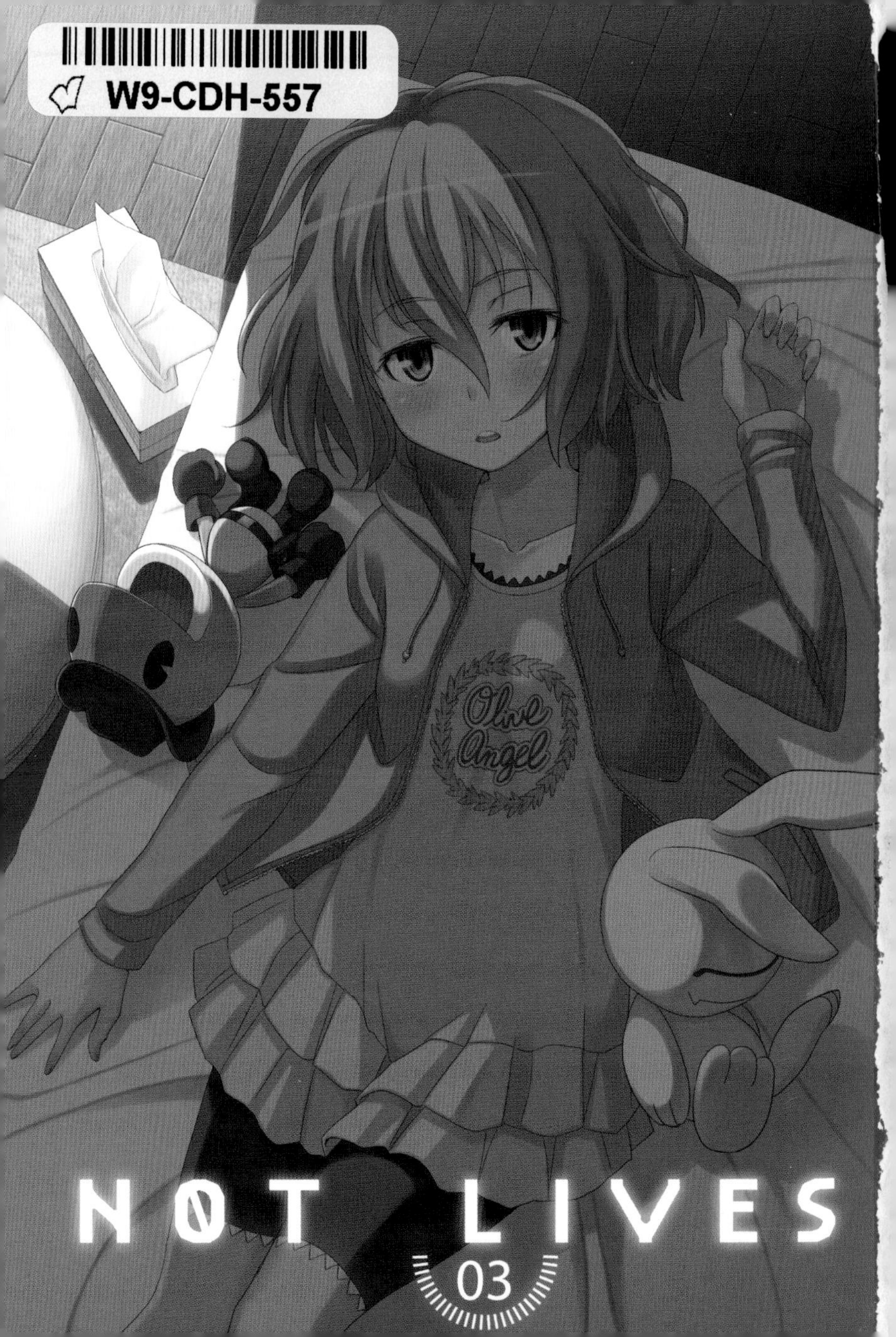
Olive Angel
N0T LIVES
03

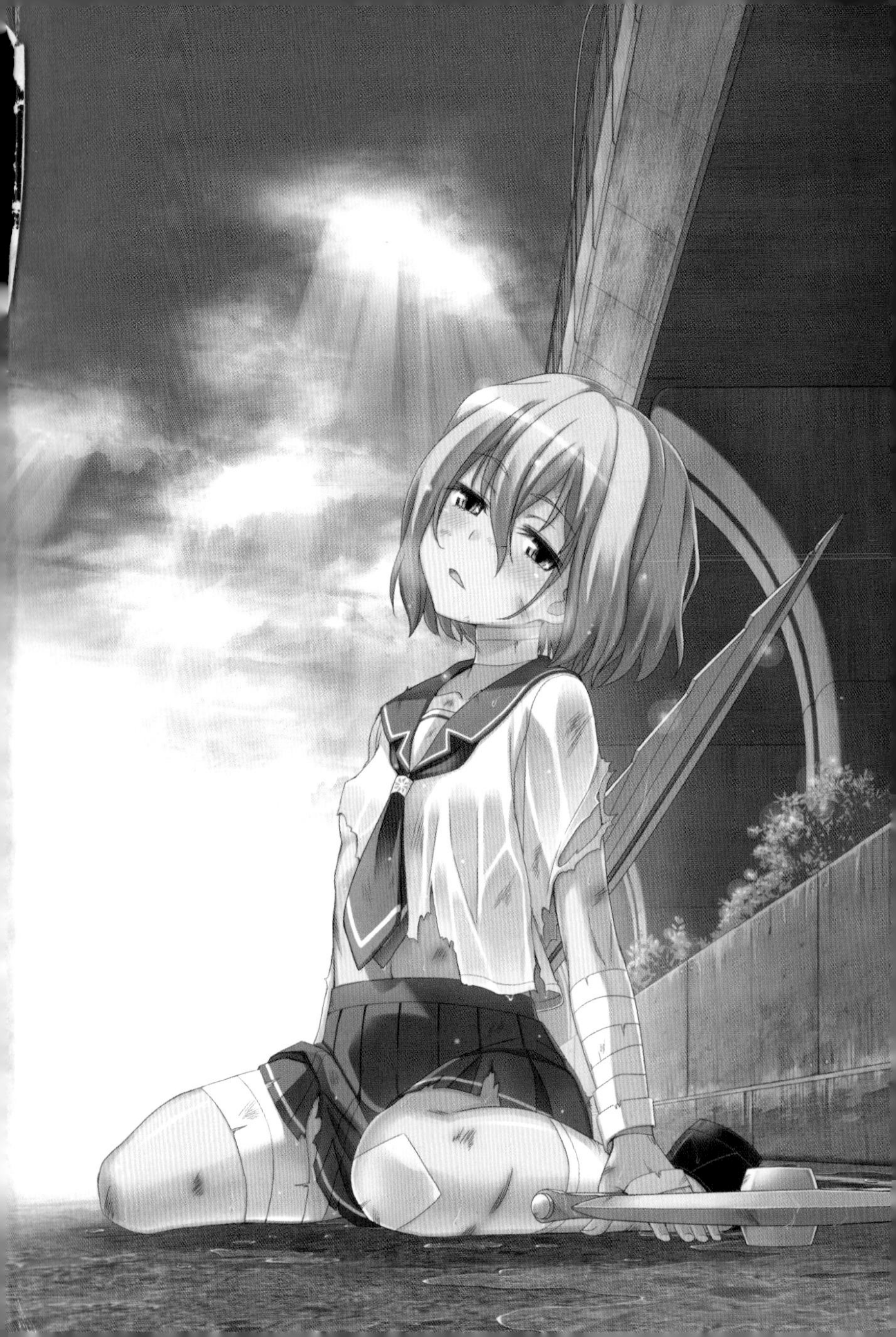

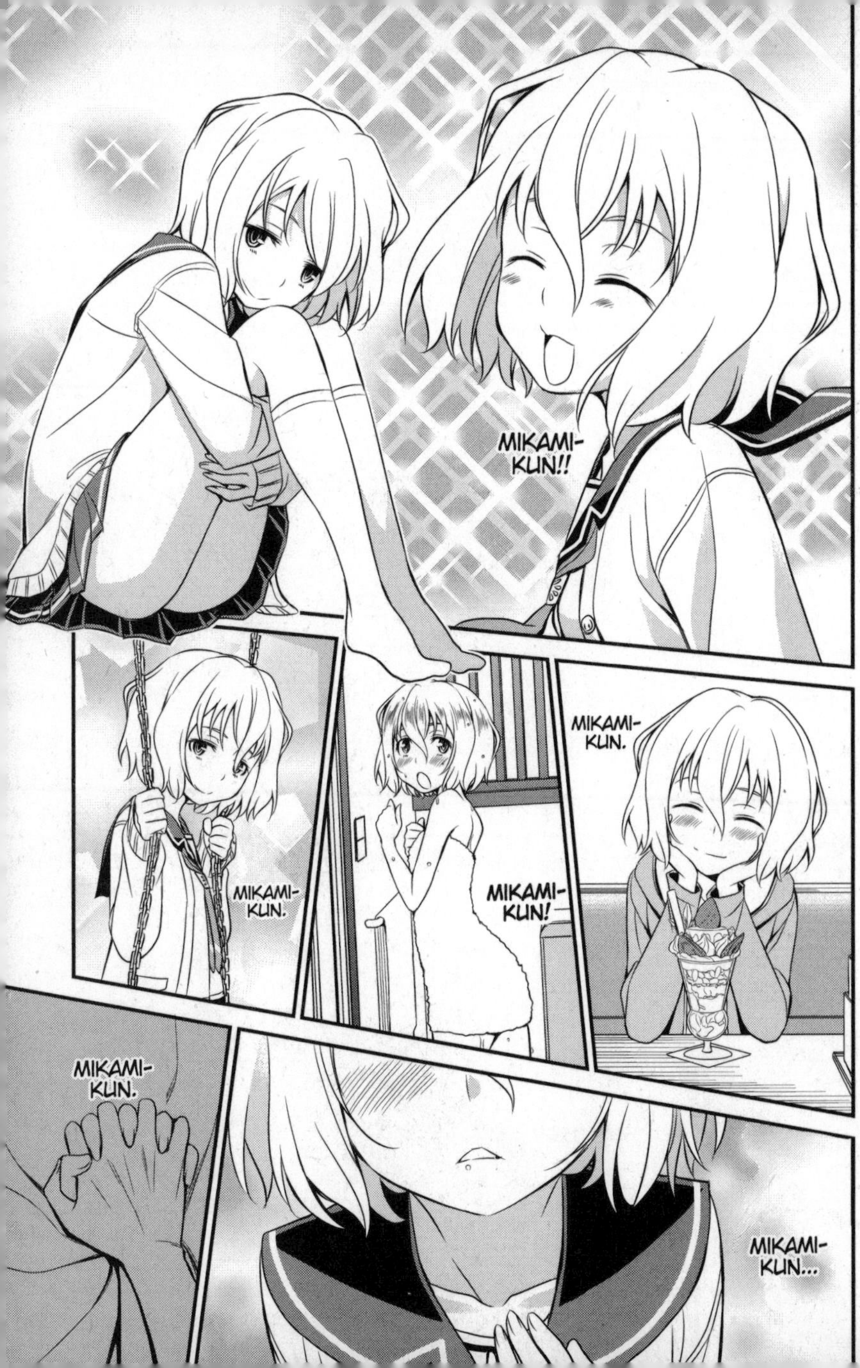
MIKAMI-KUN!!
MIKAMI-KUN.
MIKAMI-KUN!
MIKAMI-KUN.
MIKAMI-KUN...
MIKAMI-KUN.

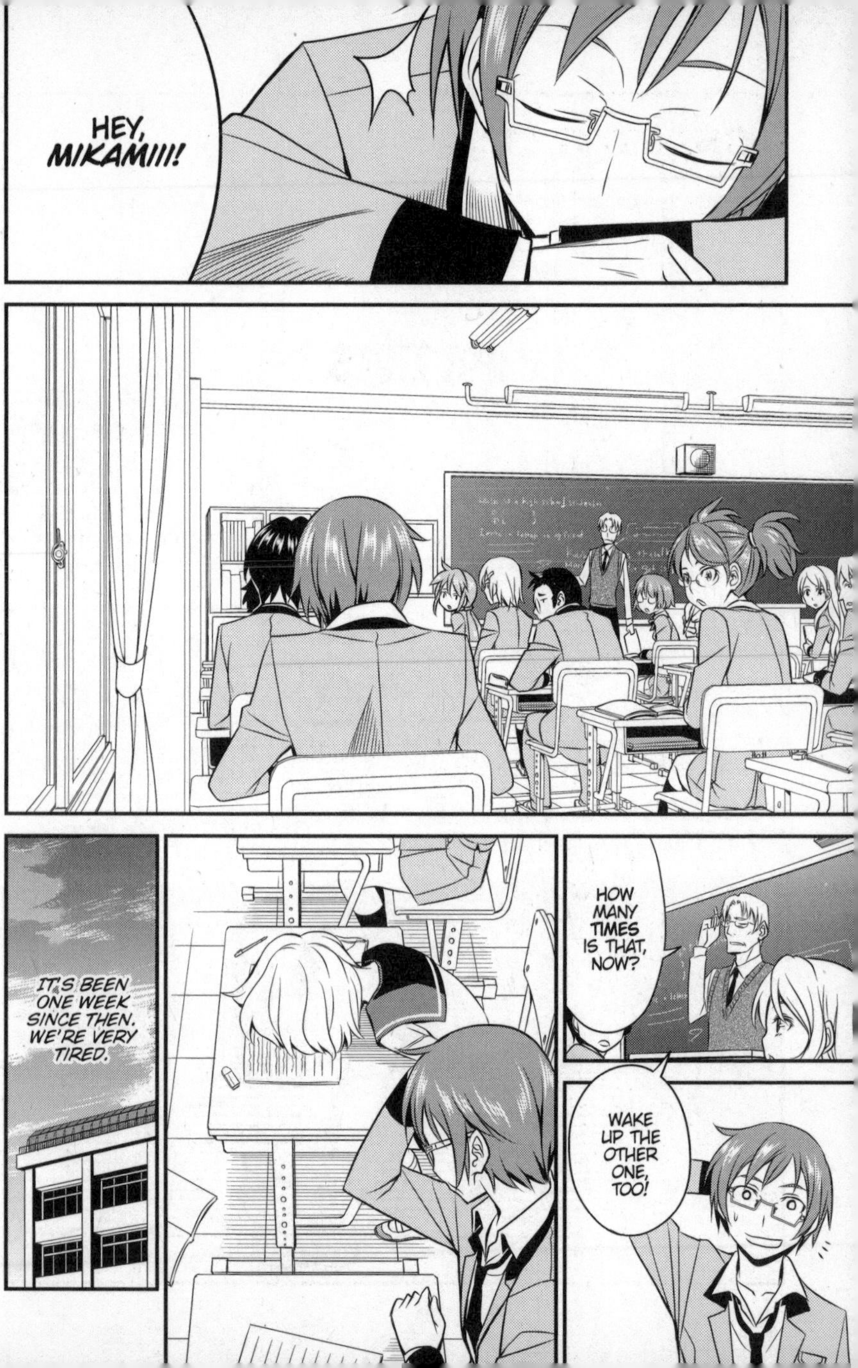
HEY, MIKAMIII!
HOW MANY TIMES IS THAT, NOW?
WAKE UP THE OTHER ONE, TOO!
IT'S BEEN ONE WEEK SINCE THEN. WE'RE VERY TIRED.

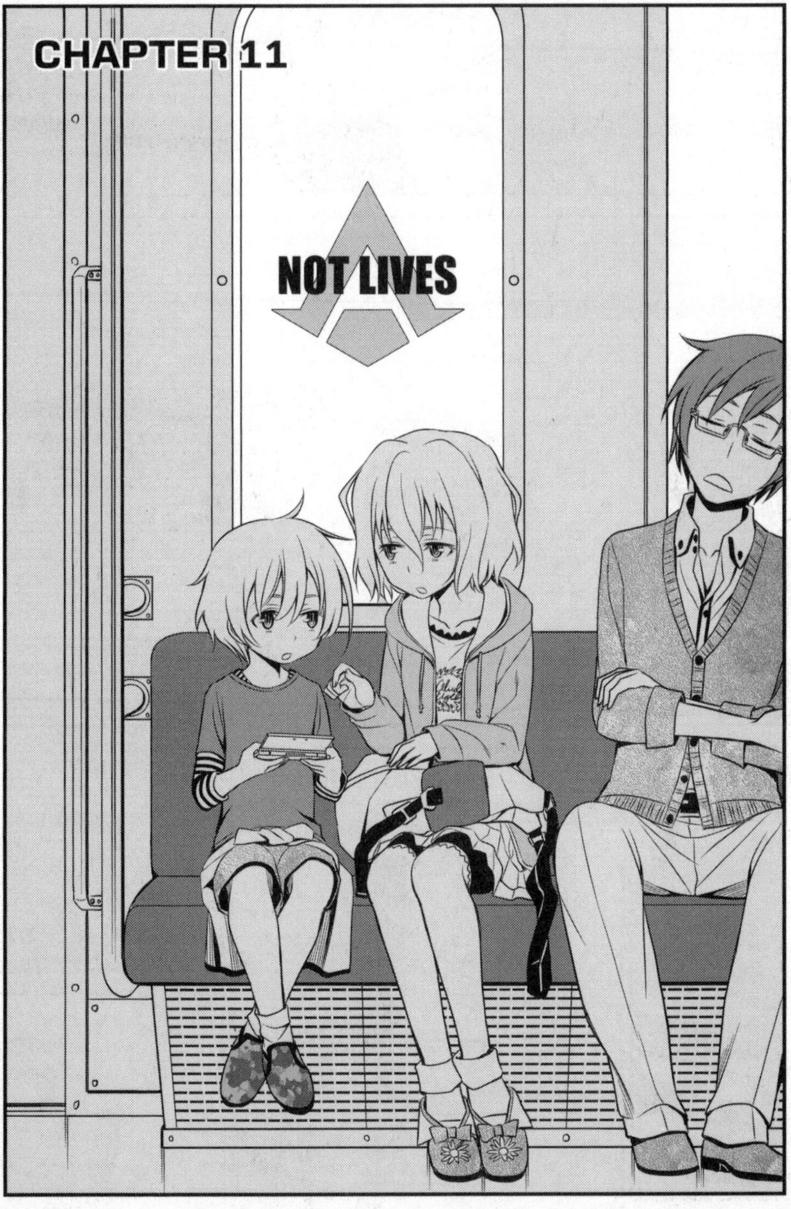
CHAPTER 11
NOT LIVES

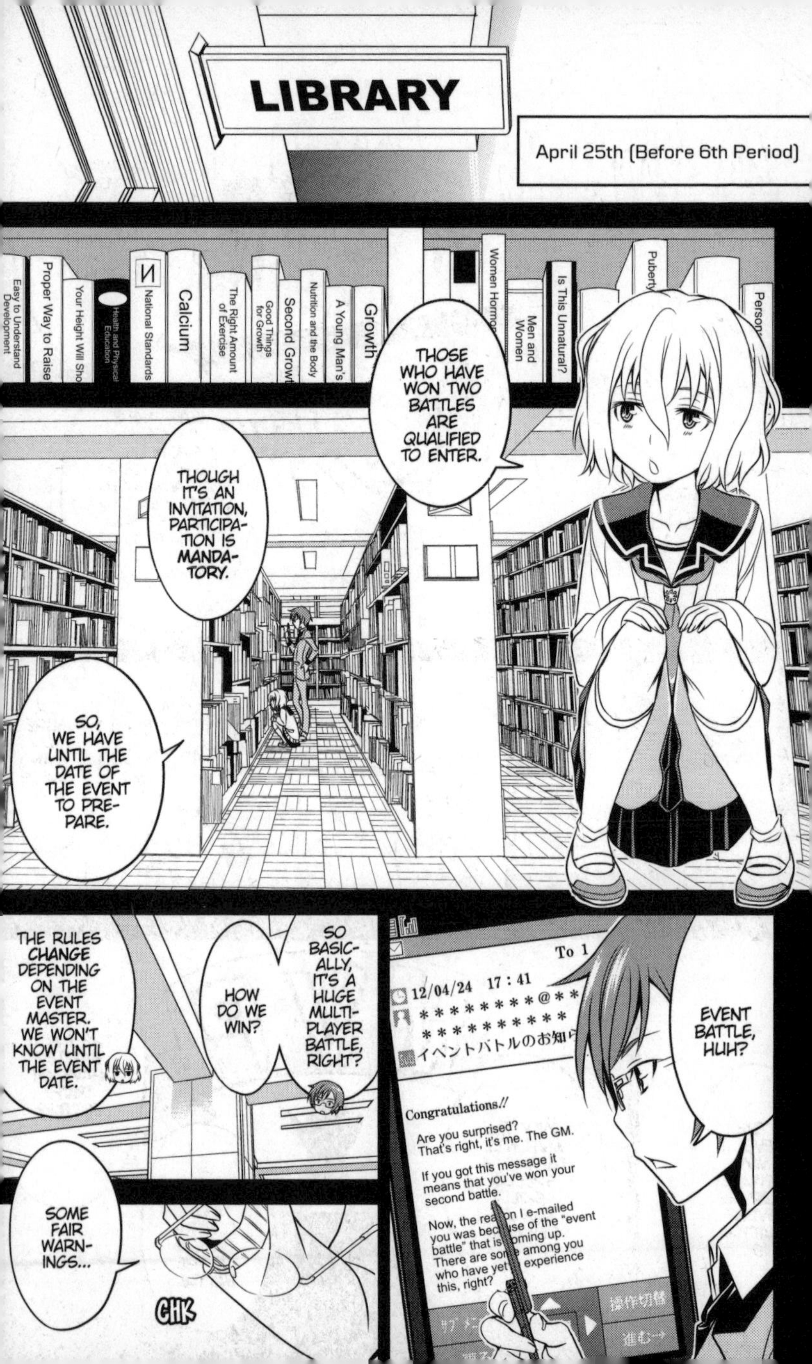
LIBRARY
April 25th (Before 6th Period)
Person
Puberty
Is This Unnatural?
Men and Women
Women Hormo
Growth
A Young Man's
Nutrition and the Body
Second Growt
Good Things for Growth
The Right Amount of Exercise
Calcium
National Standards
Health and Physical Education
Your Height Will Sho
Proper Way to Raise
Easy to Understand Development
THOSE WHO HAVE WON TWO BATTLES ARE QUALIFIED TO ENTER.
THOUGH IT'S AN INVITATION, PARTICIPATION IS MANDATORY.
SO, WE HAVE UNTIL THE DATE OF THE EVENT TO PREPARE.
EVENT BATTLE, HUH?
To 1
12/04/24 17:41
********@**
**********
イベントバトルのお知ら
Congratulations.!!
Are you surprised? That's right, it's me. The GM.
If you got this message it means that you've won your second battle.
Now, the rea on I e-mailed you was bec use of the "event battle" that is oming up. There are so e among you who have yet experience this, right?
操作切替
進む→
SO BASICALLY, IT'S A HUGE MULTIPLAYER BATTLE, RIGHT?
HOW DO WE WIN?
THE RULES CHANGE DEPENDING ON THE EVENT MASTER. WE WON'T KNOW UNTIL THE EVENT DATE.
SOME FAIR WARNINGS...
CHK

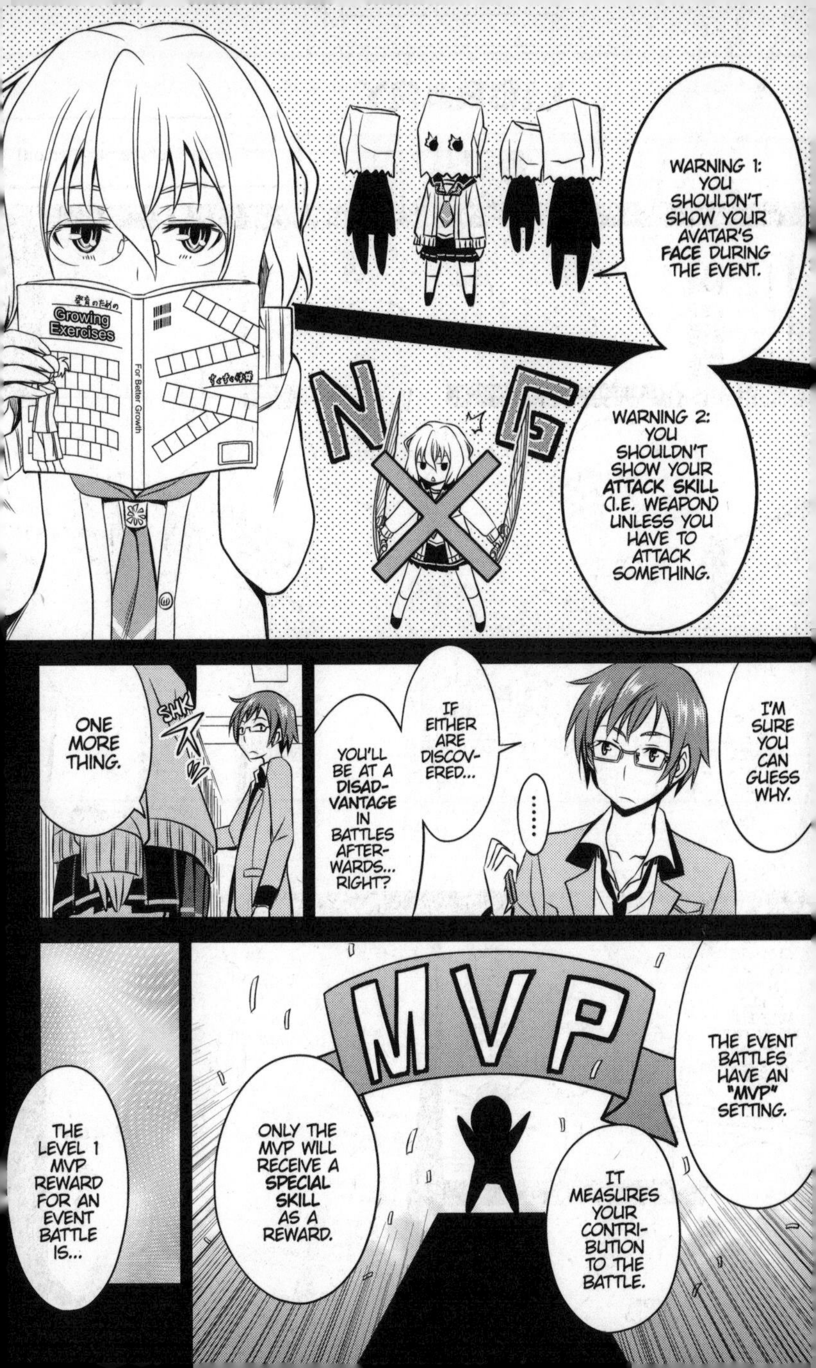
WARNING 1: YOU SHOULDN'T SHOW YOUR AVATAR'S FACE DURING THE EVENT.
WARNING 2: YOU SHOULDN'T SHOW YOUR ATTACK SKILL (I.E. WEAPON) UNLESS YOU HAVE TO ATTACK SOMETHING.
NG
Growing Exercises
For Better Growth
I'M SURE YOU CAN GUESS WHY.
IF EITHER ARE DISCOVERED...
......
YOU'LL BE AT A DISADVANTAGE IN BATTLES AFTERWARDS... RIGHT?
SHK
ONE MORE THING.
THE EVENT BATTLES HAVE AN "MVP" SETTING.
MVP
IT MEASURES YOUR CONTRIBUTION TO THE BATTLE.
ONLY THE MVP WILL RECEIVE A SPECIAL SKILL AS A REWARD.
THE LEVEL 1 MVP REWARD FOR AN EVENT BATTLE IS...

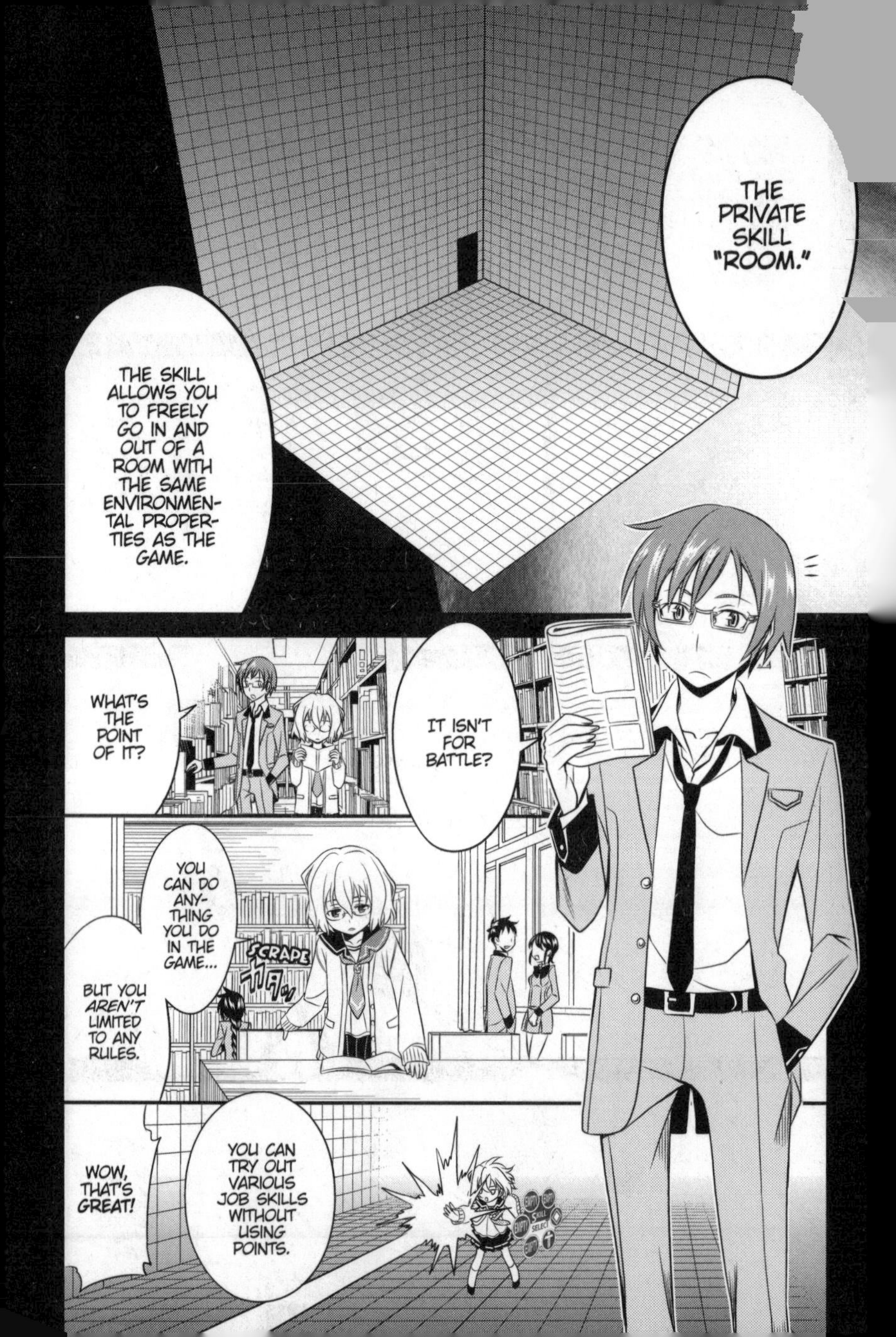
THE PRIVATE SKILL "ROOM."
THE SKILL ALLOWS YOU TO FREELY GO IN AND OUT OF A ROOM WITH THE SAME ENVIRONMENTAL PROPERTIES AS THE GAME.
IT ISN'T FOR BATTLE?
WHAT'S THE POINT OF IT?
YOU CAN DO ANYTHING YOU DO IN THE GAME...
SCRAPE
ガタッ
BUT YOU AREN'T LIMITED TO ANY RULES.
YOU CAN TRY OUT VARIOUS JOB SKILLS WITHOUT USING POINTS.
WOW, THAT'S GREAT!

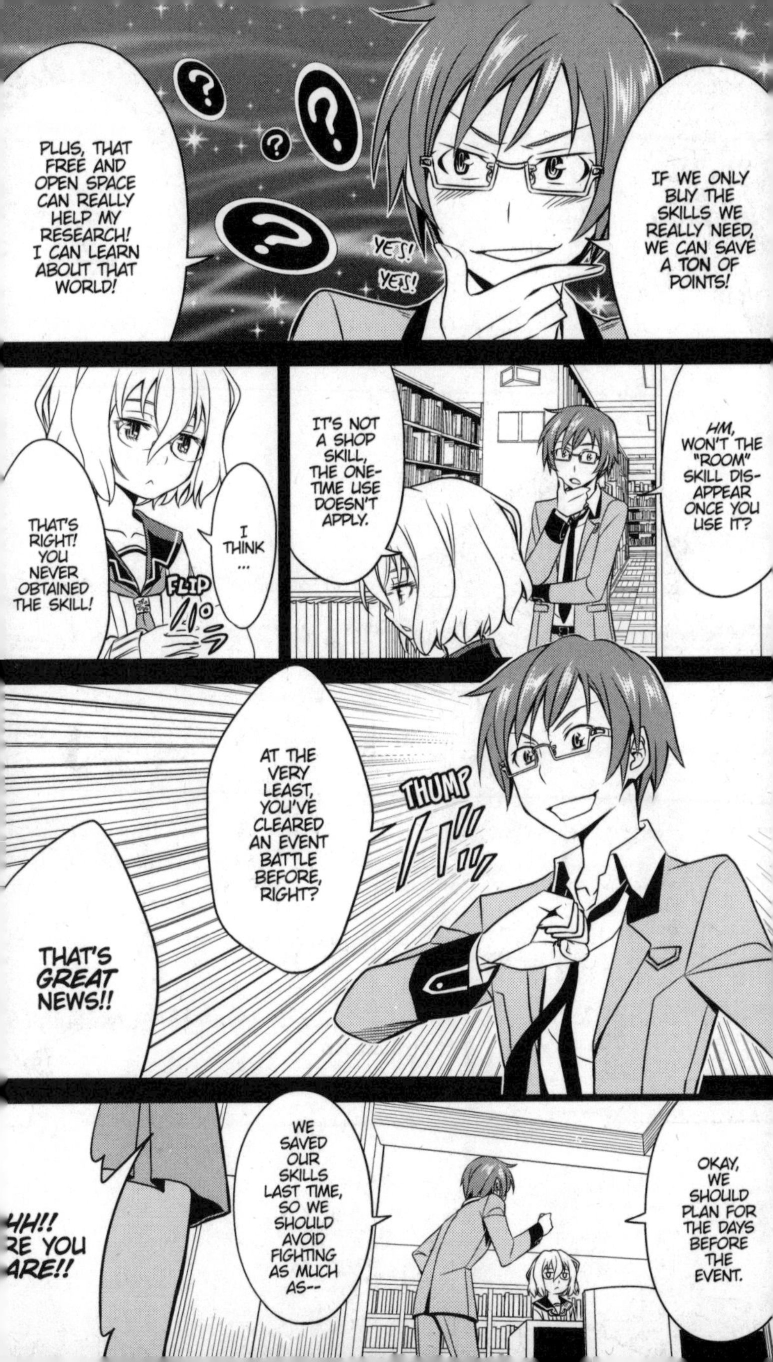
IF WE ONLY BUY THE SKILLS WE REALLY NEED, WE CAN SAVE A TON OF POINTS!
YES! YES!
PLUS, THAT FREE AND OPEN SPACE CAN REALLY HELP MY RESEARCH! I CAN LEARN ABOUT THAT WORLD!
HM, WON'T THE "ROOM" SKILL DISAPPEAR ONCE YOU USE IT?
IT'S NOT A SHOP SKILL, THE ONE-TIME USE DOESN'T APPLY.
I THINK ...
FLIP
THAT'S RIGHT! YOU NEVER OBTAINED THE SKILL!
THUMP
AT THE VERY LEAST, YOU'VE CLEARED AN EVENT BATTLE BEFORE, RIGHT?
THAT'S GREAT NEWS!!
OKAY, WE SHOULD PLAN FOR THE DAYS BEFORE THE EVENT.
WE SAVED OUR SKILLS LAST TIME, SO WE SHOULD AVOID FIGHTING AS MUCH AS--
HH!! RE YOU ARE!!

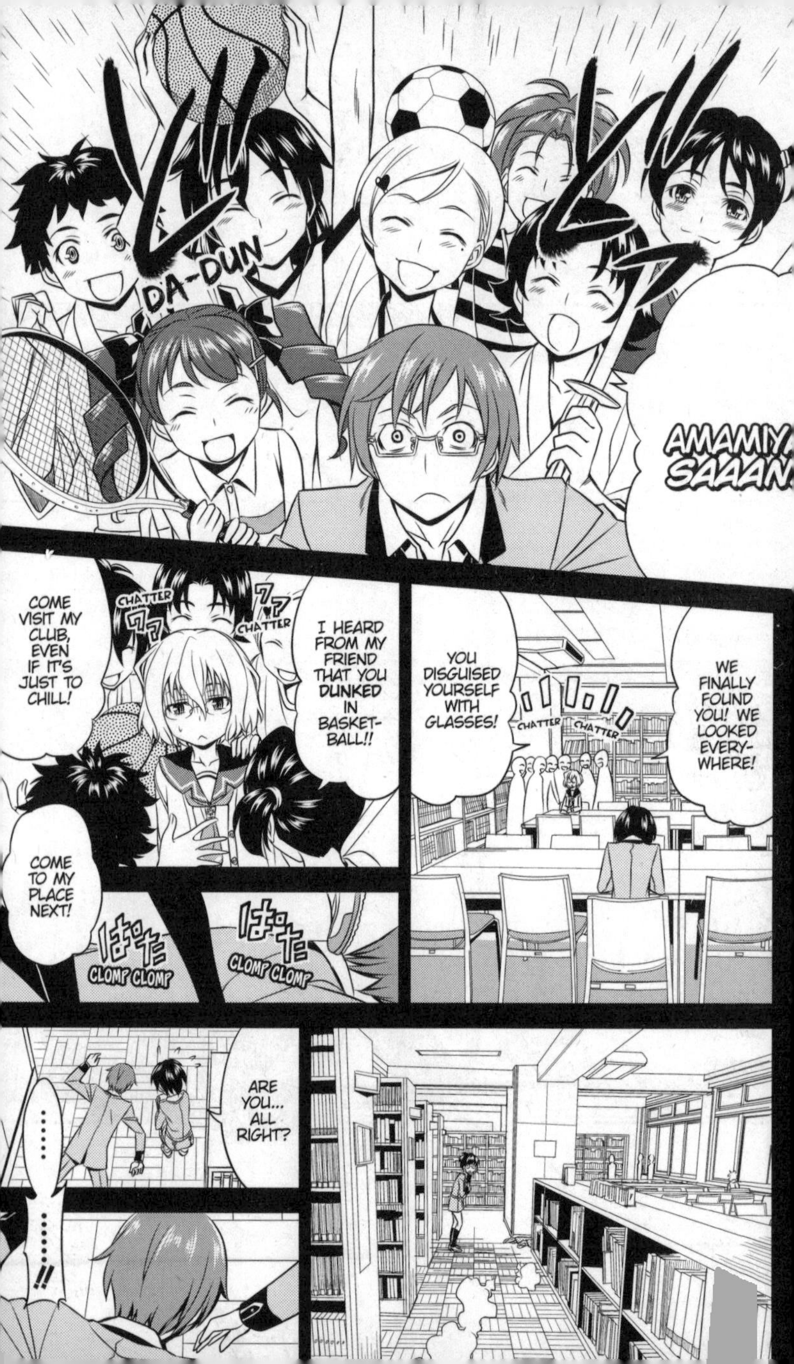
AMAMIY
SAAAN
DA-DUN
WE FINALLY FOUND YOU! WE LOOKED EVERY-WHERE!
YOU DISGUISED YOURSELF WITH GLASSES!
CHATTER
CHATTER
I HEARD FROM MY FRIEND THAT YOU DUNKED IN BASKET-BALL!!
CHATTER
CHATTER
COME VISIT MY CLUB, EVEN IF IT'S JUST TO CHILL!
COME TO MY PLACE NEXT!
CLOMP CLOMP
CLOMP CLOMP
ARE YOU... ALL RIGHT?
......
......!!

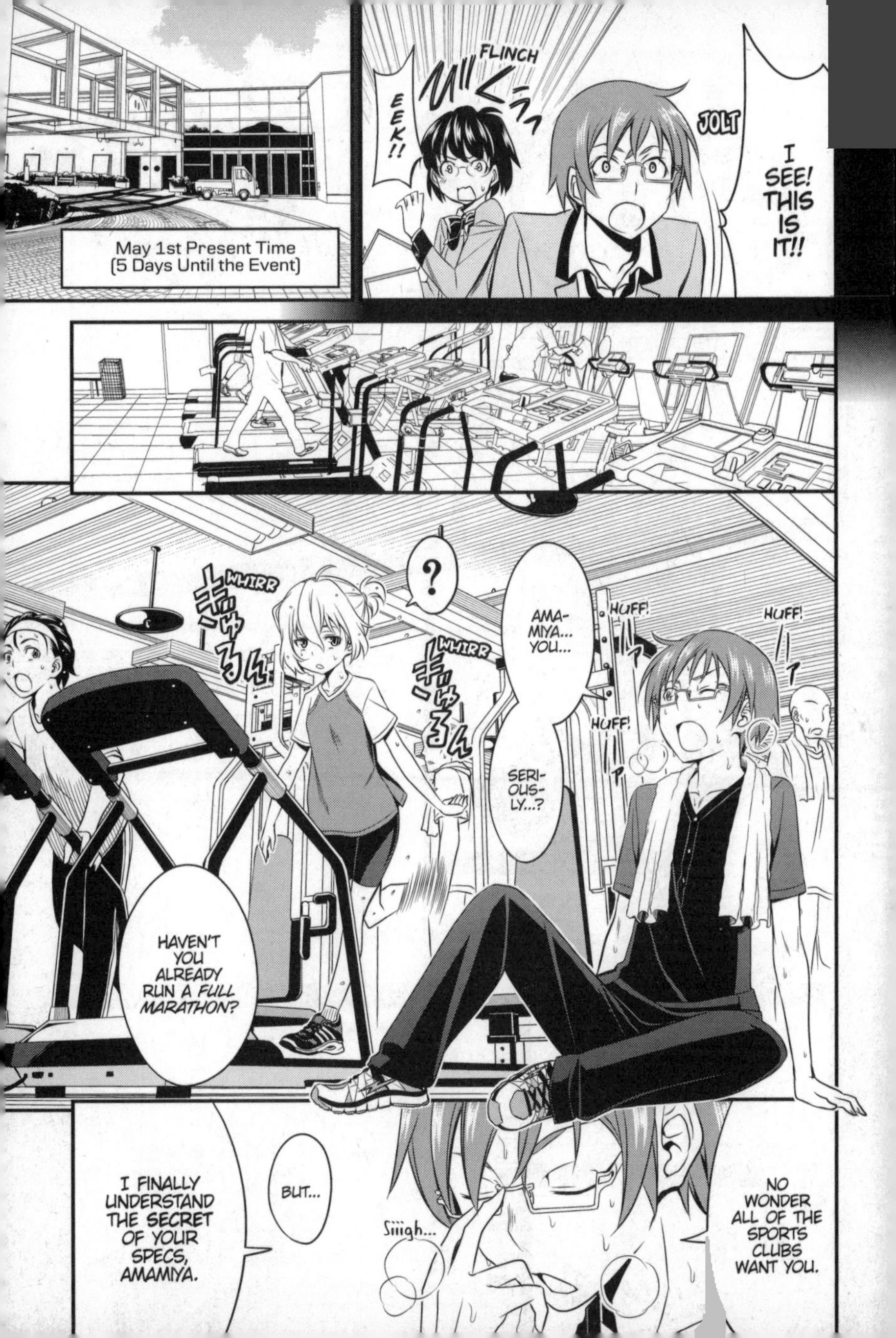
I SEE! THIS IS IT!!
JOLT
FLINCH
EEK!!
May 1st Present Time
(5 Days Until the Event)
HUFF!
HUFF!
AMA-MIYA... YOU...
HUFF!
SERI-OUS-LY...?
?
WHIRR
WHIRR
HAVEN'T YOU ALREADY RUN A *FULL MARATHON*?
NO WONDER ALL OF THE SPORTS CLUBS WANT YOU.
Siiigh...
BUT...
I FINALLY UNDERSTAND THE SECRET OF YOUR SPECS, AMAMIYA.

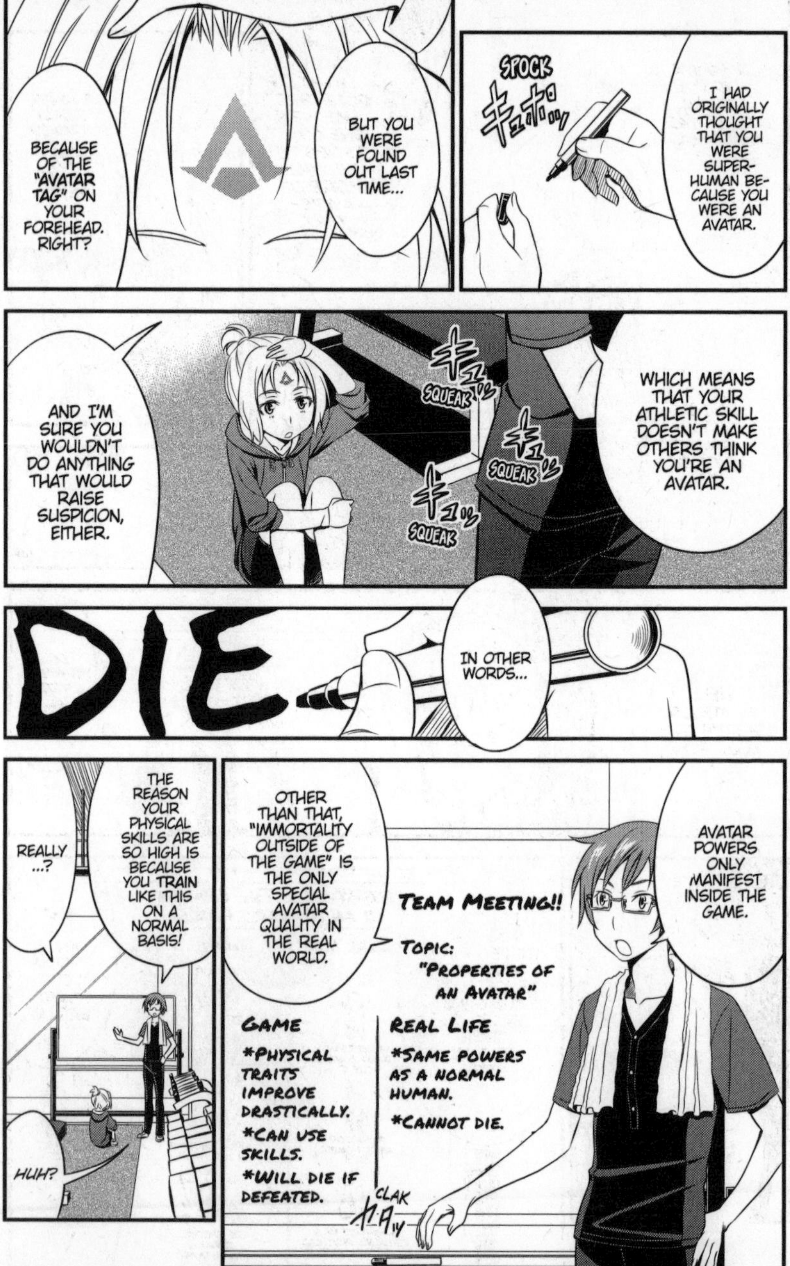
SPOCK
I HAD ORIGINALLY THOUGHT THAT YOU WERE SUPER-HUMAN BECAUSE YOU WERE AN AVATAR.
BUT YOU WERE FOUND OUT LAST TIME...
BECAUSE OF THE "AVATAR TAG" ON YOUR FOREHEAD. RIGHT?
WHICH MEANS THAT YOUR ATHLETIC SKILL DOESN'T MAKE OTHERS THINK YOU'RE AN AVATAR.
SQUEAK
SQUEAK
SQUEAK
AND I'M SURE YOU WOULDN'T DO ANYTHING THAT WOULD RAISE SUSPICION, EITHER.
IN OTHER WORDS...
DIE
AVATAR POWERS ONLY MANIFEST INSIDE THE GAME.
OTHER THAN THAT, "IMMORTALITY OUTSIDE OF THE GAME" IS THE ONLY SPECIAL AVATAR QUALITY IN THE REAL WORLD.
TEAM MEETING!!
TOPIC: "PROPERTIES OF AN AVATAR"
REAL LIFE
*SAME POWERS AS A NORMAL HUMAN.
*CANNOT DIE.
GAME
*PHYSICAL TRAITS IMPROVE DRASTICALLY.
*CAN USE SKILLS.
*WILL DIE IF DEFEATED.
CLAK
THE REASON YOUR PHYSICAL SKILLS ARE SO HIGH IS BECAUSE YOU TRAIN LIKE THIS ON A NORMAL BASIS!
REALLY ...?
HUH?

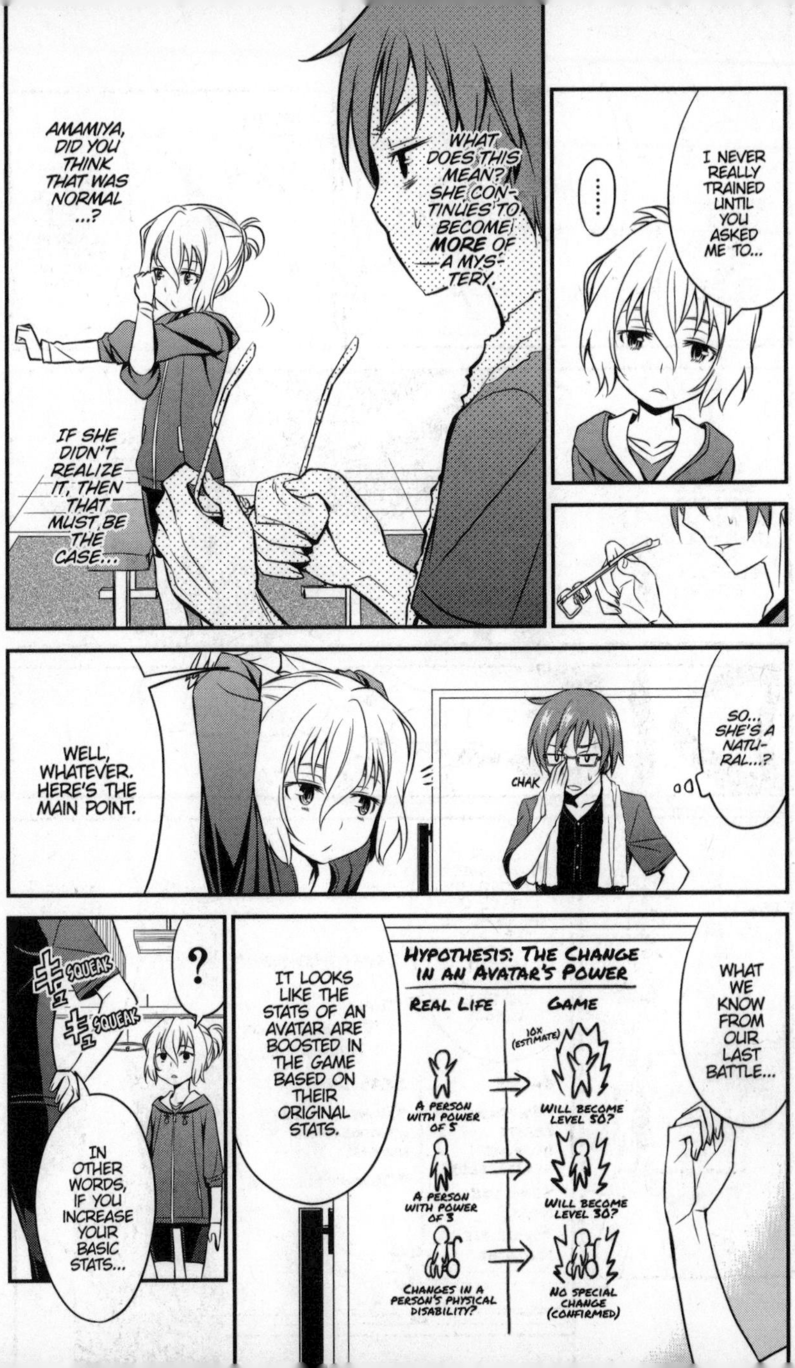
I NEVER REALLY TRAINED UNTIL YOU ASKED ME TO...
……
WHAT DOES THIS MEAN? SHE CONTINUES TO BECOME MORE OF A MYSTERY.
AMAMIYA, DID YOU THINK THAT WAS NORMAL ...?
IF SHE DIDN'T REALIZE IT, THEN THAT MUST BE THE CASE...
SO... SHE'S A NATURAL...?
CHAK
WELL, WHATEVER. HERE'S THE MAIN POINT.
WHAT WE KNOW FROM OUR LAST BATTLE...
HYPOTHESIS: THE CHANGE IN AN AVATAR'S POWER
REAL LIFE
GAME
10X (ESTIMATE)
A PERSON WITH POWER OF 5
WILL BECOME LEVEL 50?
A PERSON WITH POWER OF 3
WILL BECOME LEVEL 30?
CHANGES IN A PERSON'S PHYSICAL DISABILITY?
NO SPECIAL CHANGE (CONFIRMED)
IT LOOKS LIKE THE STATS OF AN AVATAR ARE BOOSTED IN THE GAME BASED ON THEIR ORIGINAL STATS.
?
SQUEAK
SQUEAK
IN OTHER WORDS, IF YOU INCREASE YOUR BASIC STATS...

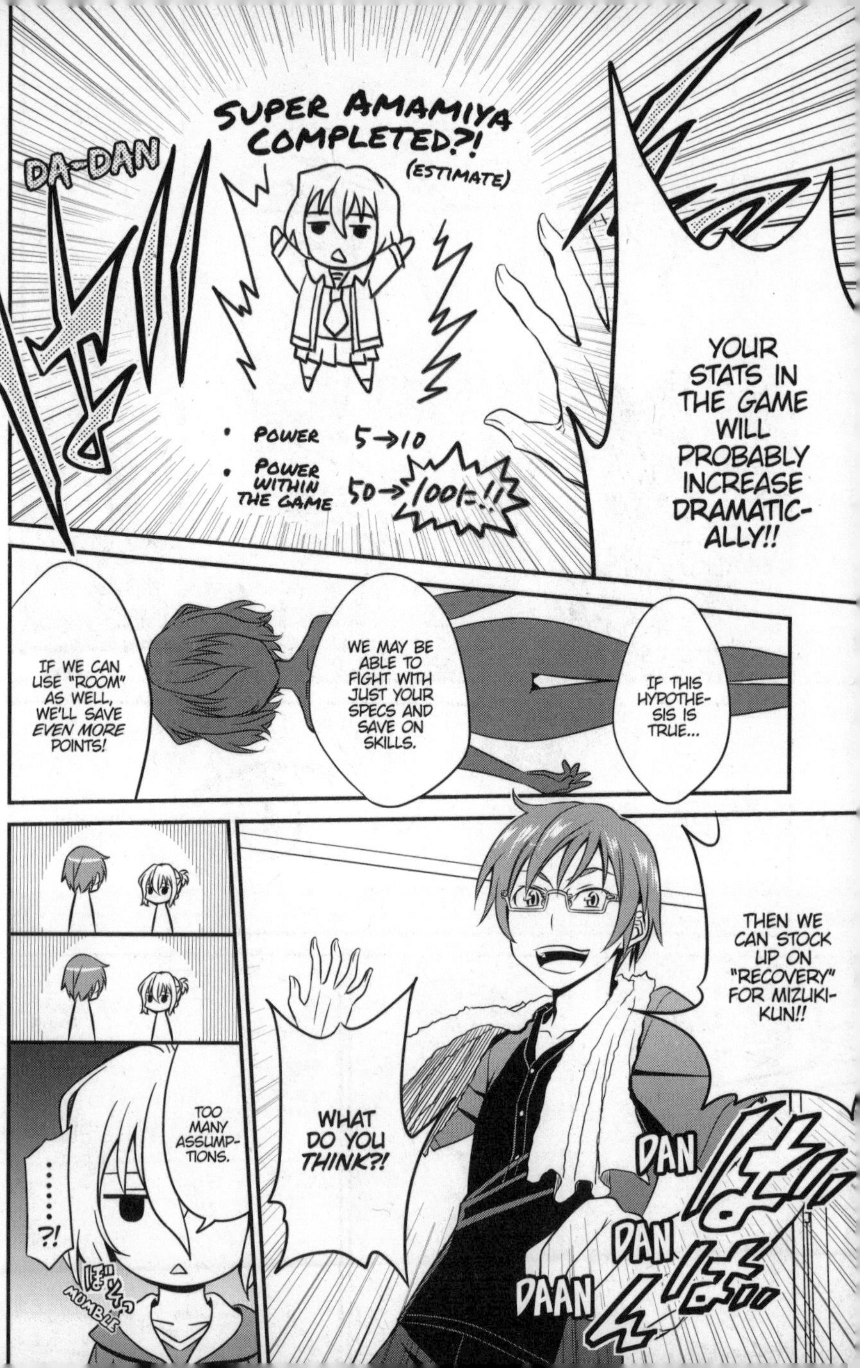
YOUR STATS IN THE GAME WILL PROBABLY INCREASE DRAMATICALLY!!
DA-DAN
SUPER AMAMIYA COMPLETED?!
(ESTIMATE)
• POWER 5→10
• POWER WITHIN THE GAME 50→100!!
IF THIS HYPOTHESIS IS TRUE...
WE MAY BE ABLE TO FIGHT WITH JUST YOUR SPECS AND SAVE ON SKILLS.
IF WE CAN USE "ROOM" AS WELL, WE'LL SAVE *EVEN MORE* POINTS!
THEN WE CAN STOCK UP ON "RECOVERY" FOR MIZUKI-KUN!!
WHAT DO YOU THINK?!
DAN
DAN
DAAN
TOO MANY ASSUMPTIONS.
......?!
MUMBLE

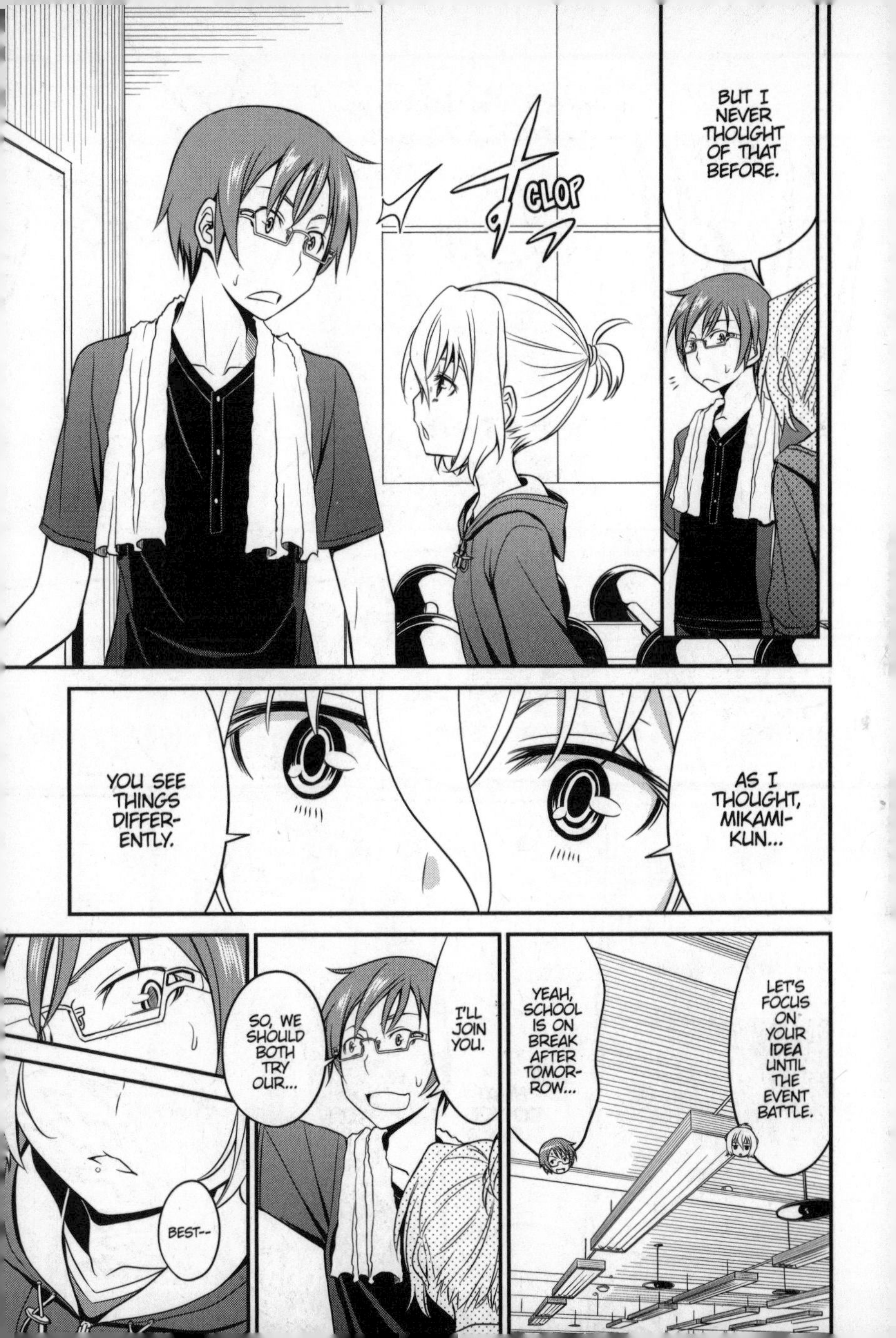
BUT I NEVER THOUGHT OF THAT BEFORE.
CLOP
AS I THOUGHT, MIKAMI-KUN...
YOU SEE THINGS DIFFER-ENTLY.
LET'S FOCUS ON YOUR IDEA UNTIL THE EVENT BATTLE.
YEAH, SCHOOL IS ON BREAK AFTER TOMOR-ROW...
I'LL JOIN YOU.
SO, WE SHOULD BOTH TRY OUR...
BEST--

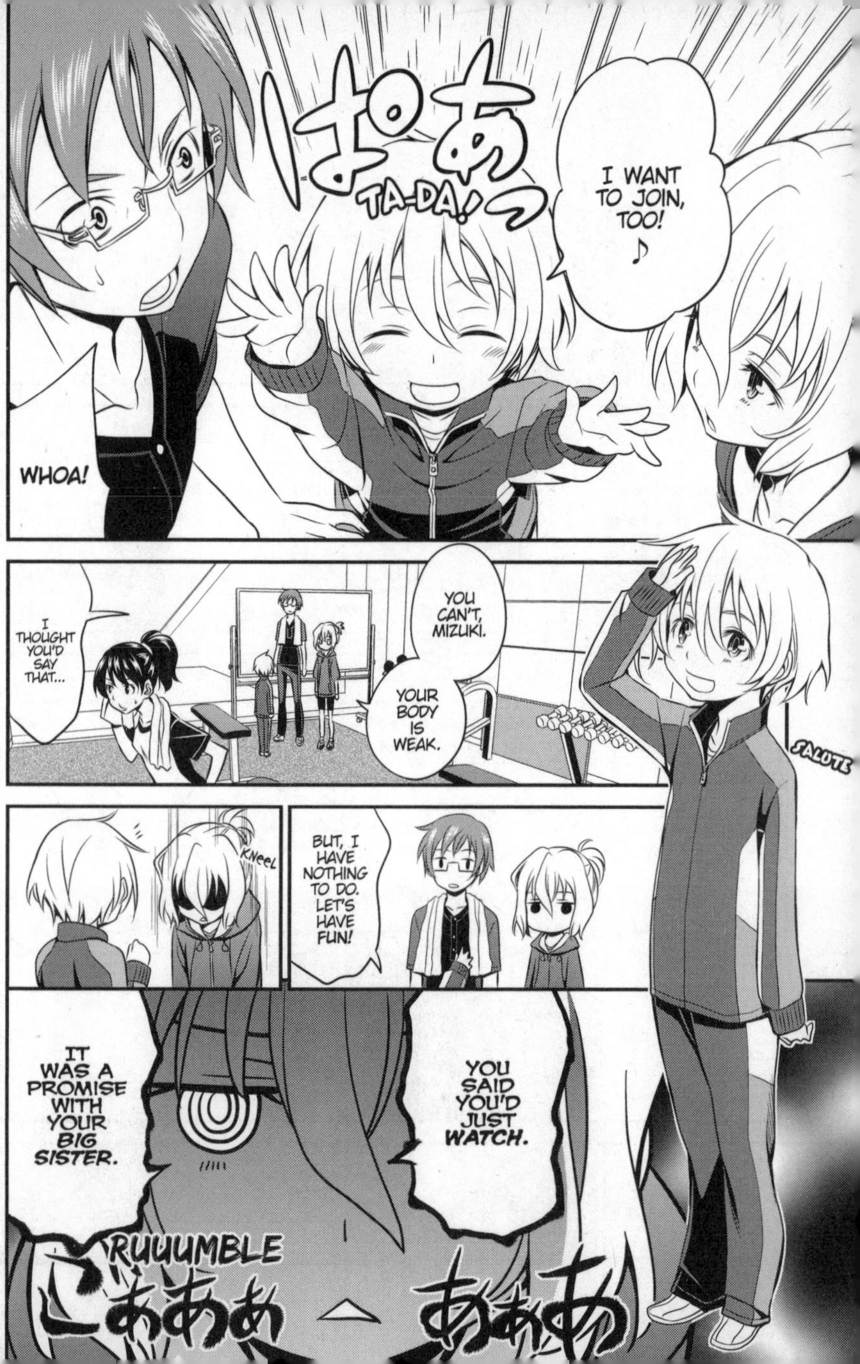
I WANT TO JOIN, TOO! ♪
ぱあっ
TA-DA!
WHOA!
SALUTE
YOU CAN'T, MIZUKI.
YOUR BODY IS WEAK.
I THOUGHT YOU'D SAY THAT...
BUT, I HAVE NOTHING TO DO. LET'S HAVE FUN!
KNEEL
YOU SAID YOU'D JUST WATCH.
IT WAS A PROMISE WITH YOUR BIG SISTER.
RUUUMBLE
ごあああ
あぁぁ

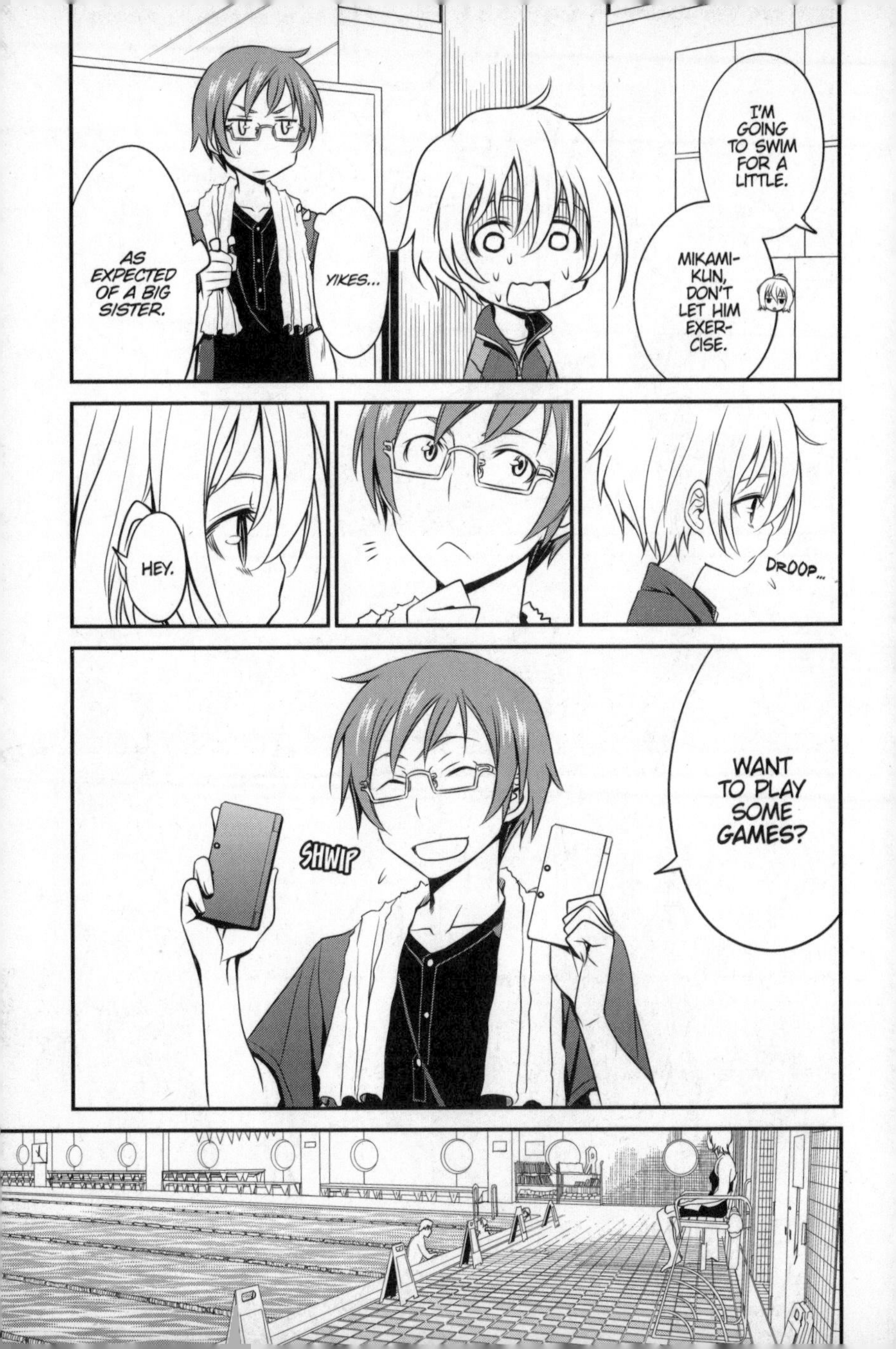
I'M GOING TO SWIM FOR A LITTLE.
MIKAMI-KUN, DON'T LET HIM EXER-CISE.
YIKES...
AS EXPECTED OF A BIG SISTER.
DROOP...
HEY.
WANT TO PLAY SOME GAMES?
SHWIP

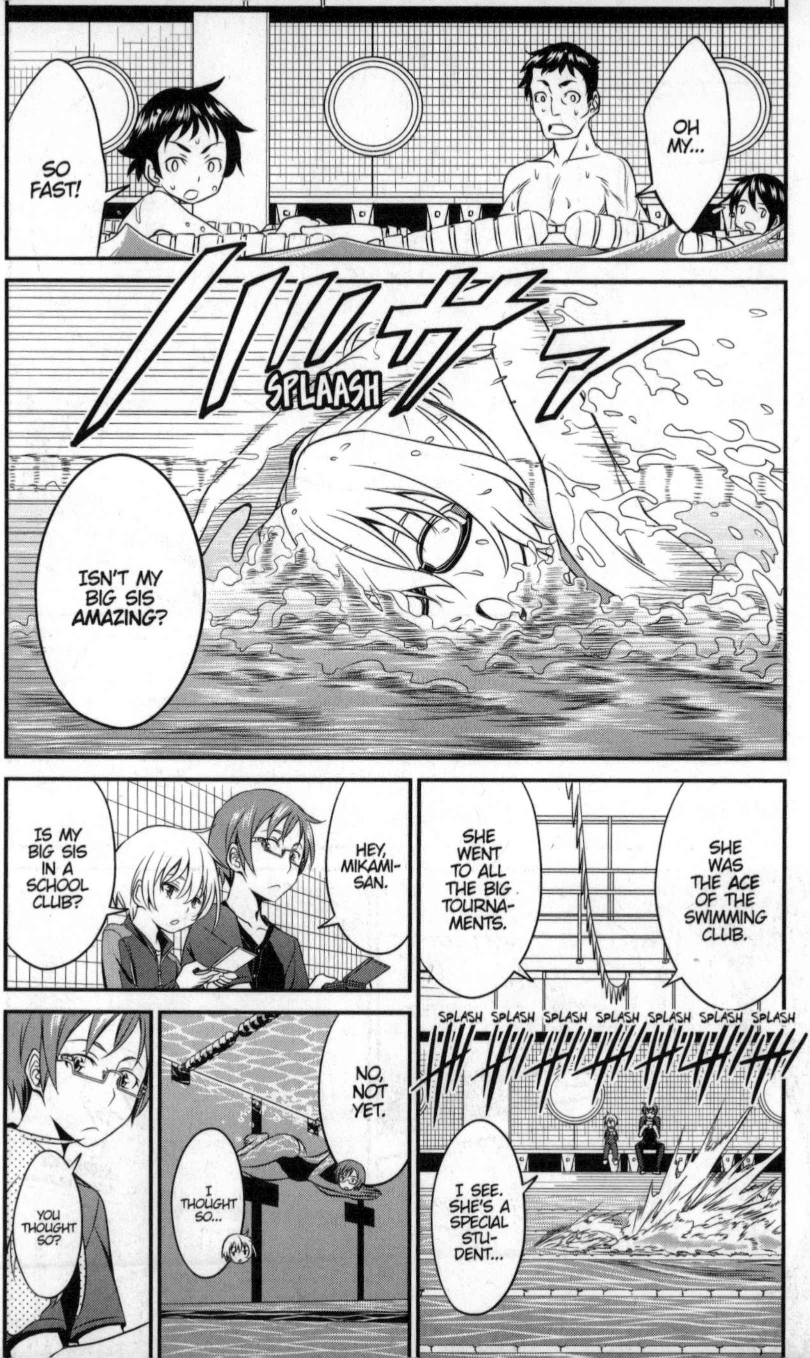
OH MY...
SO FAST!
SPLAASH
ISN'T MY BIG SIS AMAZING?
SHE WAS THE ACE OF THE SWIMMING CLUB.
SHE WENT TO ALL THE BIG TOURNA-MENTS.
SPLASH SPLASH SPLASH SPLASH SPLASH SPLASH SPLASH
I SEE. SHE'S A SPECIAL STU-DENT...
HEY, MIKAMI-SAN.
IS MY BIG SIS IN A SCHOOL CLUB?
NO, NOT YET.
I THOUGHT SO...
YOU THOUGHT SO?

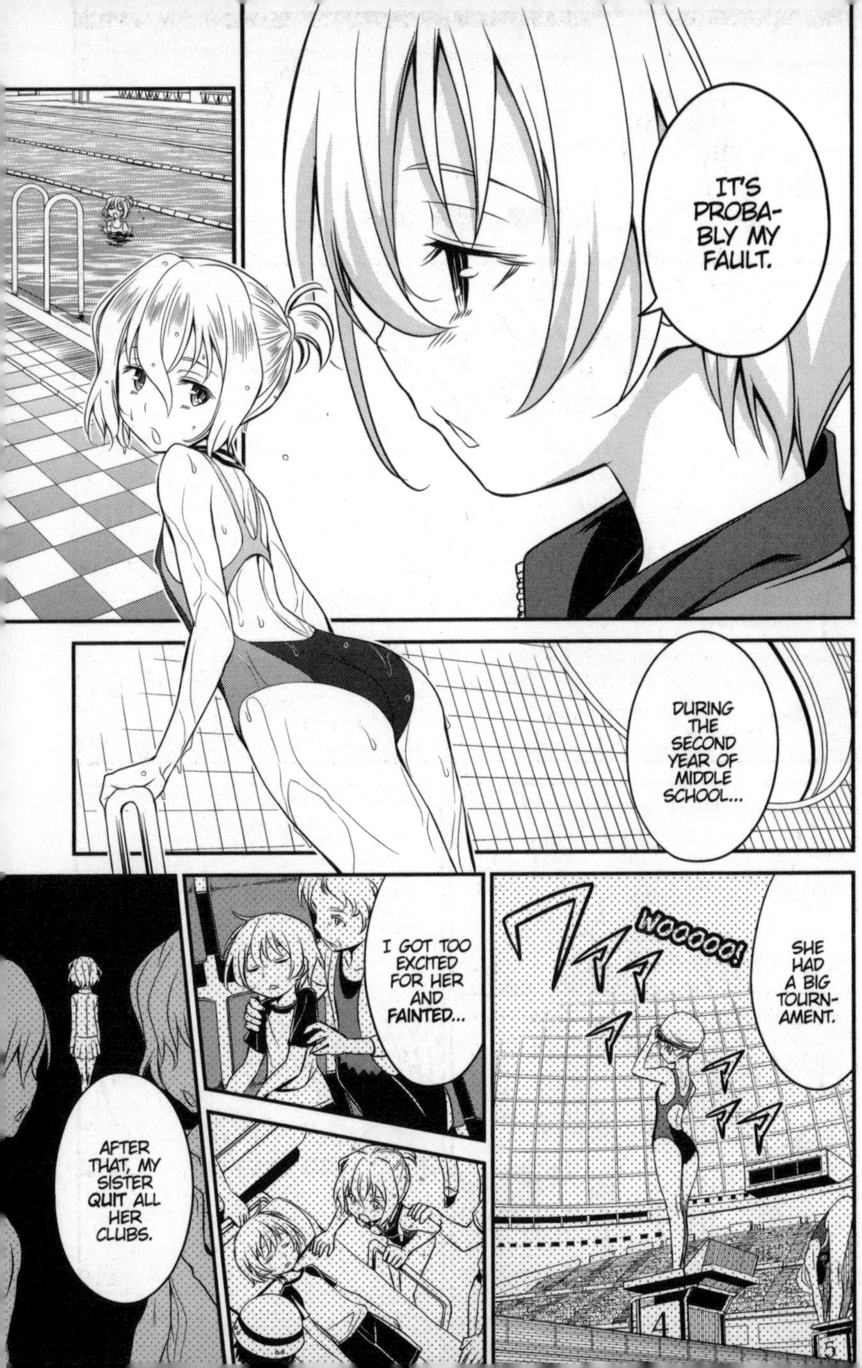
IT'S PROBABLY MY FAULT.
DURING THE SECOND YEAR OF MIDDLE SCHOOL...
SHE HAD A BIG TOURNAMENT.
WOOOOOO!
4
5
I GOT TOO EXCITED FOR HER AND FAINTED...
AFTER THAT, MY SISTER QUIT ALL HER CLUBS.

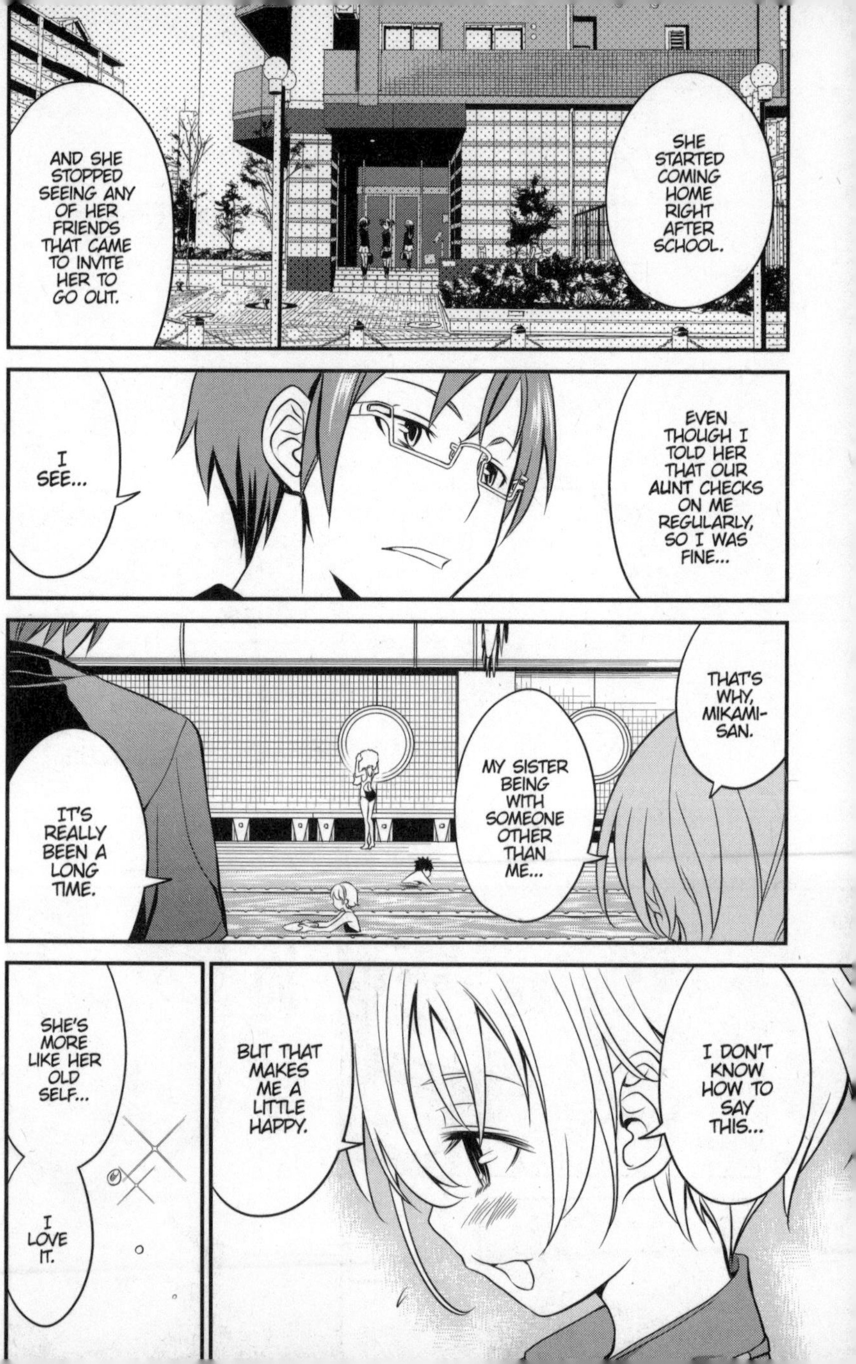
SHE STARTED COMING HOME RIGHT AFTER SCHOOL.
AND SHE STOPPED SEEING ANY OF HER FRIENDS THAT CAME TO INVITE HER TO GO OUT.
EVEN THOUGH I TOLD HER THAT OUR AUNT CHECKS ON ME REGULARLY, SO I WAS FINE...
I SEE...
THAT'S WHY, MIKAMI-SAN.
MY SISTER BEING WITH SOMEONE OTHER THAN ME...
IT'S REALLY BEEN A LONG TIME.
I DON'T KNOW HOW TO SAY THIS...
BUT THAT MAKES ME A LITTLE HAPPY.
SHE'S MORE LIKE HER OLD SELF...
I LOVE IT.

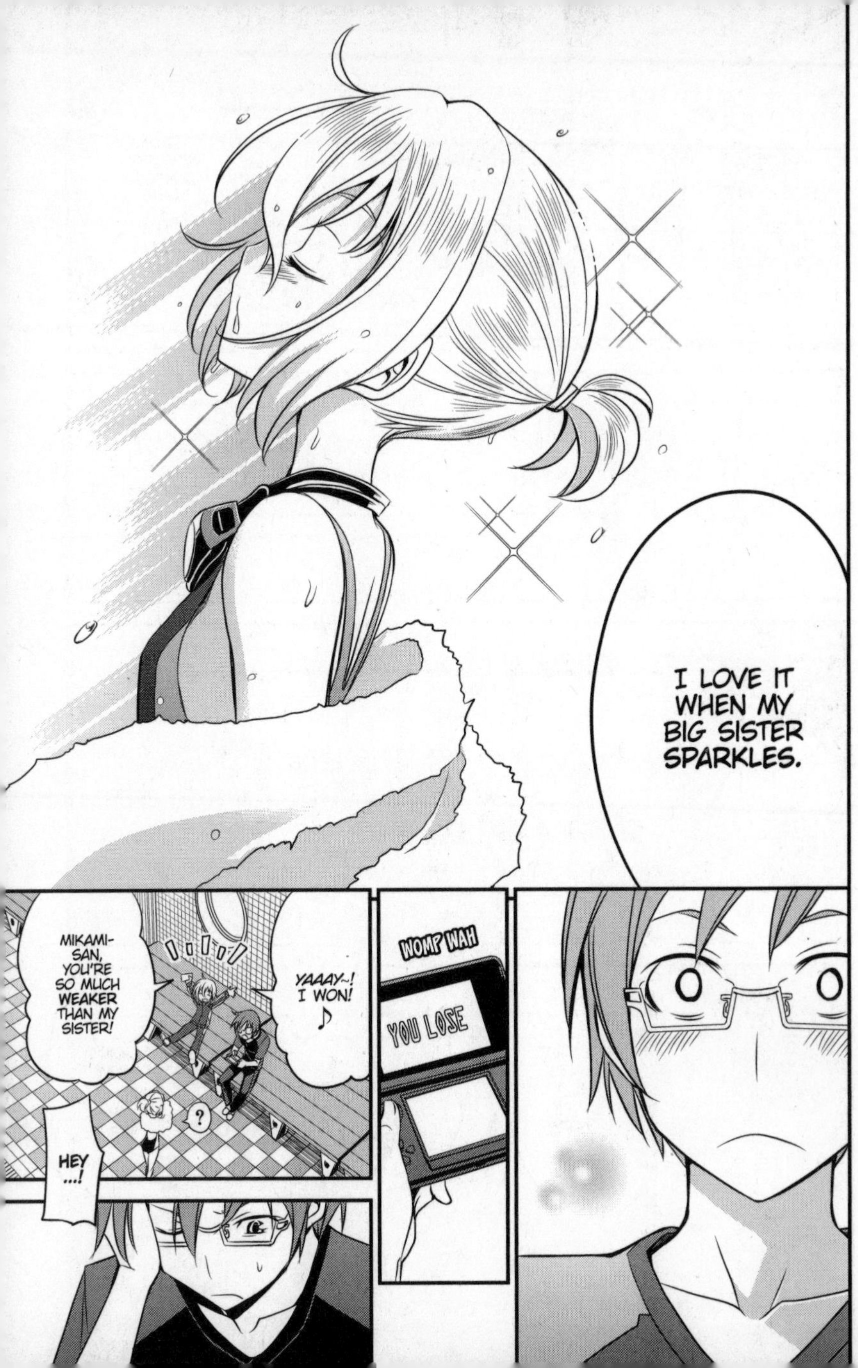
I LOVE IT WHEN MY BIG SISTER SPARKLES.
WOMP WAH
YOU LOSE
YAAAY~! I WON! ♪
MIKAMI-SAN, YOU'RE SO MUCH WEAKER THAN MY SISTER!
?
HEY ...!

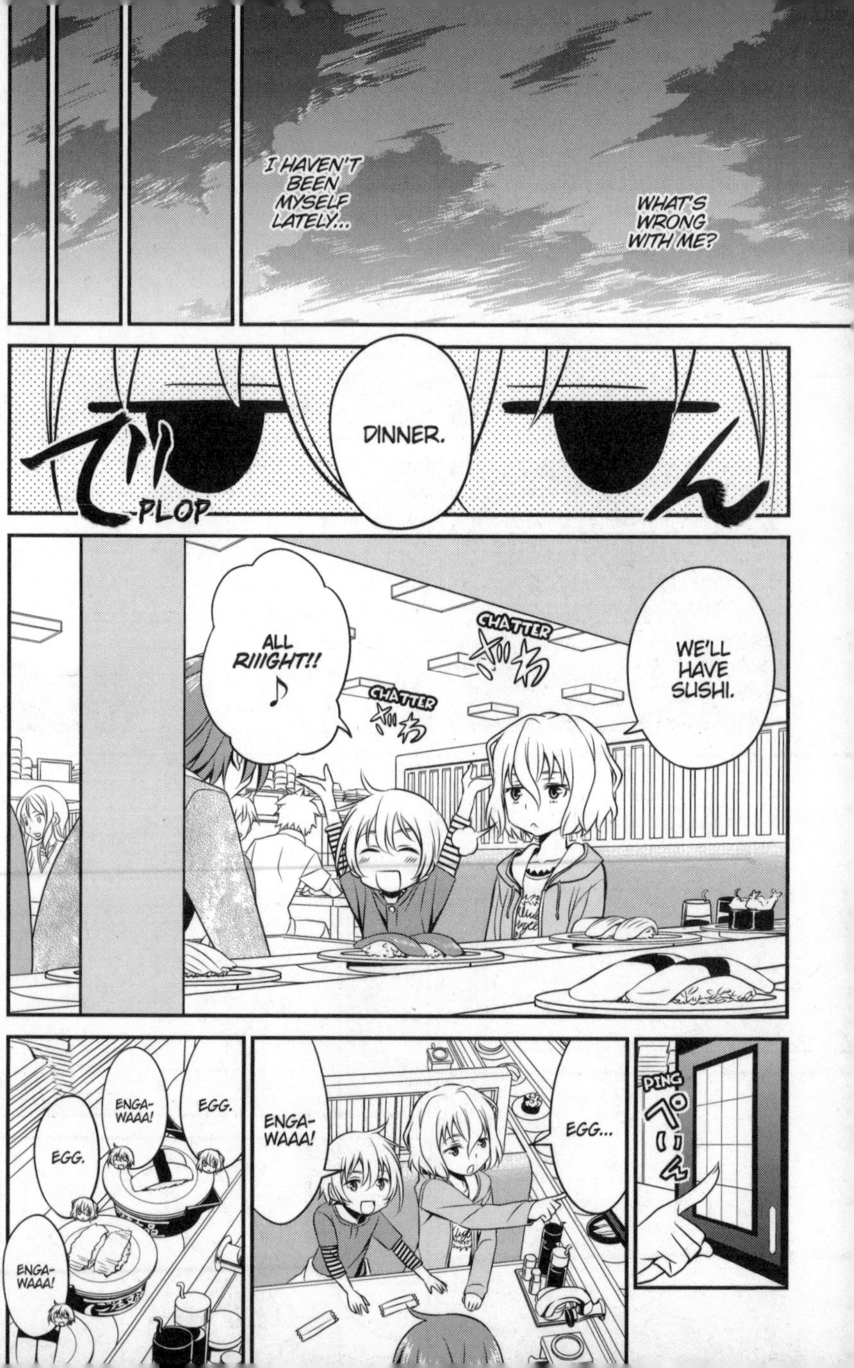
WHAT'S WRONG WITH ME?
I HAVEN'T BEEN MYSELF LATELY...
DINNER.
PLOP
WE'LL HAVE SUSHI.
CHATTER
CHATTER
ALL RIIIGHT!! ♪
PING
EGG...
ENGA-WAAA!
EGG.
ENGA-WAAA!
EGG.
ENGA-WAAA!

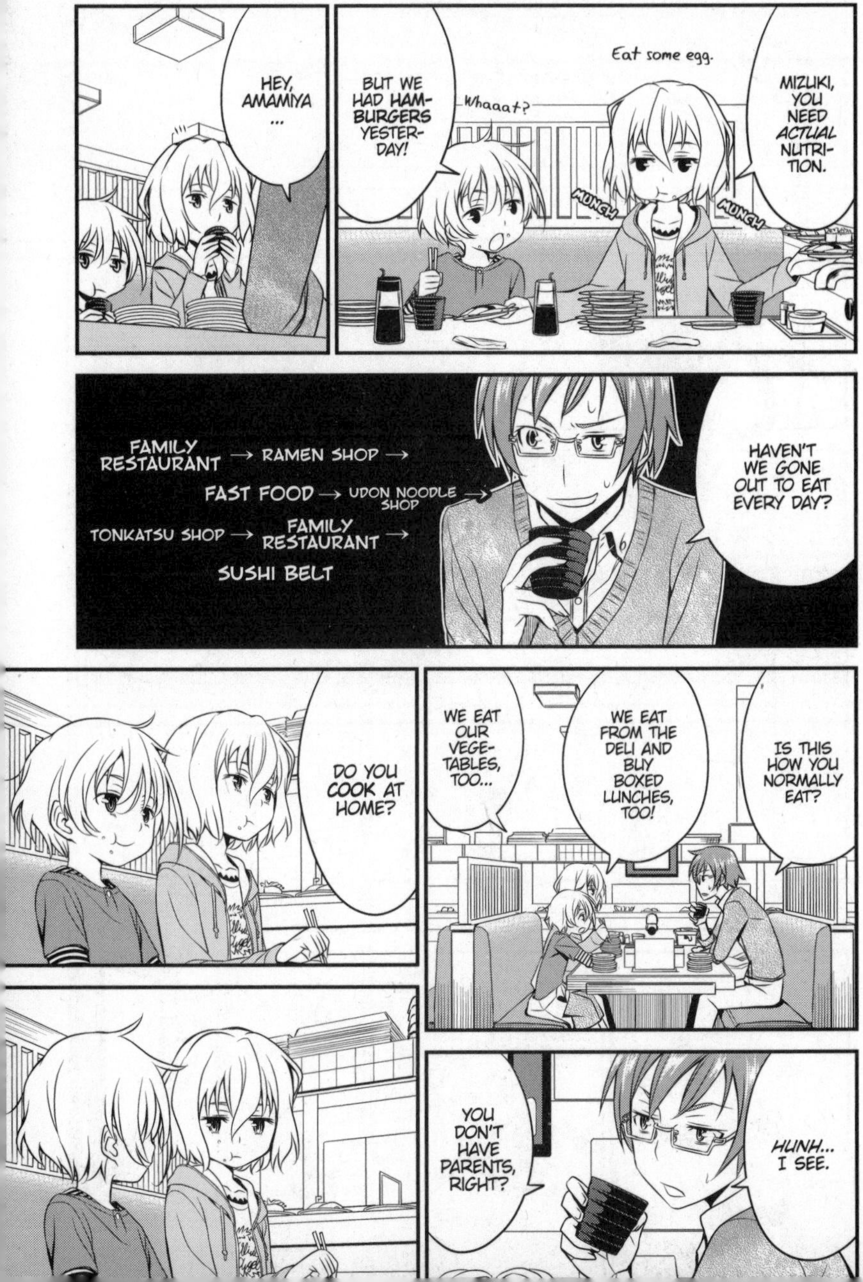
MIZUKI, YOU NEED ACTUAL NUTRITION.
Eat some egg.
MUNCH
MUNCH
Whaaat?
BUT WE HAD HAMBURGERS YESTERDAY!
HEY, AMAMIYA ...
HAVEN'T WE GONE OUT TO EAT EVERY DAY?
FAMILY RESTAURANT → RAMEN SHOP → FAST FOOD → UDON NOODLE SHOP → TONKATSU SHOP → FAMILY RESTAURANT → SUSHI BELT
IS THIS HOW YOU NORMALLY EAT?
WE EAT FROM THE DELI AND BUY BOXED LUNCHES, TOO!
WE EAT OUR VEGETABLES, TOO...
DO YOU COOK AT HOME?
HUNH... I SEE.
YOU DON'T HAVE PARENTS, RIGHT?

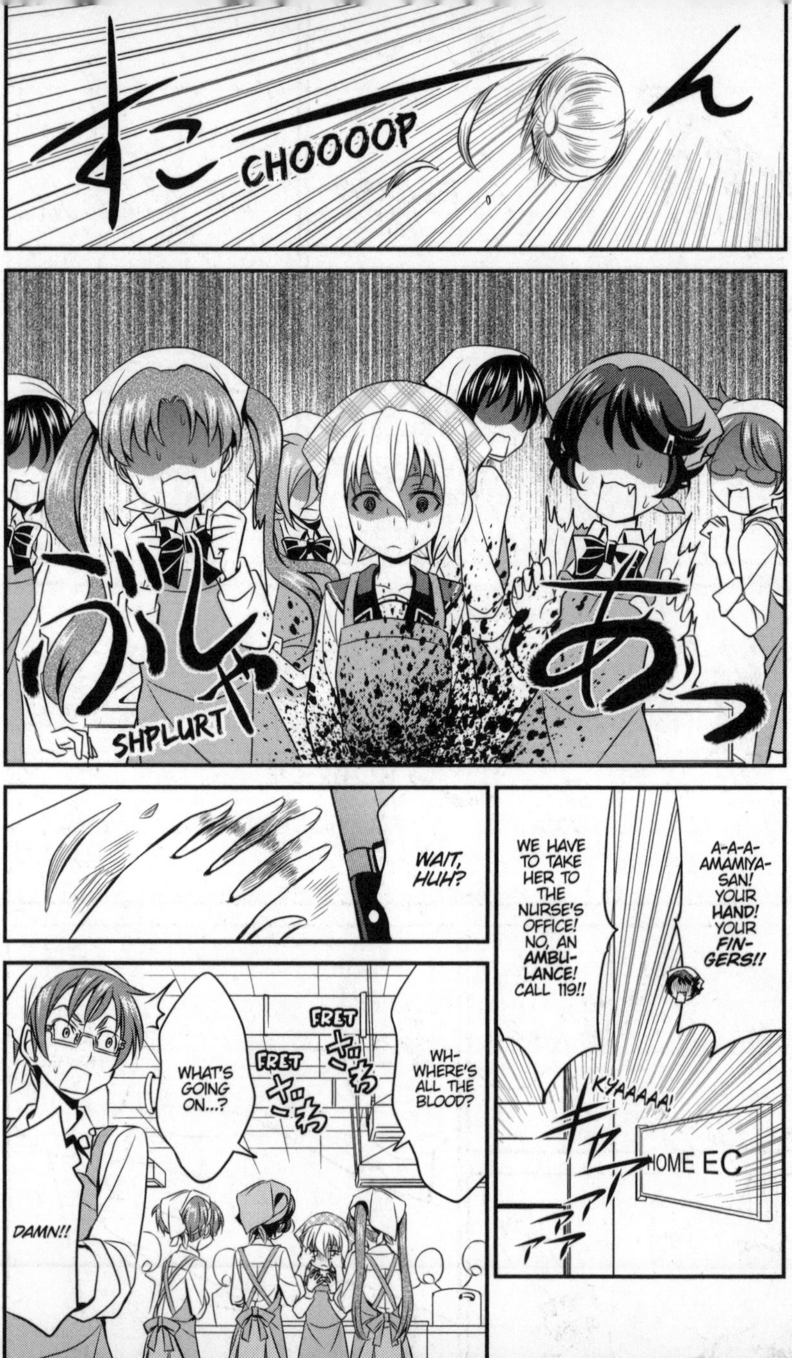
すこーーん
CHOOOOP
ぶしゃあっ
SHPLURT
A-A-A-AMAMIYA-SAN! YOUR HAND! YOUR FINGERS!!
WE HAVE TO TAKE HER TO THE NURSE'S OFFICE! NO, AN AMBULANCE! CALL 119!!
KYAAAAA!
キャアアアア
HOME EC
WAIT, HUH?
WH-WHERE'S ALL THE BLOOD?
FRET
ざわ
FRET
ざわ
WHAT'S GOING ON...?
DAMN!!

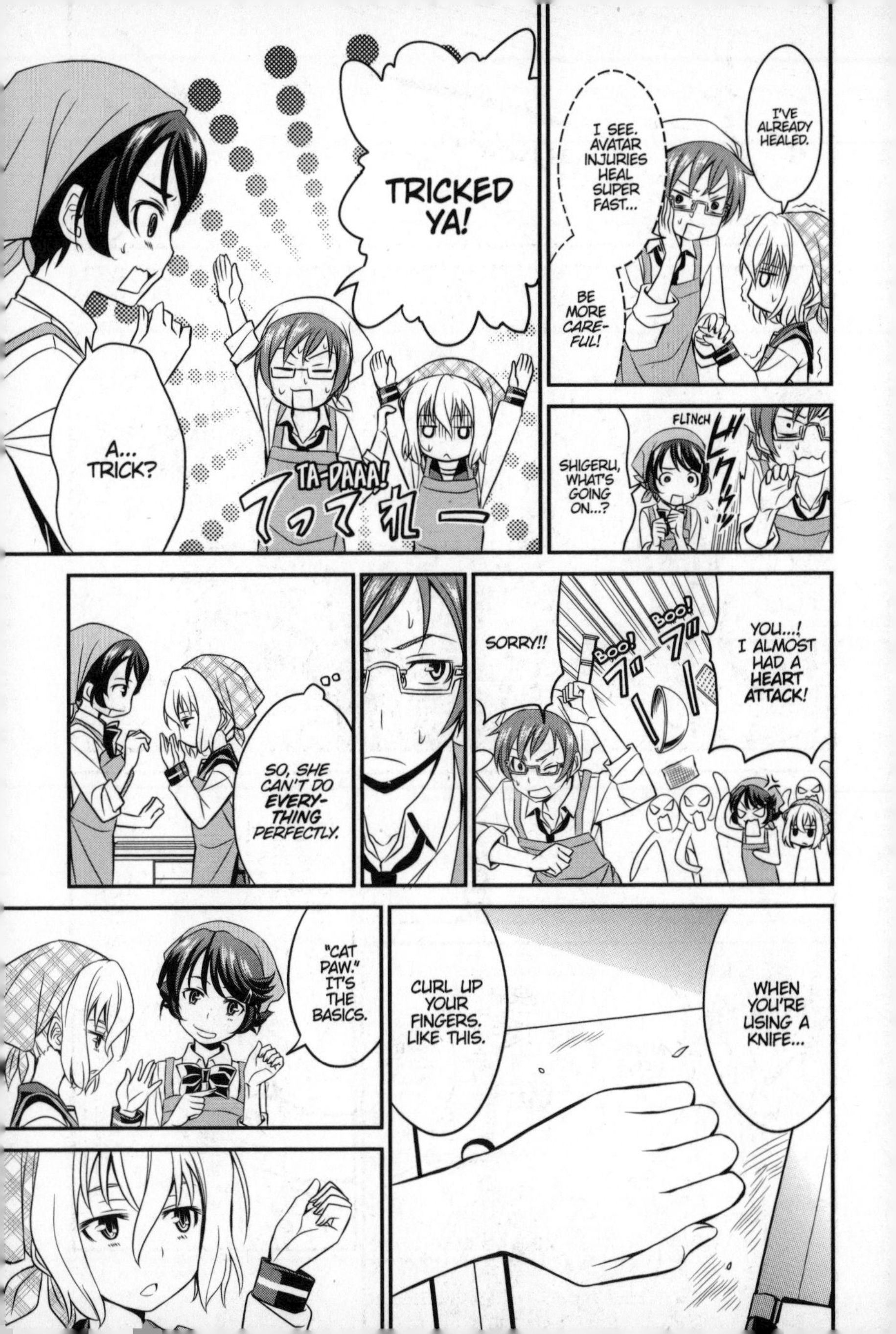
I'VE ALREADY HEALED.
I SEE. AVATAR INJURIES HEAL SUPER FAST...
BE MORE CARE-FUL!
FLINCH
SHIGERU, WHAT'S GOING ON...?
TRICKED YA!
TA-DAAA!
A... TRICK?
YOU...! I ALMOST HAD A HEART ATTACK!
BOO!
BOO!
SORRY!!
SO, SHE CAN'T DO EVERY-THING PERFECTLY.
WHEN YOU'RE USING A KNIFE...
CURL UP YOUR FINGERS. LIKE THIS.
"CAT PAW." IT'S THE BASICS.

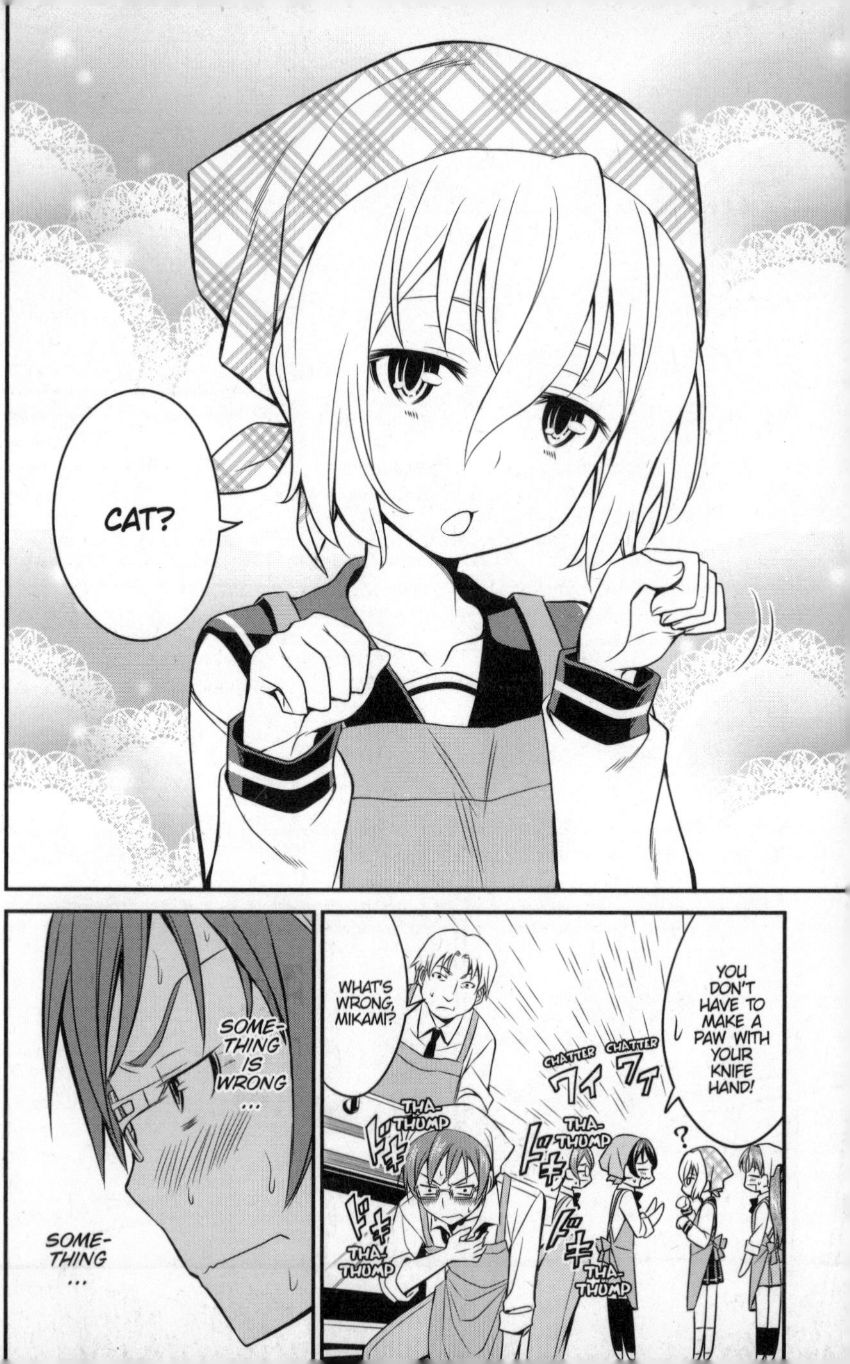
CAT?
YOU DON'T HAVE TO MAKE A PAW WITH YOUR KNIFE HAND!
WHAT'S WRONG, MIKAMI?
CHATTER CHATTER
THA-THUMP
THA-THUMP
THA-THUMP
THA-THUMP
SOME-THING IS WRONG ...
SOME-THING ...

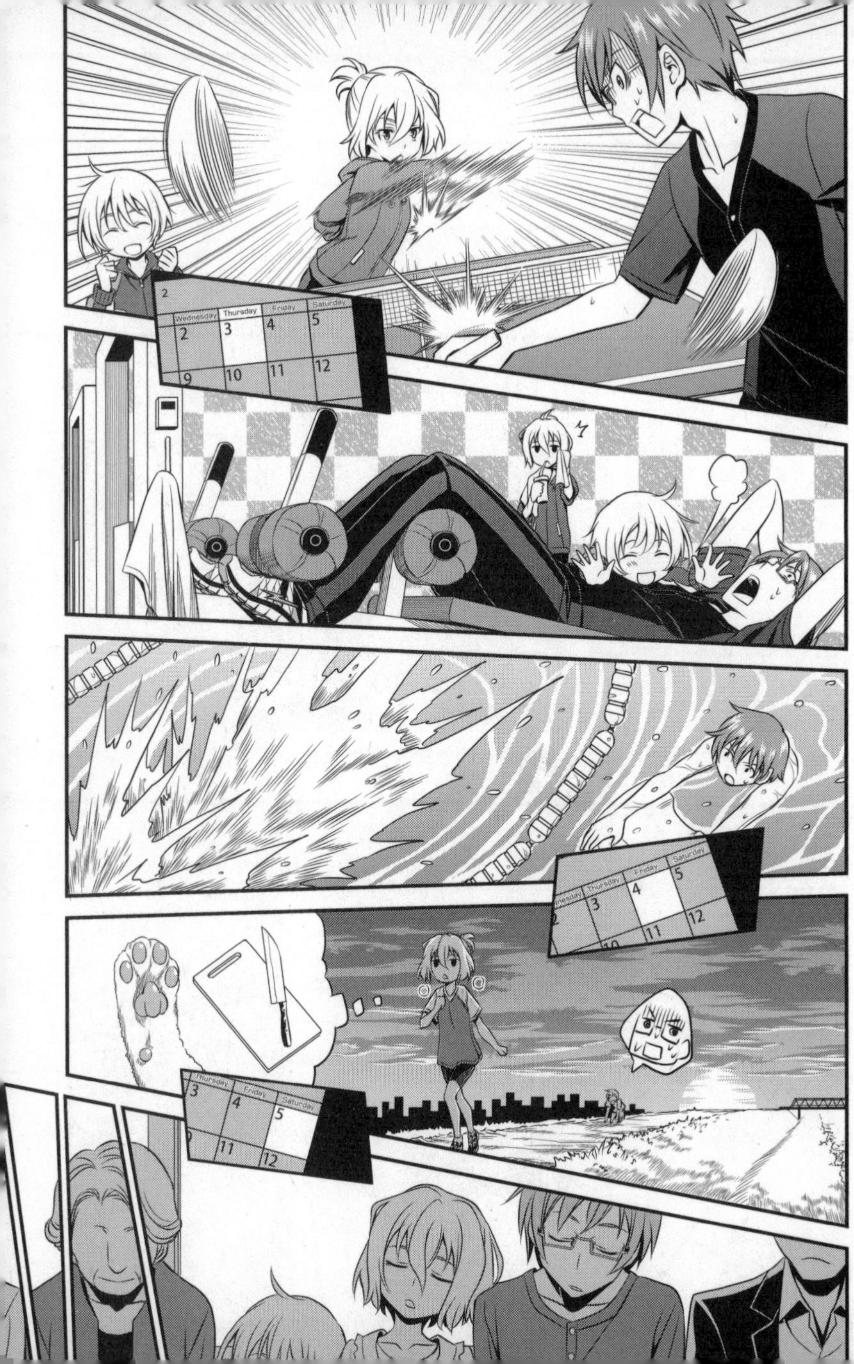
2
Wednesday
Thursday
Friday
Saturday
2 3 4 5
9 10 11 12
Thursday
Friday
Saturday
3 4 5
11 12
Thursday
Friday
Saturday
3 4 5
11 12

May 6th (Sunday) Day of Event Battle

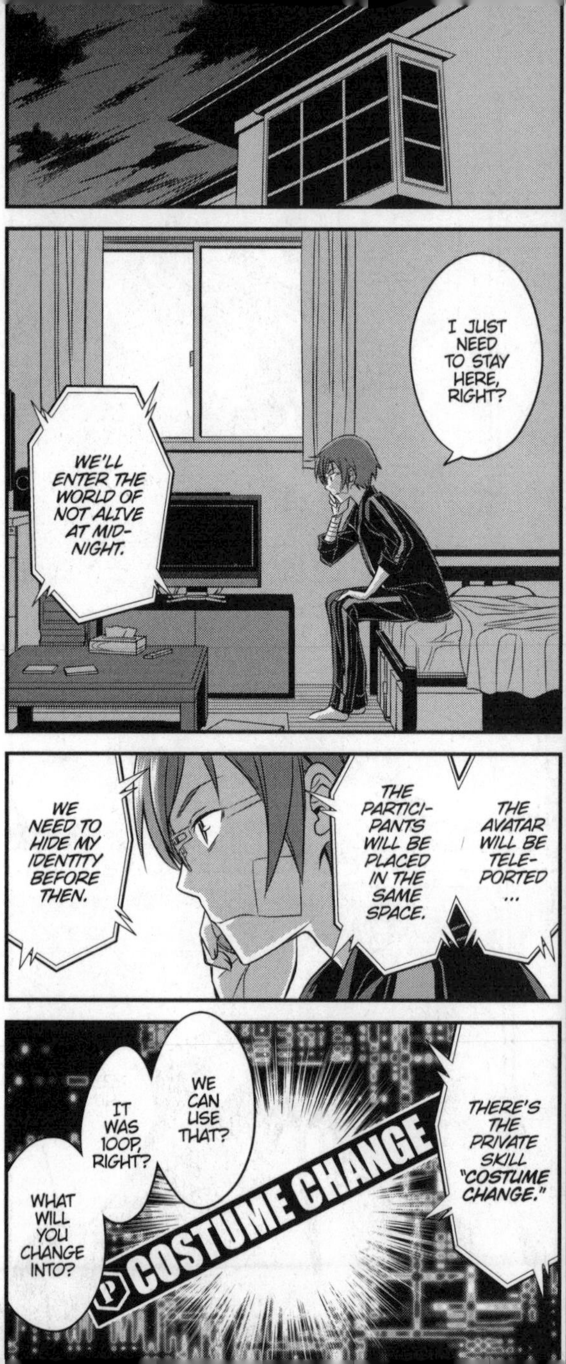
I JUST NEED TO STAY HERE, RIGHT?
WE'LL ENTER THE WORLD OF NOT ALIVE AT MID-NIGHT.
THE AVATAR WILL BE TELE-PORTED ...
THE PARTICI-PANTS WILL BE PLACED IN THE SAME SPACE.
WE NEED TO HIDE MY IDENTITY BEFORE THEN.
THERE'S THE PRIVATE SKILL "COSTUME CHANGE."
P COSTUME CHANGE
WE CAN USE THAT?
IT WAS 100P, RIGHT?
WHAT WILL YOU CHANGE INTO?

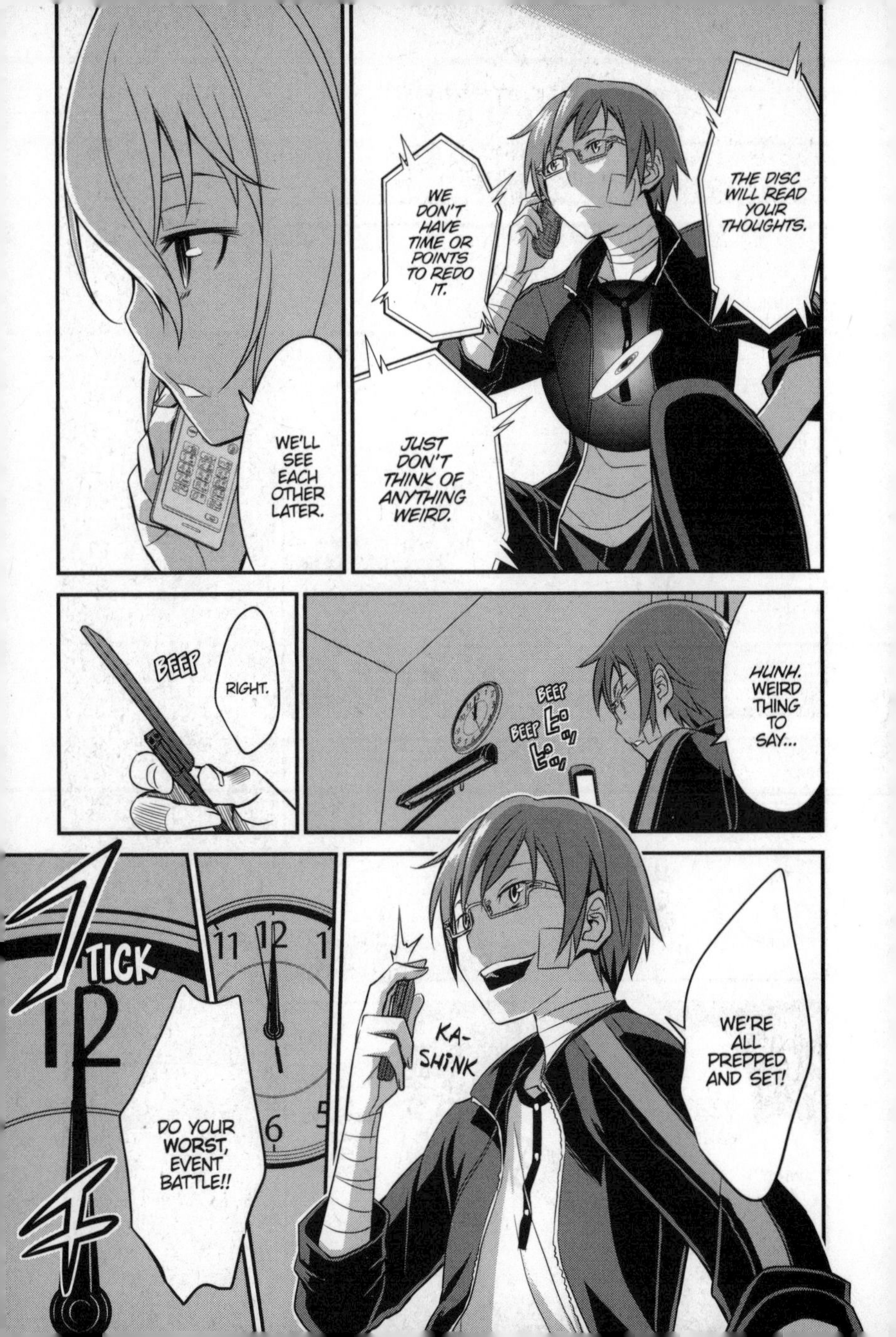
THE DISC WILL READ YOUR THOUGHTS.
WE DON'T HAVE TIME OR POINTS TO REDO IT.
JUST DON'T THINK OF ANYTHING WEIRD.
WE'LL SEE EACH OTHER LATER.
HUNH. WEIRD THING TO SAY...
BEEP
BEEP
BEEP
RIGHT.
KA-SHINK
WE'RE ALL PREPPED AND SET!
TICK
DO YOUR WORST, EVENT BATTLE!!

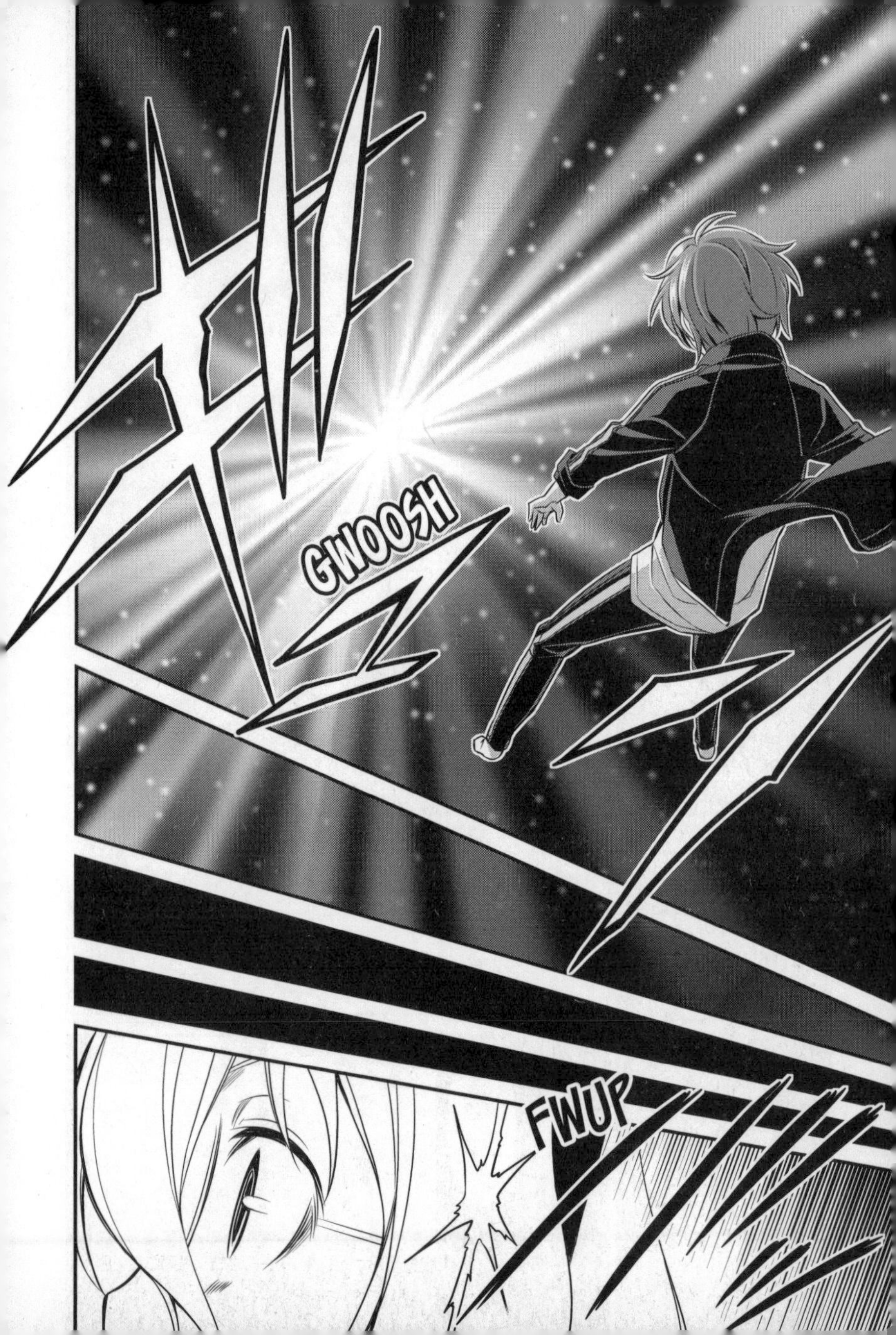
GWOOSH
FWUP

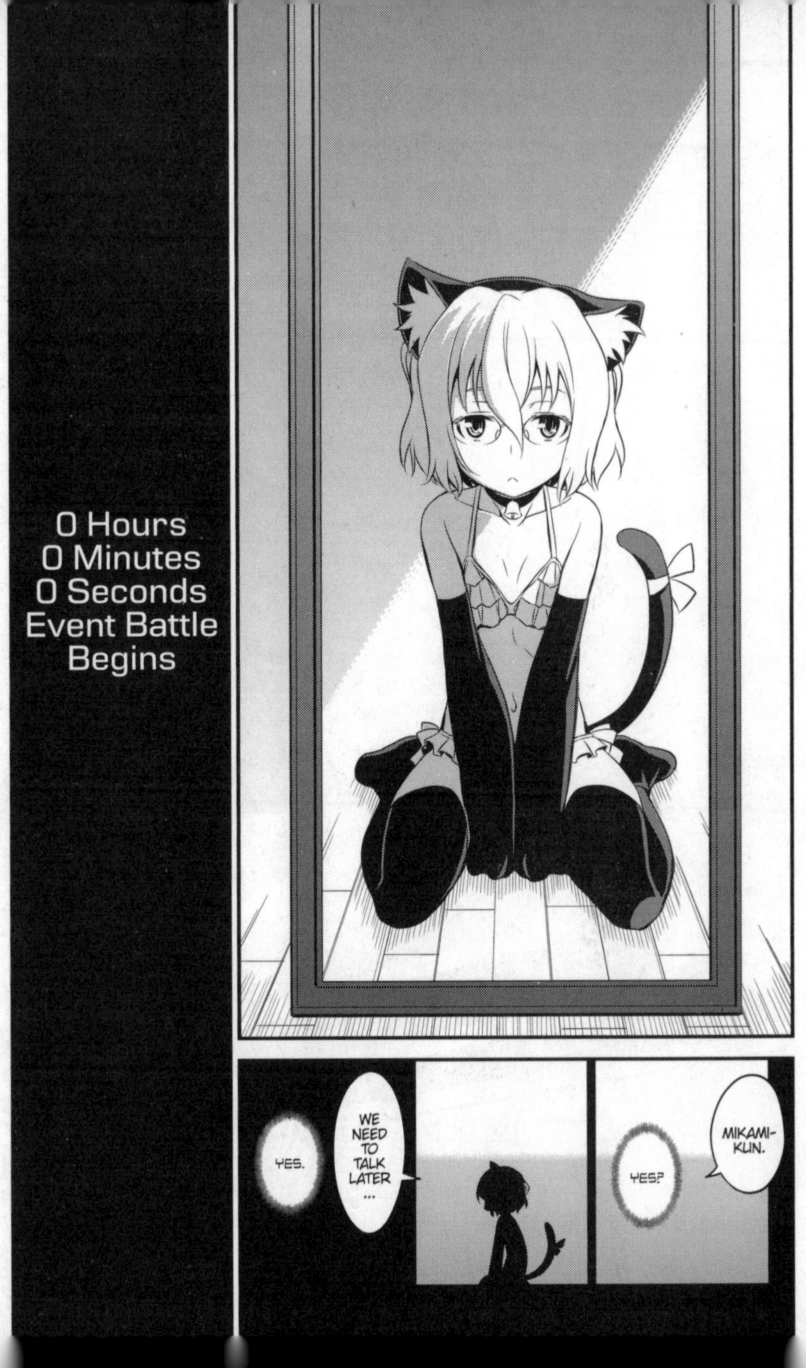
MIKAMI-KUN.
YES?
WE NEED TO TALK LATER...
YES.
0 Hours 0 Minutes 0 Seconds Event Battle Begins

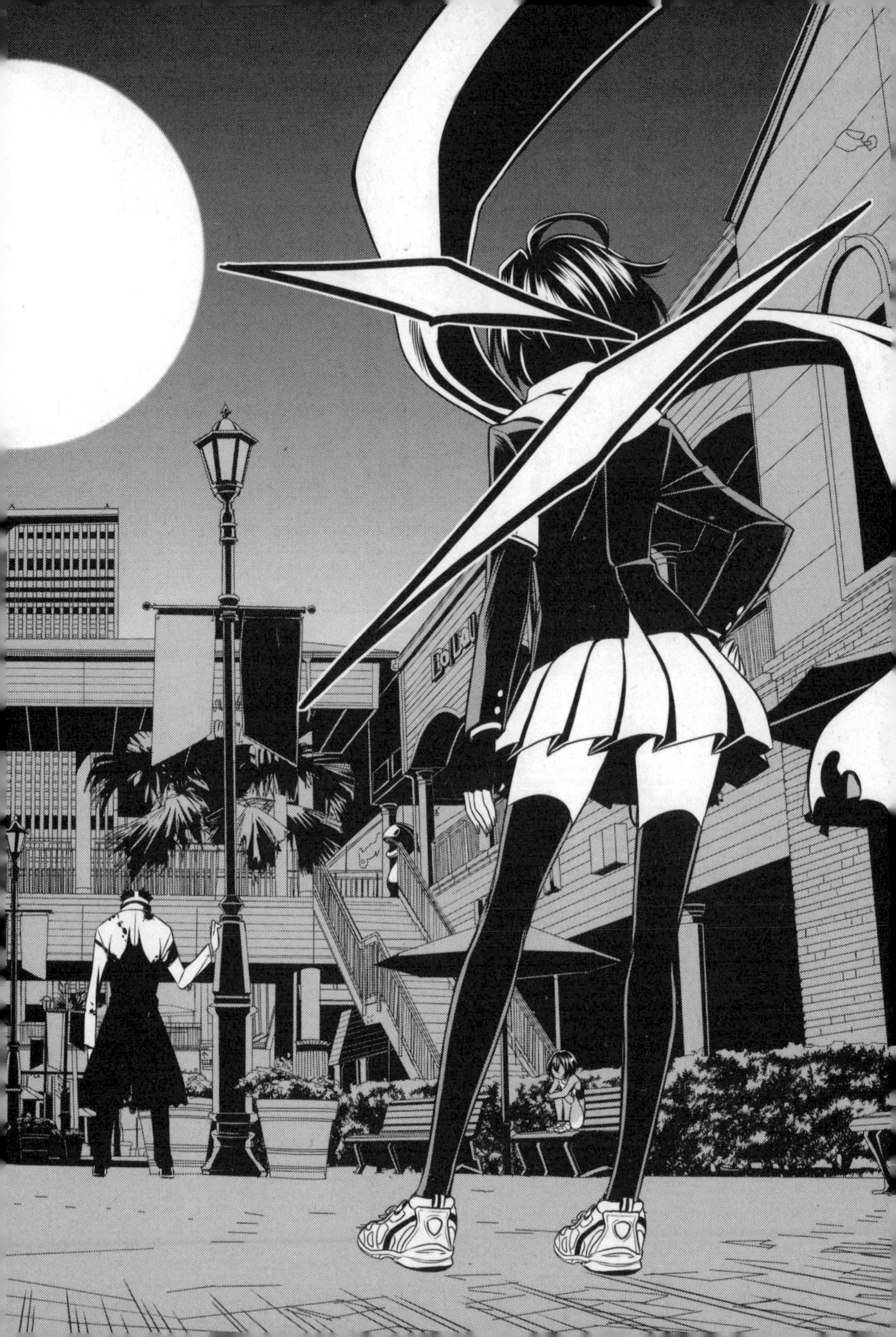

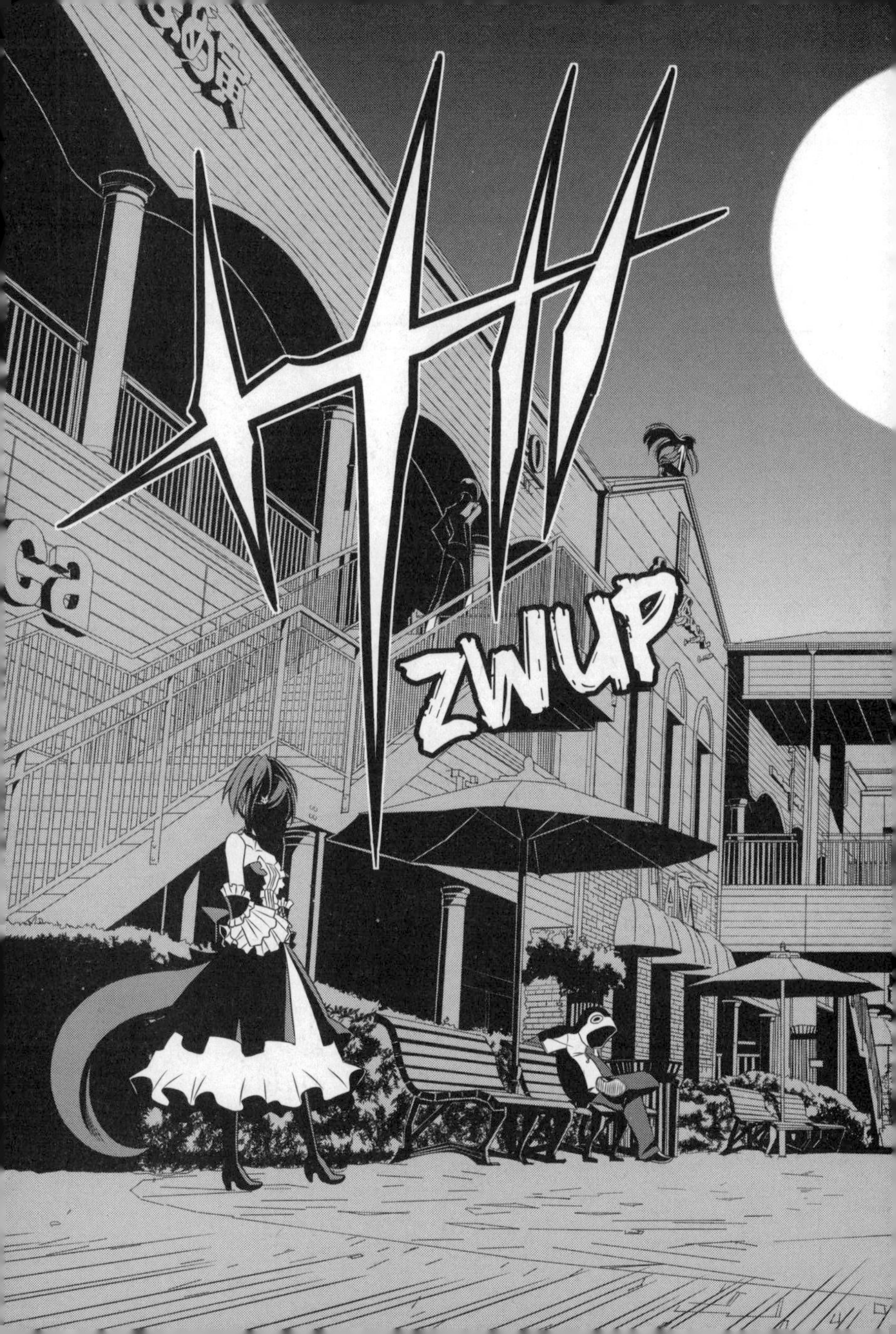
ZWUP

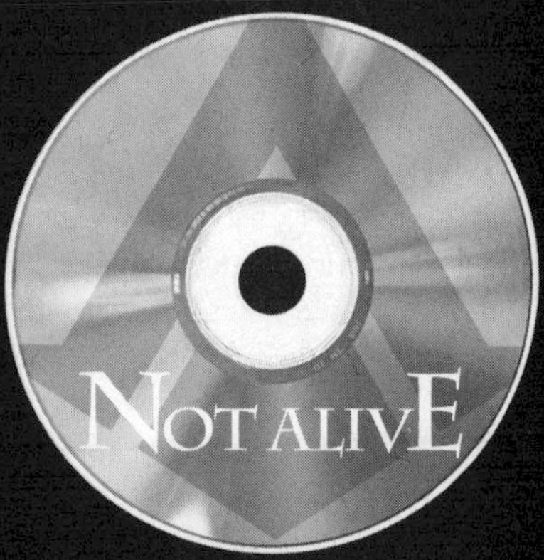
NOT ALIVE

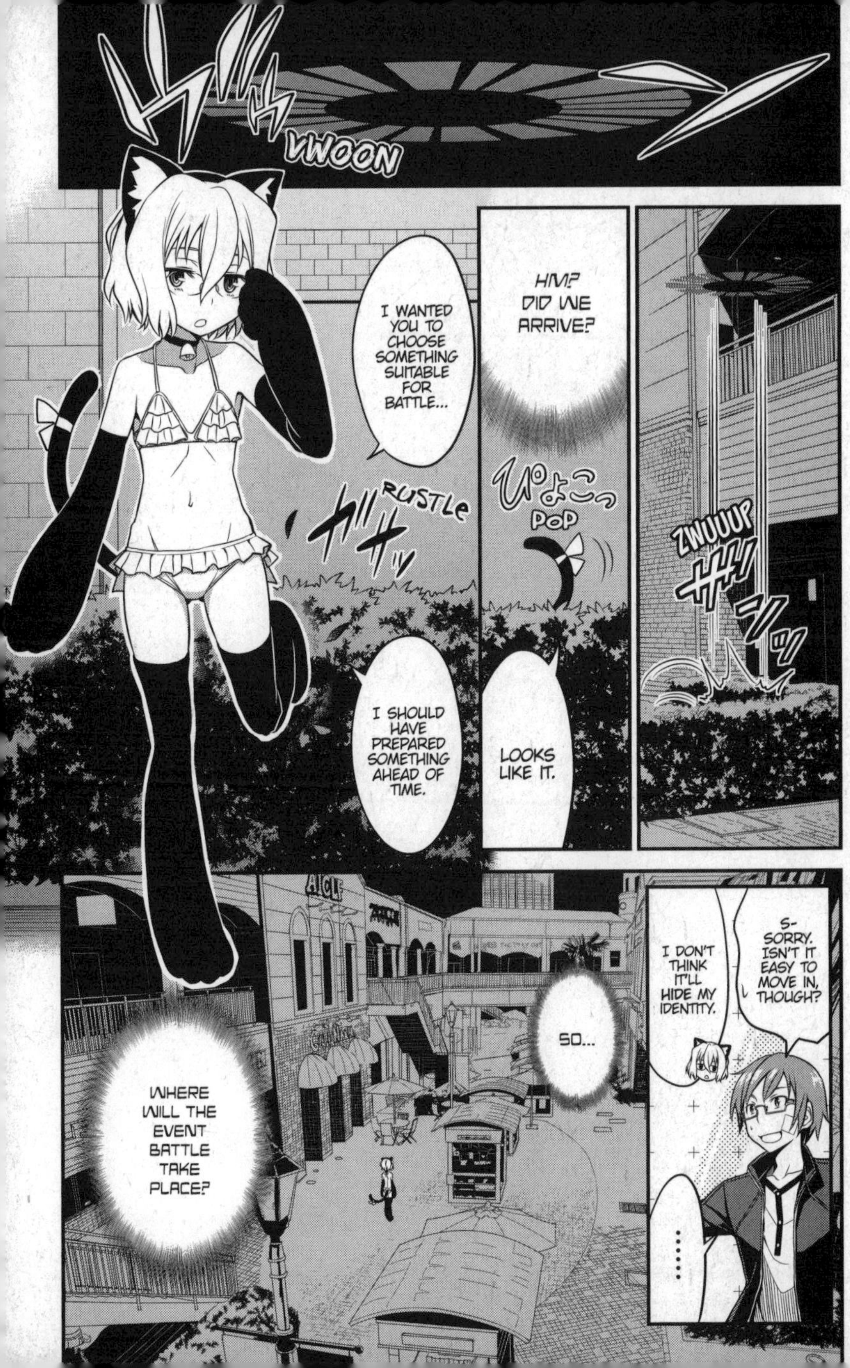
VWOON
ZWUUUP
HM? DID WE ARRIVE?
ぴよこっ
POP
LOOKS LIKE IT.
I WANTED YOU TO CHOOSE SOMETHING SUITABLE FOR BATTLE...
RUSTLE
I SHOULD HAVE PREPARED SOMETHING AHEAD OF TIME.
S-SORRY. ISN'T IT EASY TO MOVE IN, THOUGH?
I DON'T THINK IT'LL HIDE MY IDENTITY.
......
SO...
WHERE WILL THE EVENT BATTLE TAKE PLACE?

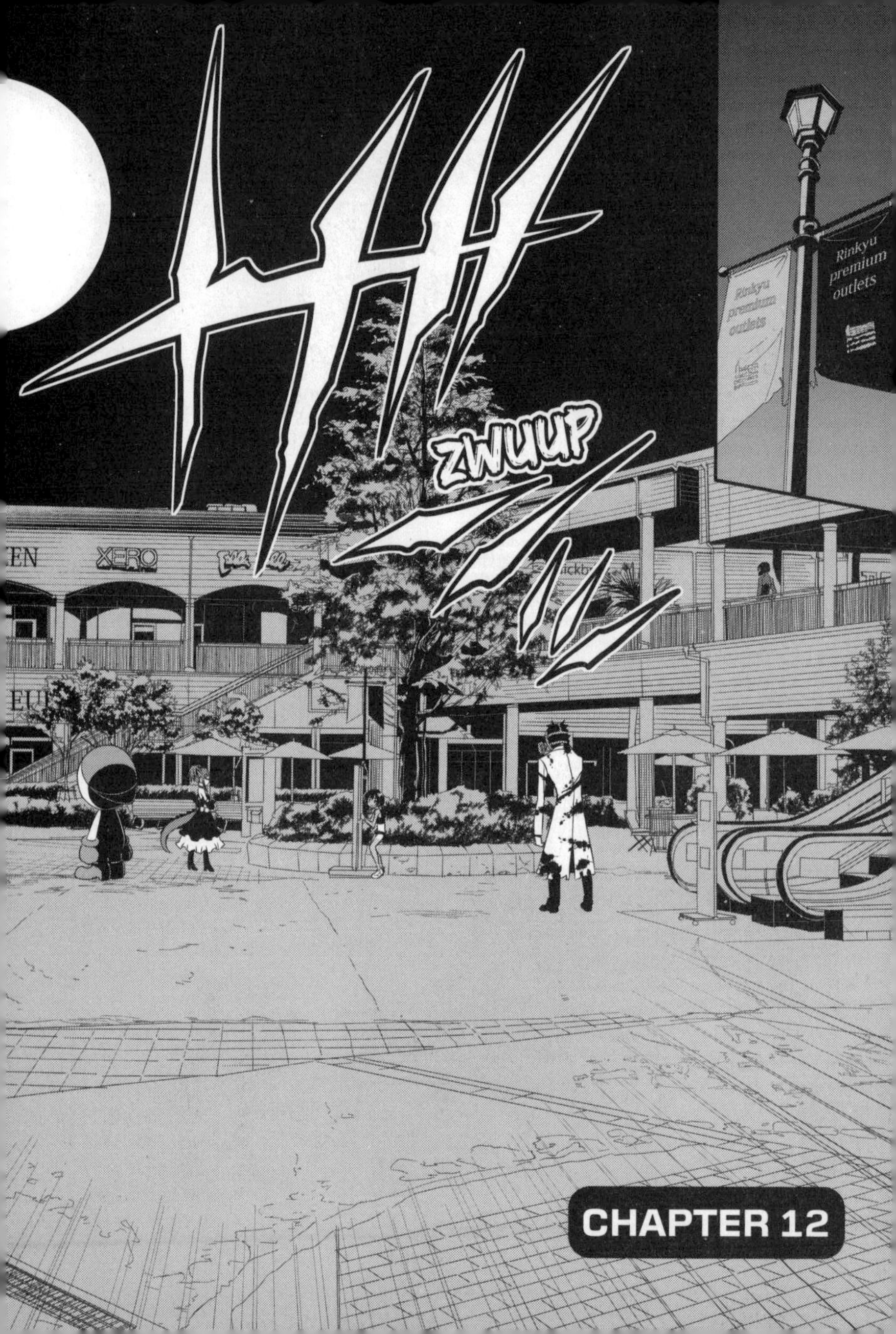

ZWUUP
Rinkyu premium outlets
Rinkyu premium outlets
XERO
CHAPTER 12

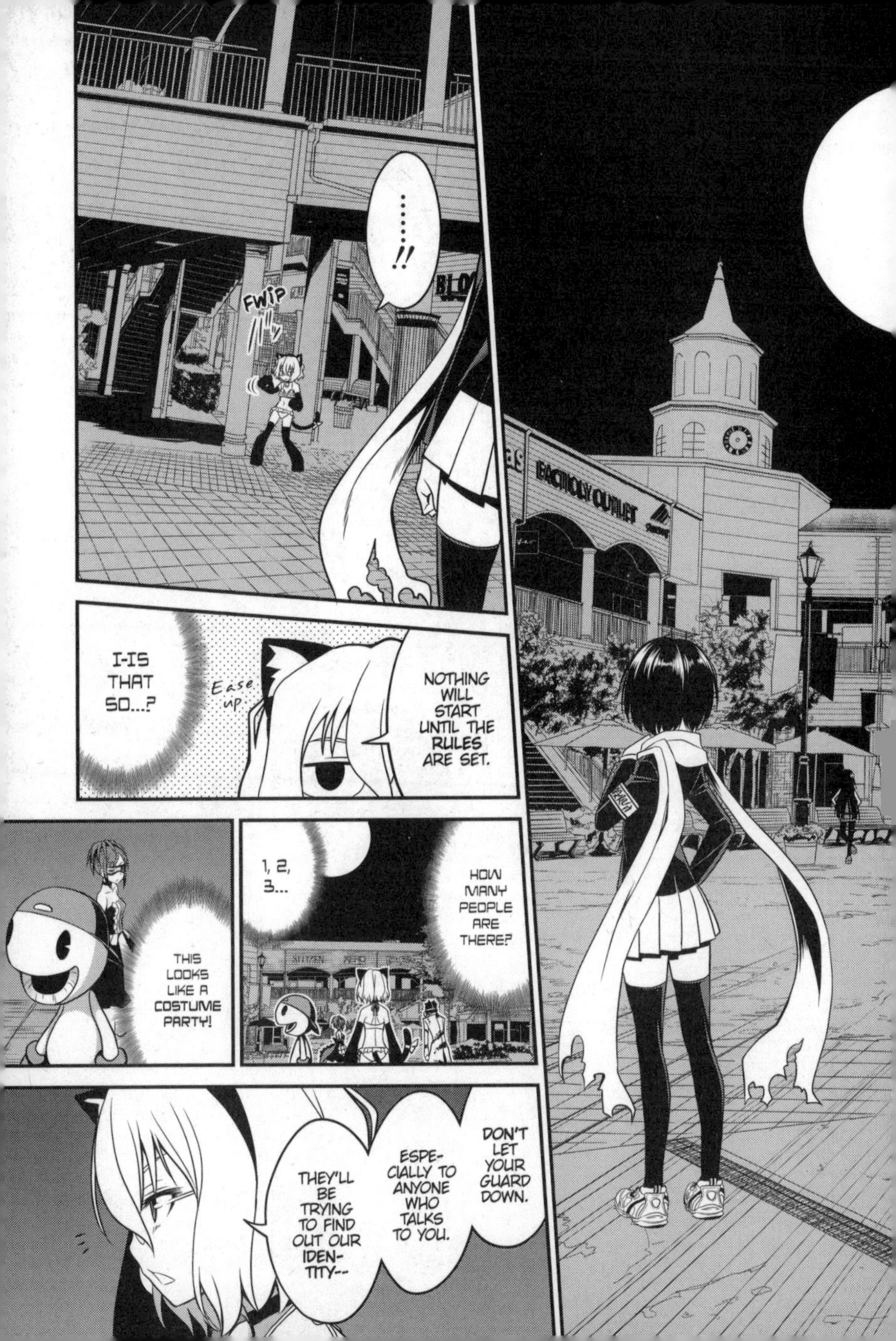
......!!
FWIP
NOTHING WILL START UNTIL THE RULES ARE SET.
Ease up
I-IS THAT SO...?
HOW MANY PEOPLE ARE THERE?
1, 2, 3...
THIS LOOKS LIKE A COSTUME PARTY!
DON'T LET YOUR GUARD DOWN.
ESPE-CIALLY TO ANYONE WHO TALKS TO YOU.
THEY'LL BE TRYING TO FIND OUT OUR IDEN-TITY--

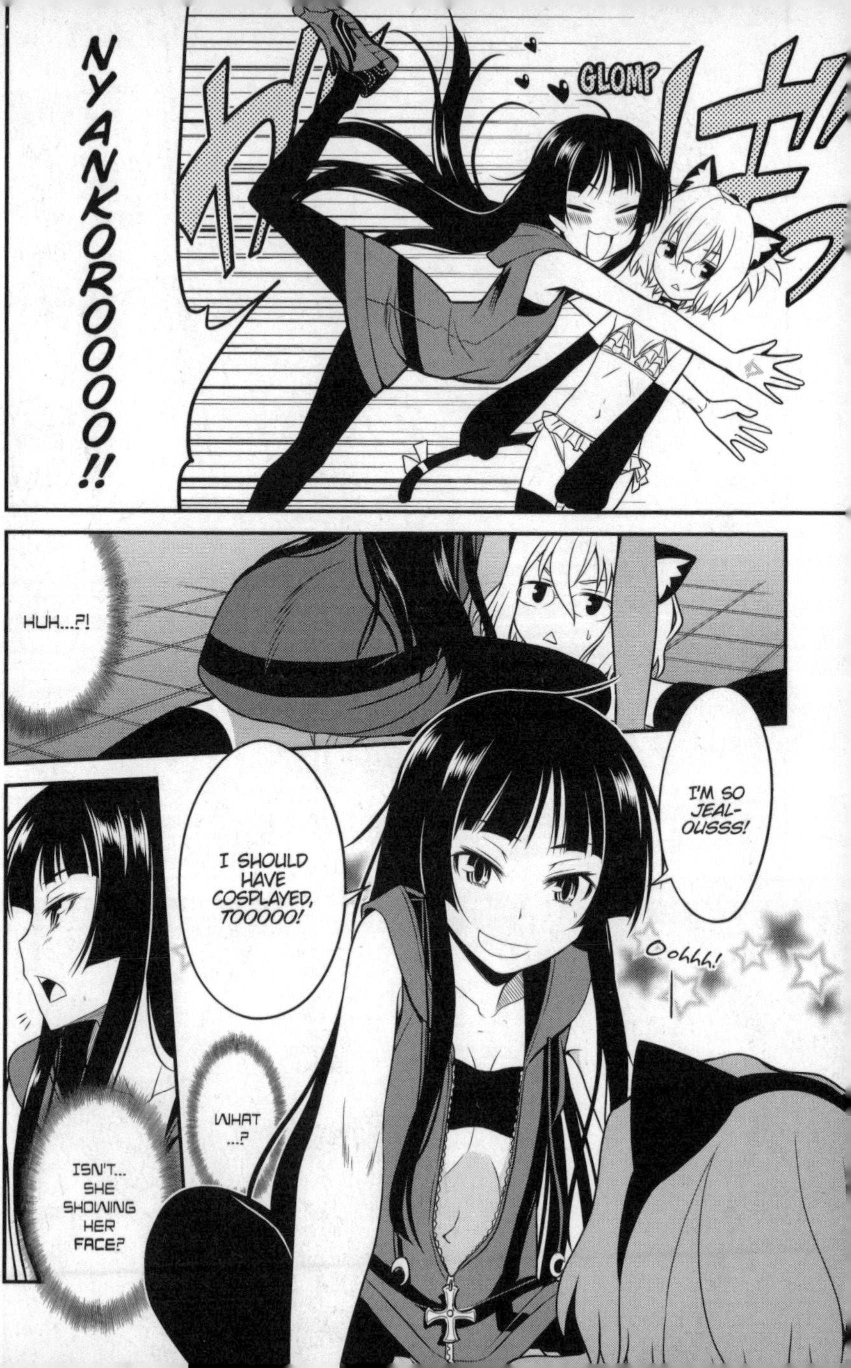
GLOMP
NYANKOROOOOO!!
HUH...?!
I'M SO JEAL-OUSSS!
I SHOULD HAVE COSPLAYED, TOOOOO!
Oohhh!
WHAT ...?
ISN'T... SHE SHOWING HER FACE?

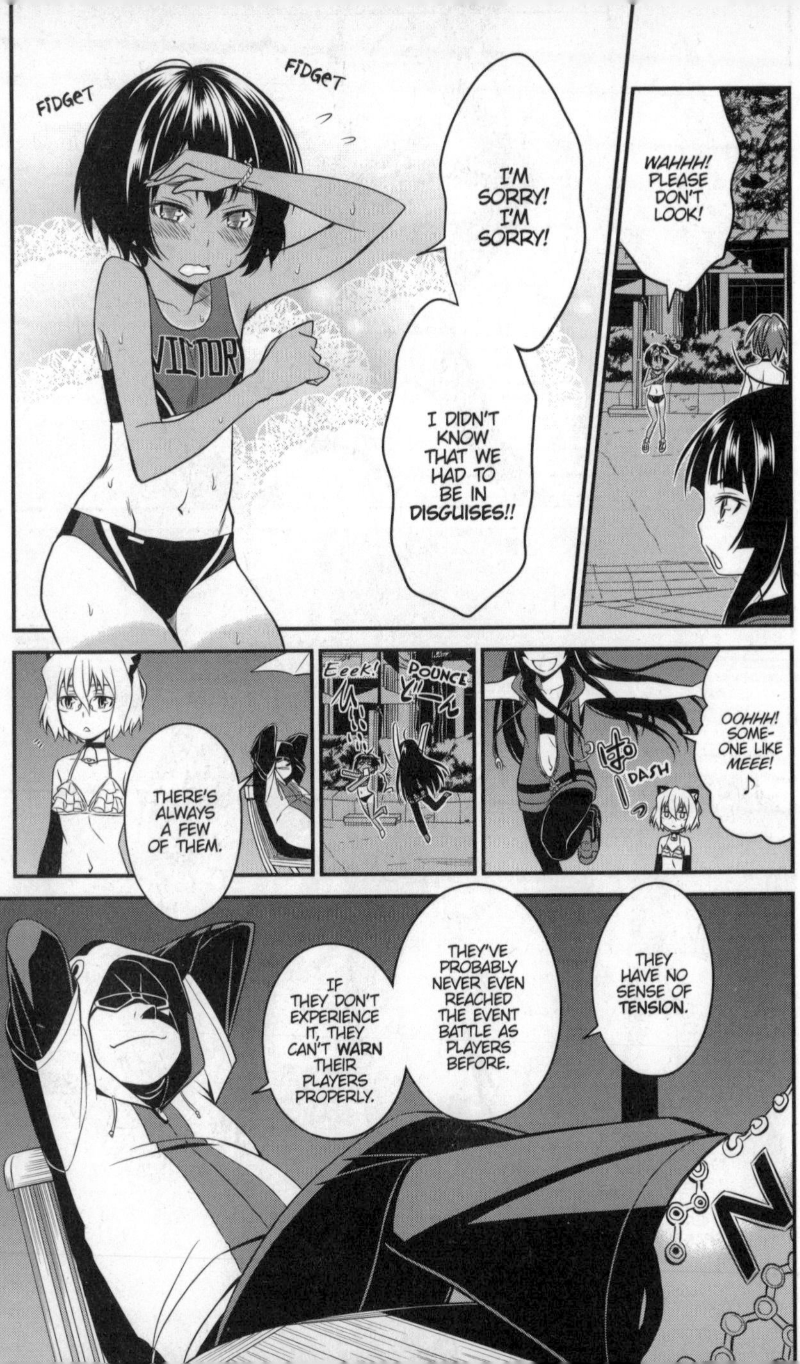
WAHHH! PLEASE DON'T LOOK!
FIDGET
FIDGET
I'M SORRY! I'M SORRY!
I DIDN'T KNOW THAT WE HAD TO BE IN DISGUISES!!
OOHHH! SOME-ONE LIKE MEEE! ♪
DASH
POUNCE
Eeek!
THERE'S ALWAYS A FEW OF THEM.
THEY HAVE NO SENSE OF TENSION.
THEY'VE PROBABLY NEVER EVEN REACHED THE EVENT BATTLE AS PLAYERS BEFORE.
IF THEY DON'T EXPERIENCE IT, THEY CAN'T WARN THEIR PLAYERS PROPERLY.

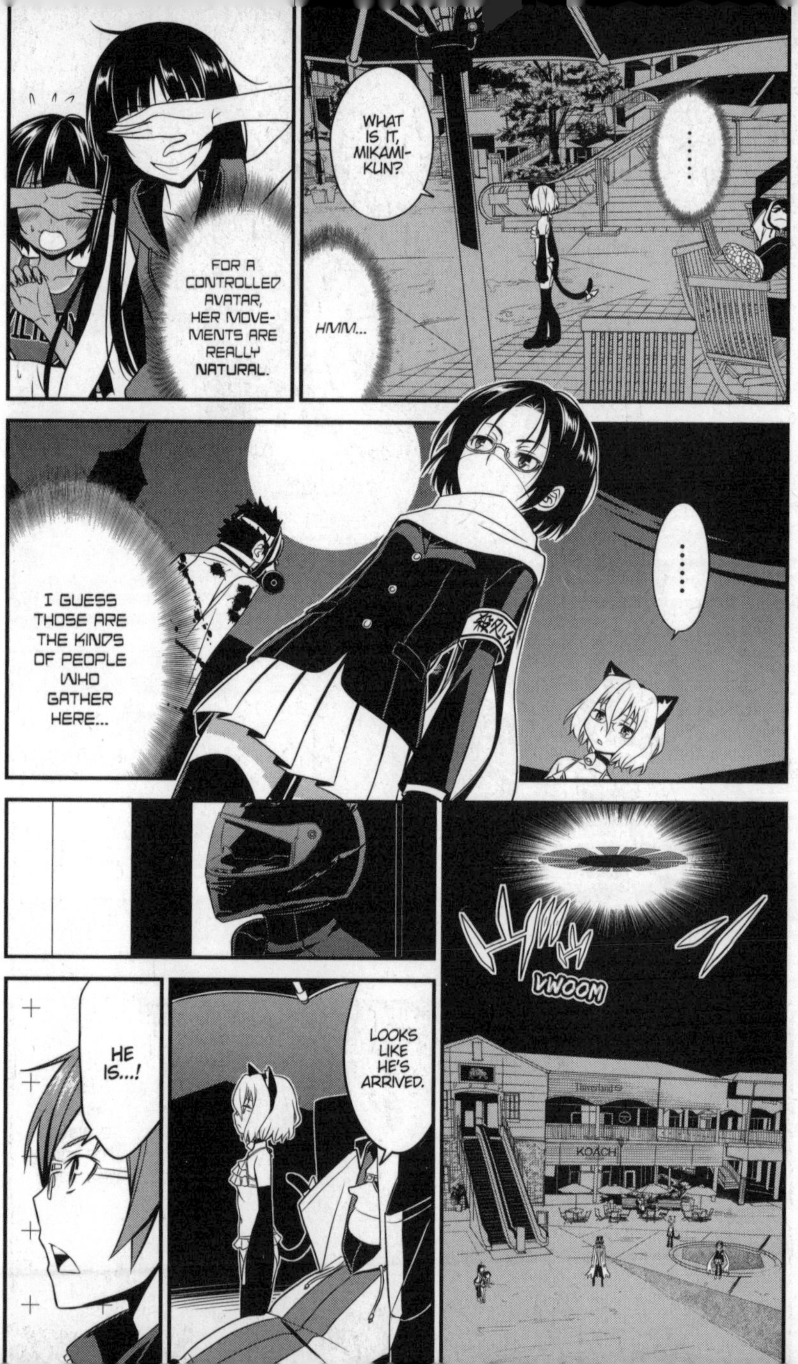
......
WHAT IS IT, MIKAMI-KUN?
HMM...
FOR A CONTROLLED AVATAR, HER MOVEMENTS ARE REALLY NATURAL.
......
I GUESS THOSE ARE THE KINDS OF PEOPLE WHO GATHER HERE...
VWOOM
KOACH
LOOKS LIKE HE'S ARRIVED.
HE IS...!

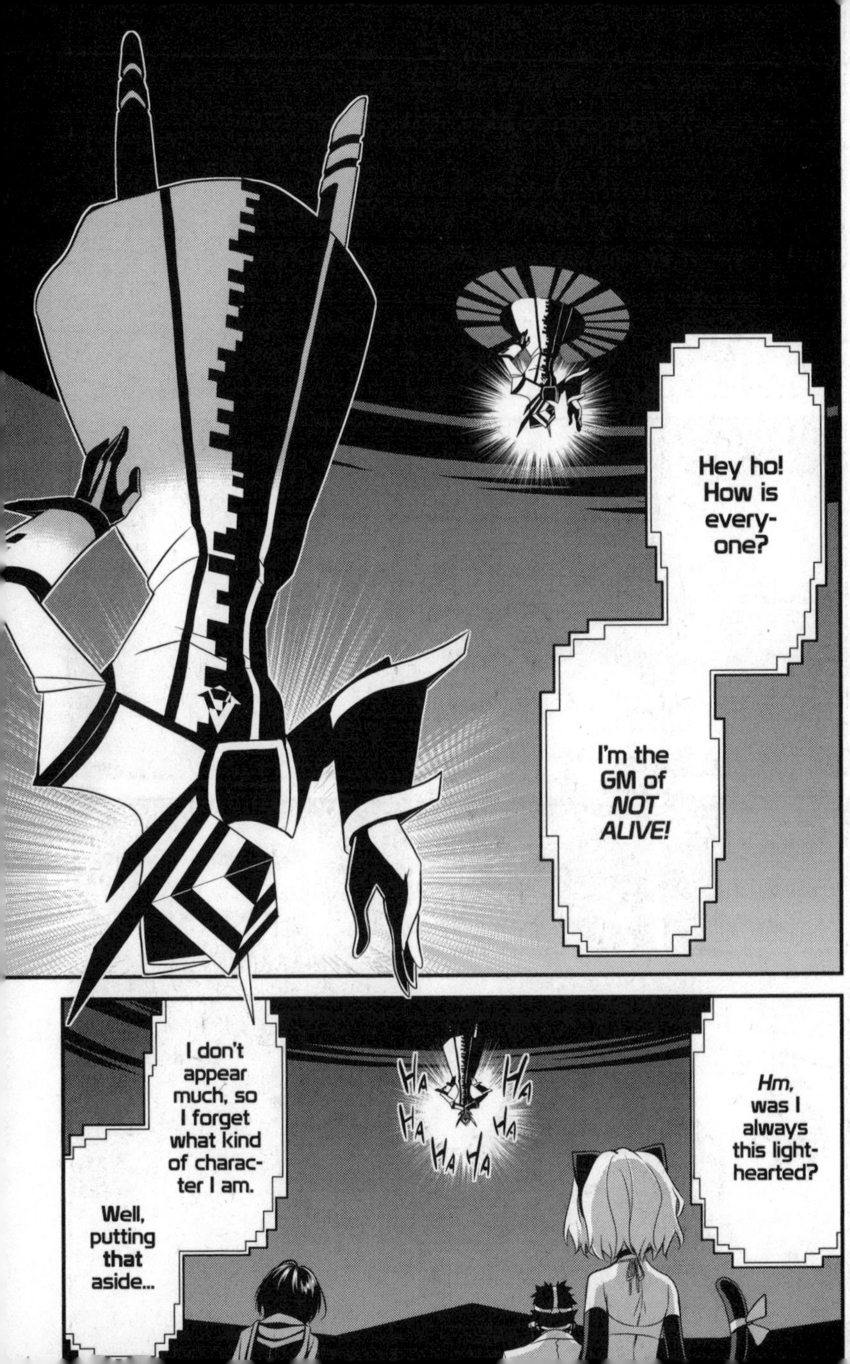
Hey ho! How is everyone?
I'm the GM of *NOT ALIVE!*
*Hm,* was I always this light-hearted?
HA HA HA HA HA HA HA
I don't appear much, so I forget what kind of character I am.
Well, putting that aside...

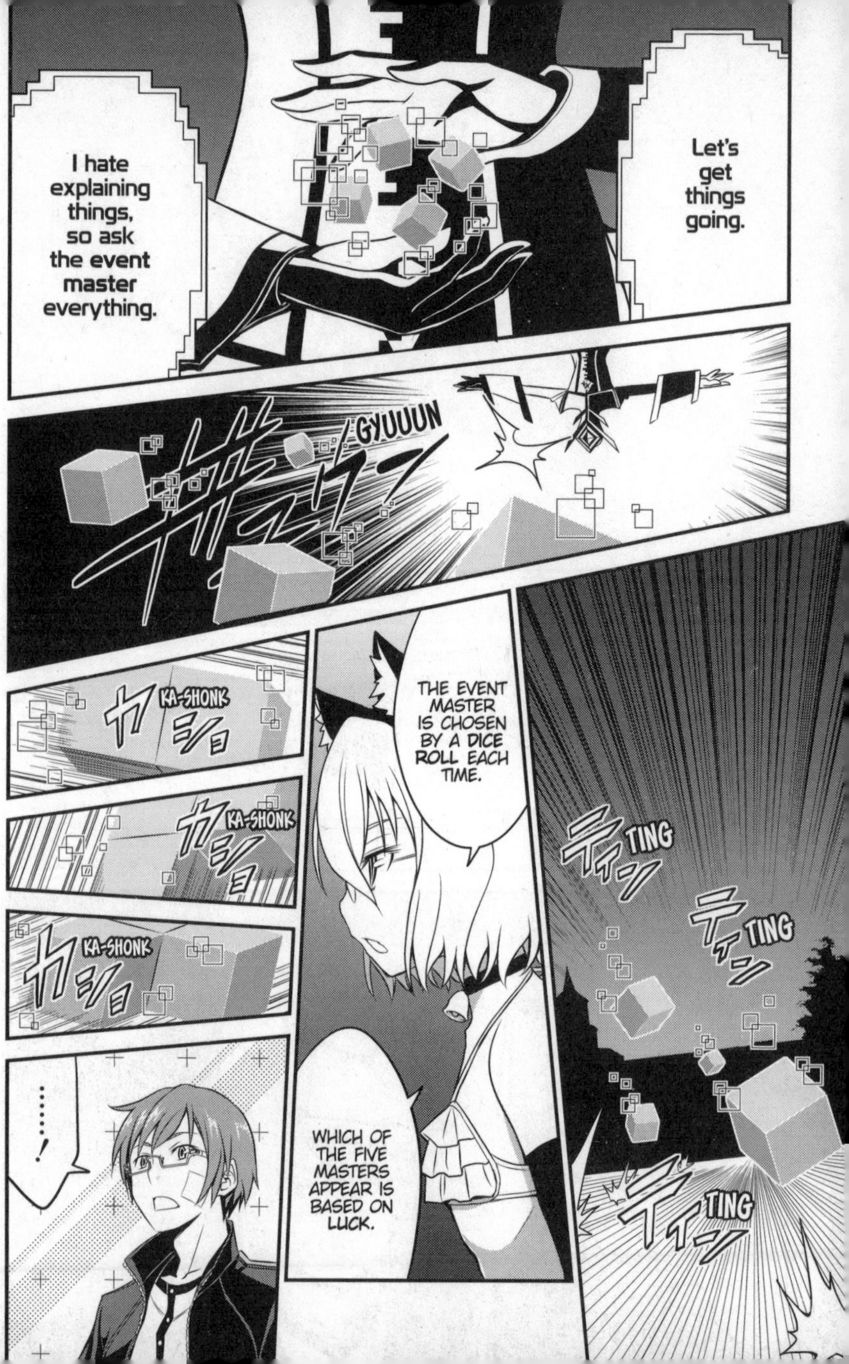
Let's get things going.
I hate explaining things, so ask the event master everything.
GYUUUN
TING
TING
TING
THE EVENT MASTER IS CHOSEN BY A DICE ROLL EACH TIME.
WHICH OF THE FIVE MASTERS APPEAR IS BASED ON LUCK.
KA-SHONK
KA-SHONK
KA-SHONK
......!

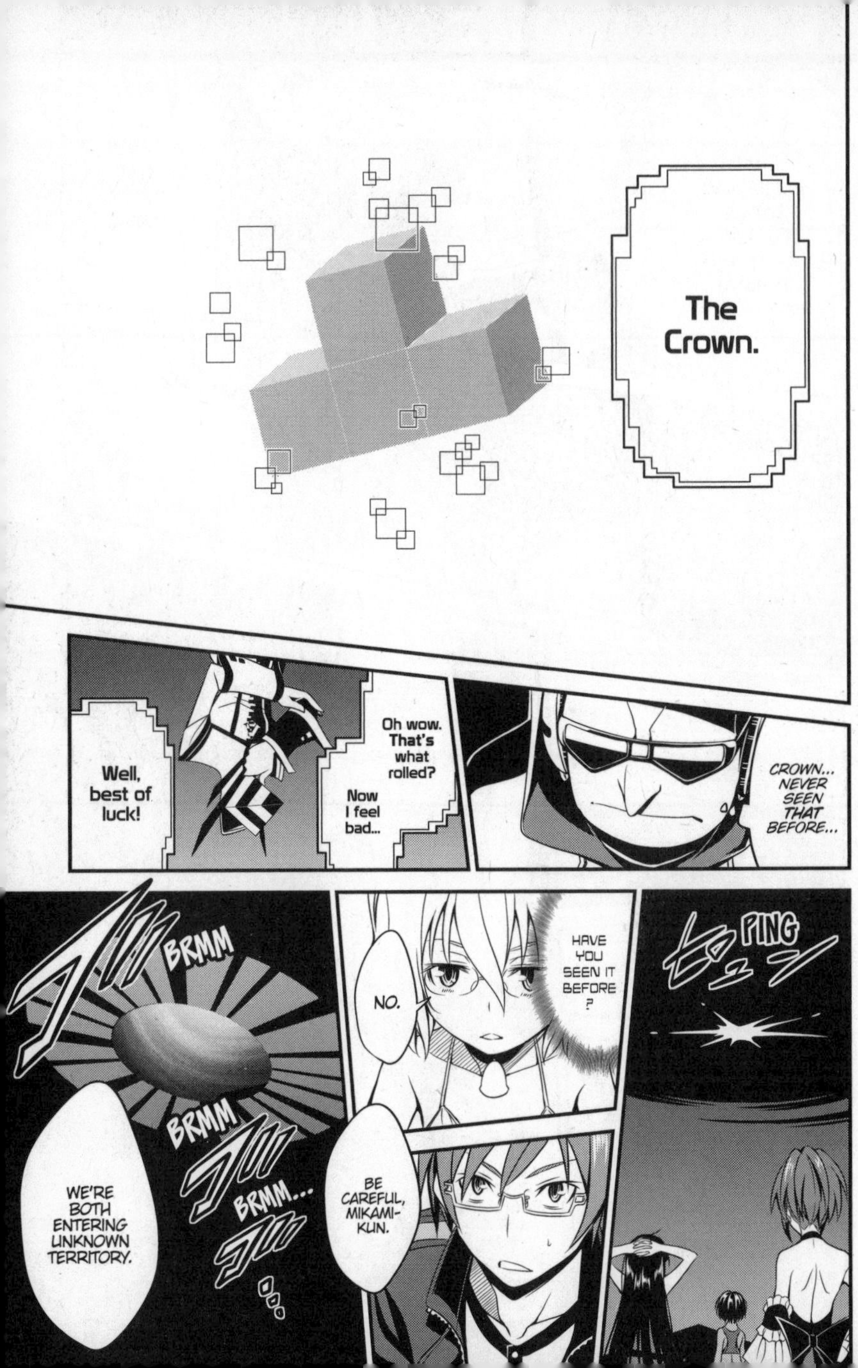
The Crown.
CROWN... NEVER SEEN THAT BEFORE...
Oh wow. That's what rolled?
Now I feel bad...
Well, best of luck!
PING
HAVE YOU SEEN IT BEFORE?
NO.
BE CAREFUL, MIKAMI-KUN.
BRMM
BRMM
BRMM...
WE'RE BOTH ENTERING UNKNOWN TERRITORY.

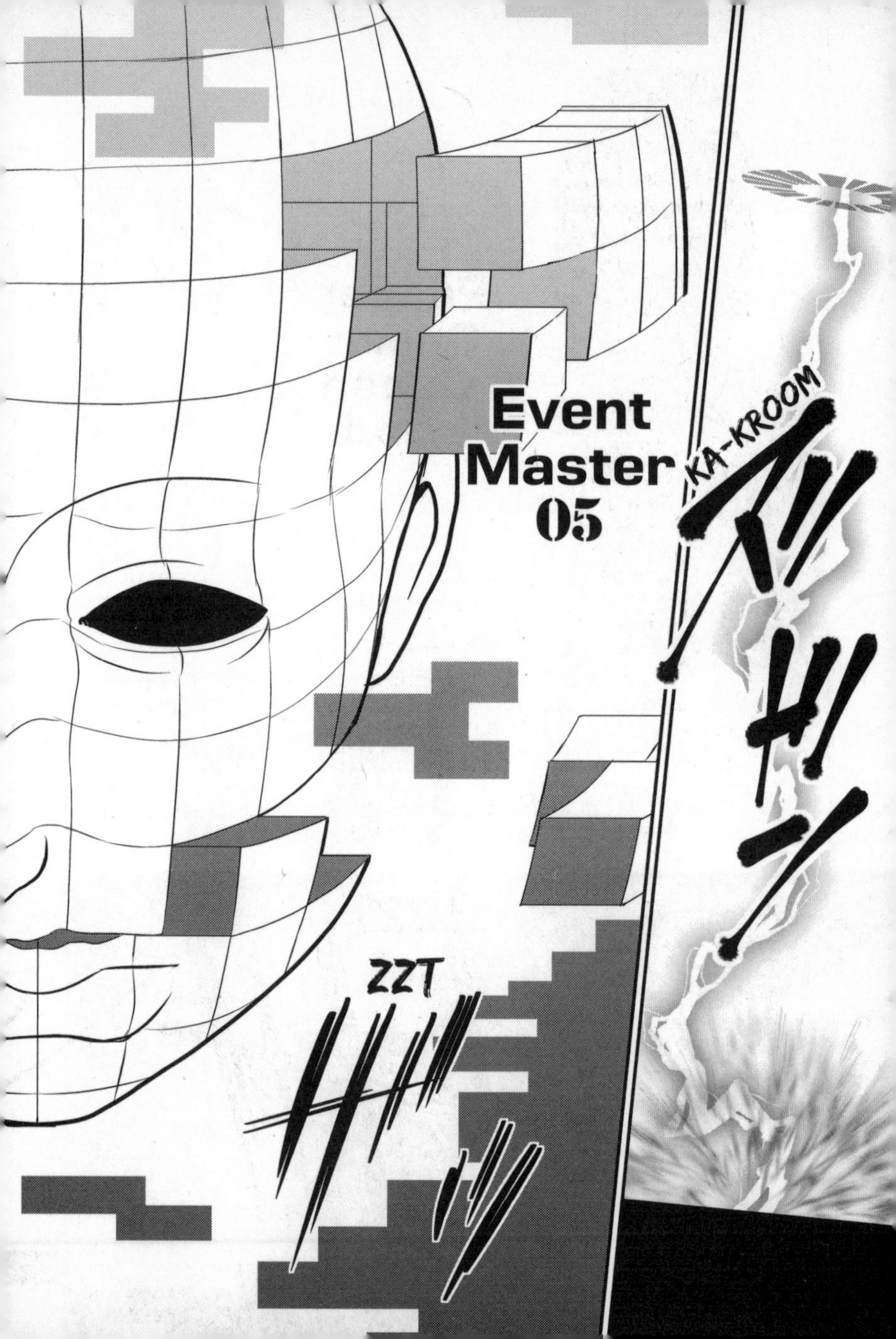
Event
Master
05
KA-KROOM
ZZT

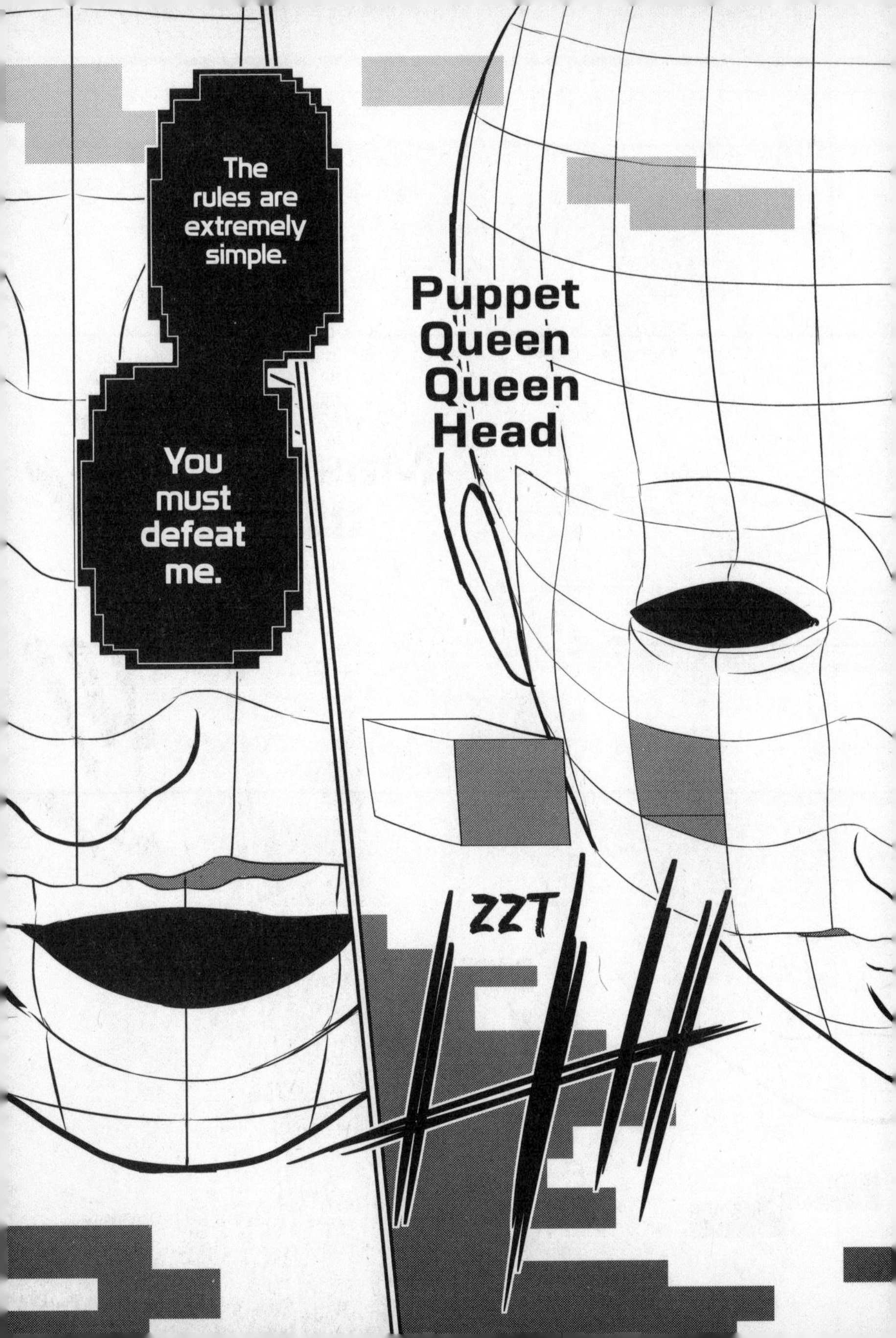
Puppet Queen Queen Head
ZZT
The rules are extremely simple.
You must defeat me.

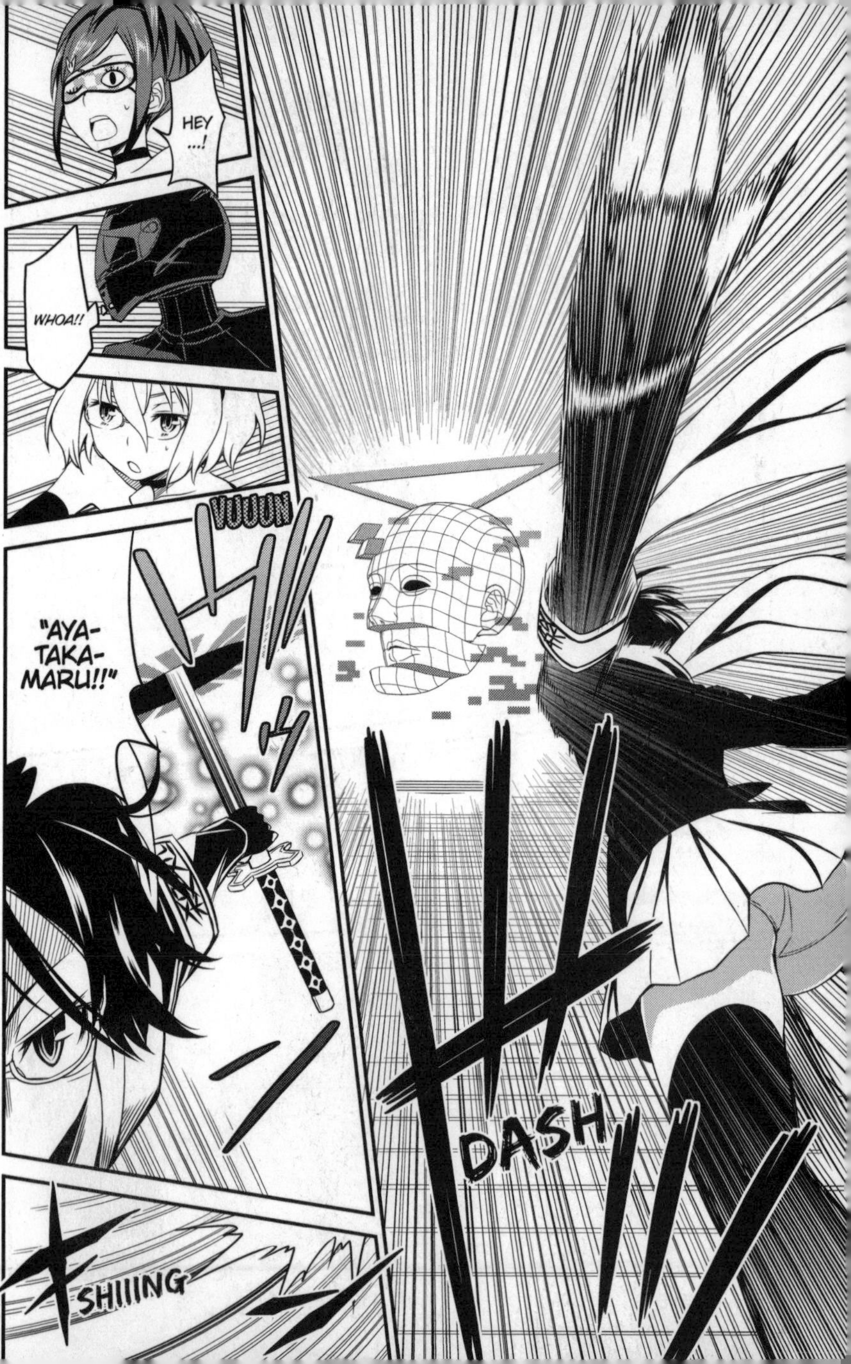
DASH
HEY ...!
WHOA!!
VUUUN
"AYA-TAKA-MARU!!"
SHIIING

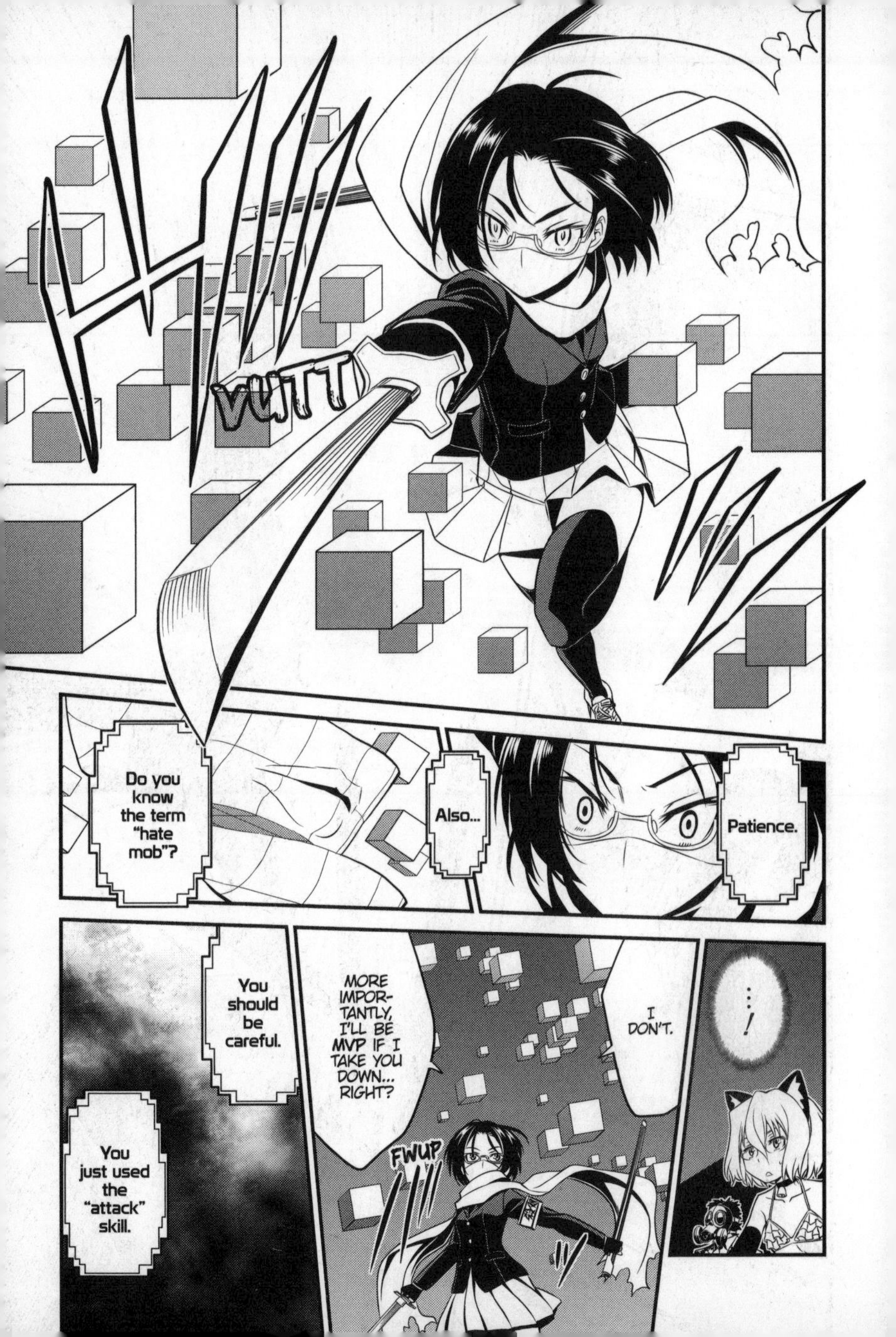
VUTT
Patience.
Also...
Do you know the term "hate mob"?
...!
I DON'T.
MORE IMPORTANTLY, I'LL BE MVP IF I TAKE YOU DOWN... RIGHT?
FWUP
You should be careful.
You just used the "attack" skill.

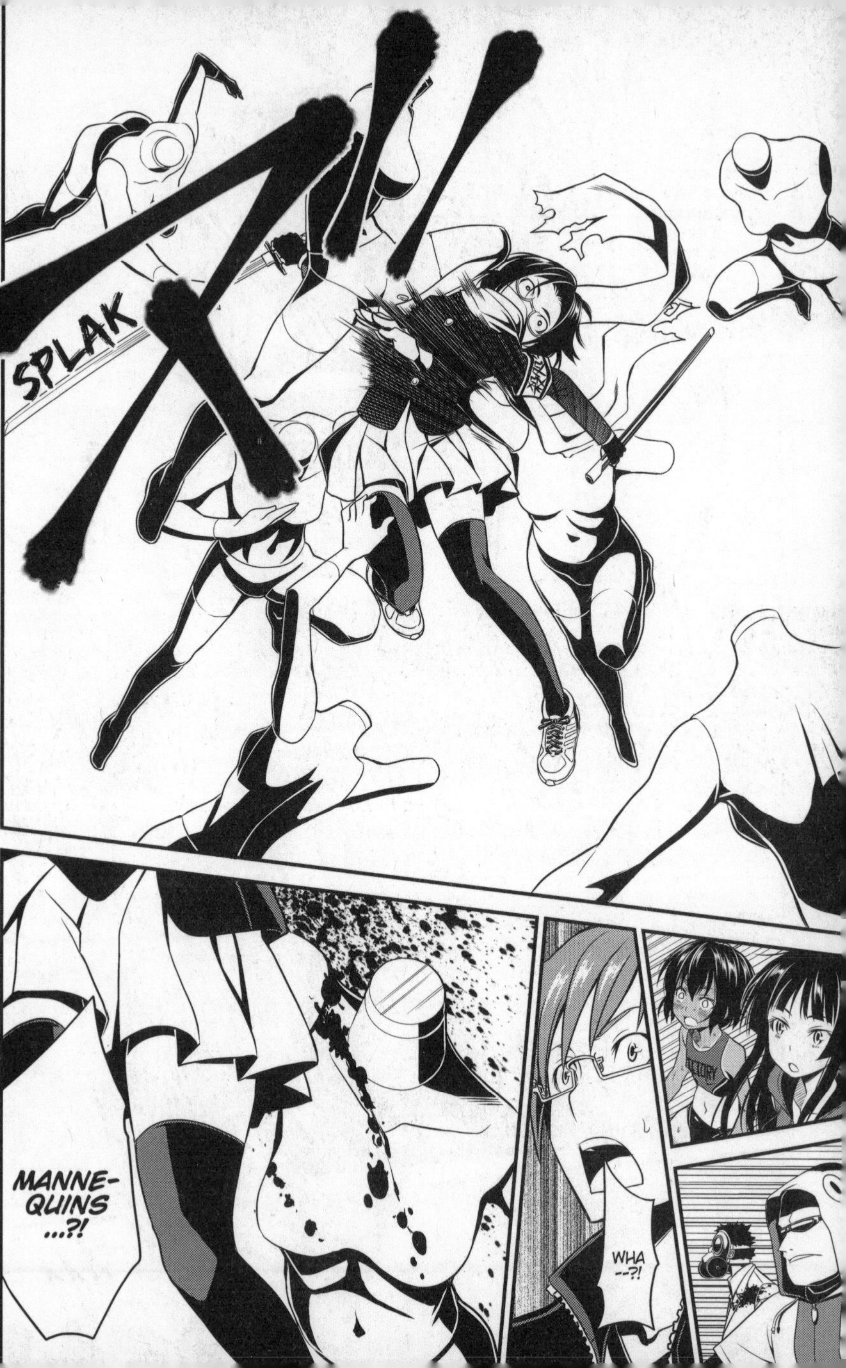
SPLAK
WHA--?!
MANNE-QUINS ...?!

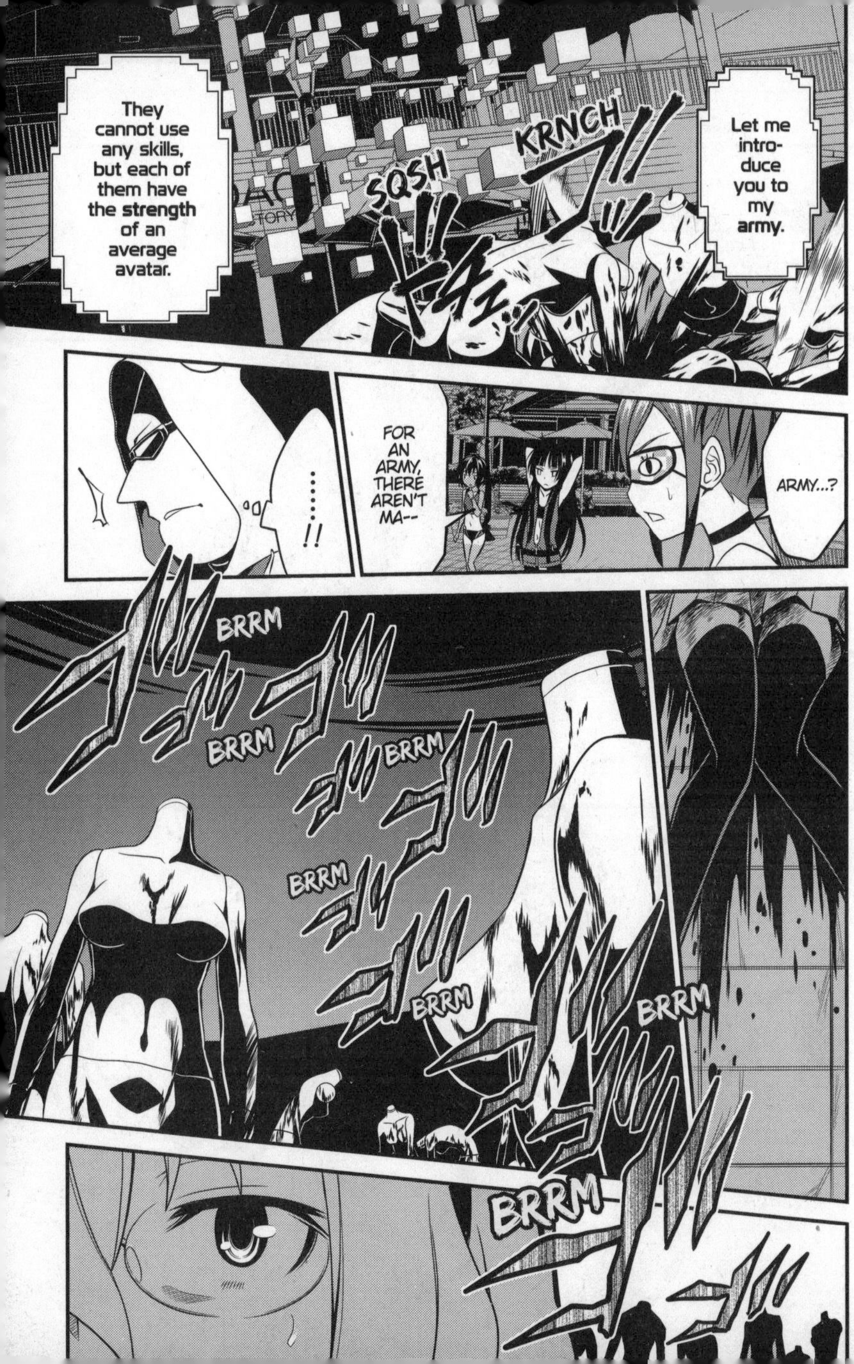
Let me intro-duce you to my army.
KRNCH
SQSH
They cannot use any skills, but each of them have the strength of an average avatar.
ARMY...?
FOR AN ARMY, THERE AREN'T MA--
......!!
BRRM
BRRM
BRRM
BRRM
BRRM
BRRM
BRRM

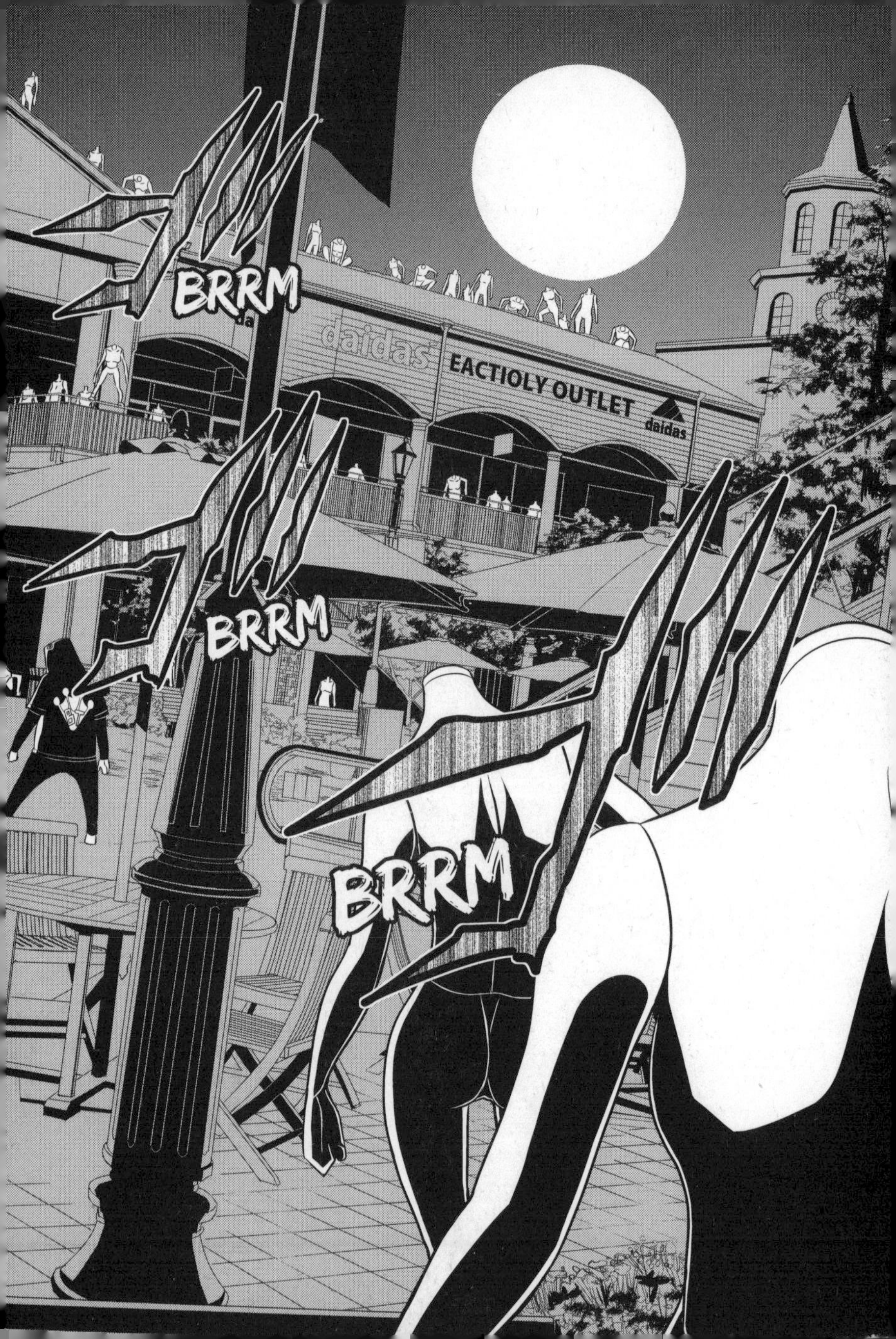
BRRM
daidas
EACTIOLY OUTLET
daidas
BRRM
BRRM

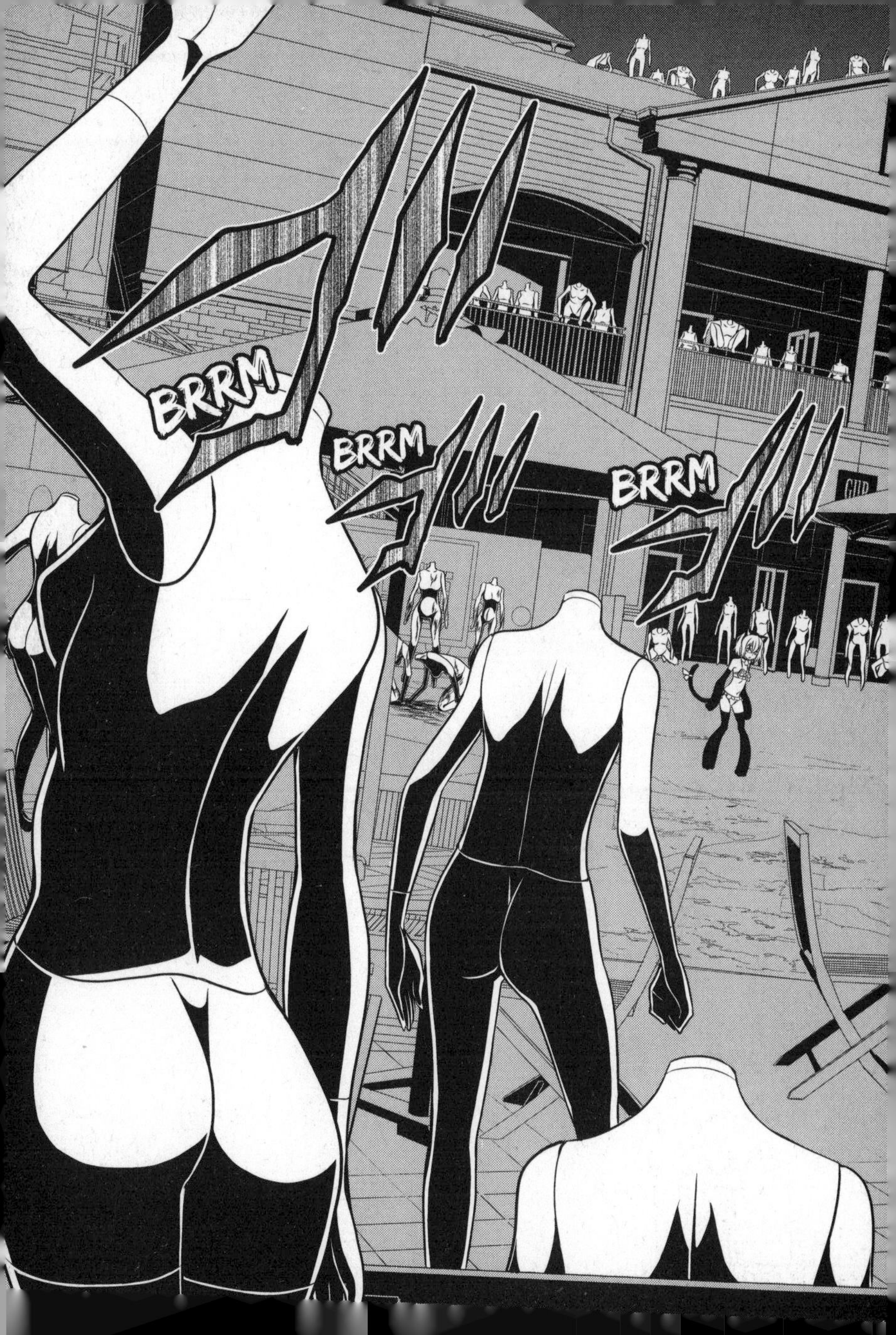
BRRM
BRRM
BRRM

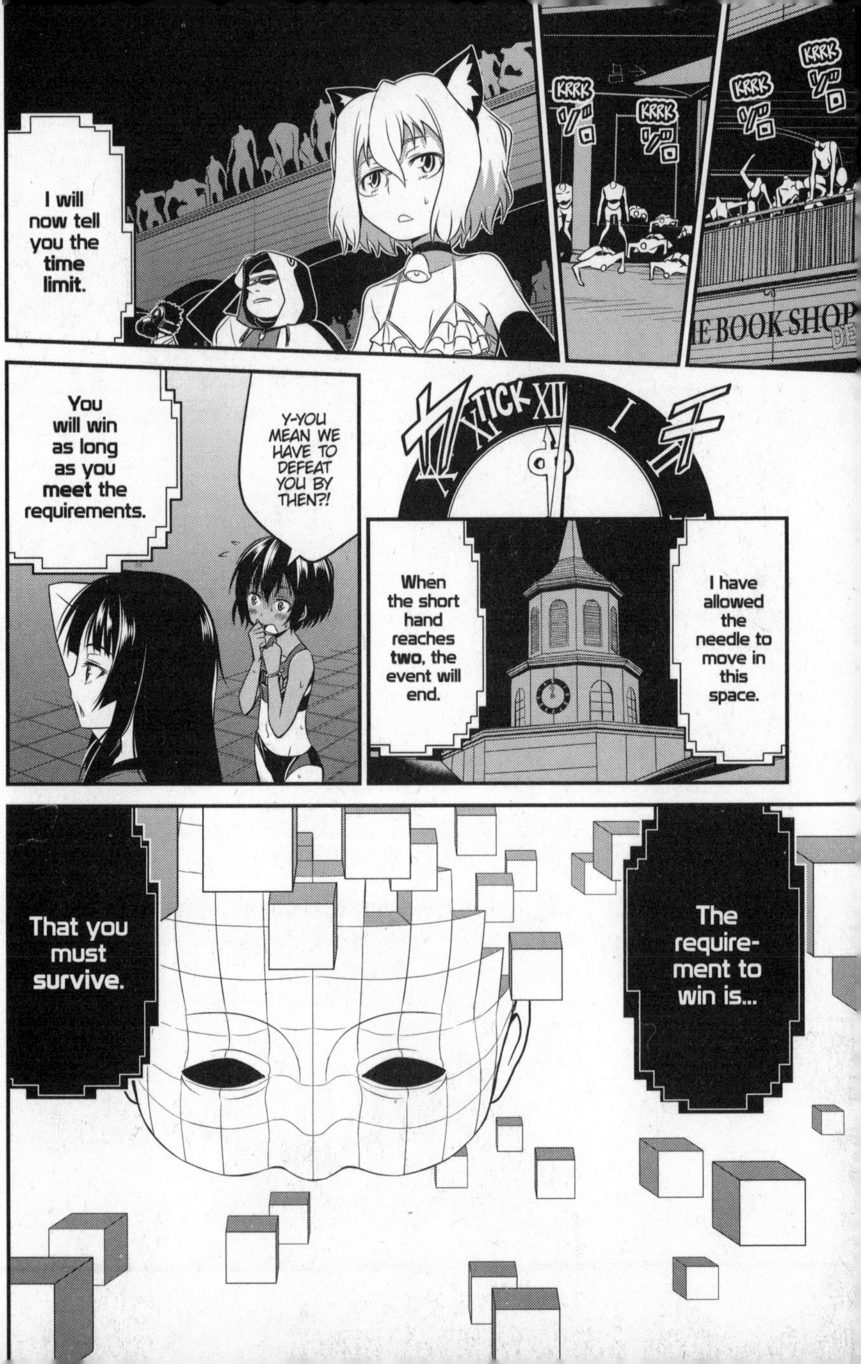
KRRK
KRRK
KRRK
KRRK
HE BOOK SHOP
I will now tell you the time limit.
TICK
I have allowed the needle to move in this space.
When the short hand reaches two, the event will end.
Y-YOU MEAN WE HAVE TO DEFEAT YOU BY THEN?!
You will win as long as you meet the requirements.
The require-ment to win is...
That you must survive.

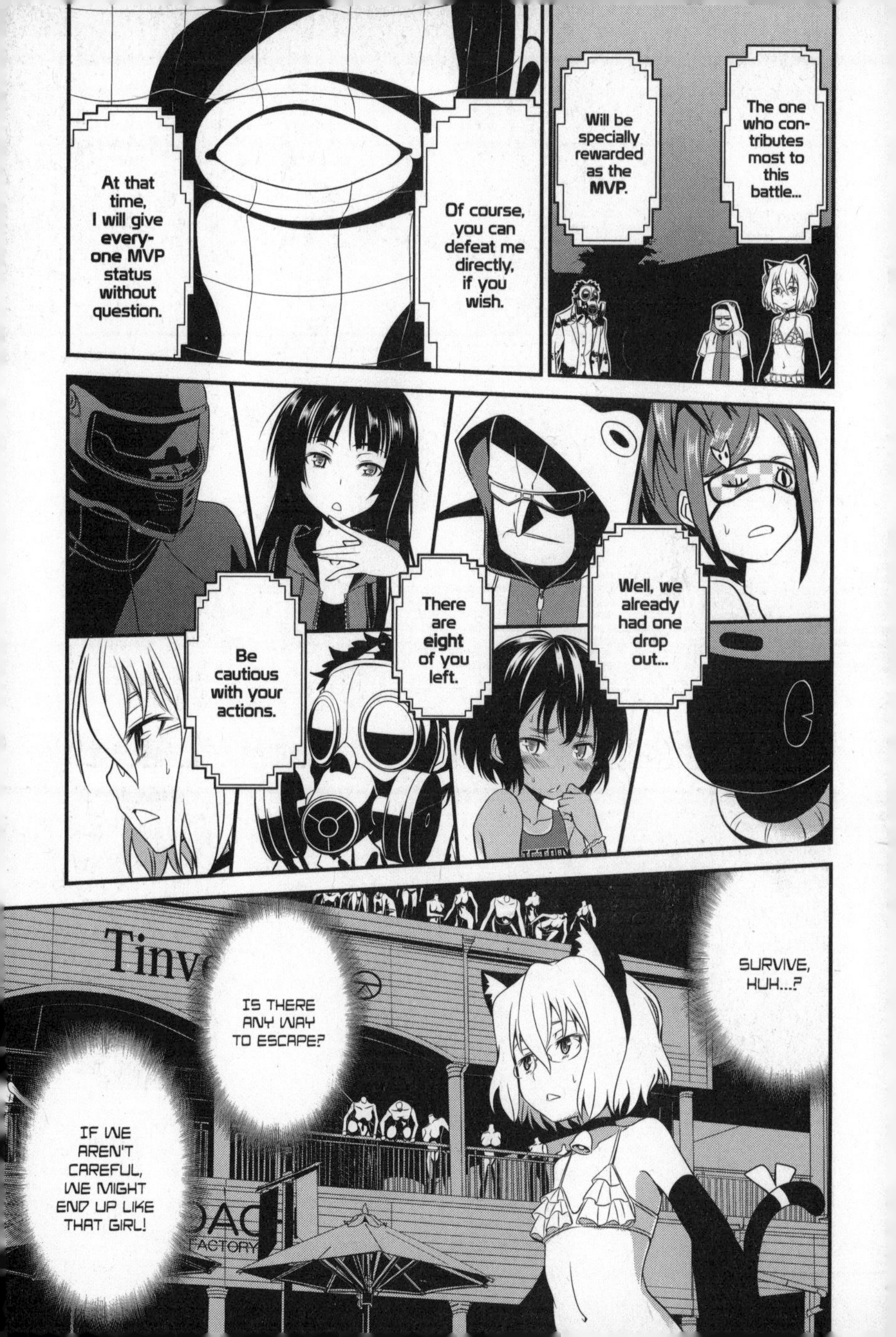
The one who con-tributes most to this battle...
Will be specially rewarded as the MVP.
Of course, you can defeat me directly, if you wish.
At that time, I will give every-one MVP status without question.
Well, we already had one drop out...
There are eight of you left.
Be cautious with your actions.
Tinv
SURVIVE, HUH...?
IS THERE ANY WAY TO ESCAPE?
IF WE AREN'T CAREFUL, WE MIGHT END UP LIKE THAT GIRL!
OACH
FACTORY

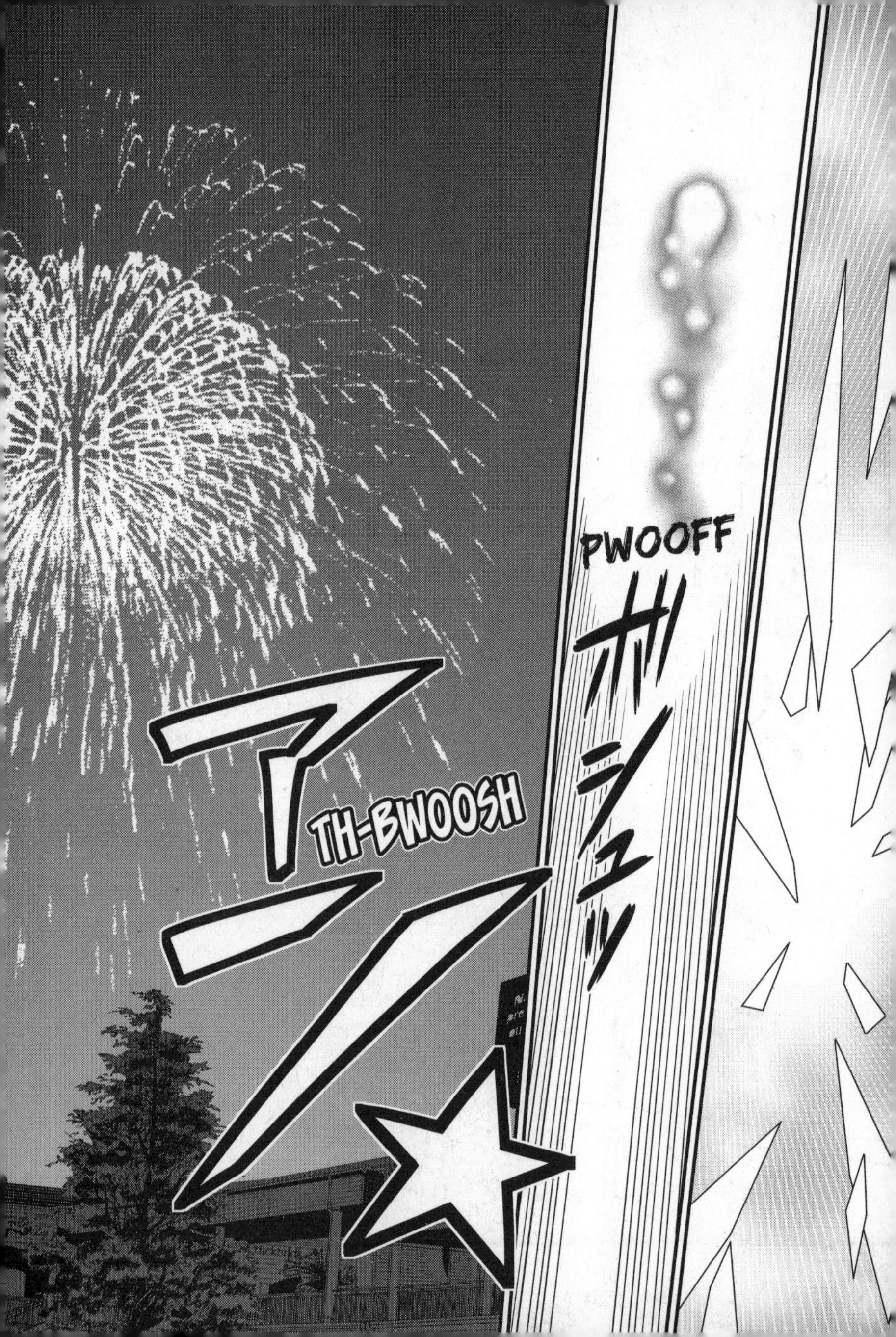
PWOOFF
TH-BWOOSH

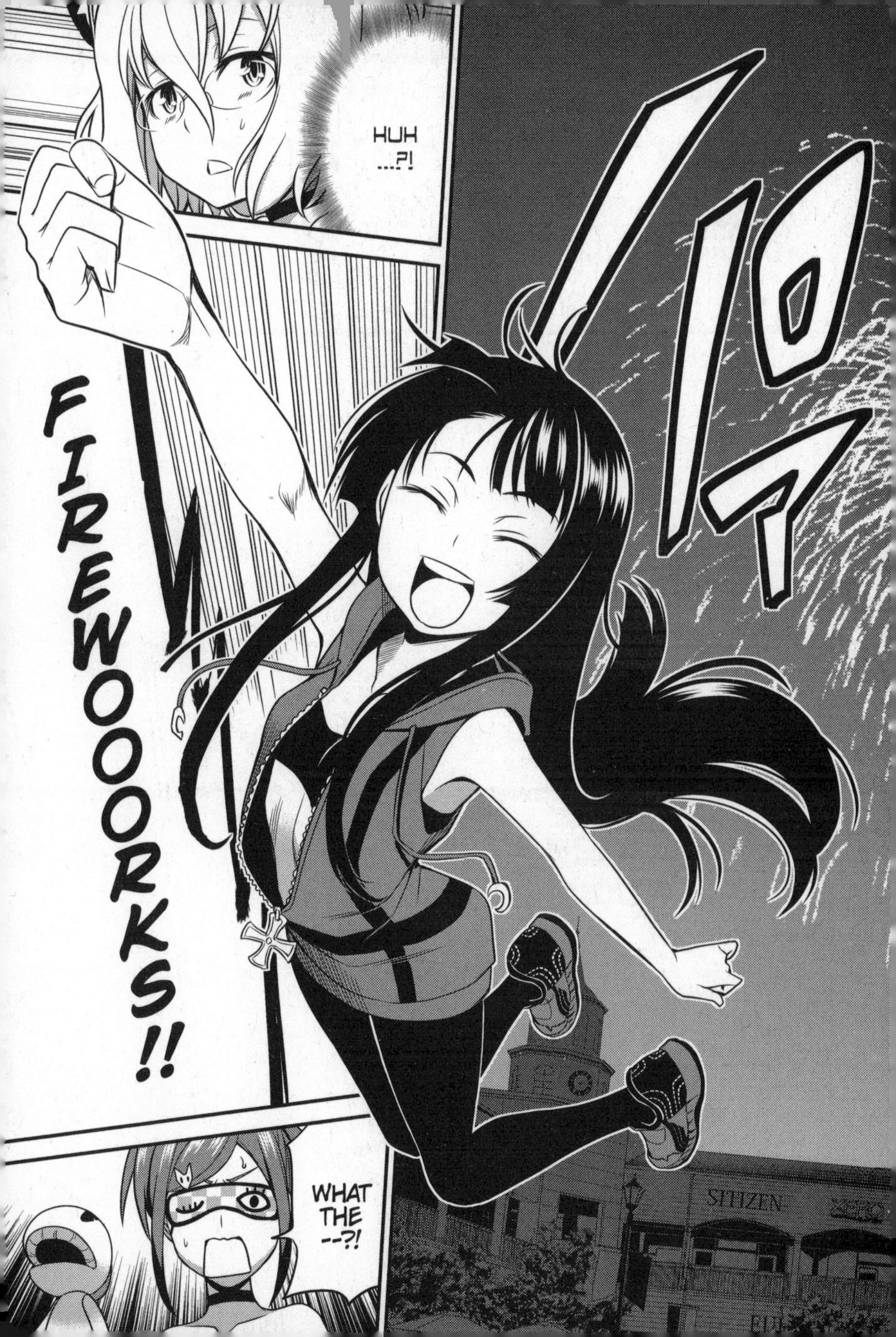
パァ
FIREWOOORKS!!
SITIZEN
HUH ...?!
WHAT THE --?!

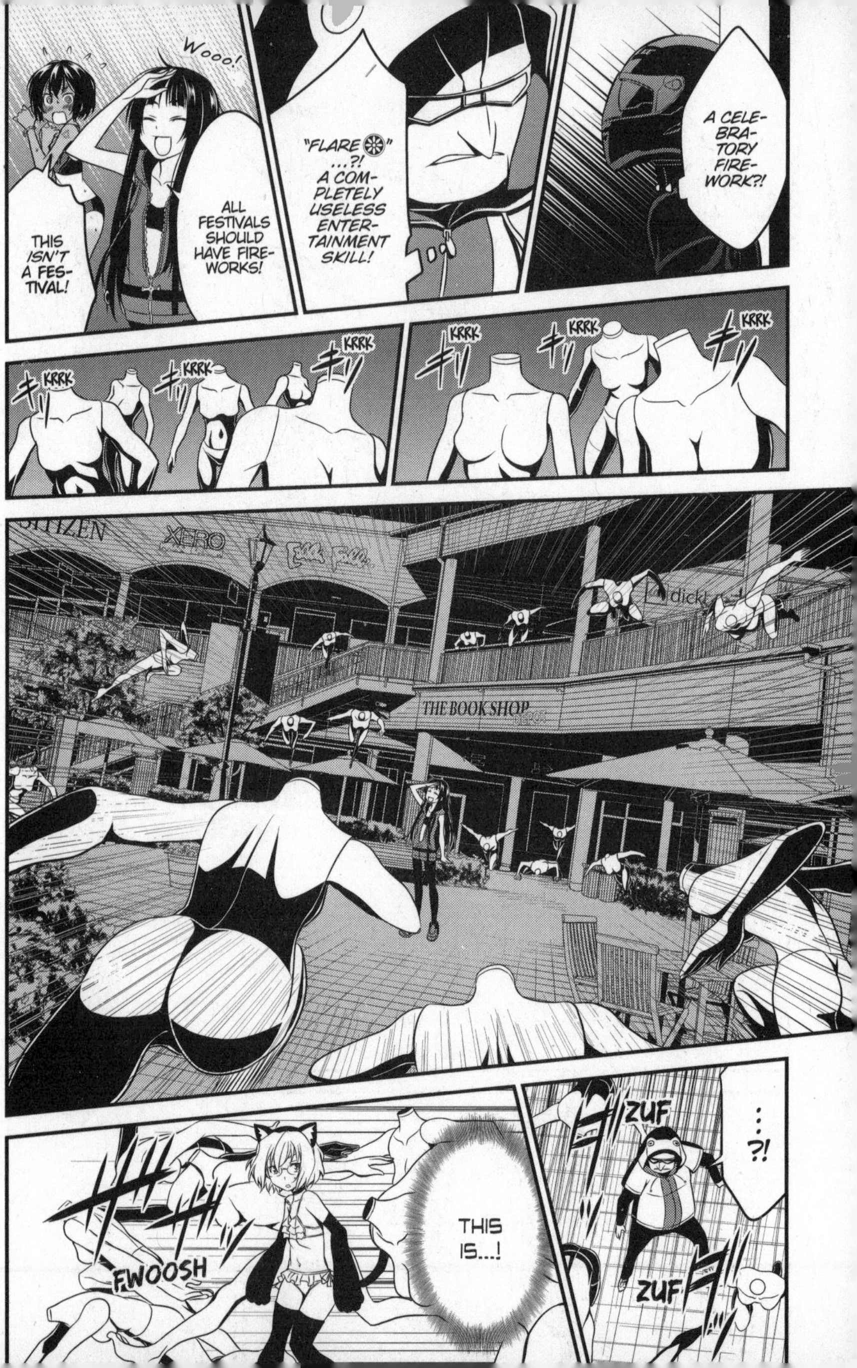
A CELEBRATORY FIREWORK?!
"FLARE ❀" ...?! A COMPLETELY USELESS ENTERTAINMENT SKILL!
Wooo!
ALL FESTIVALS SHOULD HAVE FIREWORKS!
THIS ISN'T A FESTIVAL!
KRRK
KRRK
KRRK
KRRK
KRRK
KRRK
KRRK
THE BOOK SHOP
...?!
ZUF
ZUF
THIS IS...!
F.WOOSH

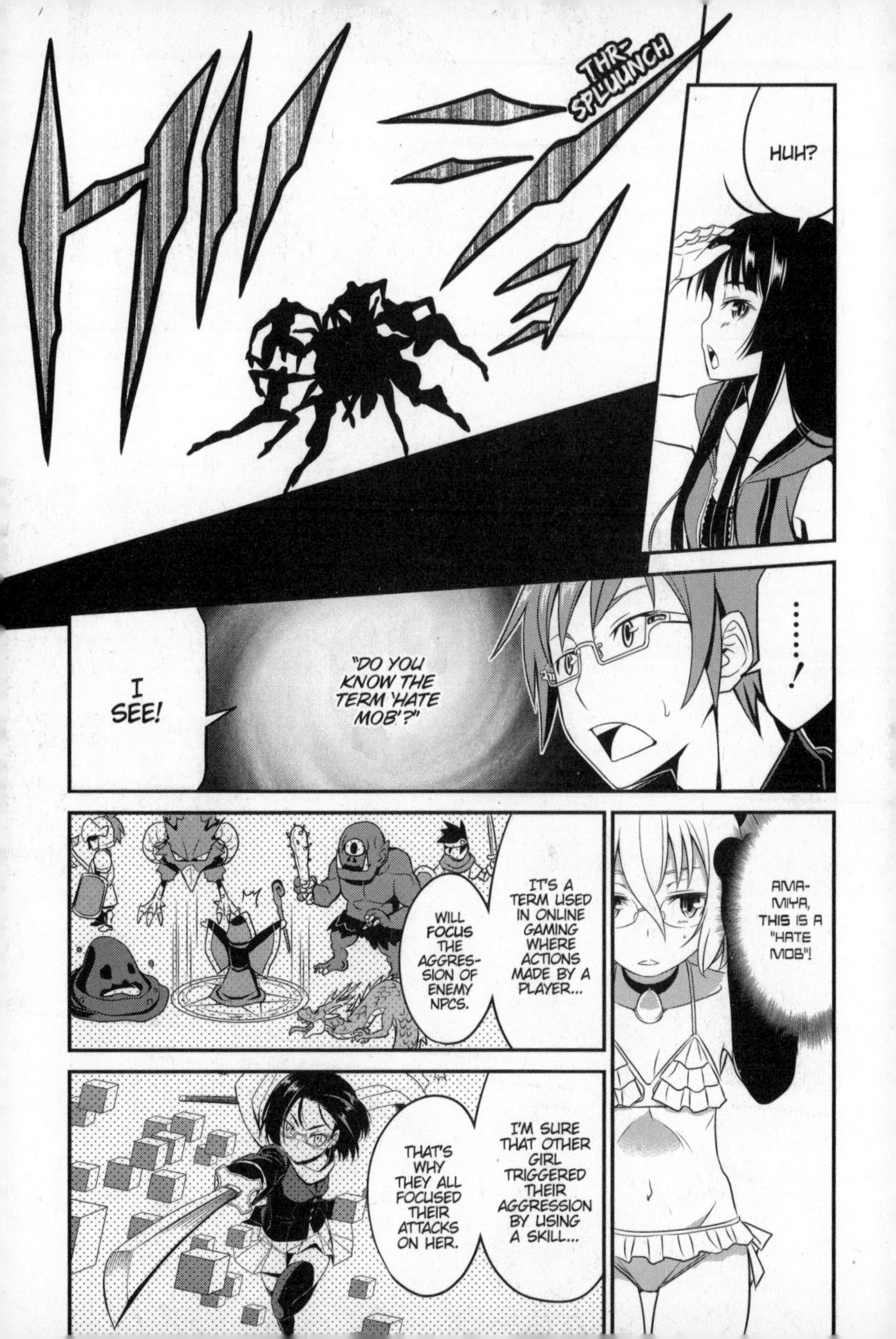
THR-SPLUUNCH
HUH?
......!
"DO YOU KNOW THE TERM 'HATE MOB'?"
I SEE!
AMA-MIYA, THIS IS A "HATE MOB"!
IT'S A TERM USED IN ONLINE GAMING WHERE ACTIONS MADE BY A PLAYER...
WILL FOCUS THE AGGRES-SION OF ENEMY NPCS.
I'M SURE THAT OTHER GIRL TRIGGERED THEIR AGGRESSION BY USING A SKILL...
THAT'S WHY THEY ALL FOCUSED THEIR ATTACKS ON HER.

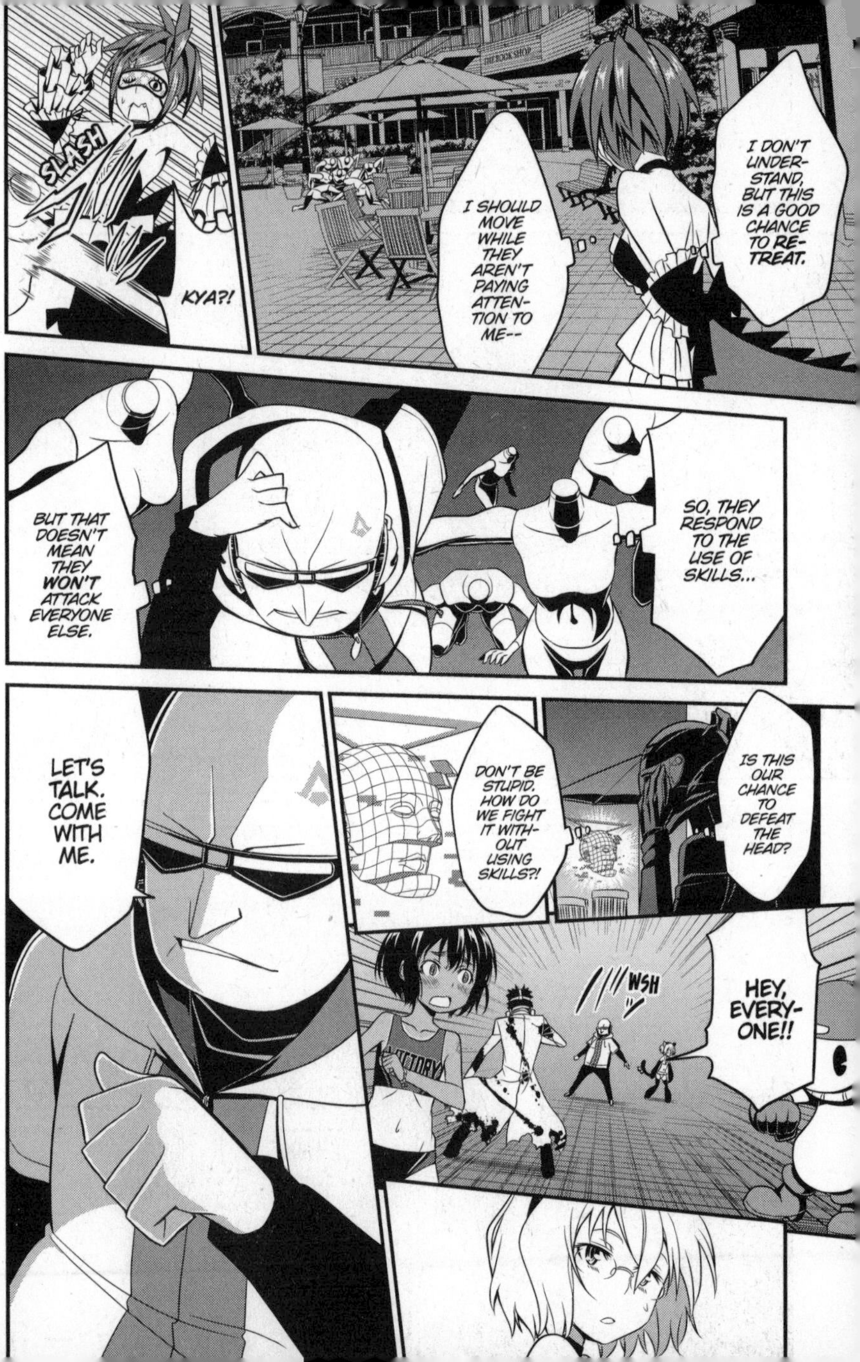
I DON'T UNDERSTAND, BUT THIS IS A GOOD CHANCE TO RETREAT.
I SHOULD MOVE WHILE THEY AREN'T PAYING ATTENTION TO ME--
SLASH
KYA?!
SO, THEY RESPOND TO THE USE OF SKILLS...
BUT THAT DOESN'T MEAN THEY WON'T ATTACK EVERYONE ELSE.
IS THIS OUR CHANCE TO DEFEAT THE HEAD?
DON'T BE STUPID. HOW DO WE FIGHT IT WITHOUT USING SKILLS?!
HEY, EVERYONE!!
WSH
LET'S TALK. COME WITH ME.

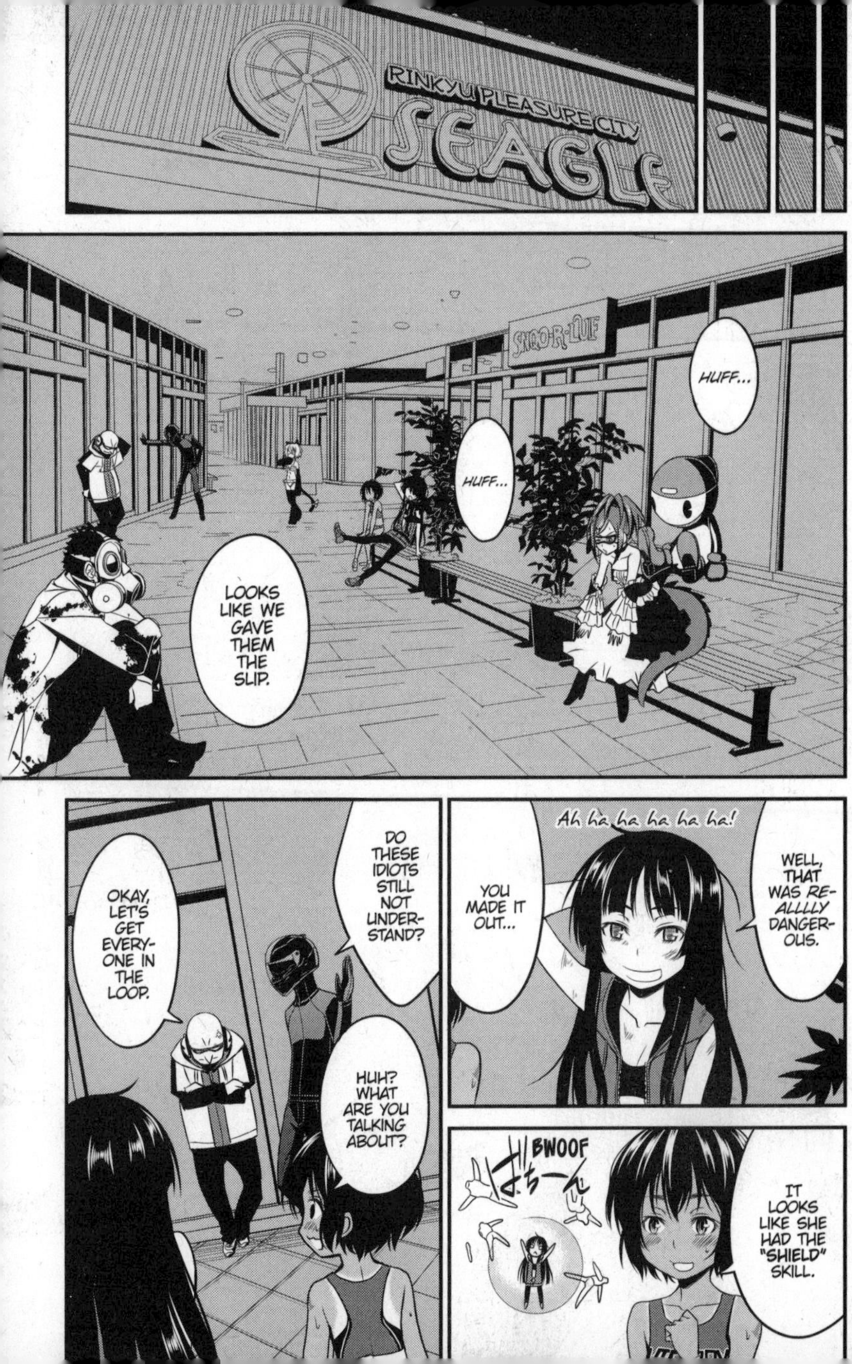

RINKYU PLEASURE CITY
SEAGLE
HUFF...
HUFF...
LOOKS LIKE WE GAVE THEM THE SLIP.
Ah ha ha ha ha ha!
WELL, THAT WAS RE-ALLLLY DANGEROUS.
YOU MADE IT OUT...
IT LOOKS LIKE SHE HAD THE "SHIELD" SKILL.
BWOOF
ぱちーん
DO THESE IDIOTS STILL NOT UNDER-STAND?
OKAY, LET'S GET EVERY-ONE IN THE LOOP.
HUH? WHAT ARE YOU TALKING ABOUT?

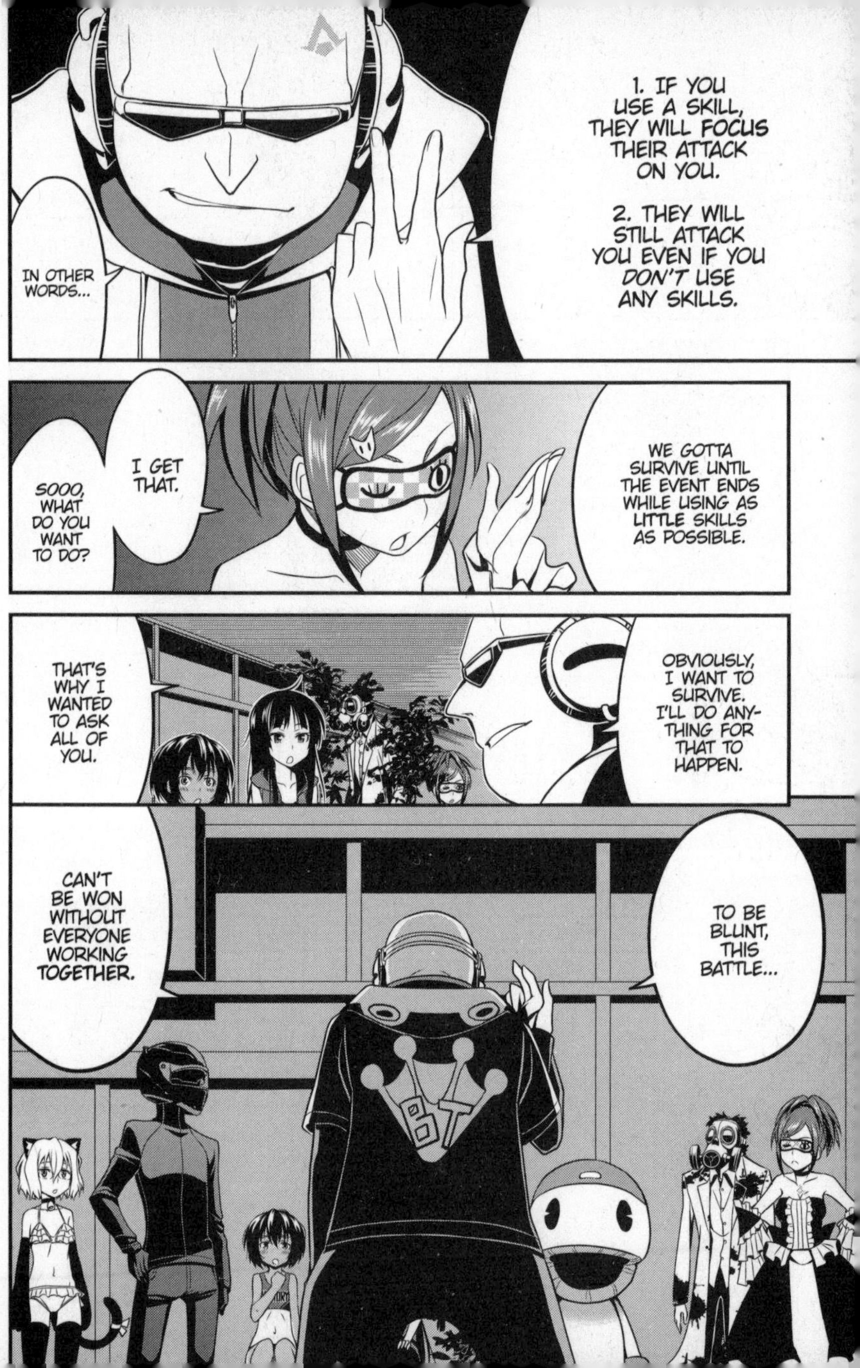
1. IF YOU USE A SKILL, THEY WILL FOCUS THEIR ATTACK ON YOU.
2. THEY WILL STILL ATTACK YOU EVEN IF YOU *DON'T* USE ANY SKILLS.
IN OTHER WORDS...
WE GOTTA SURVIVE UNTIL THE EVENT ENDS WHILE USING AS LITTLE SKILLS AS POSSIBLE.
I GET THAT.
SOOO, WHAT DO YOU WANT TO DO?
OBVIOUSLY, I WANT TO SURVIVE. I'LL DO ANY-THING FOR THAT TO HAPPEN.
THAT'S WHY I WANTED TO ASK ALL OF YOU.
TO BE BLUNT, THIS BATTLE...
CAN'T BE WON WITHOUT EVERYONE WORKING TOGETHER.

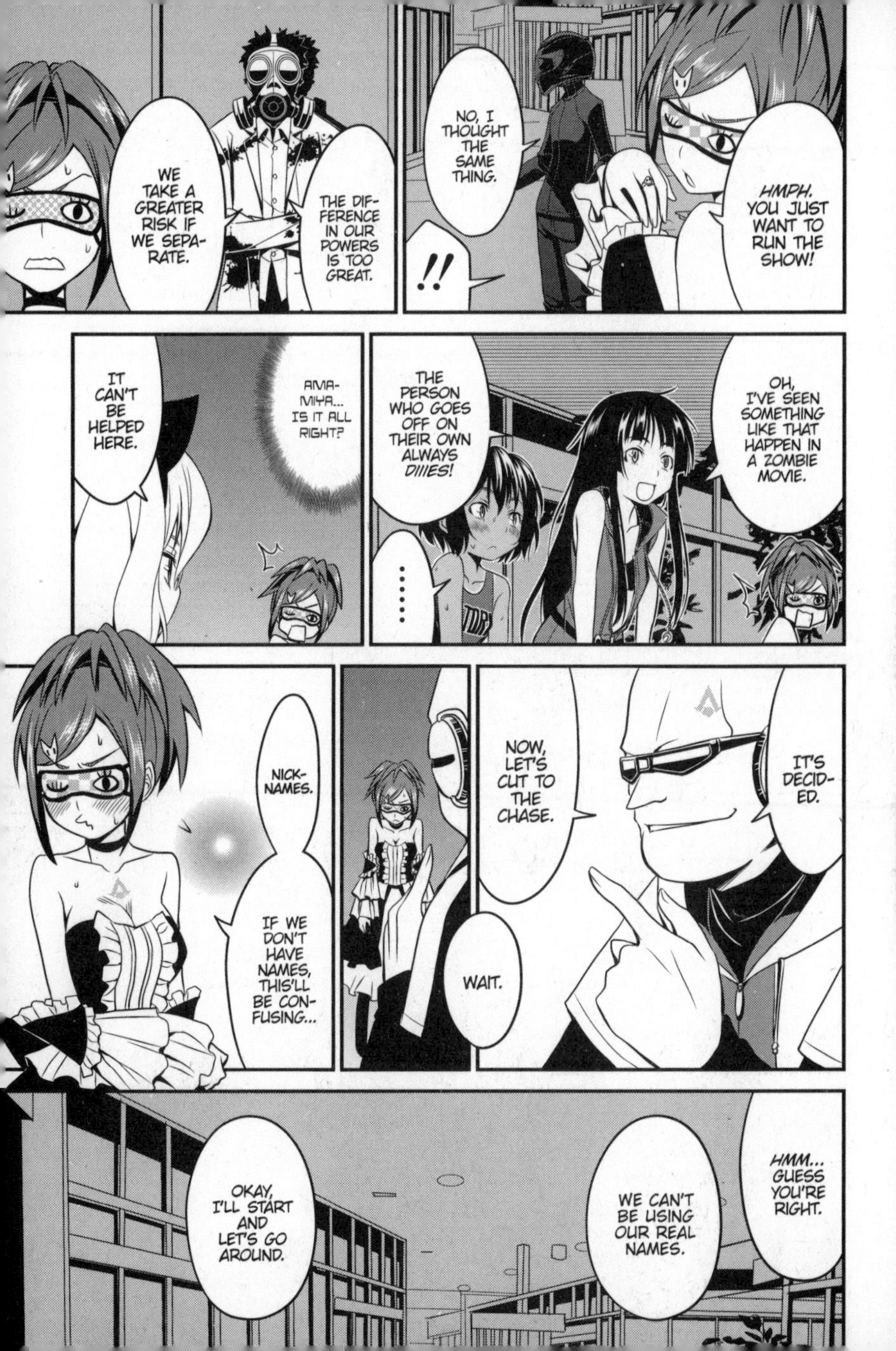

HMPH. YOU JUST WANT TO RUN THE SHOW!
NO, I THOUGHT THE SAME THING.
!!
THE DIFFERENCE IN OUR POWERS IS TOO GREAT.
WE TAKE A GREATER RISK IF WE SEPARATE.
OH, I'VE SEEN SOMETHING LIKE THAT HAPPEN IN A ZOMBIE MOVIE.
THE PERSON WHO GOES OFF ON THEIR OWN ALWAYS DIIIES!
......
AMAMIYA... IS IT ALL RIGHT?
IT CAN'T BE HELPED HERE.
IT'S DECIDED.
NOW, LET'S CUT TO THE CHASE.
WAIT.
NICKNAMES.
IF WE DON'T HAVE NAMES, THIS'LL BE CONFUSING...
HMM... GUESS YOU'RE RIGHT.
WE CAN'T BE USING OUR REAL NAMES.
OKAY, I'LL START AND LET'S GO AROUND.

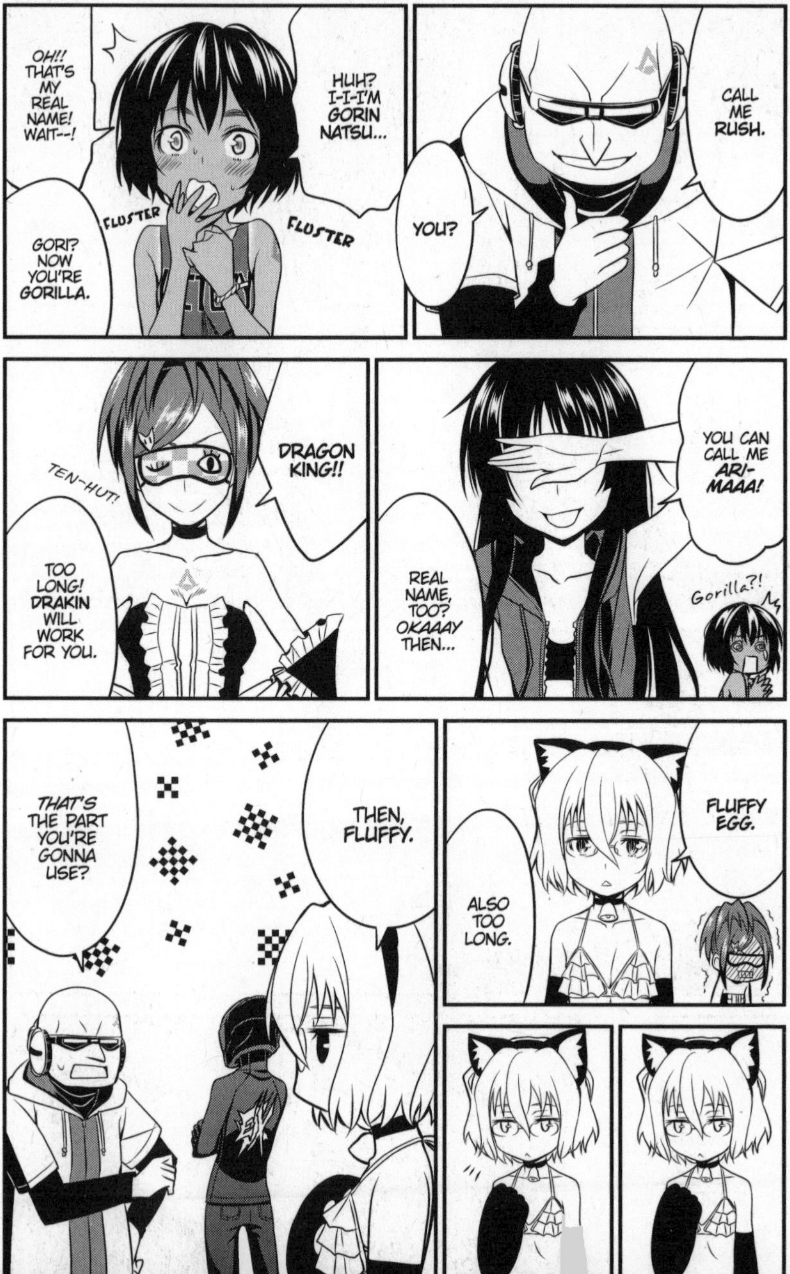
CALL ME RUSH.
YOU?
HUH? I-I-I'M GORIN NATSU...
OH!! THAT'S MY REAL NAME! WAIT--!
FLUSTER
FLUSTER
GORI? NOW YOU'RE GORILLA.
YOU CAN CALL ME ARI-MAAA!
REAL NAME, TOO? OKAAAY THEN...
Gorilla?!
DRAGON KING!!
TEN-HUT!
TOO LONG! DRAKIN WILL WORK FOR YOU.
FLUFFY EGG.
ALSO TOO LONG.
THEN, FLUFFY.
THAT'S THE PART YOU'RE GONNA USE?

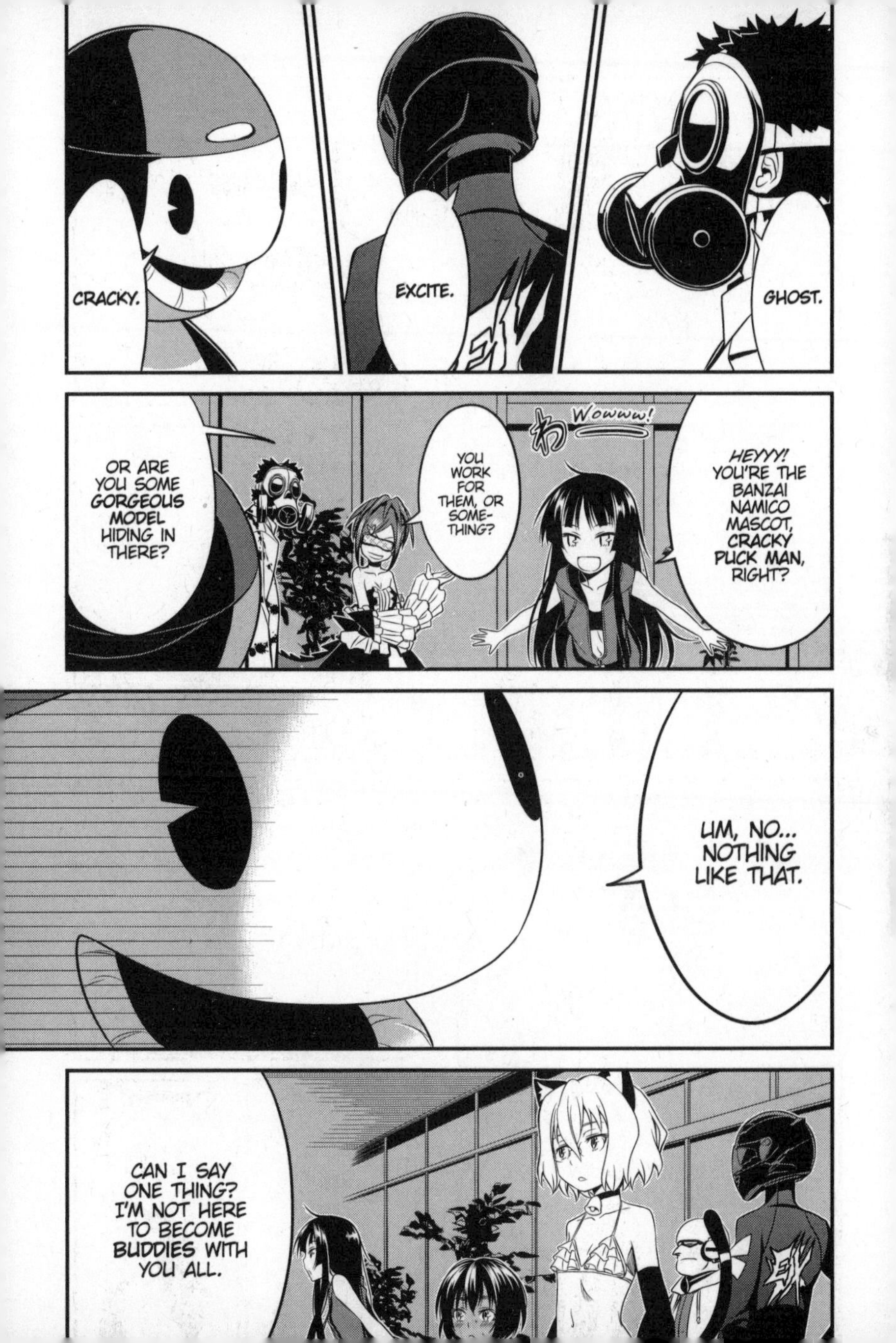
GHOST.
EXCITE.
CRACKY.
HEYYY! YOU'RE THE BANZAI NAMICO MASCOT, CRACKY PUCK MAN, RIGHT?
わー Wowww!
YOU WORK FOR THEM, OR SOME-THING?
OR ARE YOU SOME GORGEOUS MODEL HIDING IN THERE?
UM, NO... NOTHING LIKE THAT.
CAN I SAY ONE THING? I'M NOT HERE TO BECOME BUDDIES WITH YOU ALL.

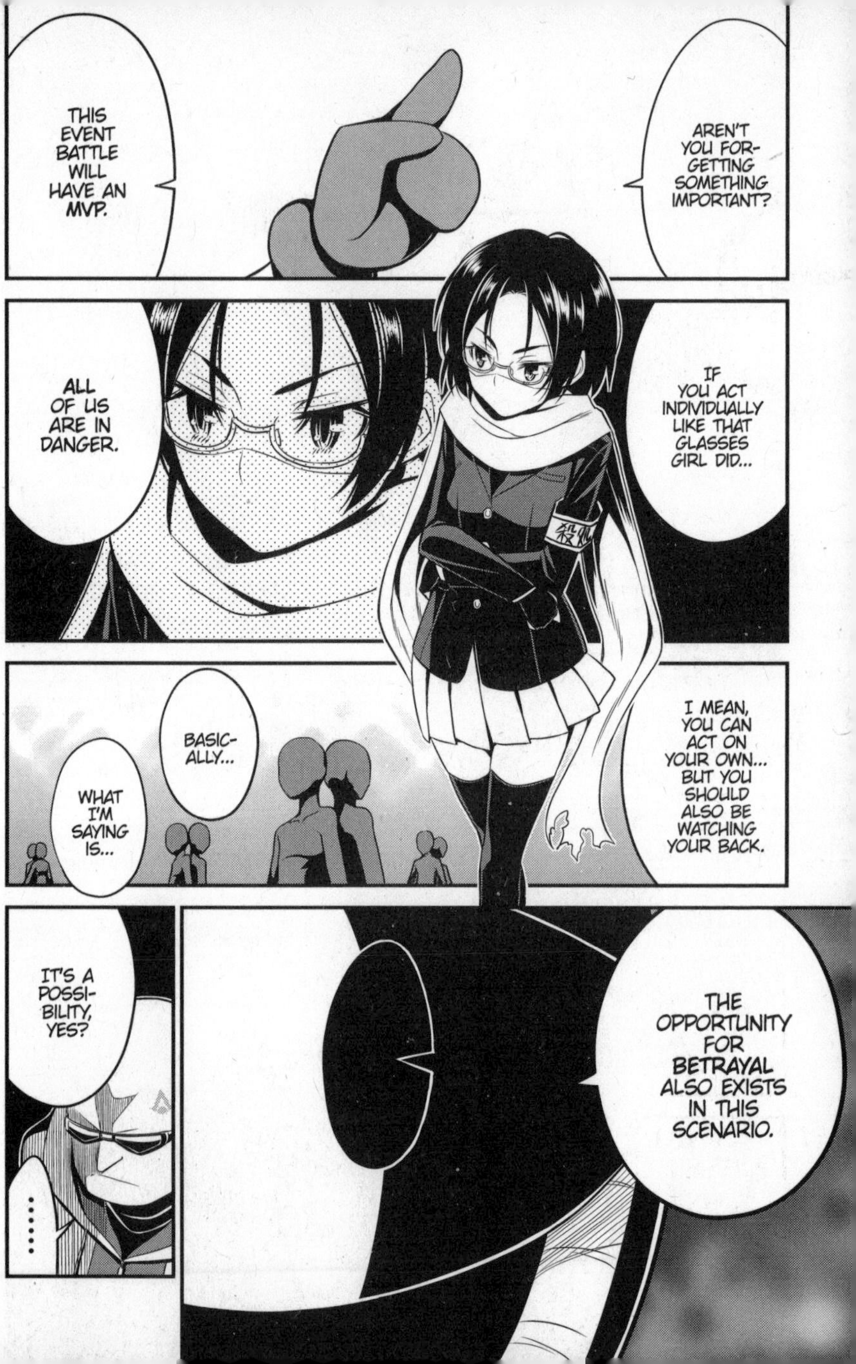
AREN'T YOU FOR-GETTING SOMETHING IMPORTANT?
THIS EVENT BATTLE WILL HAVE AN MVP.
IF YOU ACT INDIVIDUALLY LIKE THAT GLASSES GIRL DID...
ALL OF US ARE IN DANGER.
I MEAN, YOU CAN ACT ON YOUR OWN... BUT YOU SHOULD ALSO BE WATCHING YOUR BACK.
BASIC-ALLY...
WHAT I'M SAYING IS...
THE OPPORTUNITY FOR BETRAYAL ALSO EXISTS IN THIS SCENARIO.
IT'S A POSSI-BILITY, YES?
......

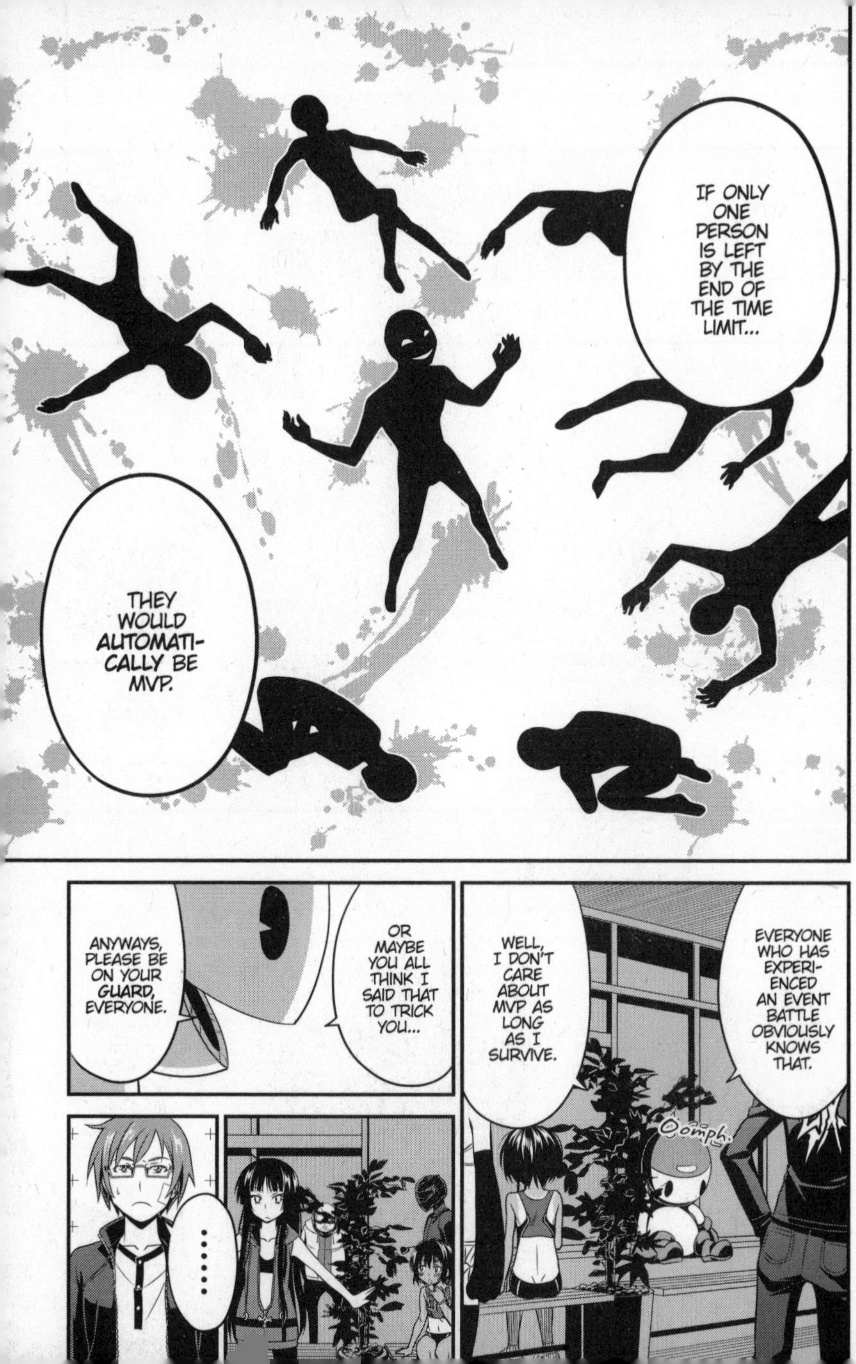
IF ONLY ONE PERSON IS LEFT BY THE END OF THE TIME LIMIT...
THEY WOULD AUTOMATI-CALLY BE MVP.
EVERYONE WHO HAS EXPERI-ENCED AN EVENT BATTLE OBVIOUSLY KNOWS THAT.
WELL, I DON'T CARE ABOUT MVP AS LONG AS I SURVIVE.
Oomph.
OR MAYBE YOU ALL THINK I SAID THAT TO TRICK YOU...
ANYWAYS, PLEASE BE ON YOUR GUARD, EVERYONE.
......

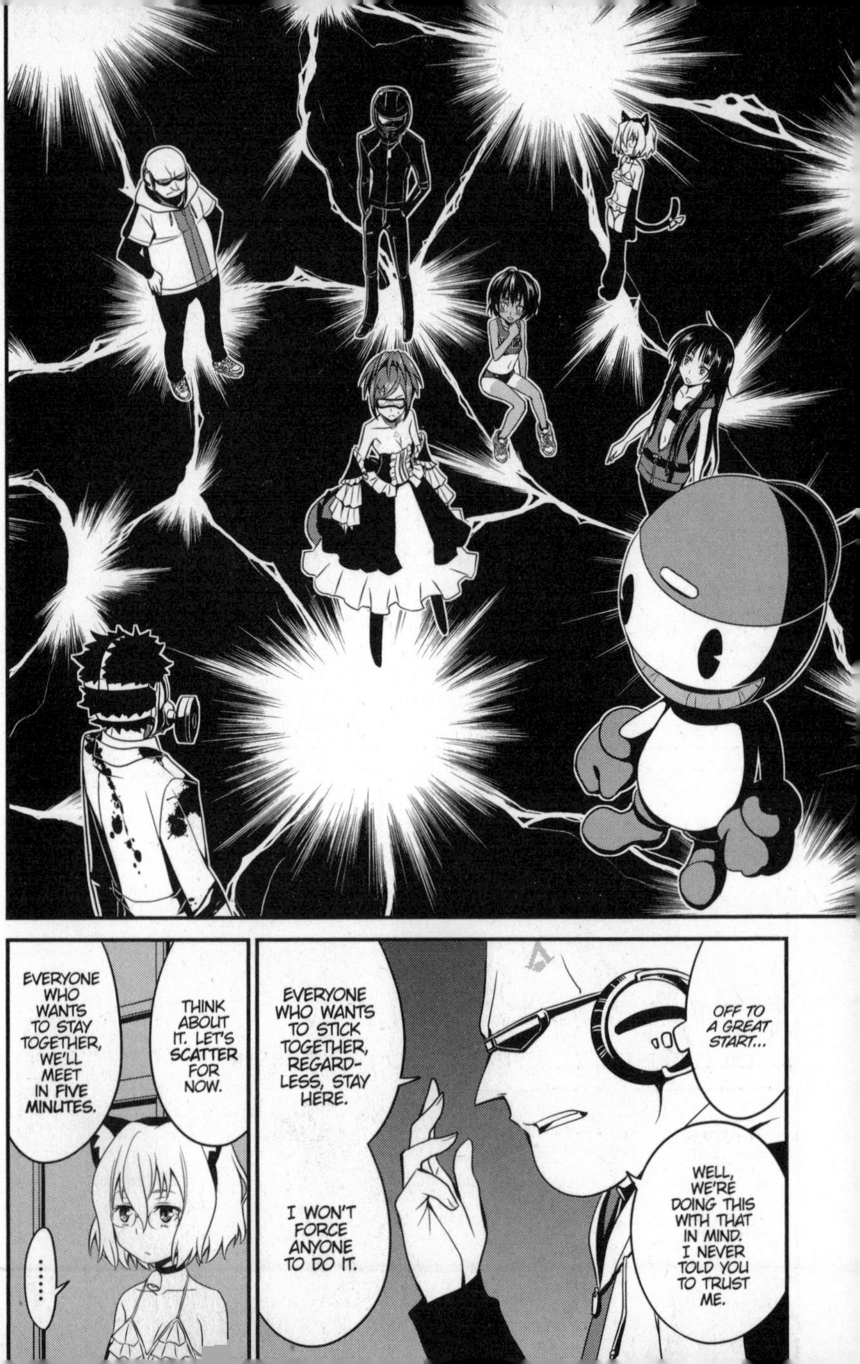
OFF TO A GREAT START...
EVERYONE WHO WANTS TO STICK TOGETHER, REGARDLESS, STAY HERE.
WELL, WE'RE DOING THIS WITH THAT IN MIND. I NEVER TOLD YOU TO TRUST ME.
I WON'T FORCE ANYONE TO DO IT.
THINK ABOUT IT. LET'S SCATTER FOR NOW.
EVERYONE WHO WANTS TO STAY TOGETHER, WE'LL MEET IN FIVE MINUTES.
......

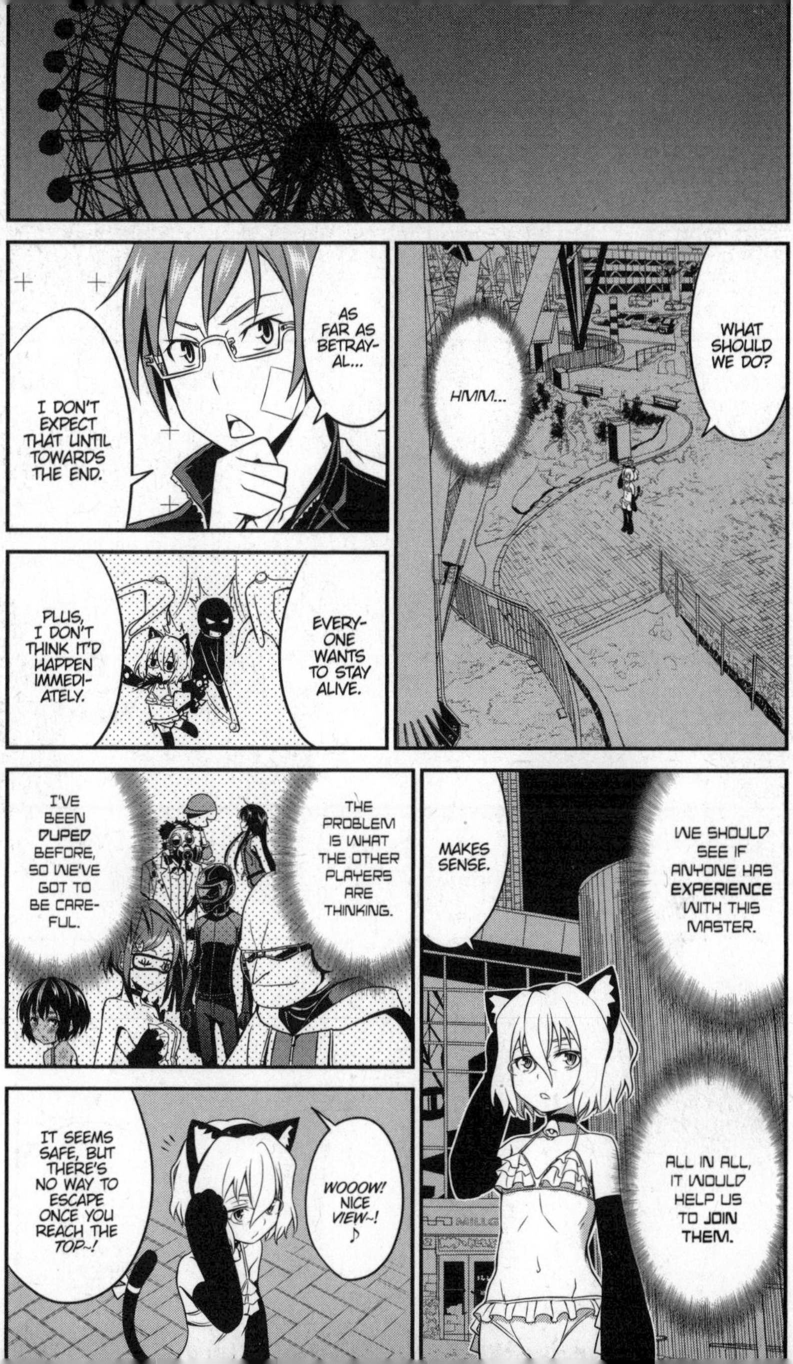
WHAT SHOULD WE DO?
HMM...
AS FAR AS BETRAY-AL...
I DON'T EXPECT THAT UNTIL TOWARDS THE END.
EVERY-ONE WANTS TO STAY ALIVE.
PLUS, I DON'T THINK IT'D HAPPEN IMMEDI-ATELY.
WE SHOULD SEE IF ANYONE HAS EXPERIENCE WITH THIS MASTER.
MAKES SENSE.
ALL IN ALL, IT WOULD HELP US TO JOIN THEM.
THE PROBLEM IS WHAT THE OTHER PLAYERS ARE THINKING.
I'VE BEEN DUPED BEFORE, SO WE'VE GOT TO BE CARE-FUL.
WOOOW! NICE VIEW~! ♪
IT SEEMS SAFE, BUT THERE'S NO WAY TO ESCAPE ONCE YOU REACH THE TOP~!

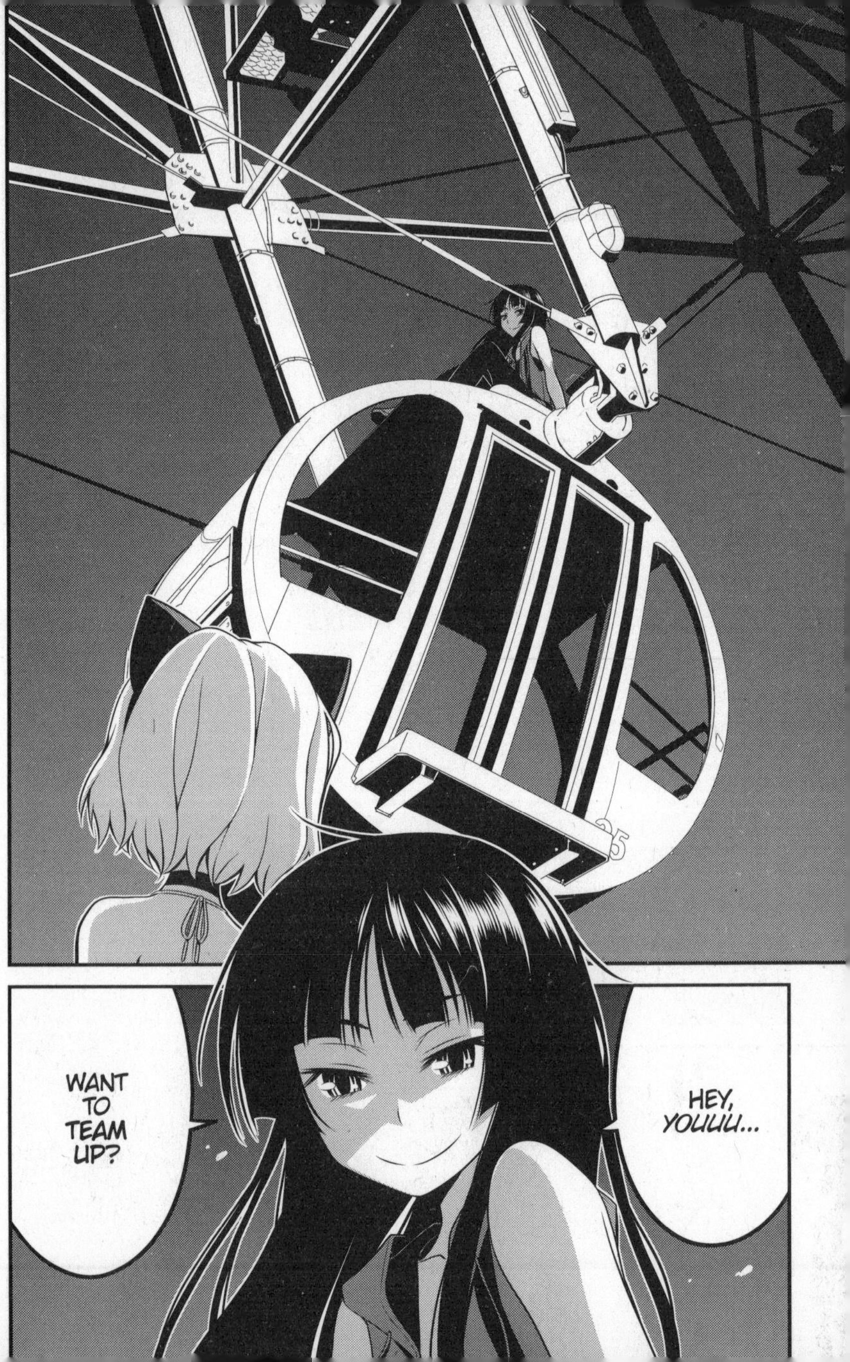
HEY, YOUUU...
WANT TO TEAM UP?

# CHAPTER 13

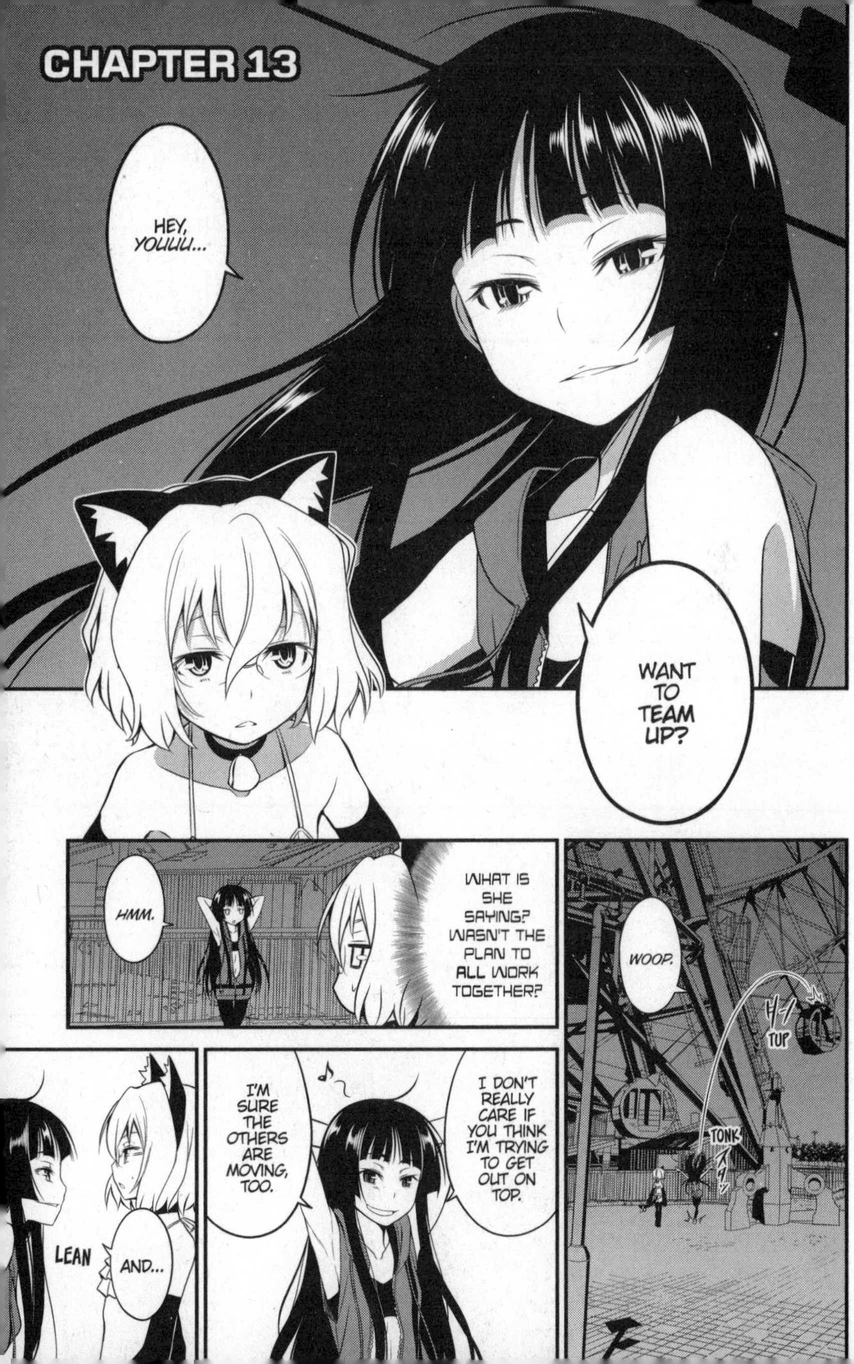
HEY, YOUUU...
WANT TO TEAM UP?
WOOP.
TUP
TONK
WHAT IS SHE SAYING? WASN'T THE PLAN TO ALL WORK TOGETHER?
HMM.
I DON'T REALLY CARE IF YOU THINK I'M TRYING TO GET OUT ON TOP.
I'M SURE THE OTHERS ARE MOVING, TOO.
LEAN
AND...

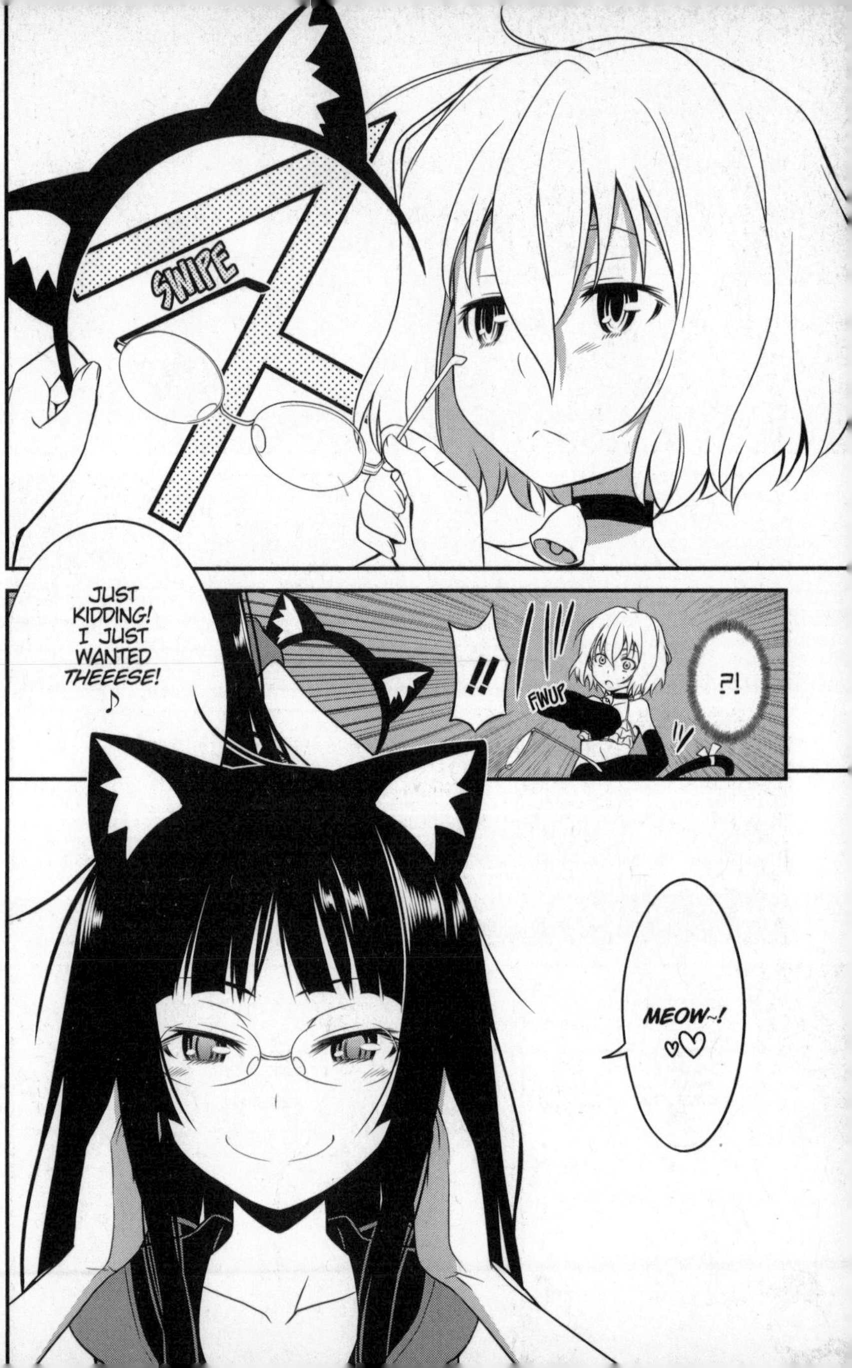
SWIPE
?!
FWUP
!!
JUST KIDDING! I JUST WANTED THEEESE! ♪
MEOW~! ♡♥

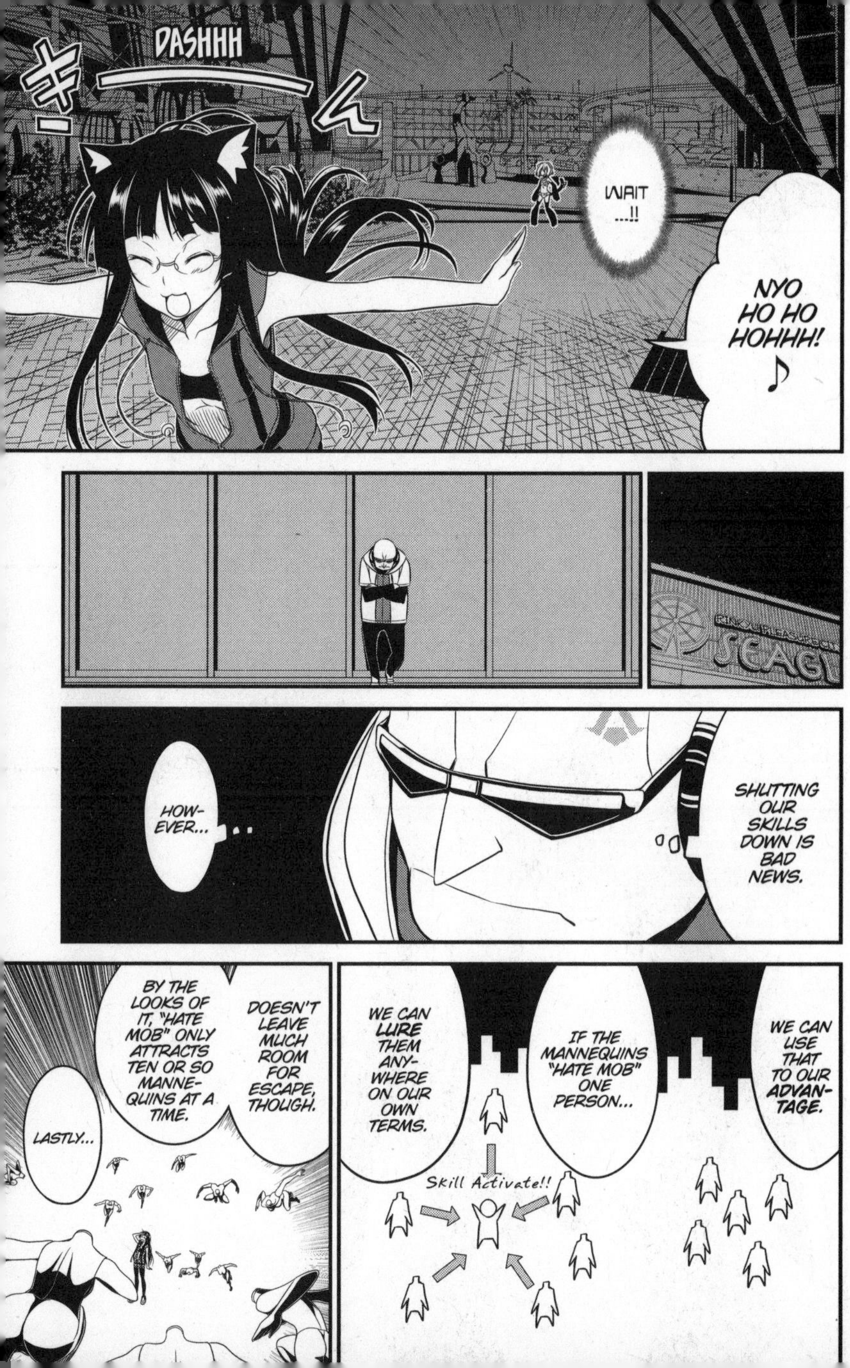
NYO HO HO HOHHH! ♪
WAIT ...!!
DASHHH
SHUTTING OUR SKILLS DOWN IS BAD NEWS.
HOW-EVER...
WE CAN USE THAT TO OUR ADVAN-TAGE.
IF THE MANNEQUINS "HATE MOB" ONE PERSON...
WE CAN LURE THEM ANY-WHERE ON OUR OWN TERMS.
Skill Activate!!
DOESN'T LEAVE MUCH ROOM FOR ESCAPE, THOUGH.
BY THE LOOKS OF IT, "HATE MOB" ONLY ATTRACTS TEN OR SO MANNE-QUINS AT A TIME.
LASTLY...

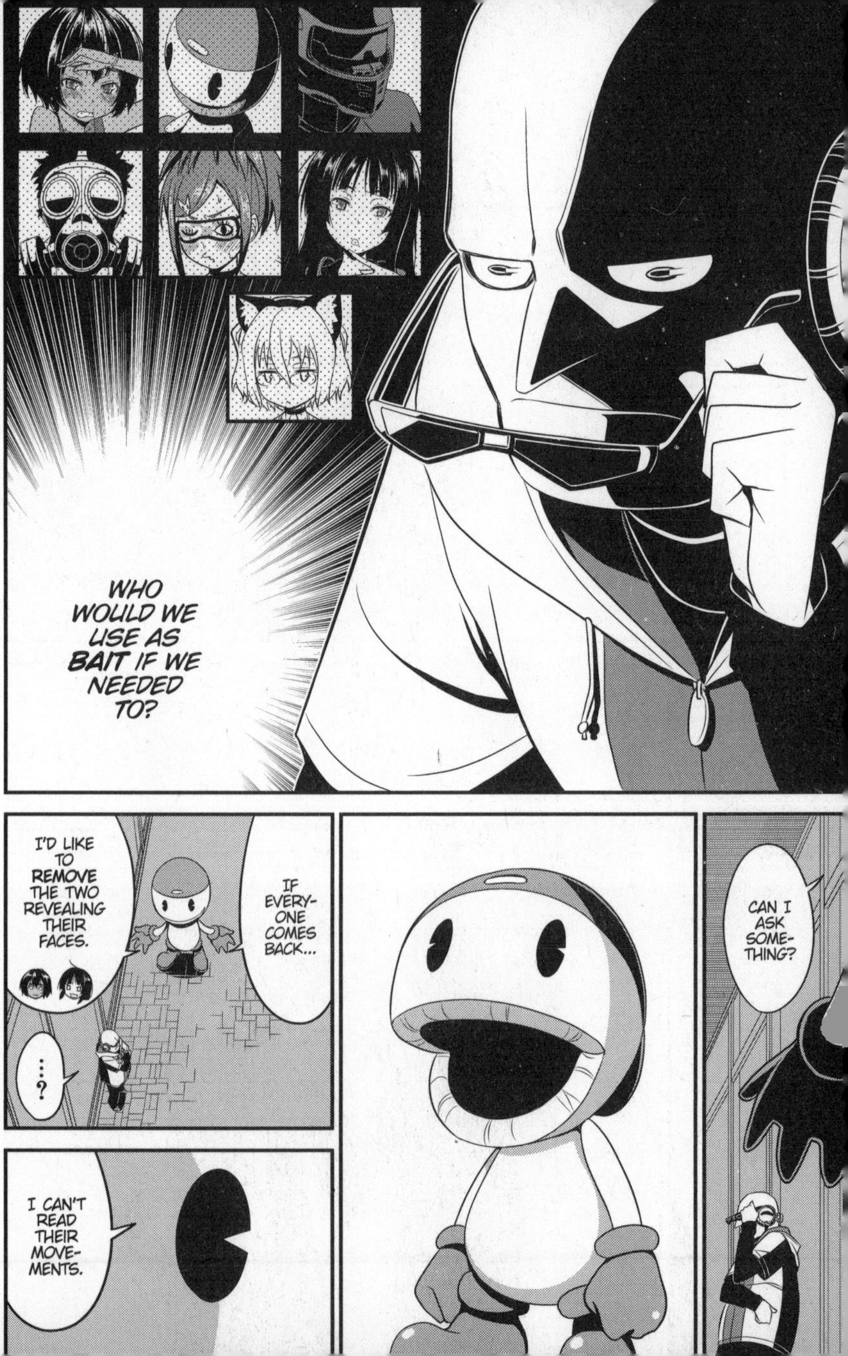
WHO WOULD WE USE AS BAIT IF WE NEEDED TO?
CAN I ASK SOMETHING?
IF EVERYONE COMES BACK...
I'D LIKE TO REMOVE THE TWO REVEALING THEIR FACES.
...?
I CAN'T READ THEIR MOVEMENTS.

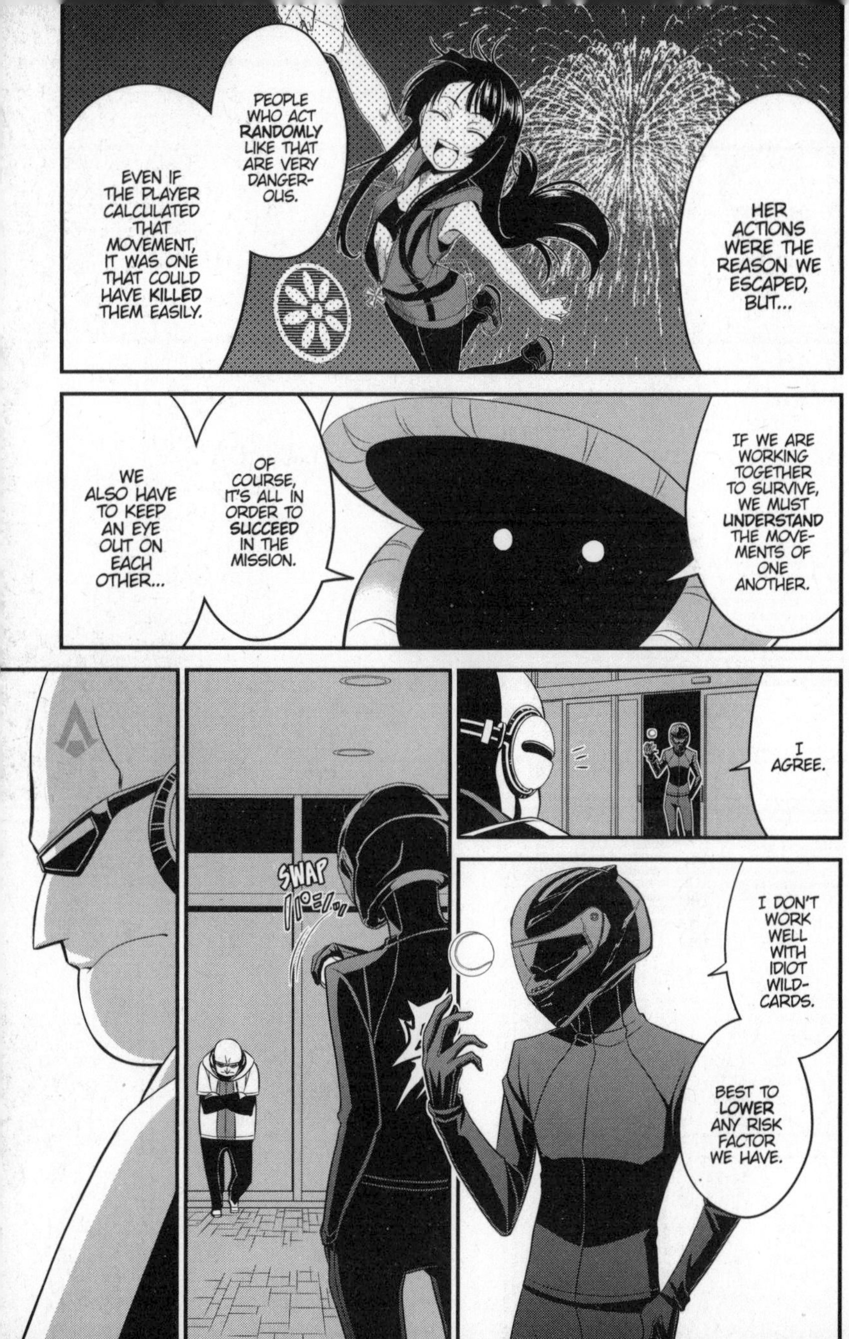
HER ACTIONS WERE THE REASON WE ESCAPED, BUT...
PEOPLE WHO ACT RANDOMLY LIKE THAT ARE VERY DANGEROUS.
EVEN IF THE PLAYER CALCULATED THAT MOVEMENT, IT WAS ONE THAT COULD HAVE KILLED THEM EASILY.
IF WE ARE WORKING TOGETHER TO SURVIVE, WE MUST UNDERSTAND THE MOVEMENTS OF ONE ANOTHER.
OF COURSE, IT'S ALL IN ORDER TO SUCCEED IN THE MISSION.
WE ALSO HAVE TO KEEP AN EYE OUT ON EACH OTHER...
I AGREE.
I DON'T WORK WELL WITH IDIOT WILD-CARDS.
BEST TO LOWER ANY RISK FACTOR WE HAVE.
SWAP

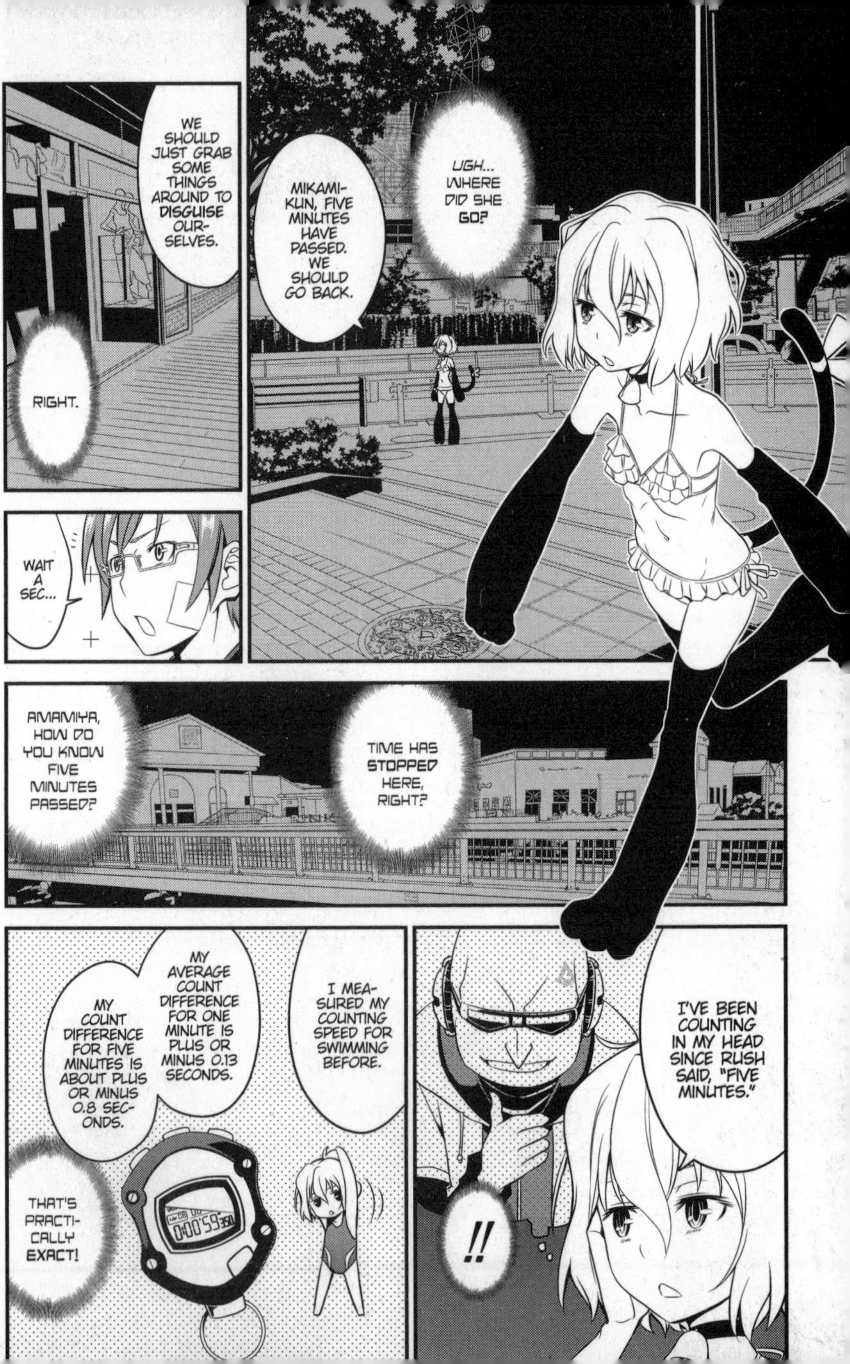
UGH... WHERE DID SHE GO?
MIKAMI-KUN, FIVE MINUTES HAVE PASSED. WE SHOULD GO BACK.
WE SHOULD JUST GRAB SOME THINGS AROUND TO DISGUISE OURSELVES.
RIGHT.
WAIT A SEC...
TIME HAS STOPPED HERE, RIGHT?
AMAMIYA, HOW DO YOU KNOW FIVE MINUTES PASSED?
I'VE BEEN COUNTING IN MY HEAD SINCE RUSH SAID, "FIVE MINUTES."
!!
I MEASURED MY COUNTING SPEED FOR SWIMMING BEFORE.
MY AVERAGE COUNT DIFFERENCE FOR ONE MINUTE IS PLUS OR MINUS 0.13 SECONDS.
MY COUNT DIFFERENCE FOR FIVE MINUTES IS ABOUT PLUS OR MINUS 0.8 SECONDS.
THAT'S PRACTICALLY EXACT!

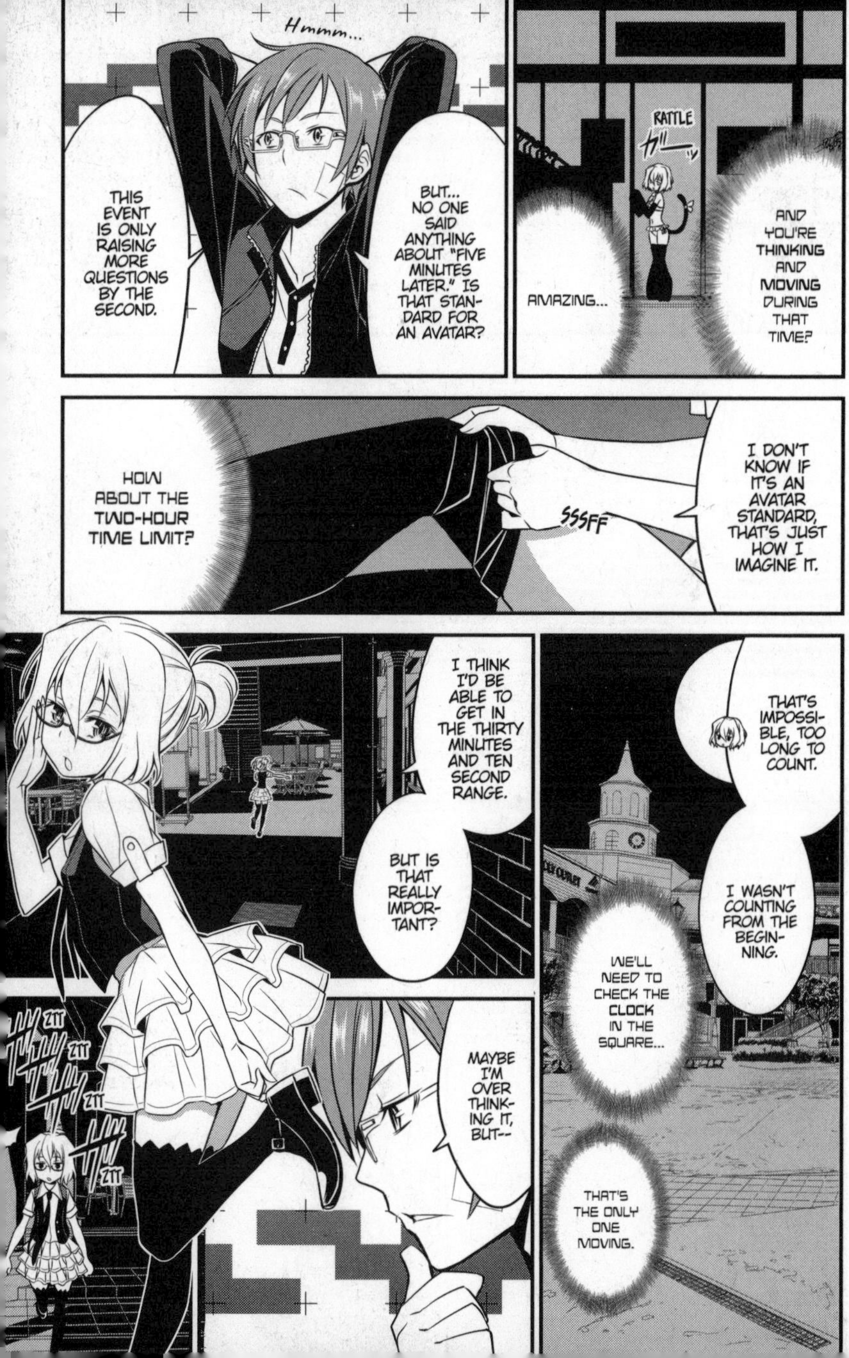
RATTLE
AND YOU'RE THINKING AND MOVING DURING THAT TIME?
AMAZING...
Hmmm...
BUT... NO ONE SAID ANYTHING ABOUT "FIVE MINUTES LATER." IS THAT STANDARD FOR AN AVATAR?
THIS EVENT IS ONLY RAISING MORE QUESTIONS BY THE SECOND.
I DON'T KNOW IF IT'S AN AVATAR STANDARD, THAT'S JUST HOW I IMAGINE IT.
SSSFF
HOW ABOUT THE TWO-HOUR TIME LIMIT?
THAT'S IMPOSSIBLE, TOO LONG TO COUNT.
I WASN'T COUNTING FROM THE BEGINNING.
WE'LL NEED TO CHECK THE CLOCK IN THE SQUARE...
THAT'S THE ONLY ONE MOVING.
I THINK I'D BE ABLE TO GET IN THE THIRTY MINUTES AND TEN SECOND RANGE.
BUT IS THAT REALLY IMPORTANT?
MAYBE I'M OVER THINKING IT, BUT--
ZIT
ZIT
ZIT
ZIT

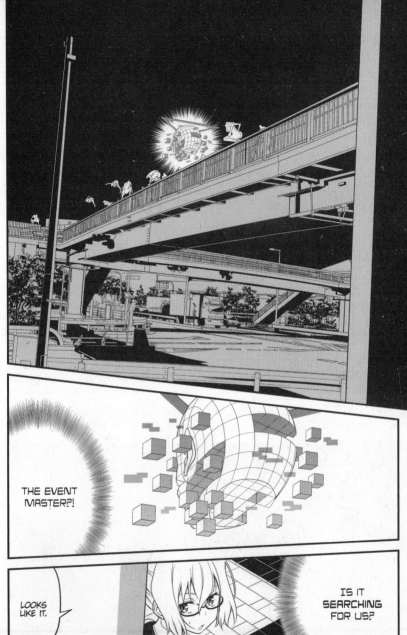

THE EVENT
MASTER?!

LOOKS
LIKE IT.

IS IT
SEARCHING
FOR US?

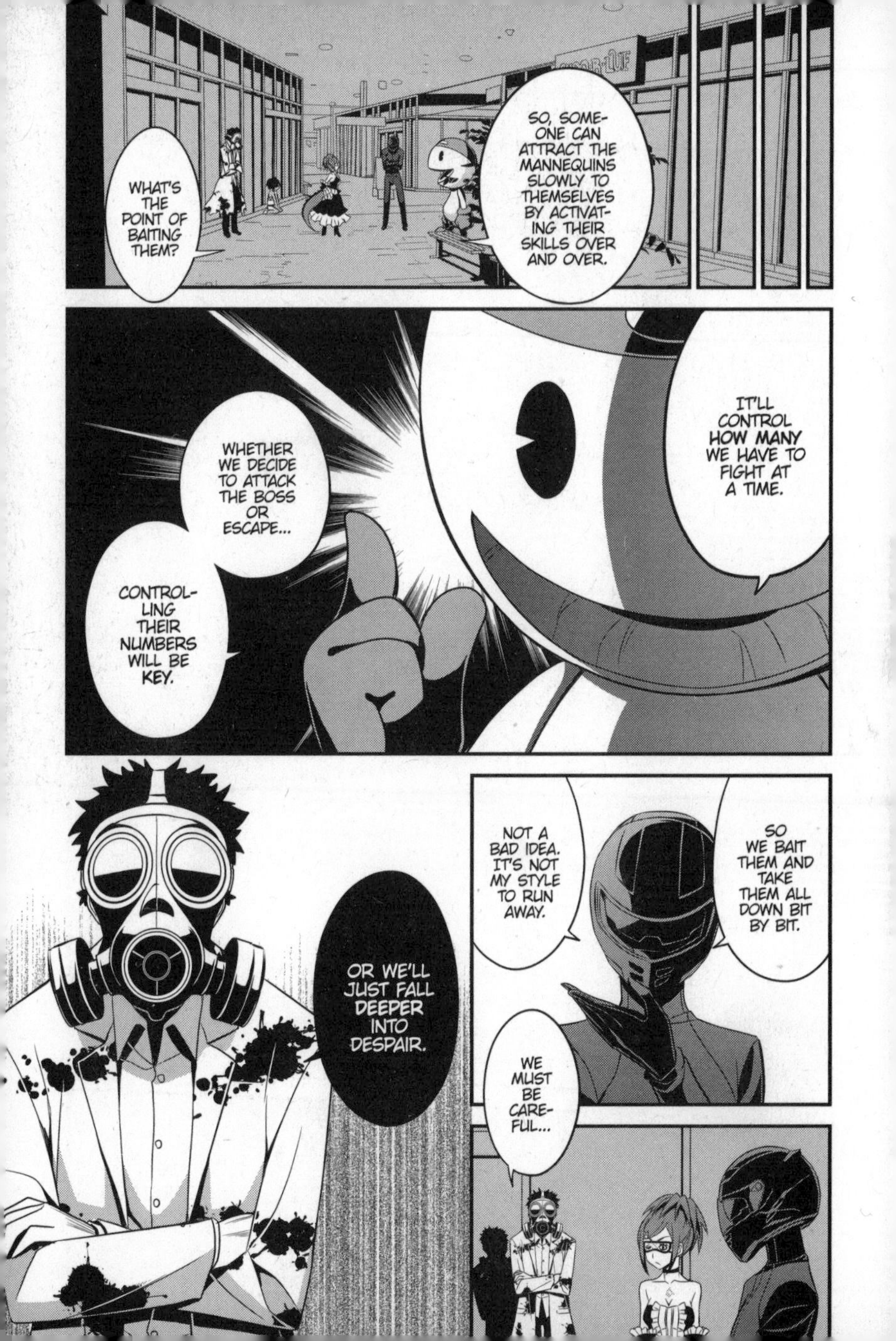
SO, SOME-ONE CAN ATTRACT THE MANNEQUINS SLOWLY TO THEMSELVES BY ACTIVAT-ING THEIR SKILLS OVER AND OVER.
WHAT'S THE POINT OF BAITING THEM?
IT'LL CONTROL HOW MANY WE HAVE TO FIGHT AT A TIME.
WHETHER WE DECIDE TO ATTACK THE BOSS OR ESCAPE...
CONTROL-LING THEIR NUMBERS WILL BE KEY.
SO WE BAIT THEM AND TAKE THEM ALL DOWN BIT BY BIT.
NOT A BAD IDEA. IT'S NOT MY STYLE TO RUN AWAY.
WE MUST BE CARE-FUL...
OR WE'LL JUST FALL DEEPER INTO DESPAIR.

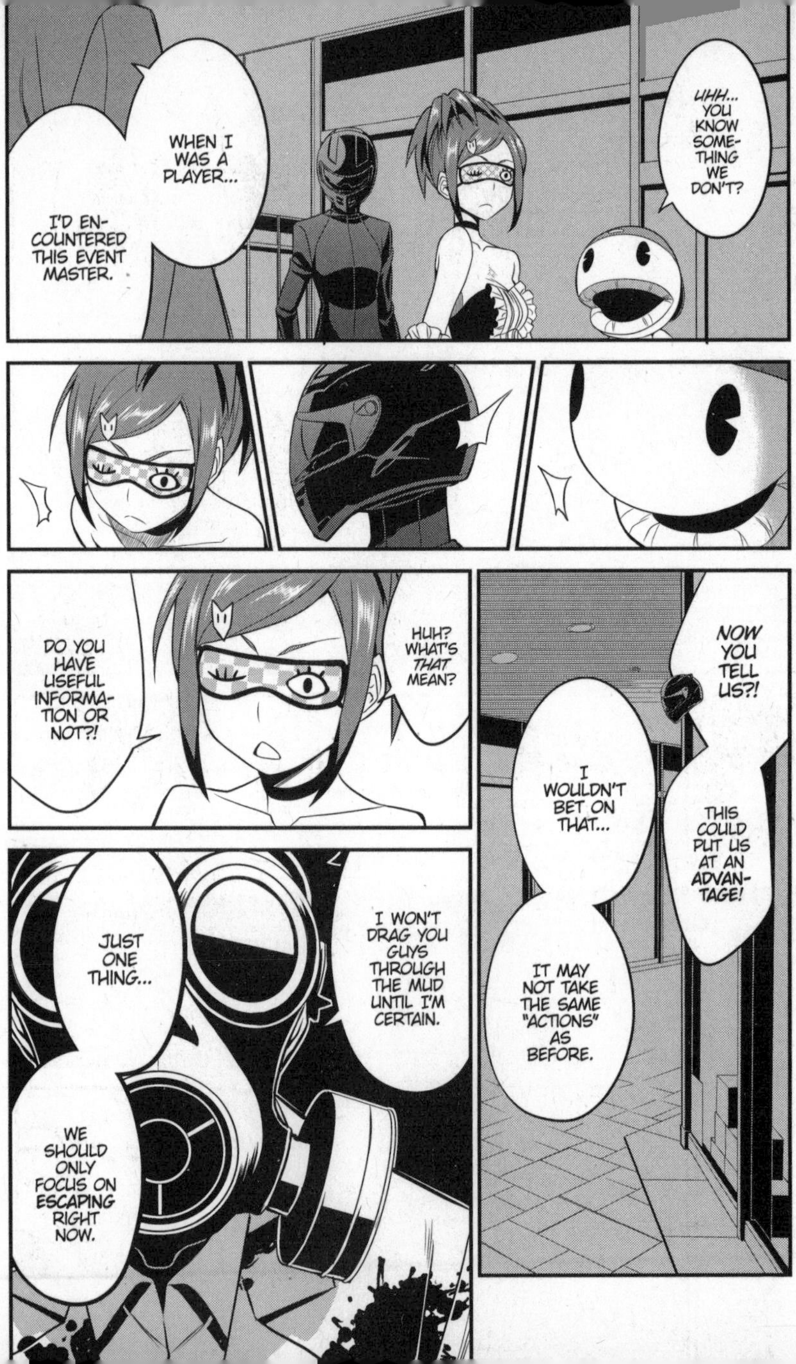
UHH... YOU KNOW SOME-THING WE DON'T?
WHEN I WAS A PLAYER...
I'D EN-COUNTERED THIS EVENT MASTER.
NOW YOU TELL US?!
THIS COULD PUT US AT AN ADVAN-TAGE!
I WOULDN'T BET ON THAT...
IT MAY NOT TAKE THE SAME "ACTIONS" AS BEFORE.
HUH? WHAT'S *THAT* MEAN?
DO YOU HAVE USEFUL INFORMA-TION OR NOT?!
I WON'T DRAG YOU GUYS THROUGH THE MUD UNTIL I'M CERTAIN.
JUST ONE THING...
WE SHOULD ONLY FOCUS ON ESCAPING RIGHT NOW.

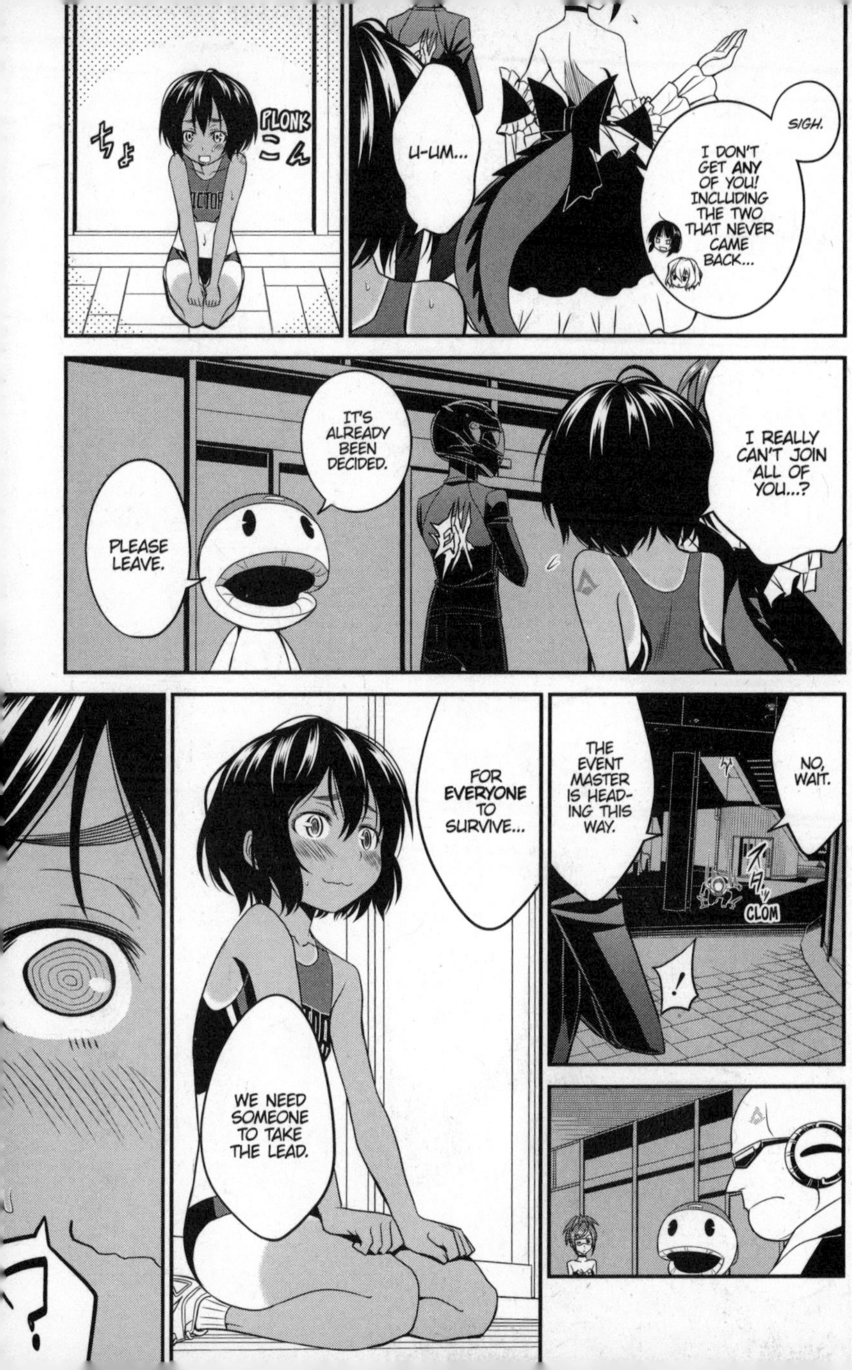
SIGH.
I DON'T GET ANY OF YOU! INCLUDING THE TWO THAT NEVER CAME BACK...
U-UM...
PLONK
ちょこん
I REALLY CAN'T JOIN ALL OF YOU...?
IT'S ALREADY BEEN DECIDED.
PLEASE LEAVE.
NO, WAIT.
THE EVENT MASTER IS HEADING THIS WAY.
CLOM
!
FOR EVERYONE TO SURVIVE...
WE NEED SOMEONE TO TAKE THE LEAD.
?

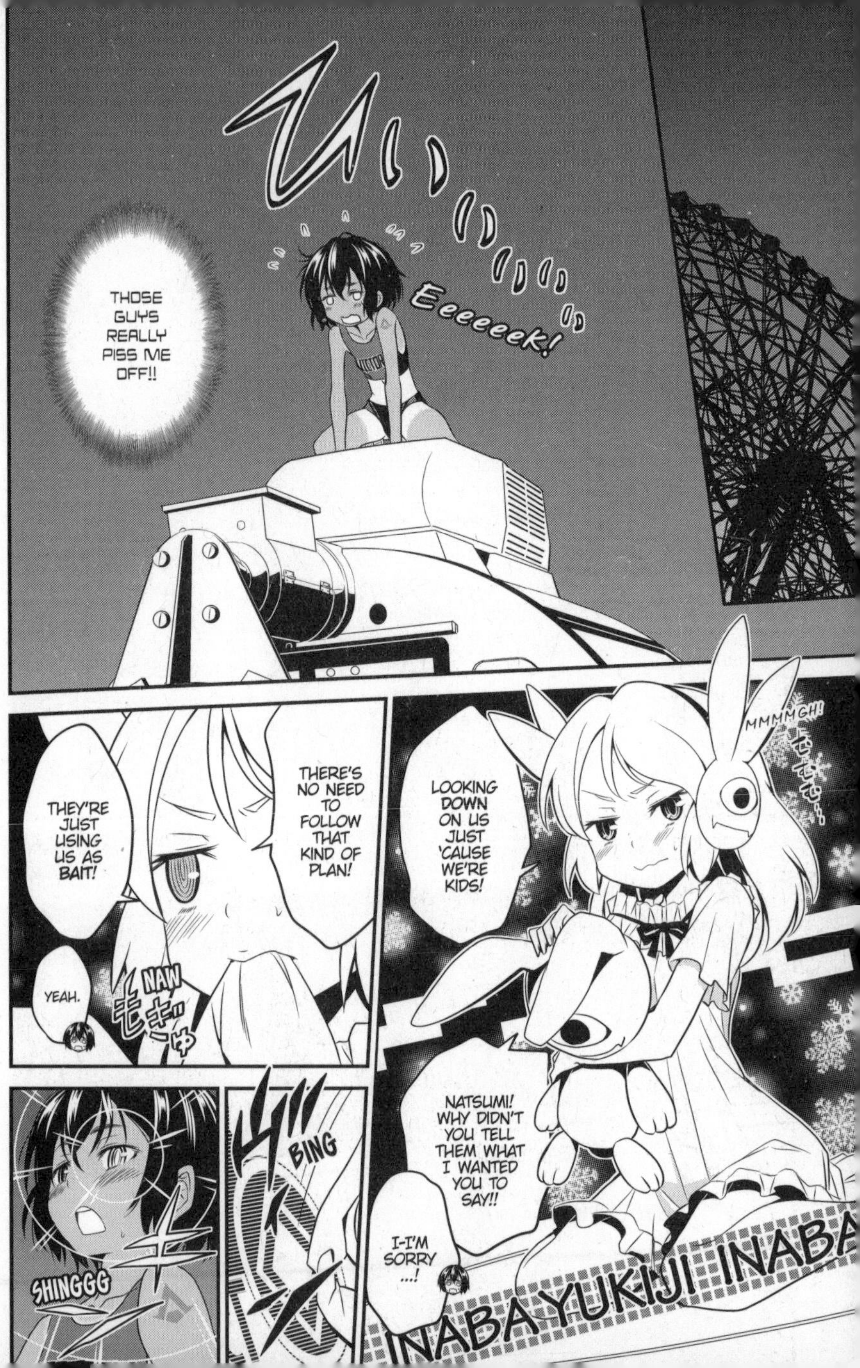
Eeeeeek!
THOSE GUYS REALLY PISS ME OFF!!
MMMMGH!
LOOKING DOWN ON US JUST 'CAUSE WE'RE KIDS!
THERE'S NO NEED TO FOLLOW THAT KIND OF PLAN!
THEY'RE JUST USING US AS BAIT!
NAW
YEAH.
NATSUMI! WHY DIDN'T YOU TELL THEM WHAT I WANTED YOU TO SAY!!
I-I'M SORRY ...!
INABA YUKIJI INABA
BING
SHINGGG

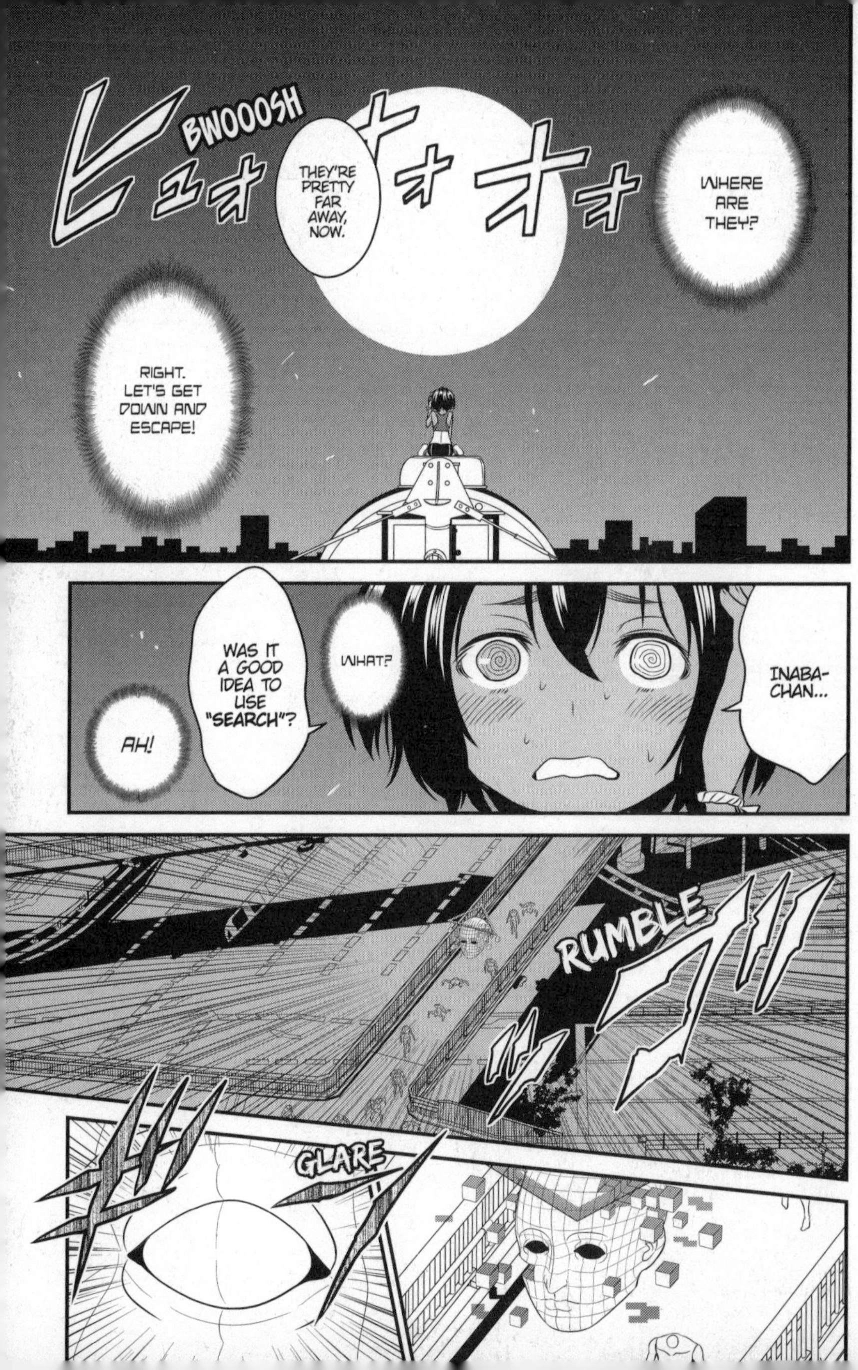
WHERE ARE THEY?
THEY'RE PRETTY FAR AWAY, NOW.
BWOOOSH
RIGHT. LET'S GET DOWN AND ESCAPE!
INABA-CHAN...
WHAT?
WAS IT A GOOD IDEA TO USE "SEARCH"?
AH!
RUMBLE
GLARE

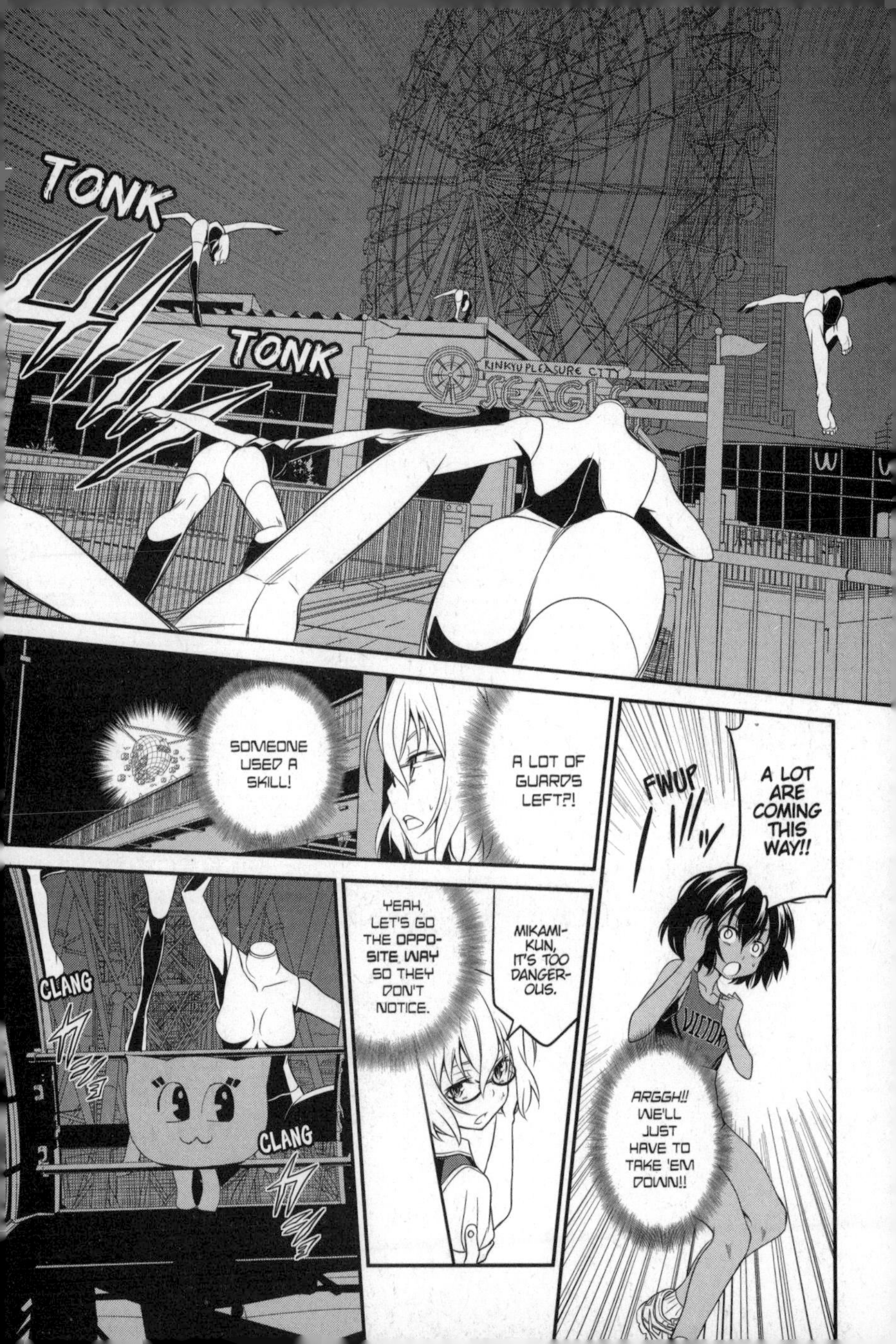
TONK
TONK
KINKYU PLEASURE CITY
FWUP
A LOT ARE COMING THIS WAY!!
ARGGH!! WE'LL JUST HAVE TO TAKE 'EM DOWN!!
A LOT OF GUARDS LEFT?!
SOMEONE USED A SKILL!
MIKAMI-KUN, IT'S TOO DANGEROUS.
YEAH, LET'S GO THE OPPOSITE WAY SO THEY DON'T NOTICE.
CLANG
CLANG

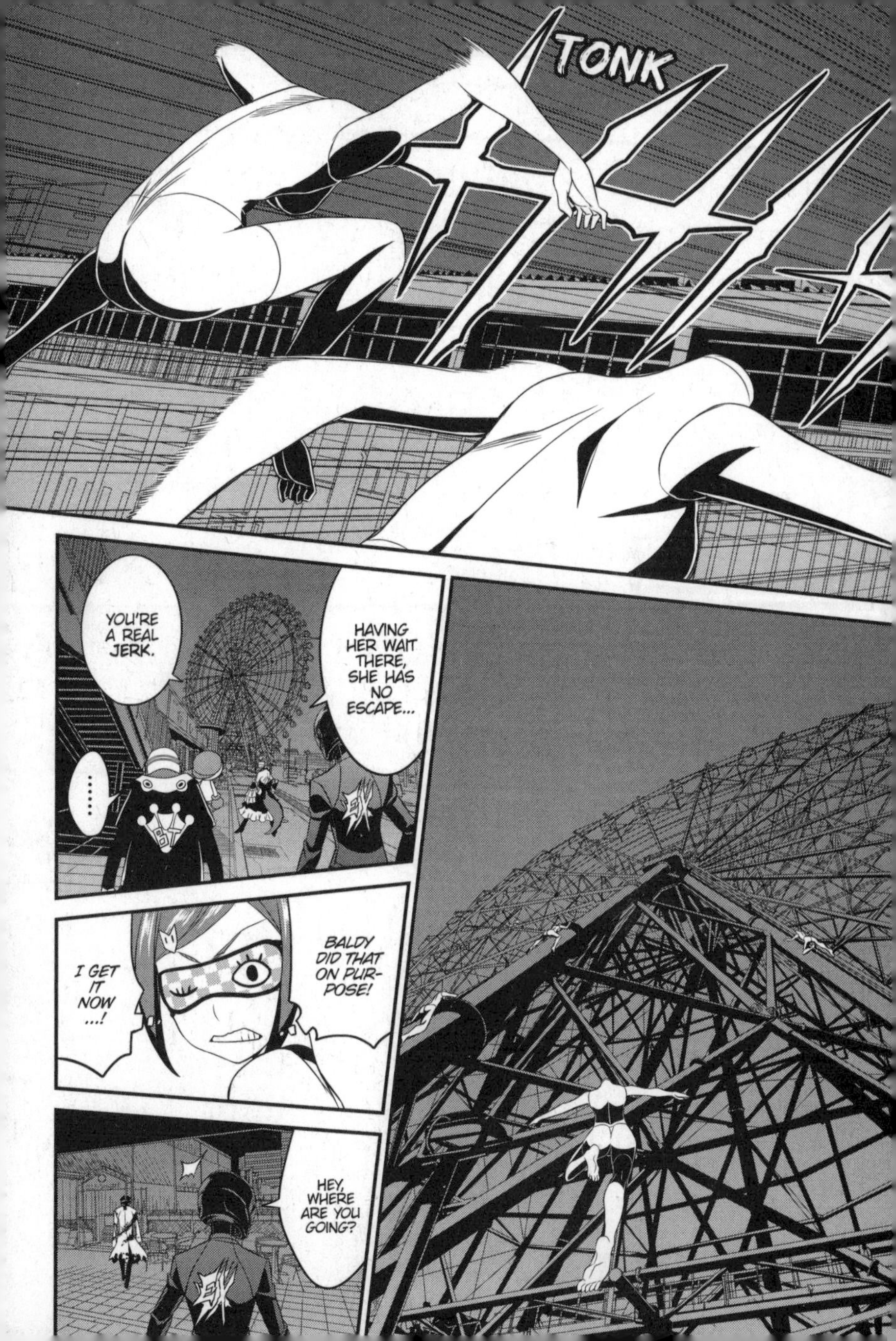
TONK
HAVING HER WAIT THERE, SHE HAS NO ESCAPE...
YOU'RE A REAL JERK.
......
BALDY DID THAT ON PUR-POSE!
I GET IT NOW ...!
HEY, WHERE ARE YOU GOING?

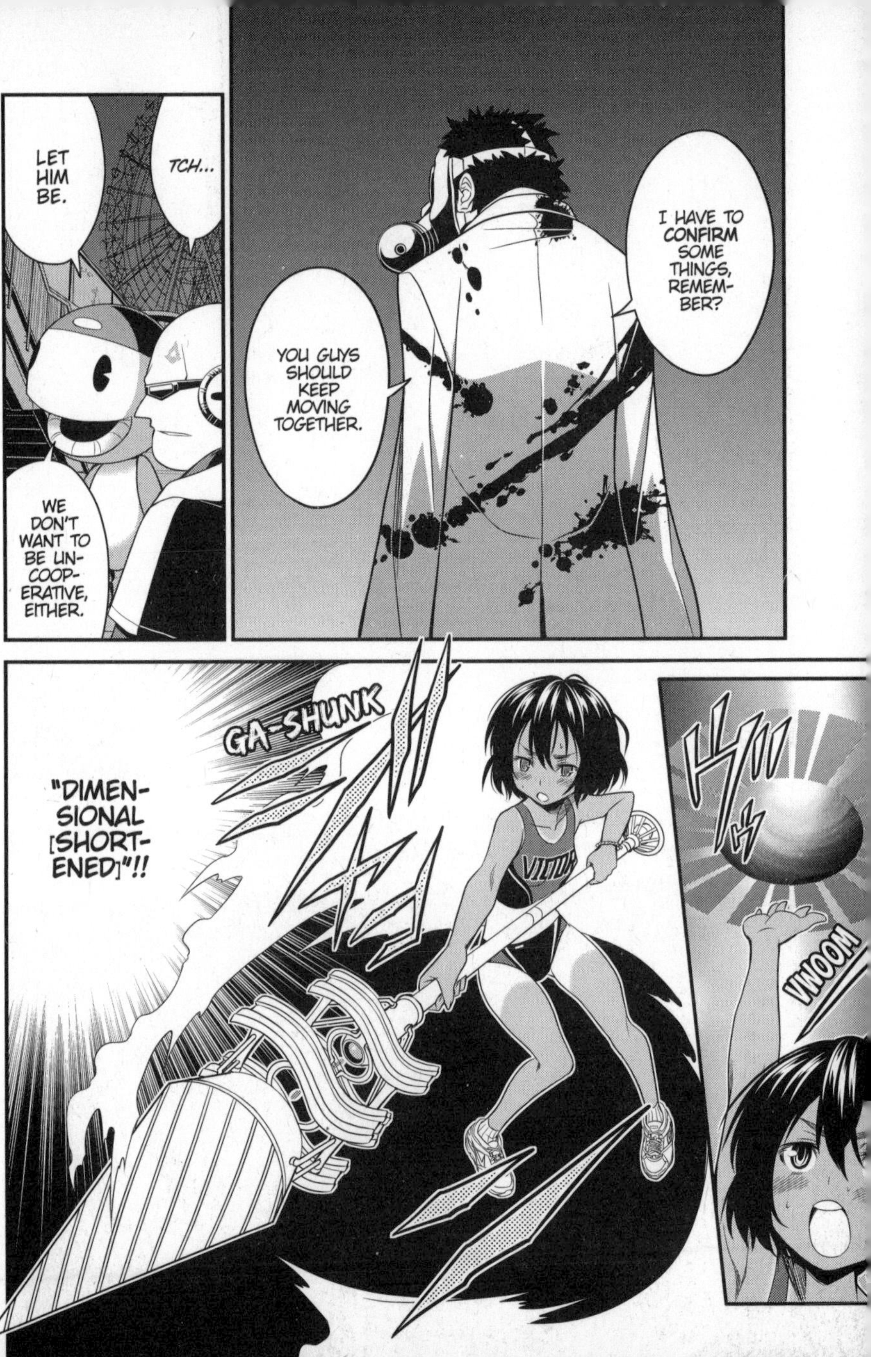

I HAVE TO CONFIRM SOME THINGS, REMEMBER?
YOU GUYS SHOULD KEEP MOVING TOGETHER.
TCH...
LET HIM BE.
WE DON'T WANT TO BE UN-COOPERATIVE, EITHER.
VWOOM
GA-SHUNK
"DIMENSIONAL [SHORTENED]"!!

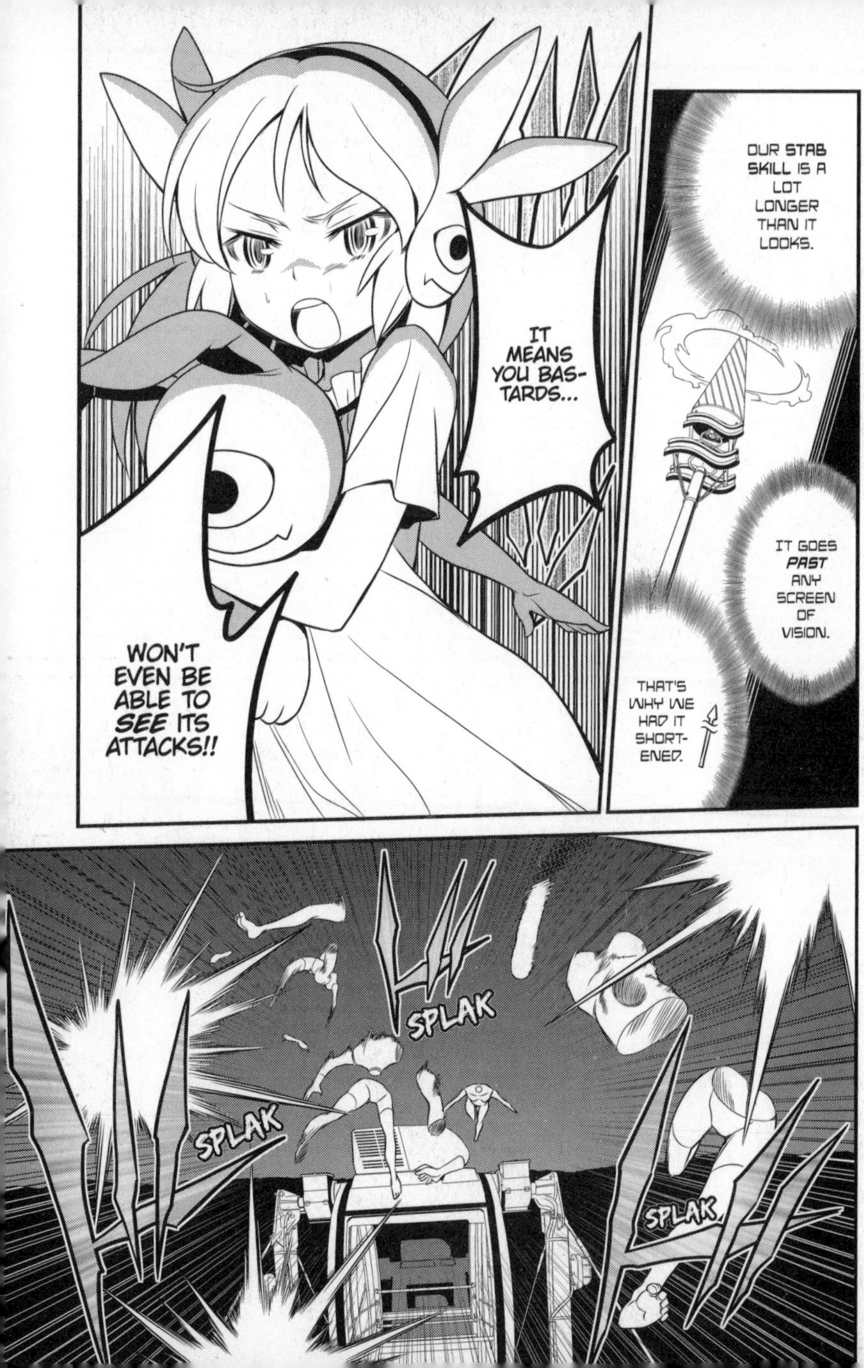
OUR STAB SKILL IS A LOT LONGER THAN IT LOOKS.
IT GOES *PAST* ANY SCREEN OF VISION.
THAT'S WHY WE HAD IT SHORTENED.
IT MEANS YOU BASTARDS...
WON'T EVEN BE ABLE TO *SEE* ITS ATTACKS!!
SPLAK
SPLAK
SPLAK

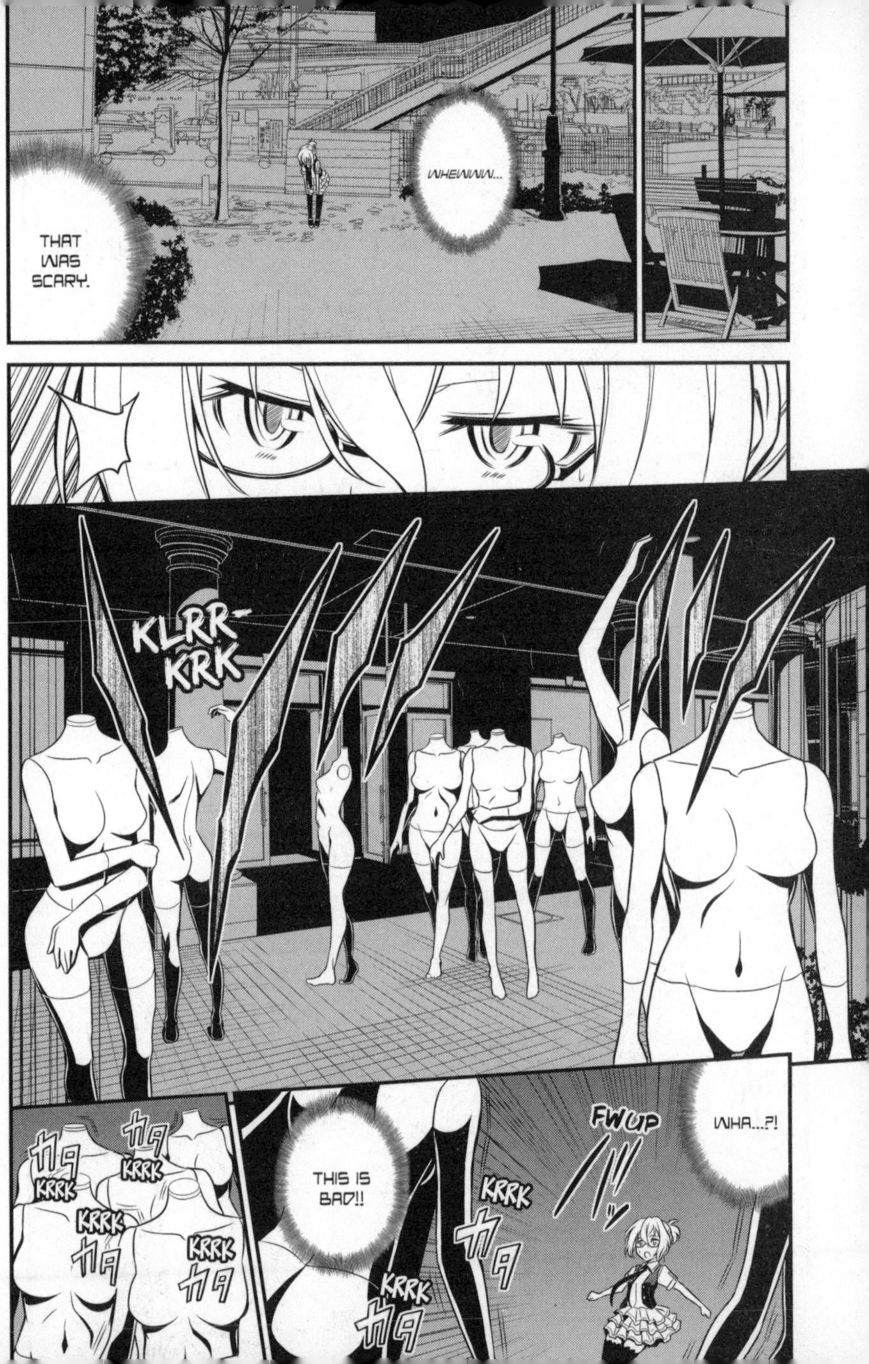
WHEWWW...
THAT WAS SCARY.
KLRR-KRK
WHA...?!
FWUP
THIS IS BAD!!
KRRK
カタ
KRRK
カタ
カタ
KRRK
カタ
KRRK
KRRK
カタ
KRRK
カタ

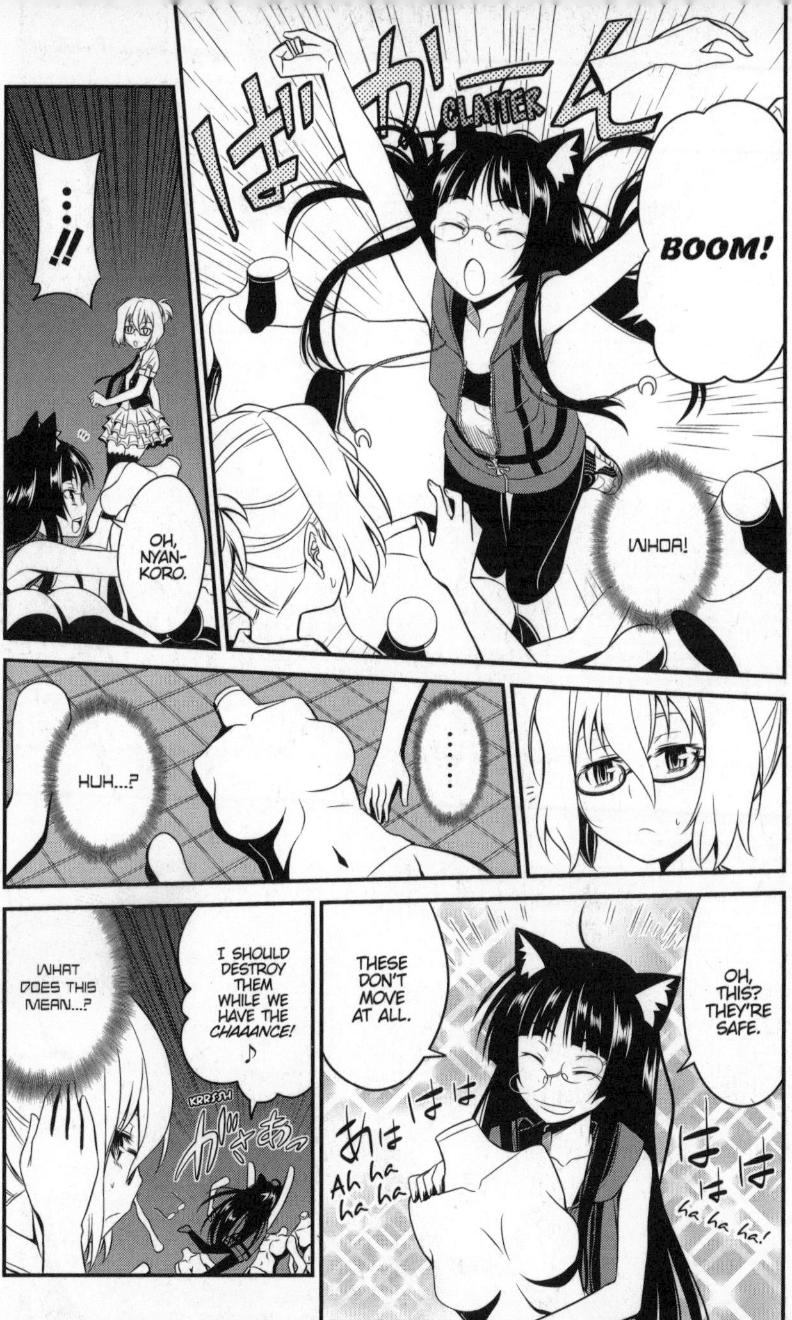
ぱかーん
CLATTER
BOOM!
WHOA!
…!!
OH, NYAN-KORO.
……
HUH…?
OH, THIS? THEY'RE SAFE.
THESE DON'T MOVE AT ALL.
ははは
ha ha ha!
あははは
Ah ha ha ha
I SHOULD DESTROY THEM WHILE WE HAVE THE CHAAANCE! ♪
WHAT DOES THIS MEAN…?
がさぁっ
KRRSSH

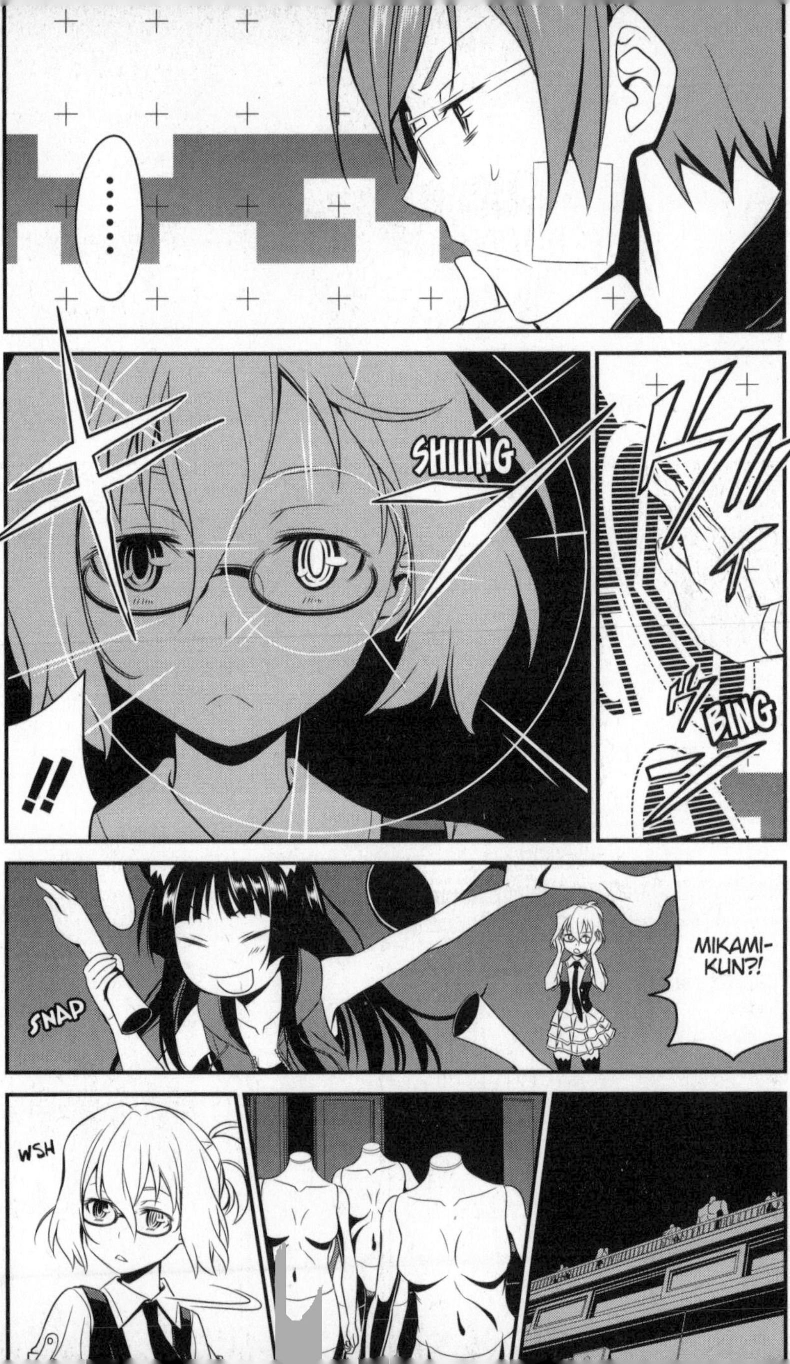
......
SHIIING
BING
!!
MIKAMI-KUN?!
SNAP
WSH

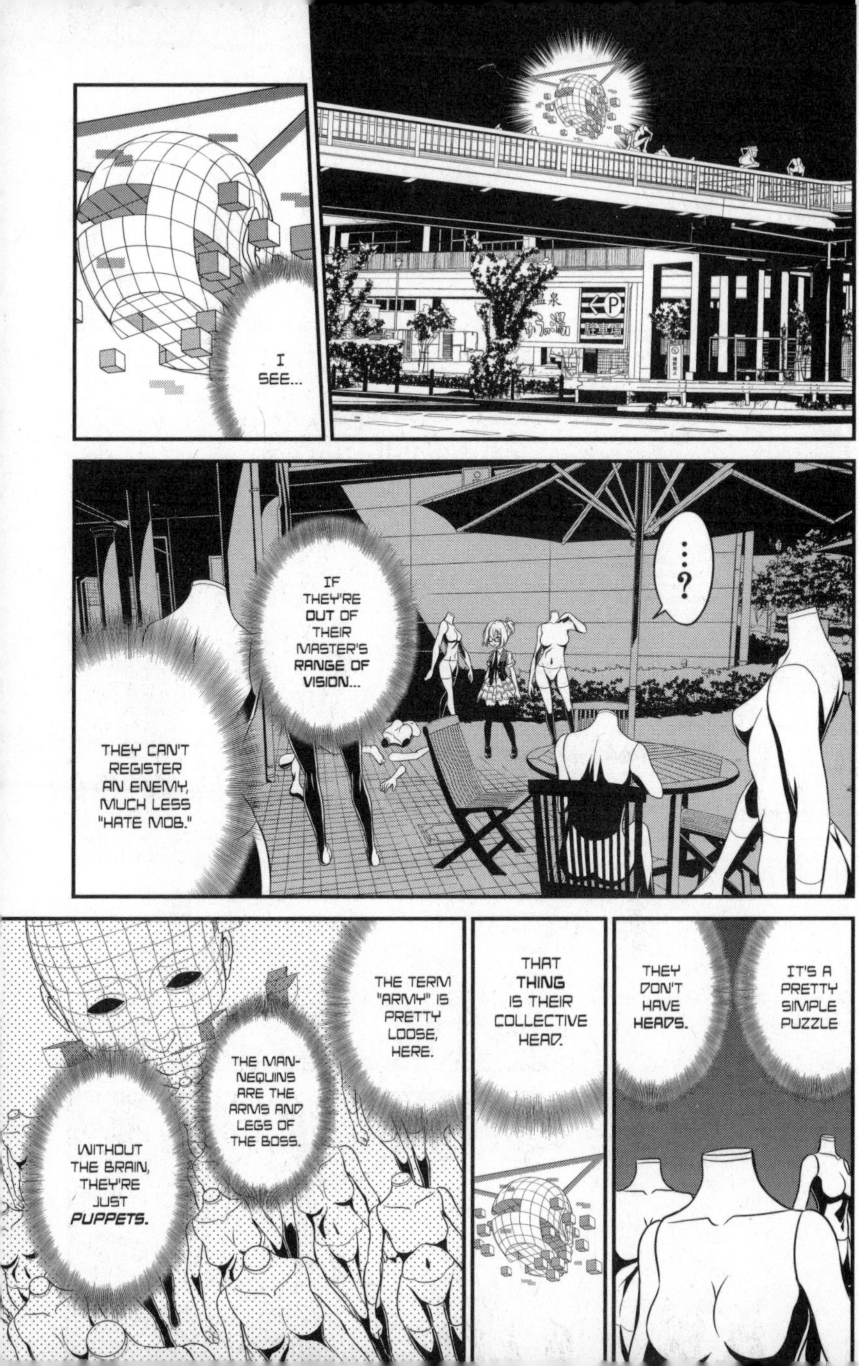
I SEE...
...?
IF THEY'RE OUT OF THEIR MASTER'S RANGE OF VISION...
THEY CAN'T REGISTER AN ENEMY, MUCH LESS "HATE MOB."
IT'S A PRETTY SIMPLE PUZZLE
THEY DON'T HAVE HEADS.
THAT THING IS THEIR COLLECTIVE HEAD.
THE TERM "ARMY" IS PRETTY LOOSE, HERE.
THE MAN-NEQUINS ARE THE ARMS AND LEGS OF THE BOSS.
WITHOUT THE BRAIN, THEY'RE JUST PUPPETS.

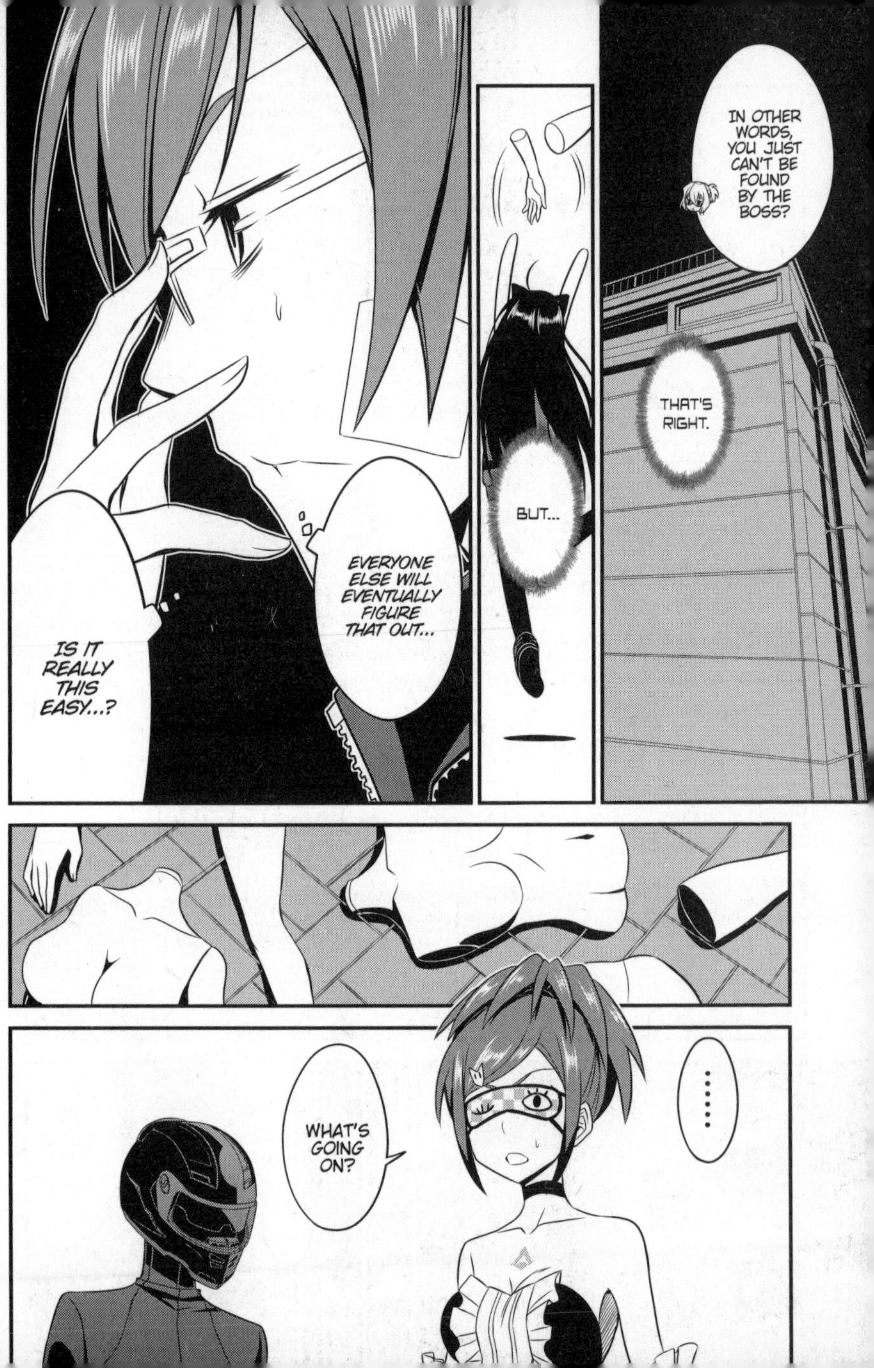
IN OTHER WORDS, YOU JUST CAN'T BE FOUND BY THE BOSS?
THAT'S RIGHT.
BUT...
EVERYONE ELSE WILL EVENTUALLY FIGURE THAT OUT...
IS IT REALLY THIS EASY...?
......
WHAT'S GOING ON?

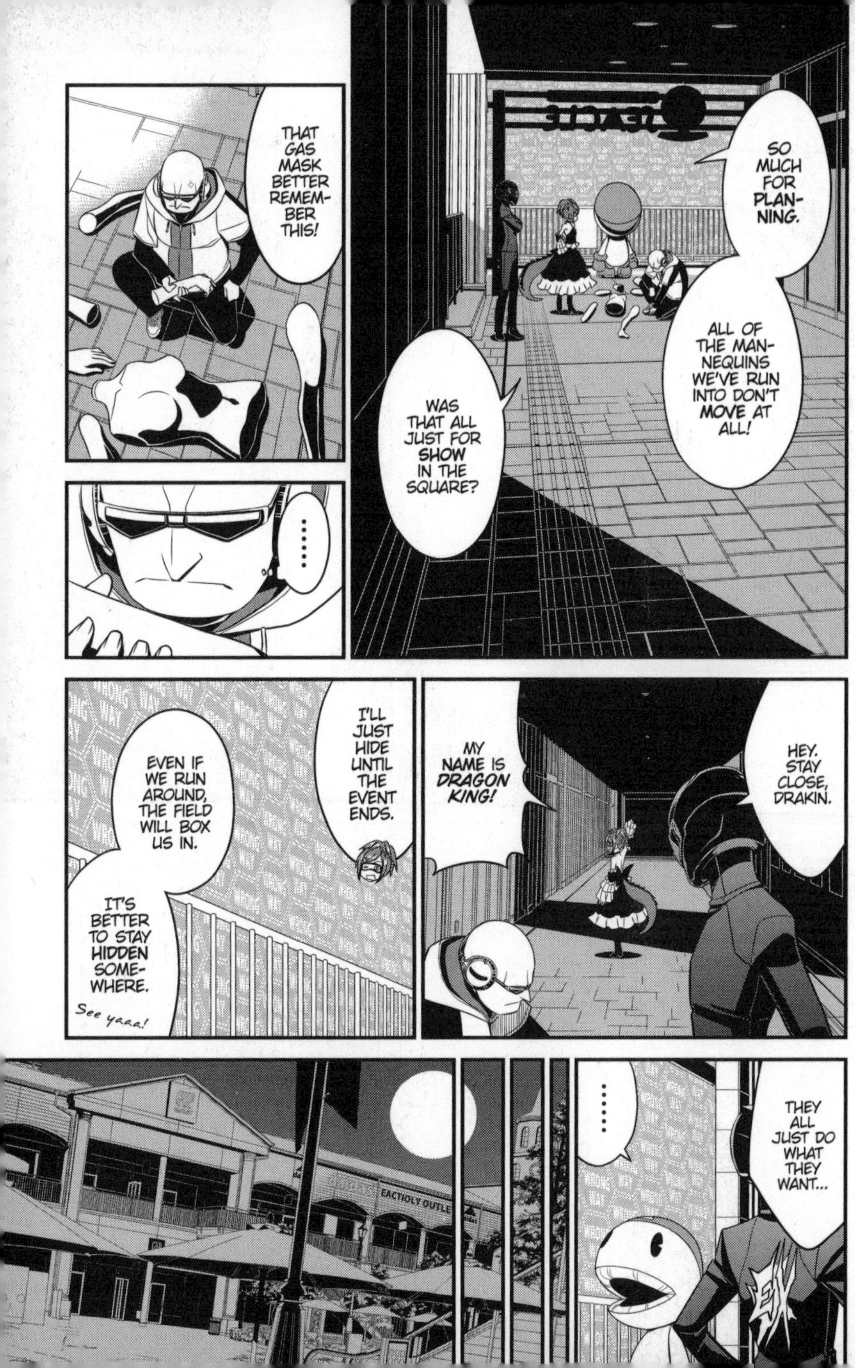
SO MUCH FOR PLAN-NING.
ALL OF THE MAN-NEQUINS WE'VE RUN INTO DON'T MOVE AT ALL!
WAS THAT ALL JUST FOR SHOW IN THE SQUARE?
THAT GAS MASK BETTER REMEM-BER THIS!
……
HEY. STAY CLOSE, DRAKIN.
MY NAME IS DRAGON KING!
I'LL JUST HIDE UNTIL THE EVENT ENDS.
EVEN IF WE RUN AROUND, THE FIELD WILL BOX US IN.
IT'S BETTER TO STAY HIDDEN SOME-WHERE.
See yaaa!
THEY ALL JUST DO WHAT THEY WANT...
……

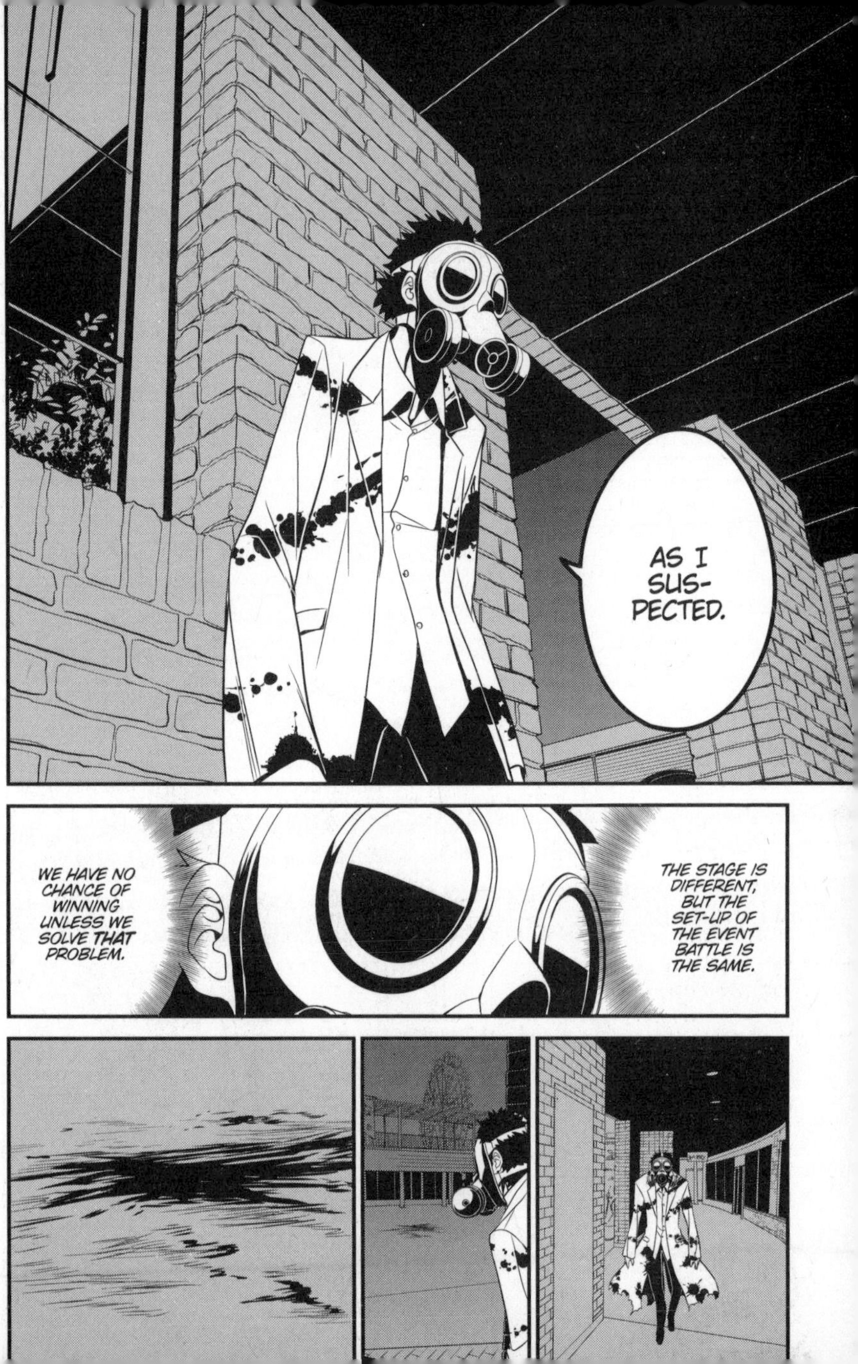
AS I SUS-PECTED.
THE STAGE IS DIFFERENT, BUT THE SET-UP OF THE EVENT BATTLE IS THE SAME.
WE HAVE NO CHANCE OF WINNING UNLESS WE SOLVE THAT PROBLEM.

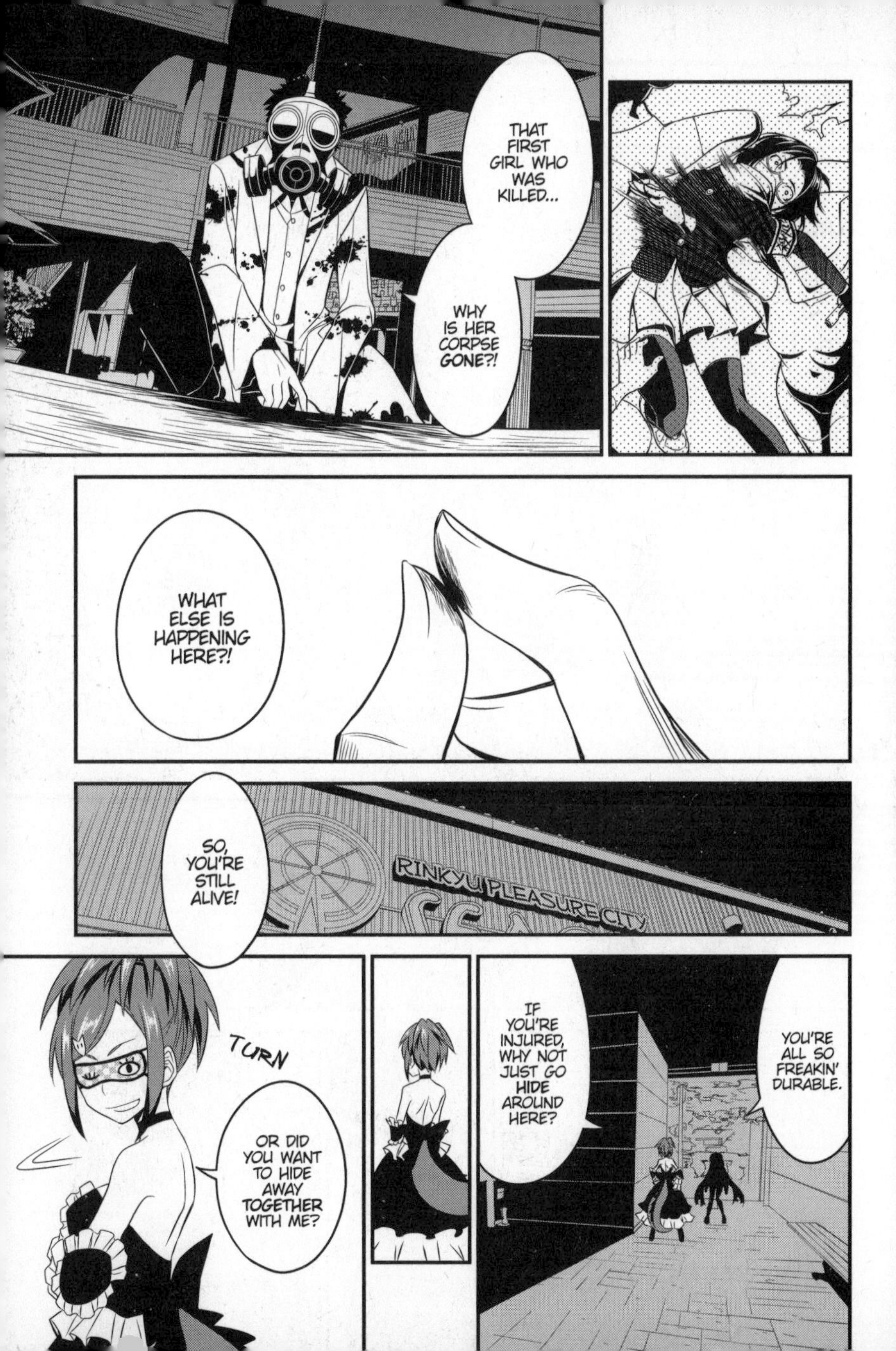
THAT FIRST GIRL WHO WAS KILLED...
WHY IS HER CORPSE GONE?!
WHAT ELSE IS HAPPENING HERE?!
SO, YOU'RE STILL ALIVE!
RINKYU PLEASURE CITY
YOU'RE ALL SO FREAKIN' DURABLE.
IF YOU'RE INJURED, WHY NOT JUST GO HIDE AROUND HERE?
TURN
OR DID YOU WANT TO HIDE AWAY TOGETHER WITH ME?

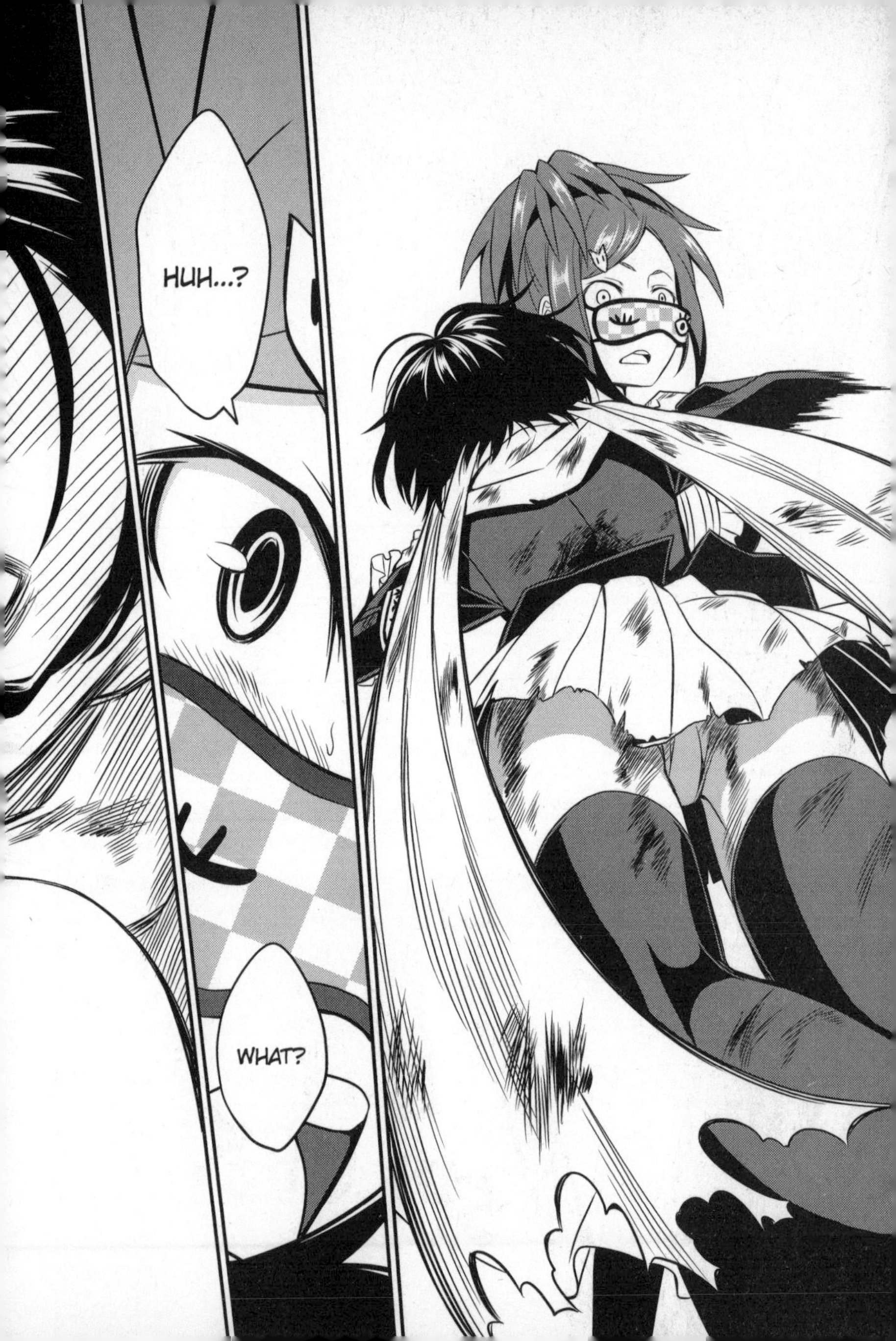
HUH...?
WHAT?

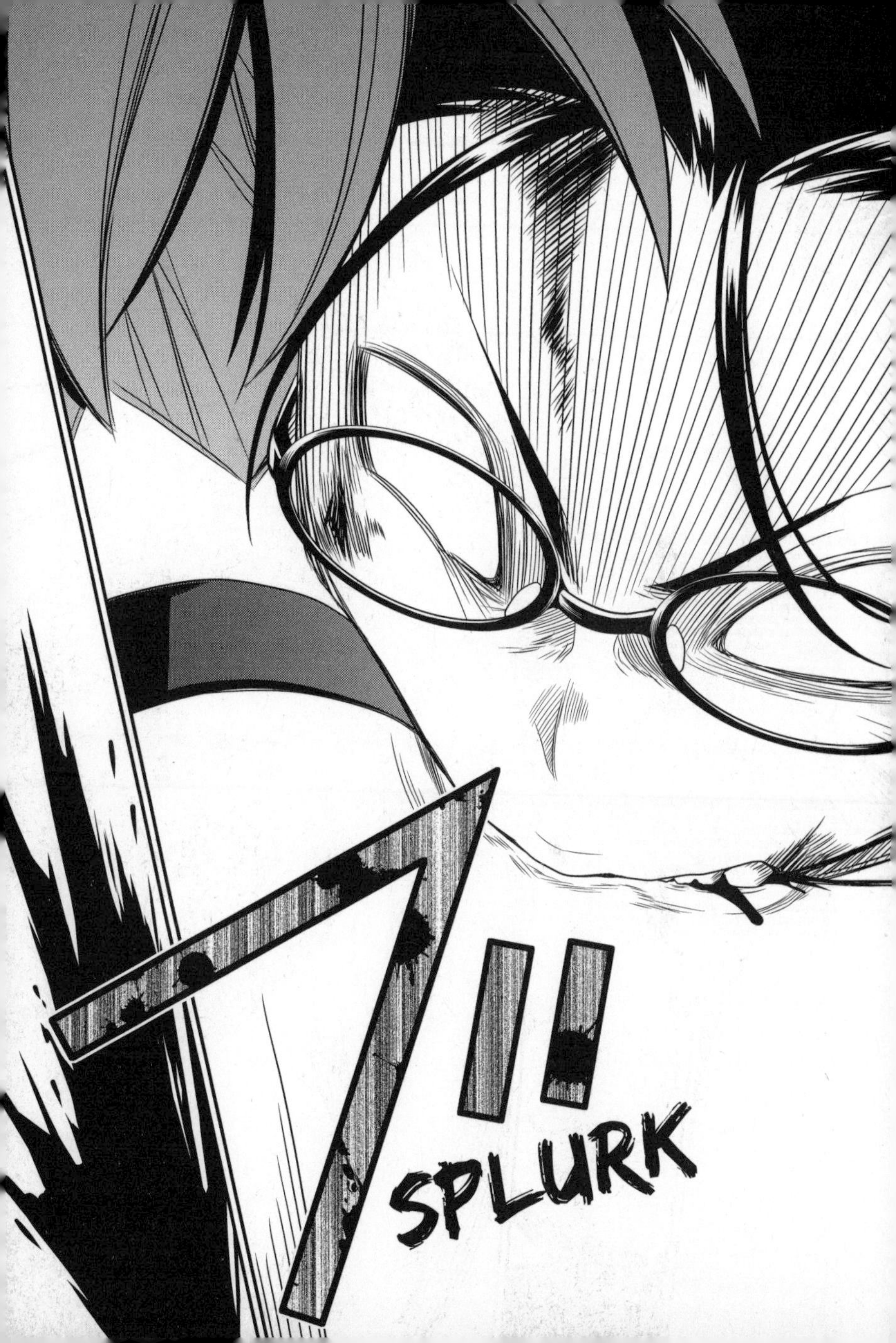
SPLURK

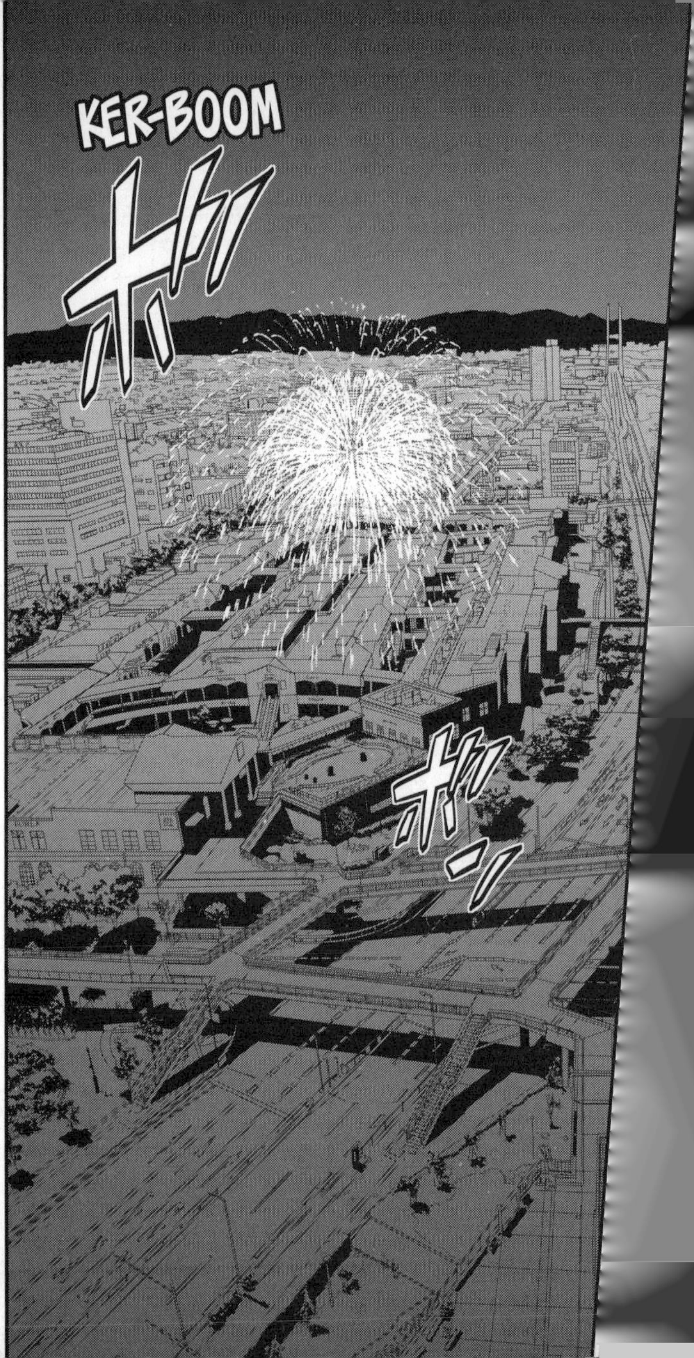

KER-BOOM
ボカン
ボボーン

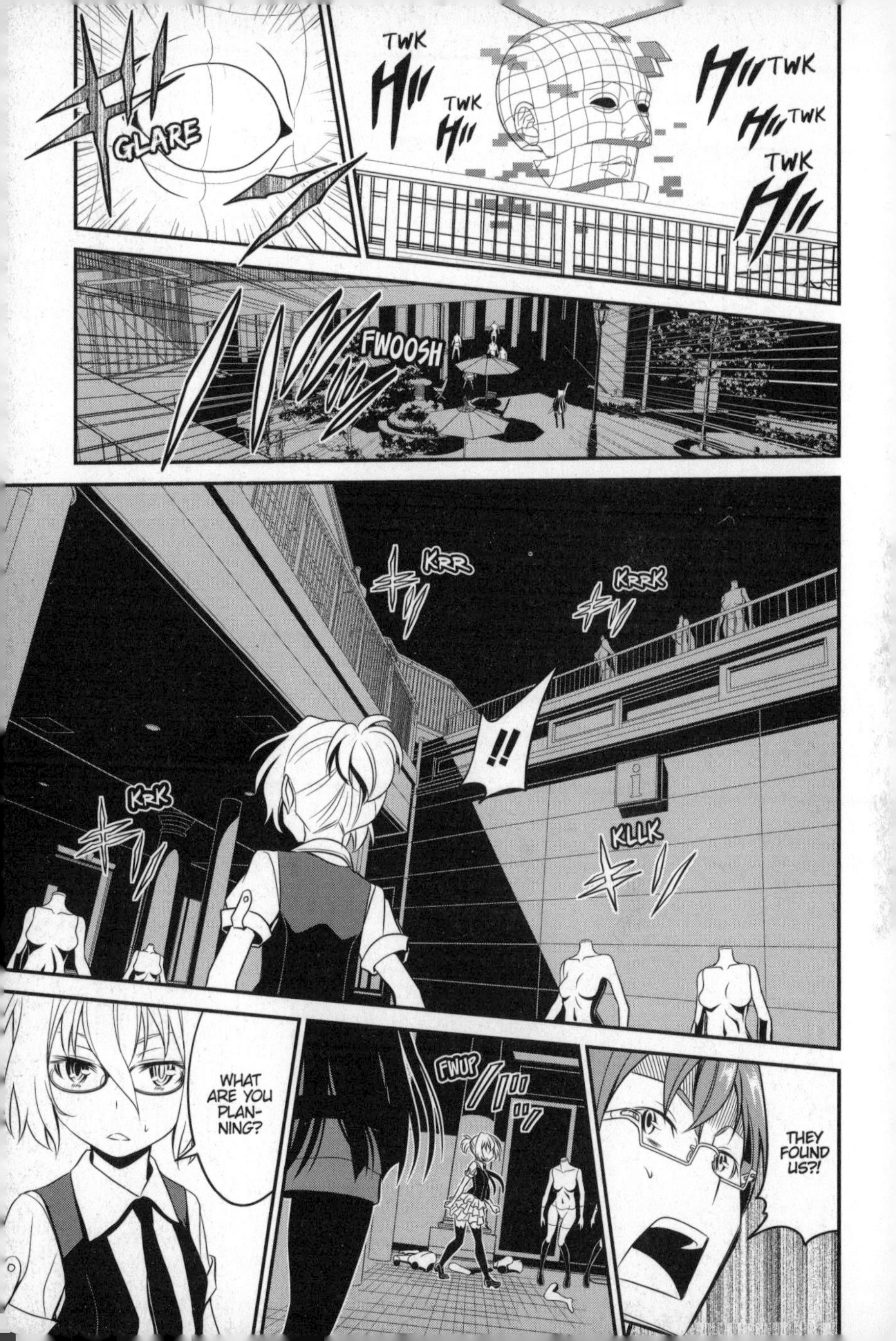
TWK
TWK
TWK
TWK
TWK
GLARE
FWOOSH
KRRK
KRR
!!
KLLK
KRK
THEY FOUND US?!
FWUP
WHAT ARE YOU PLAN-NING?

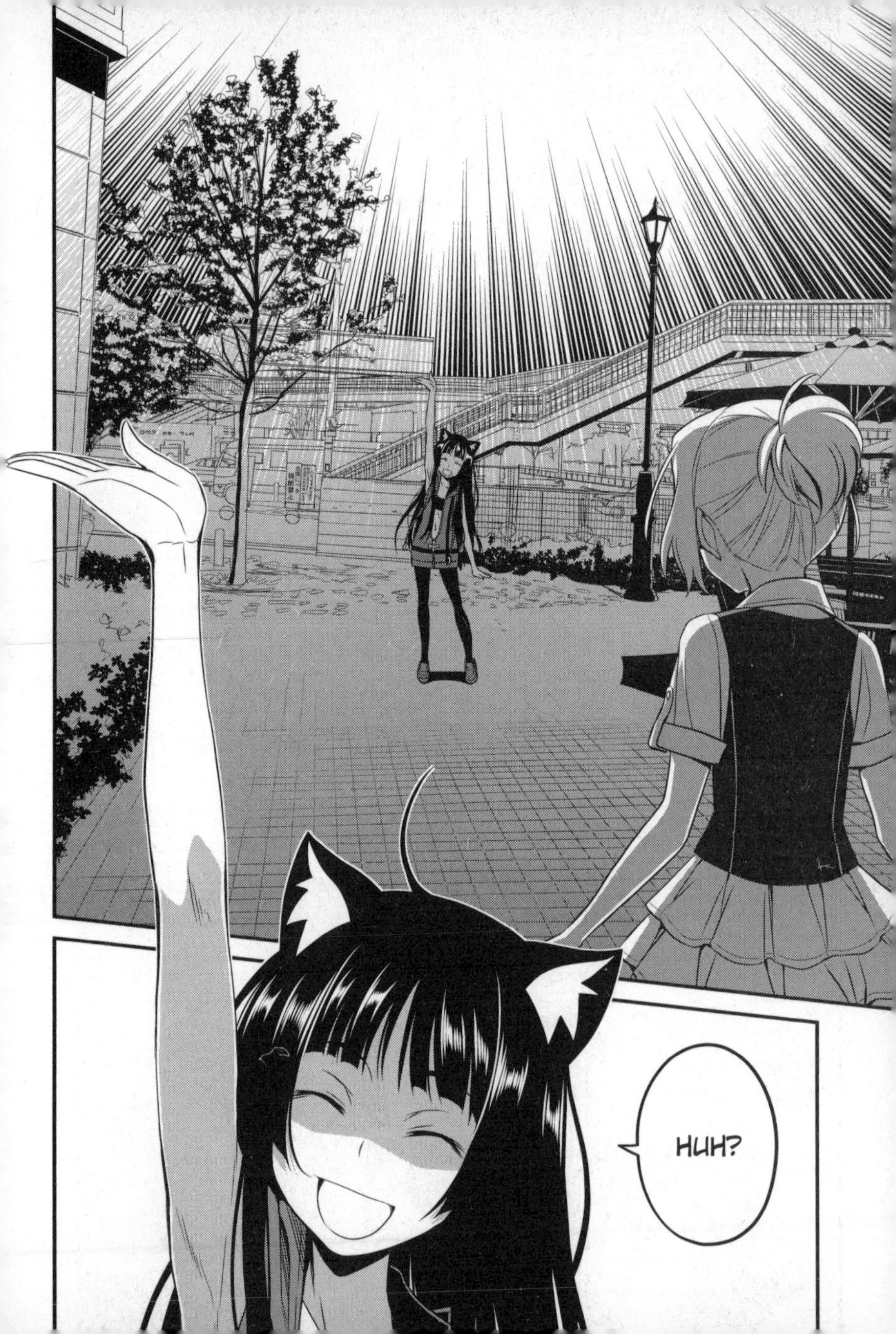
HUH?

# CHAPTER 14

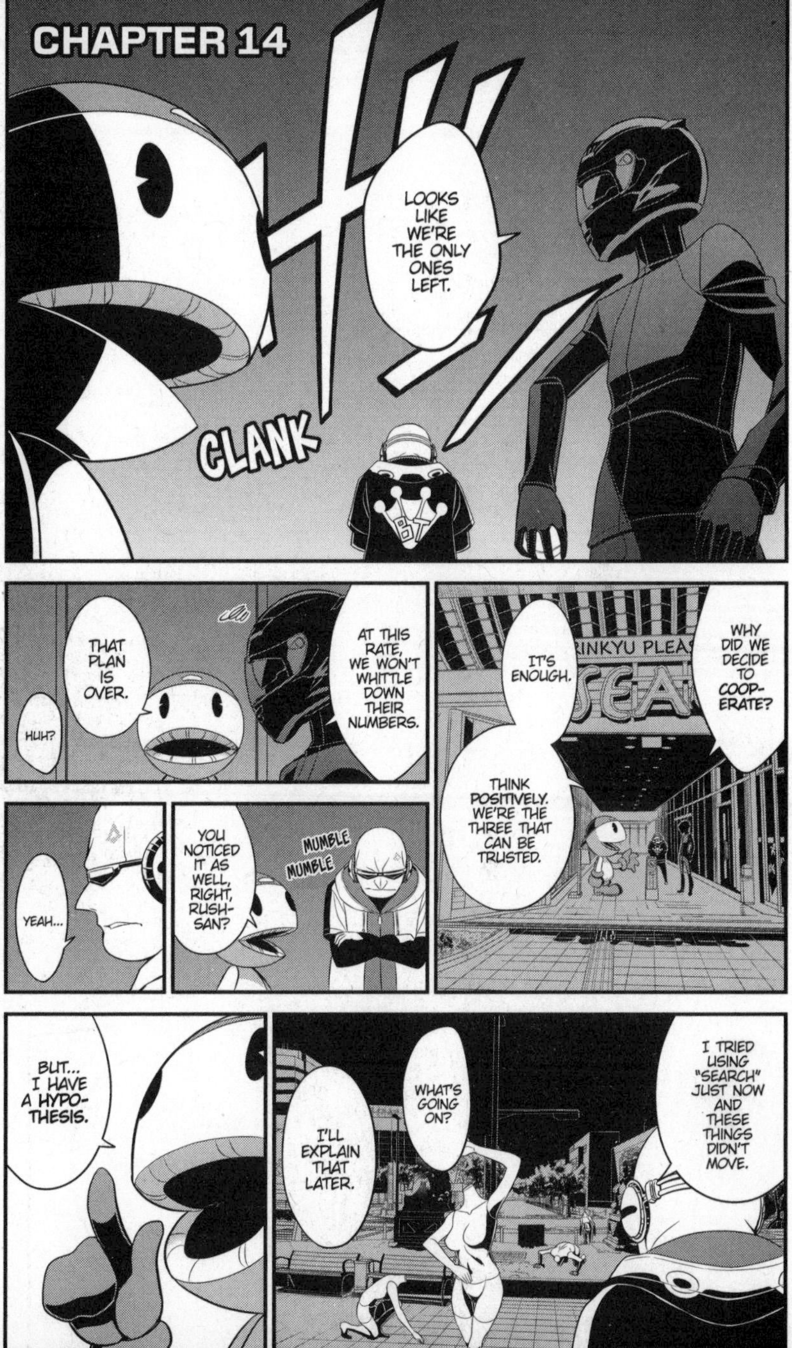
LOOKS LIKE WE'RE THE ONLY ONES LEFT.
CLANK
WHY DID WE DECIDE TO COOP-ERATE?
IT'S ENOUGH.
THINK POSITIVELY. WE'RE THE THREE THAT CAN BE TRUSTED.
AT THIS RATE, WE WON'T WHITTLE DOWN THEIR NUMBERS.
THAT PLAN IS OVER.
HUH?
MUMBLE MUMBLE
YOU NOTICED IT AS WELL, RIGHT, RUSH-SAN?
YEAH...
I TRIED USING "SEARCH" JUST NOW AND THESE THINGS DIDN'T MOVE.
WHAT'S GOING ON?
I'LL EXPLAIN THAT LATER.
BUT... I HAVE A HYPO-THESIS.

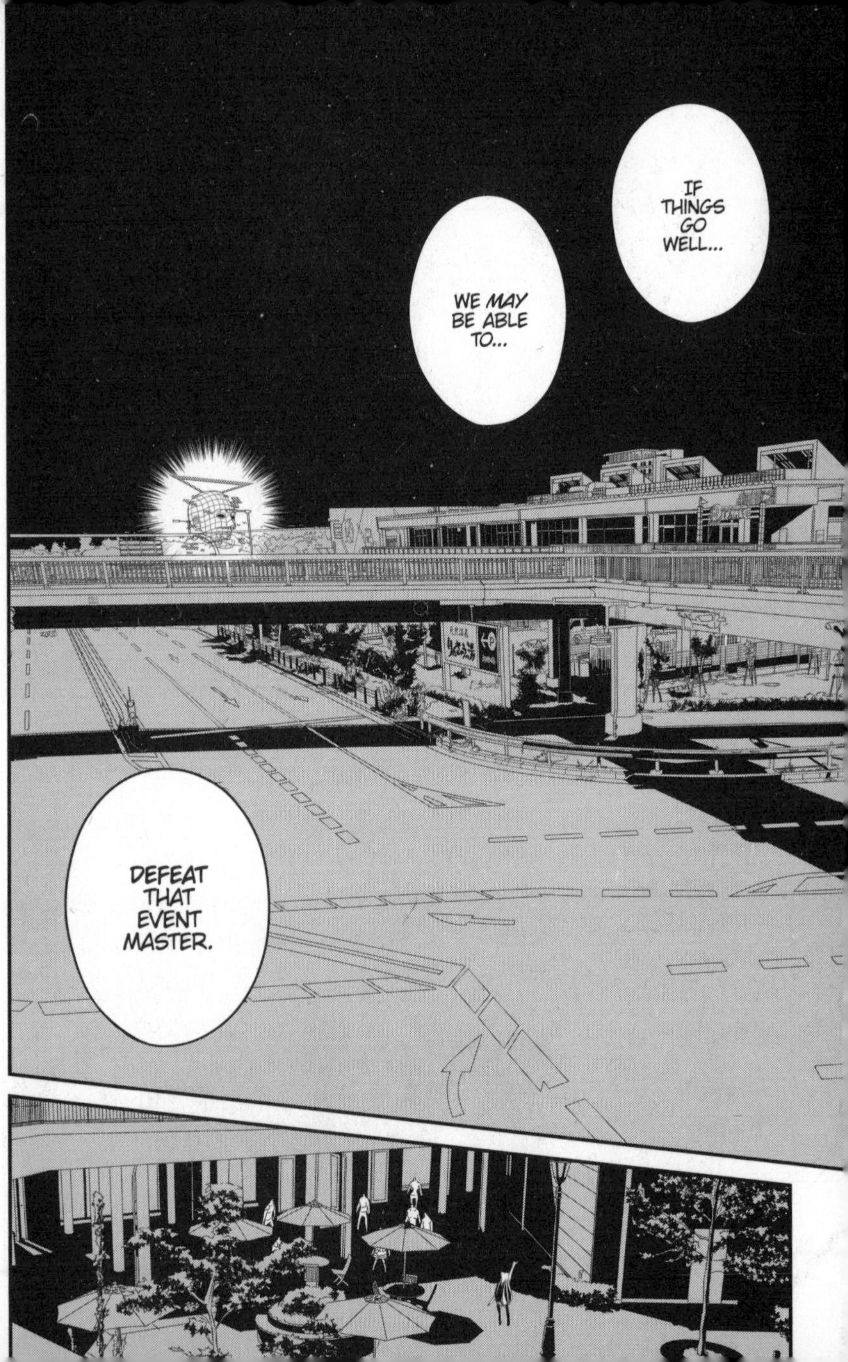
IF THINGS GO WELL...
WE MAY BE ABLE TO...
DEFEAT THAT EVENT MASTER.

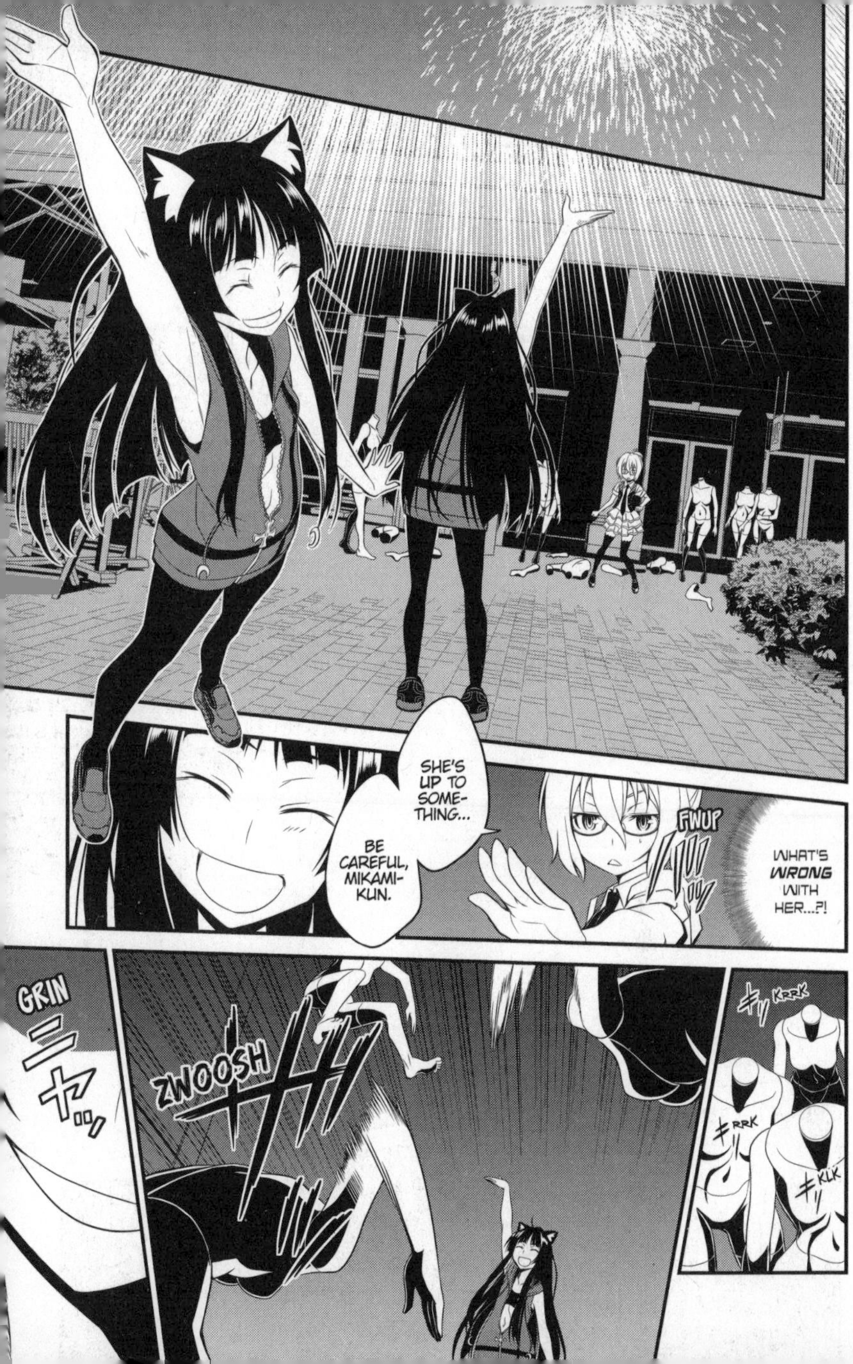
WHAT'S WRONG WITH HER...?!
FWUP
SHE'S UP TO SOME-THING...
BE CAREFUL, MIKAMI-KUN.
KRRK
RRK
KLIK
ZWOOSH
GRIN

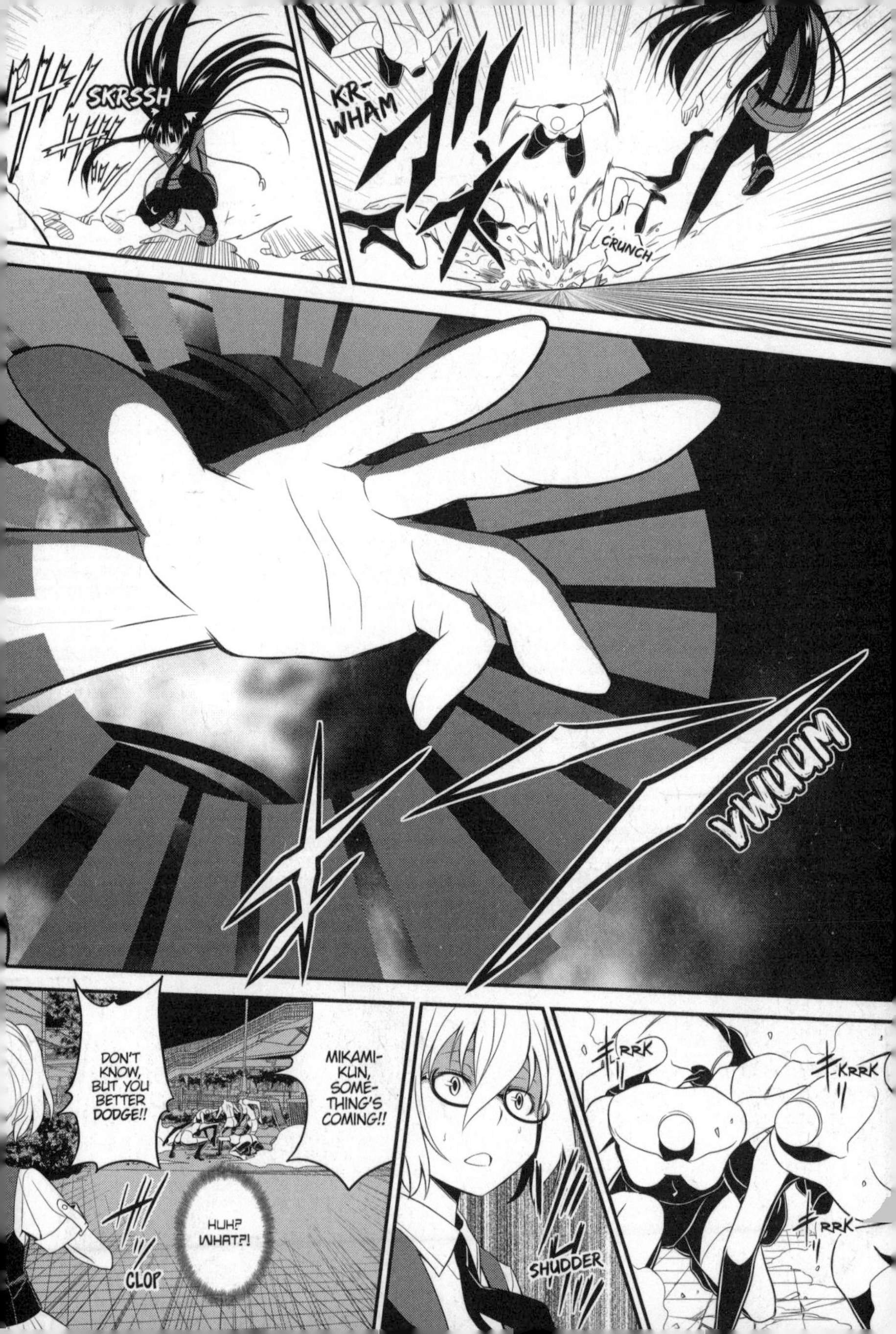
KR-WHAM
CRUNCH
SKRSSH
VWUUM
RRK
KRRK
RRK
SHUDDER
MIKAMI-KUN, SOMETHING'S COMING!!
DON'T KNOW, BUT YOU BETTER DODGE!!
HUH? WHAT?!
CLOP

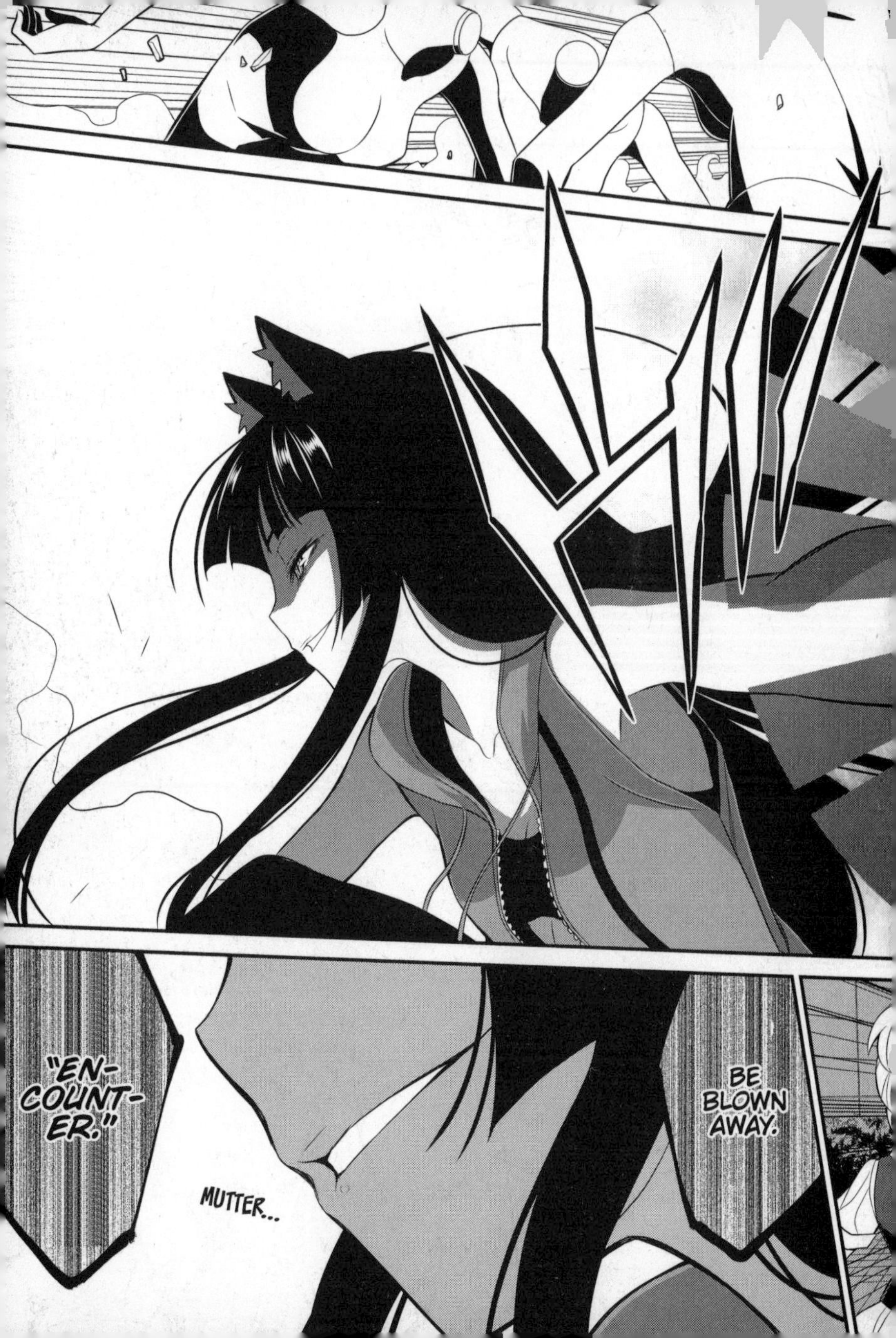
BE BLOWN AWAY.
"EN-COUNT-ER."
MUTTER...

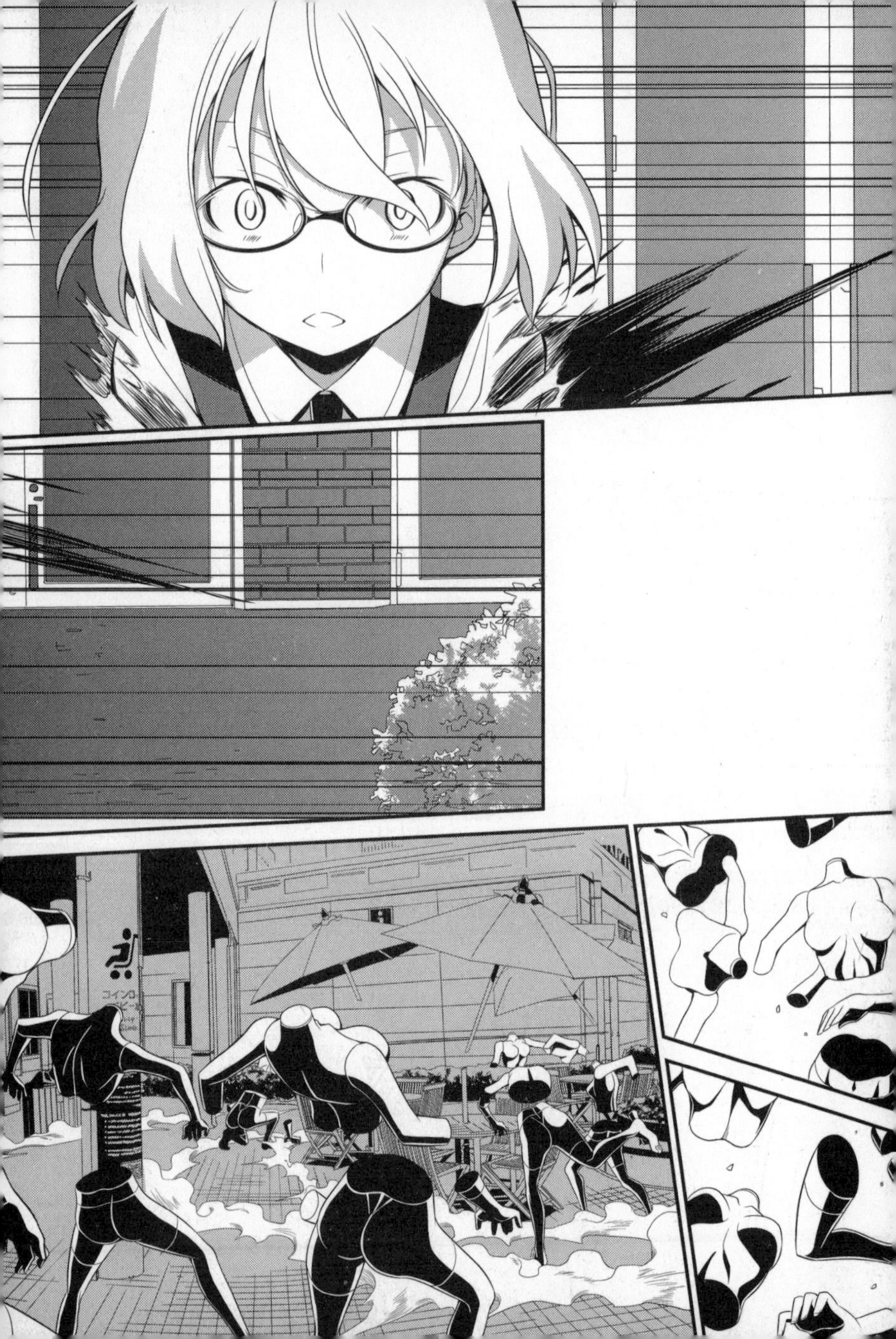

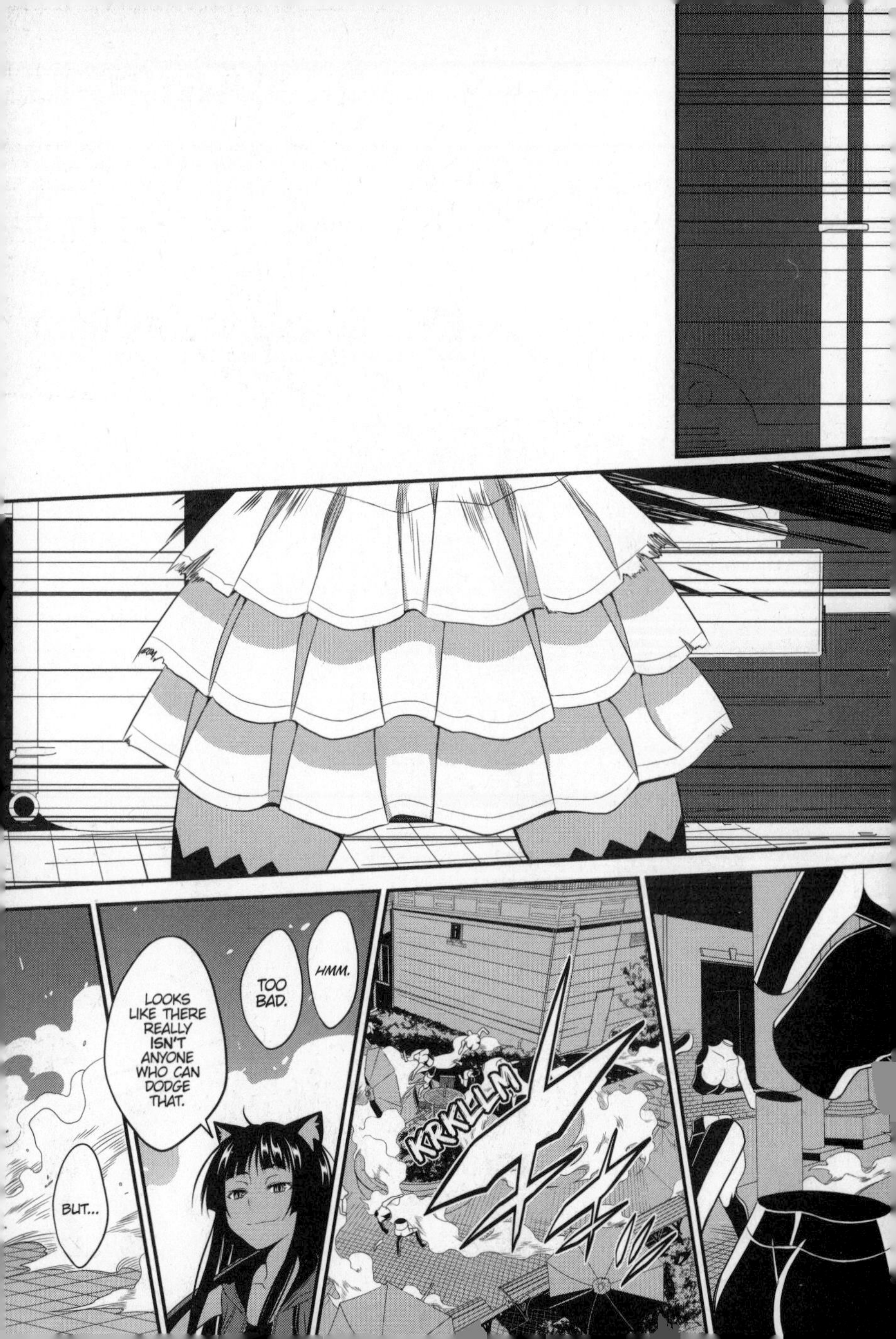
KRKLLM
HMM.
TOO BAD.
LOOKS LIKE THERE REALLY ISN'T ANYONE WHO CAN DODGE THAT.
BUT...

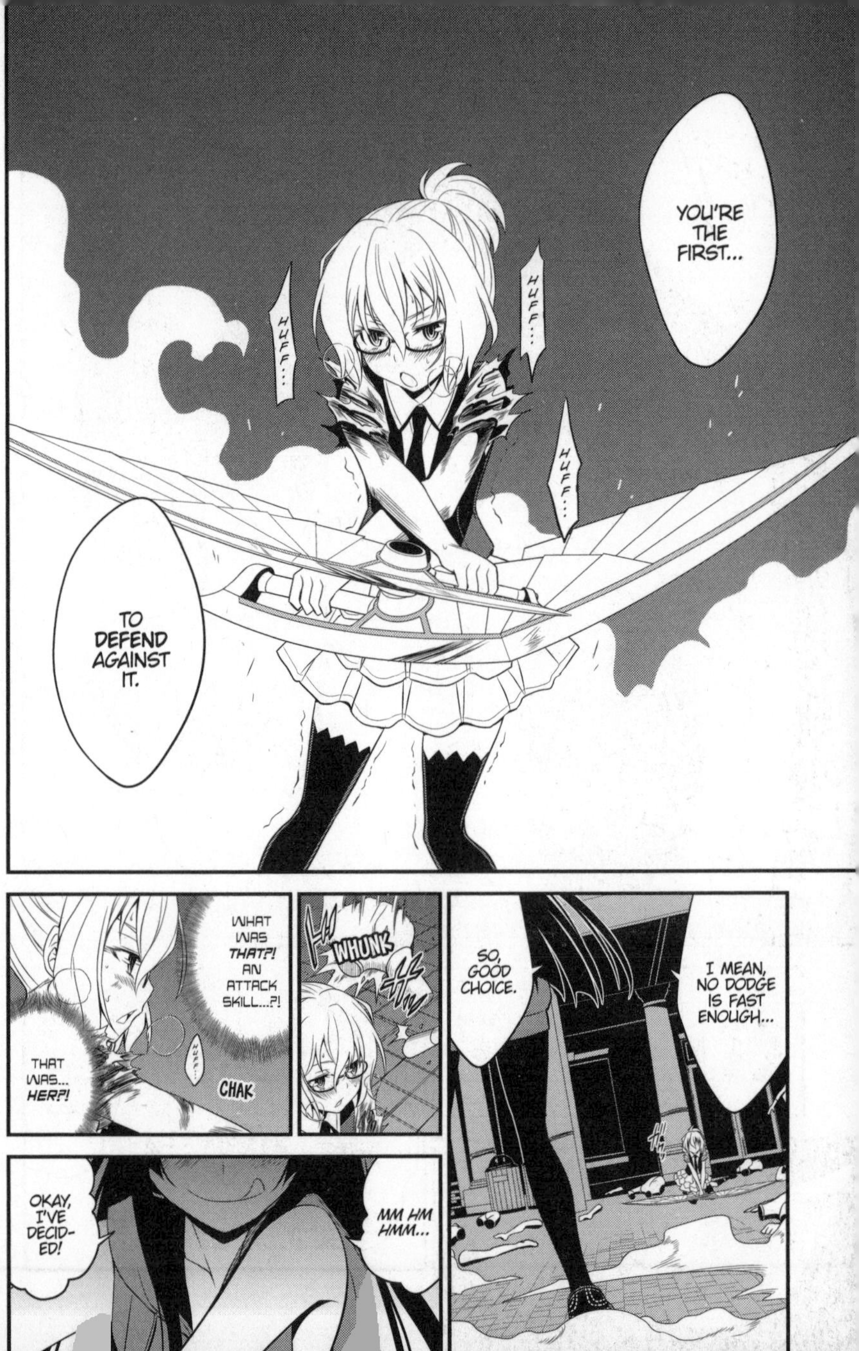

YOU'RE THE FIRST...
HUFF...
HUFF...
HUFF...
TO DEFEND AGAINST IT.
I MEAN, NO DODGE IS FAST ENOUGH...
SO, GOOD CHOICE.
WHUNK
WHAT WAS THAT?! AN ATTACK SKILL...?!
HUFF...
THAT WAS... HER?!
CHAK
MM HM HMM...
OKAY, I'VE DECID-ED!

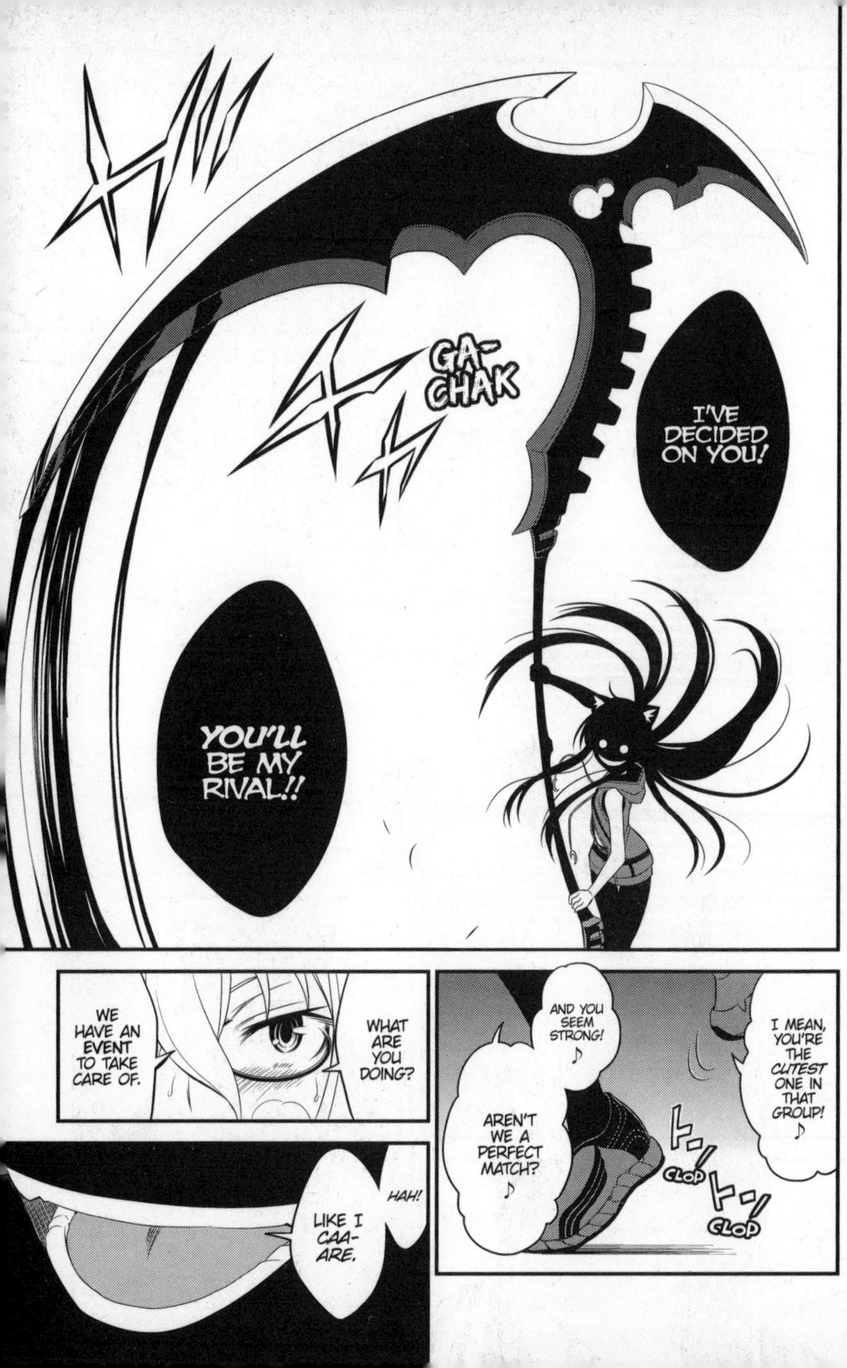
I'VE DECIDED ON YOU!
GA-CHAK
YOU'LL BE MY RIVAL!!
I MEAN, YOU'RE THE CUTEST ONE IN THAT GROUP! ♪
AND YOU SEEM STRONG! ♪
AREN'T WE A PERFECT MATCH? ♪
CLOP
CLOP
WHAT ARE YOU DOING?
WE HAVE AN EVENT TO TAKE CARE OF.
HAH!
LIKE I CAA-ARE.

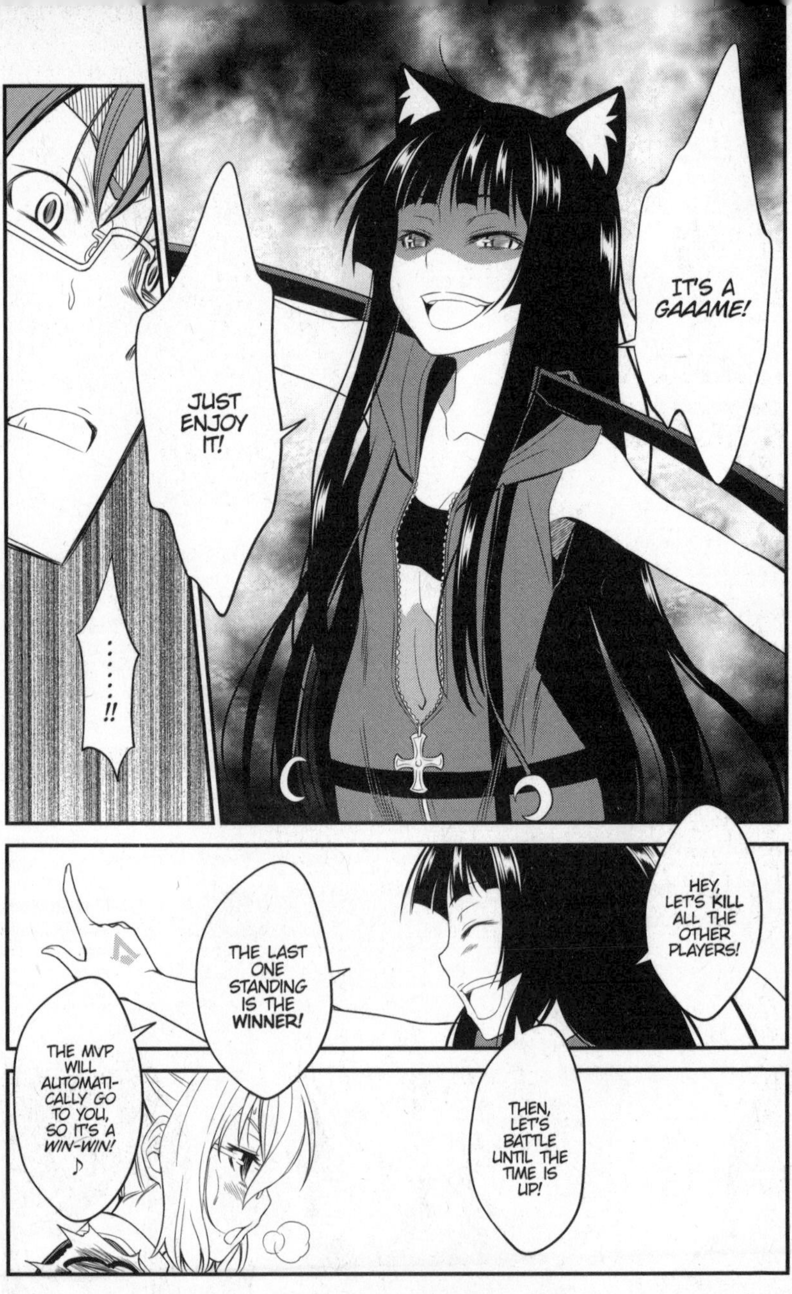
IT'S A GAAAME!
JUST ENJOY IT!
......!!
HEY, LET'S KILL ALL THE OTHER PLAYERS!
THE LAST ONE STANDING IS THE WINNER!
THEN, LET'S BATTLE UNTIL THE TIME IS UP!
THE MVP WILL AUTOMATICALLY GO TO YOU, SO IT'S A *WIN-WIN!* ♪

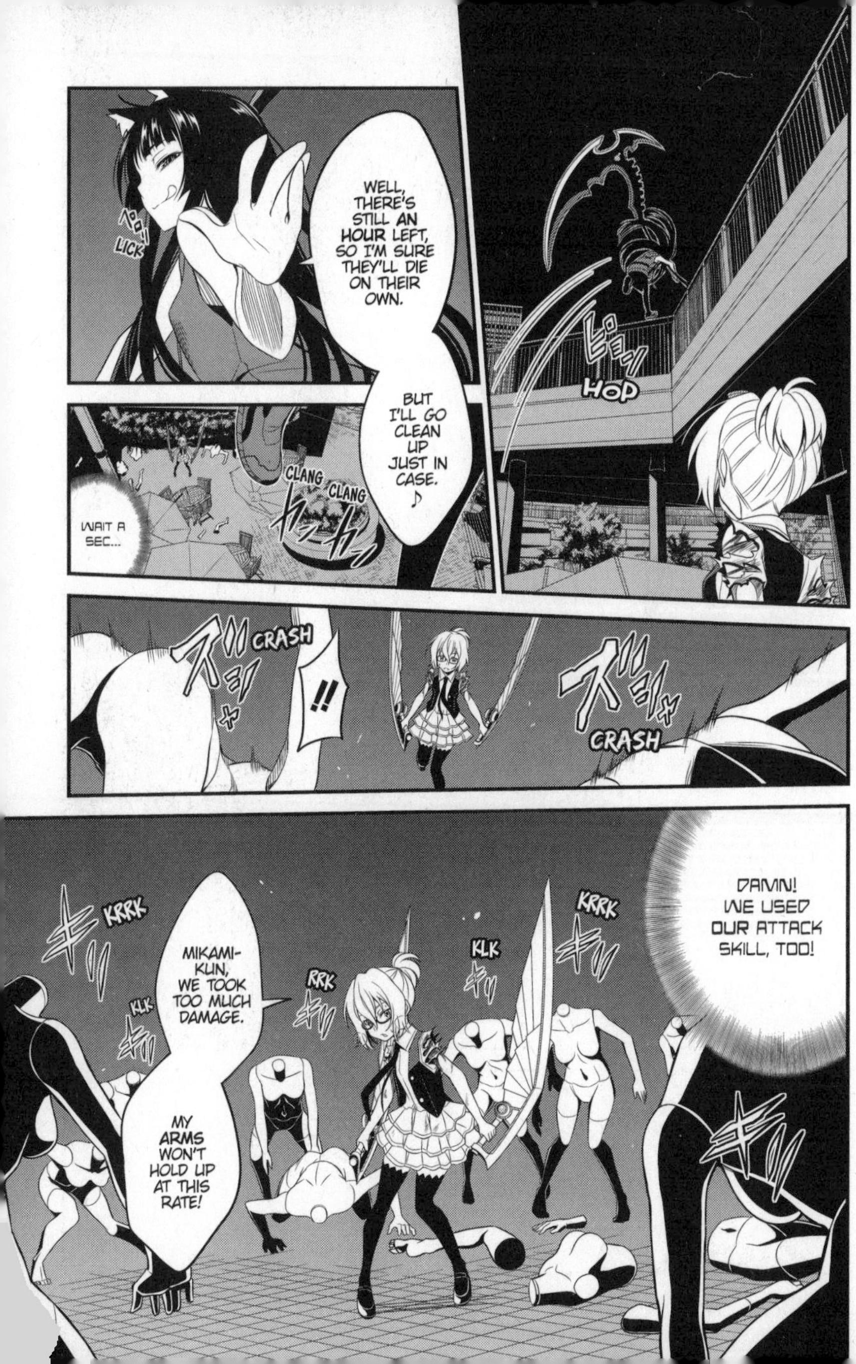
HOP
WELL, THERE'S STILL AN HOUR LEFT, SO I'M SURE THEY'LL DIE ON THEIR OWN.
LICK
BUT I'LL GO CLEAN UP JUST IN CASE. ♪
CLANG CLANG
WAIT A SEC...
CRASH
!!
CRASH
DAMN! WE USED OUR ATTACK SKILL, TOO!
KRRK
KLK
MIKAMI-KUN, WE TOOK TOO MUCH DAMAGE.
RRK
KLK
KRRK
MY ARMS WON'T HOLD UP AT THIS RATE!

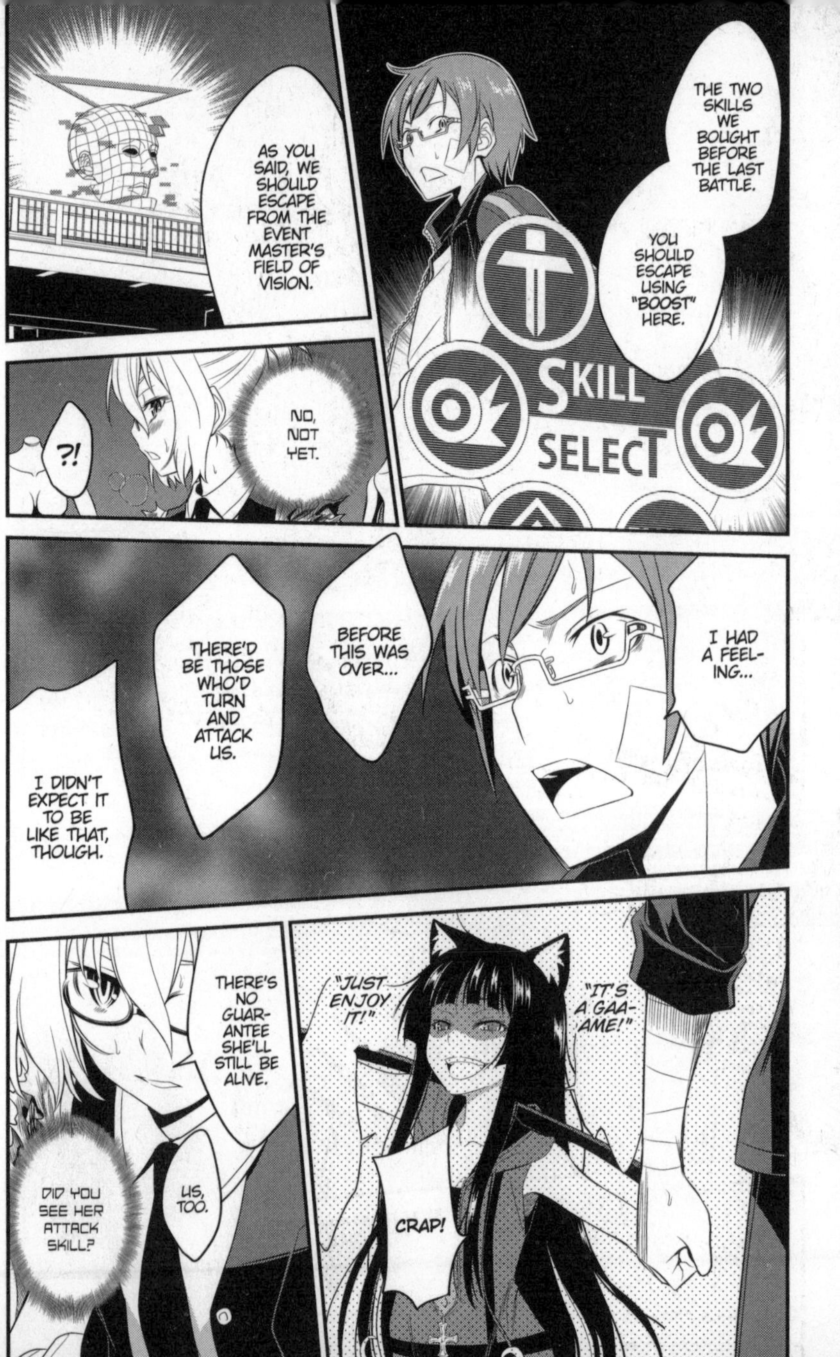
THE TWO SKILLS WE BOUGHT BEFORE THE LAST BATTLE.
YOU SHOULD ESCAPE USING "BOOST" HERE.
SKILL SELECT
AS YOU SAID, WE SHOULD ESCAPE FROM THE EVENT MASTER'S FIELD OF VISION.
NO, NOT YET.
?!
I HAD A FEEL-ING...
BEFORE THIS WAS OVER...
THERE'D BE THOSE WHO'D TURN AND ATTACK US.
I DIDN'T EXPECT IT TO BE LIKE THAT, THOUGH.
"IT'S A GAA-AME!"
"JUST ENJOY IT!"
CRAP!
THERE'S NO GUAR-ANTEE SHE'LL STILL BE ALIVE.
US, TOO.
DID YOU SEE HER ATTACK SKILL?

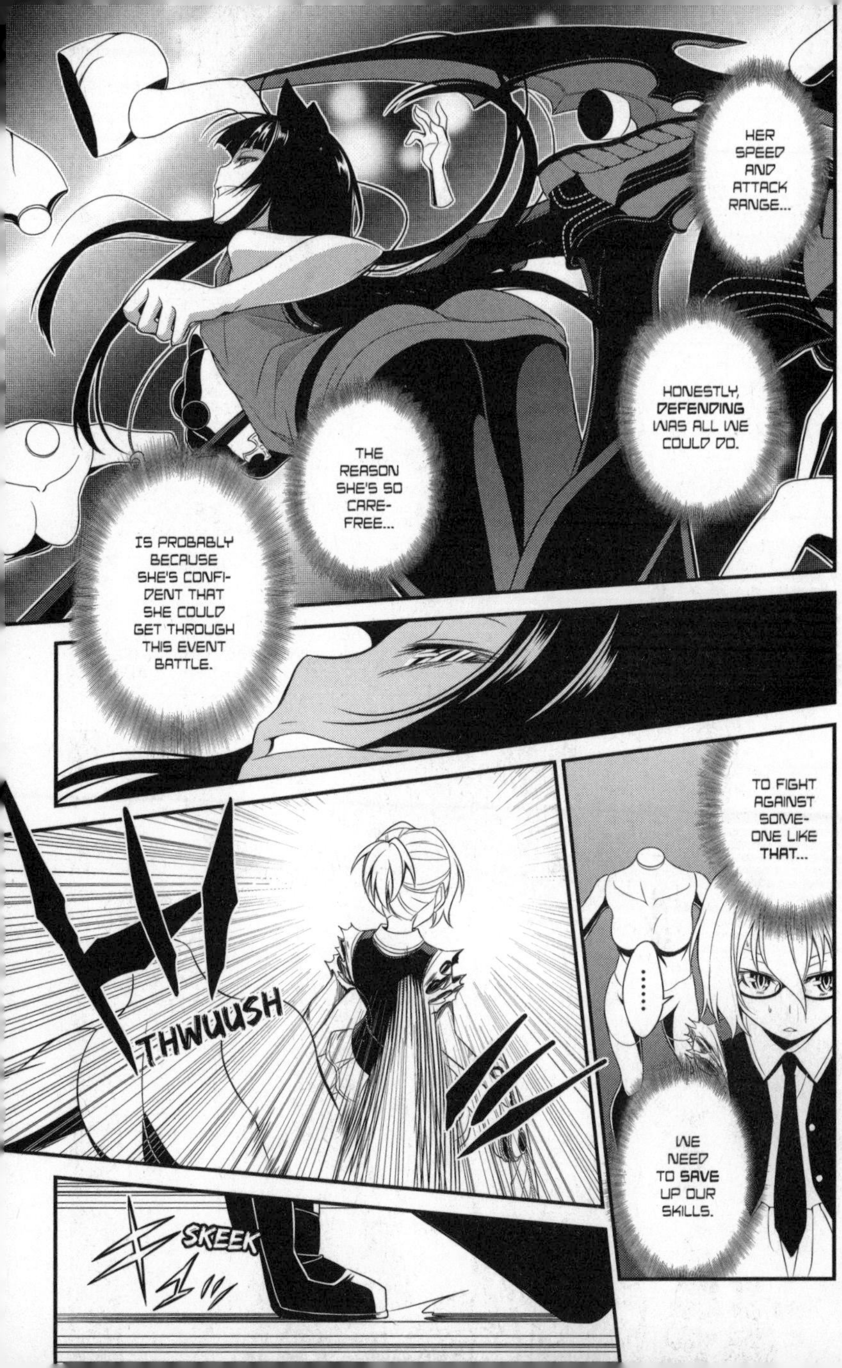
HER SPEED AND ATTACK RANGE...
HONESTLY, DEFENDING WAS ALL WE COULD DO.
THE REASON SHE'S SO CARE-FREE...
IS PROBABLY BECAUSE SHE'S CONFI-DENT THAT SHE COULD GET THROUGH THIS EVENT BATTLE.
TO FIGHT AGAINST SOME-ONE LIKE THAT...
......
WE NEED TO SAVE UP OUR SKILLS.
THWUUSH
SKEEK

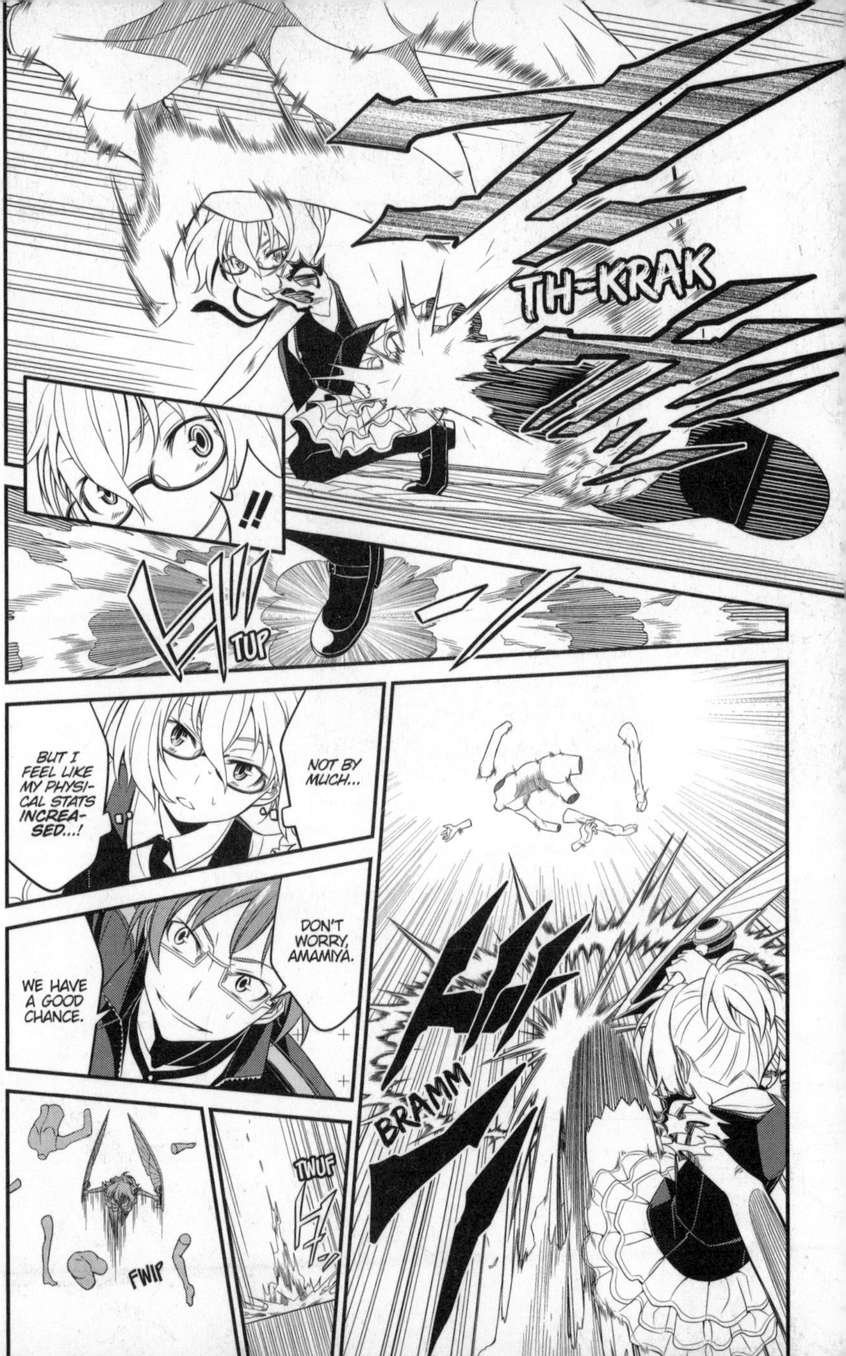
TH-KRAK
!!
TUP
BRAMM
NOT BY MUCH...
BUT I FEEL LIKE MY PHYSICAL STATS INCREASED...!
DON'T WORRY, AMAMIYA.
WE HAVE A GOOD CHANCE.
TWUF
FWIP

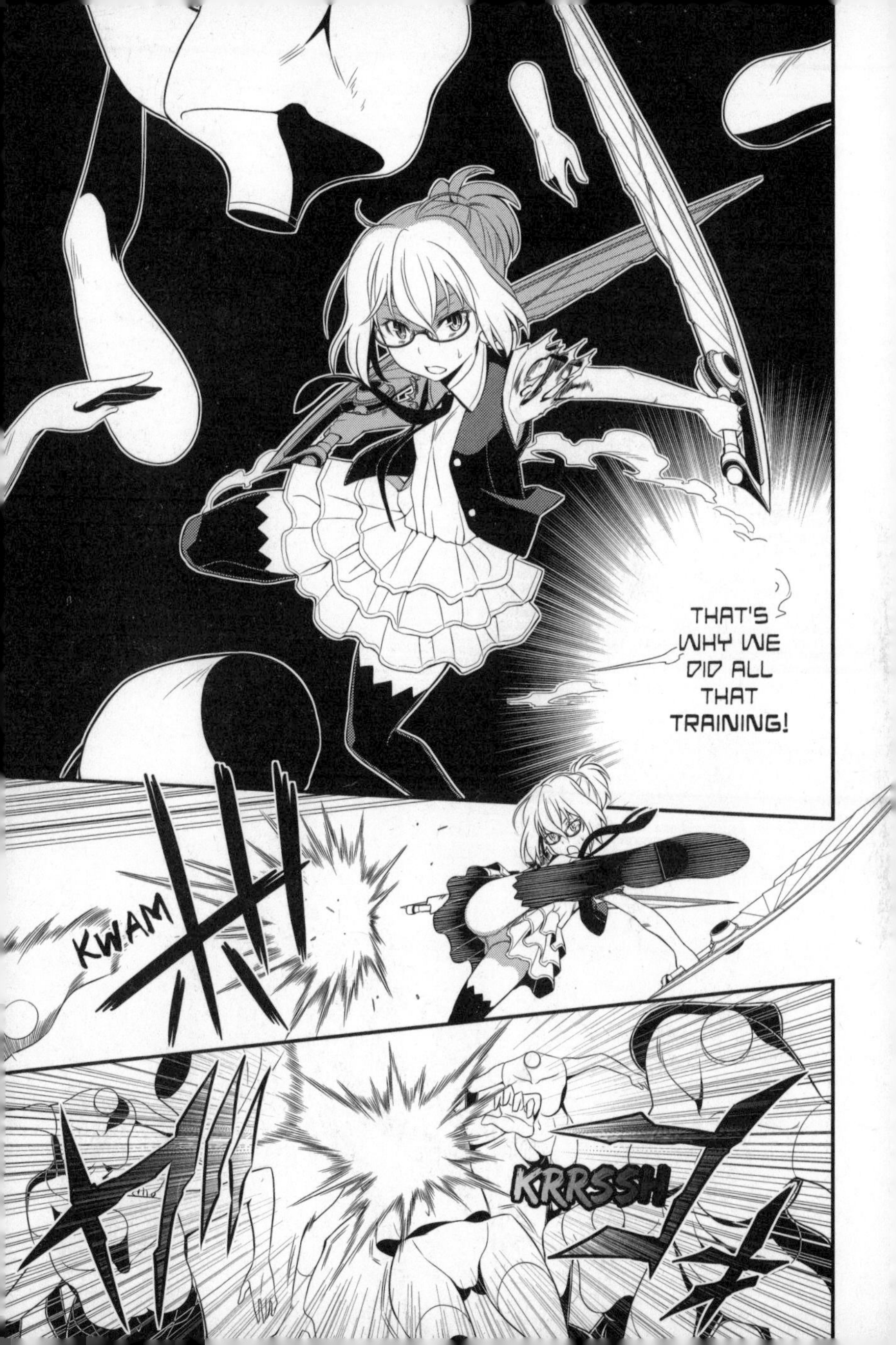
THAT'S WHY WE DID ALL THAT TRAINING!
KWAM
KRRSSH

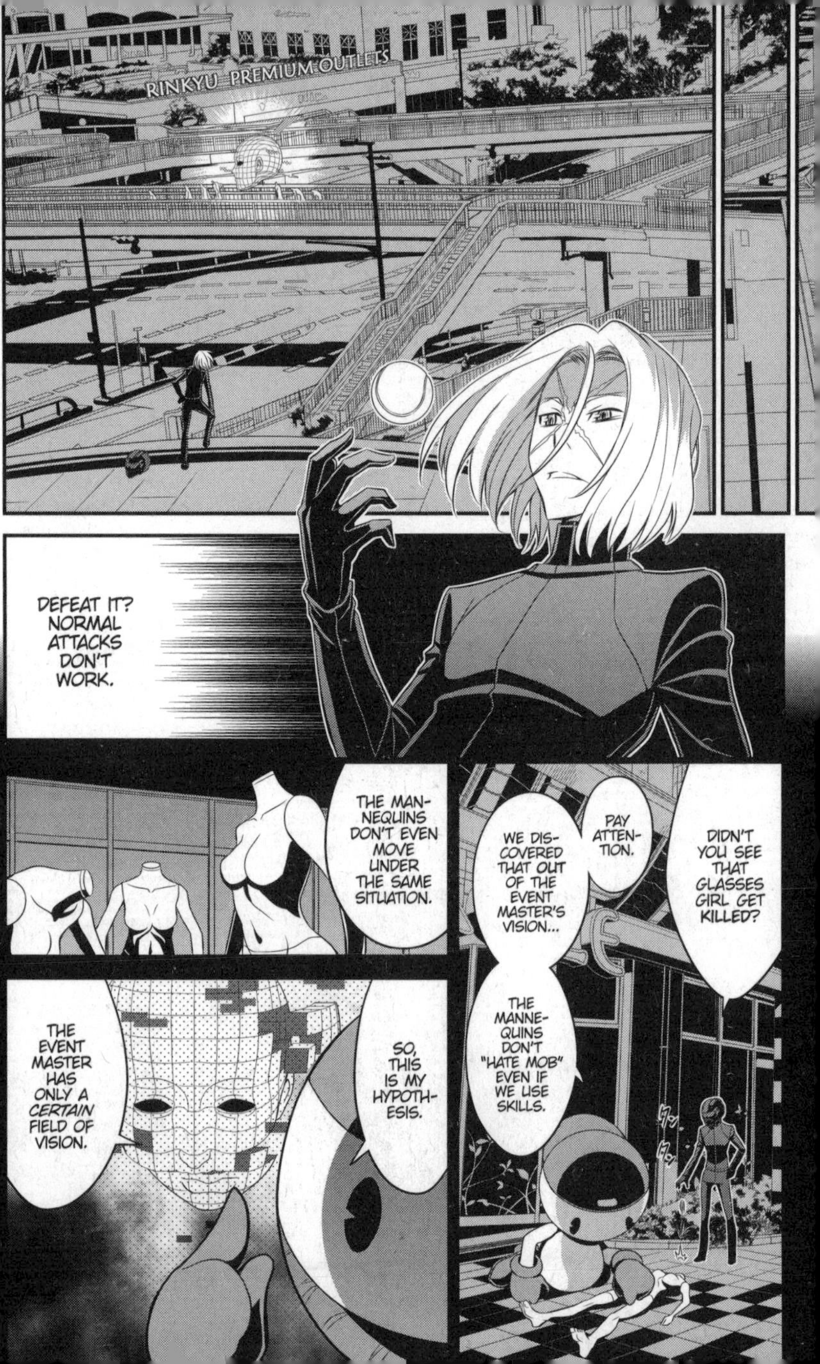
RINKYU PREMIUM OUTLETS
DEFEAT IT? NORMAL ATTACKS DON'T WORK.
DIDN'T YOU SEE THAT GLASSES GIRL GET KILLED?
PAY ATTENTION.
WE DISCOVERED THAT OUT OF THE EVENT MASTER'S VISION...
THE MANNEQUINS DON'T "HATE MOB" EVEN IF WE USE SKILLS.
THE MANNEQUINS DON'T EVEN MOVE UNDER THE SAME SITUATION.
SO, THIS IS MY HYPOTHESIS.
THE EVENT MASTER HAS ONLY A *CERTAIN* FIELD OF VISION.

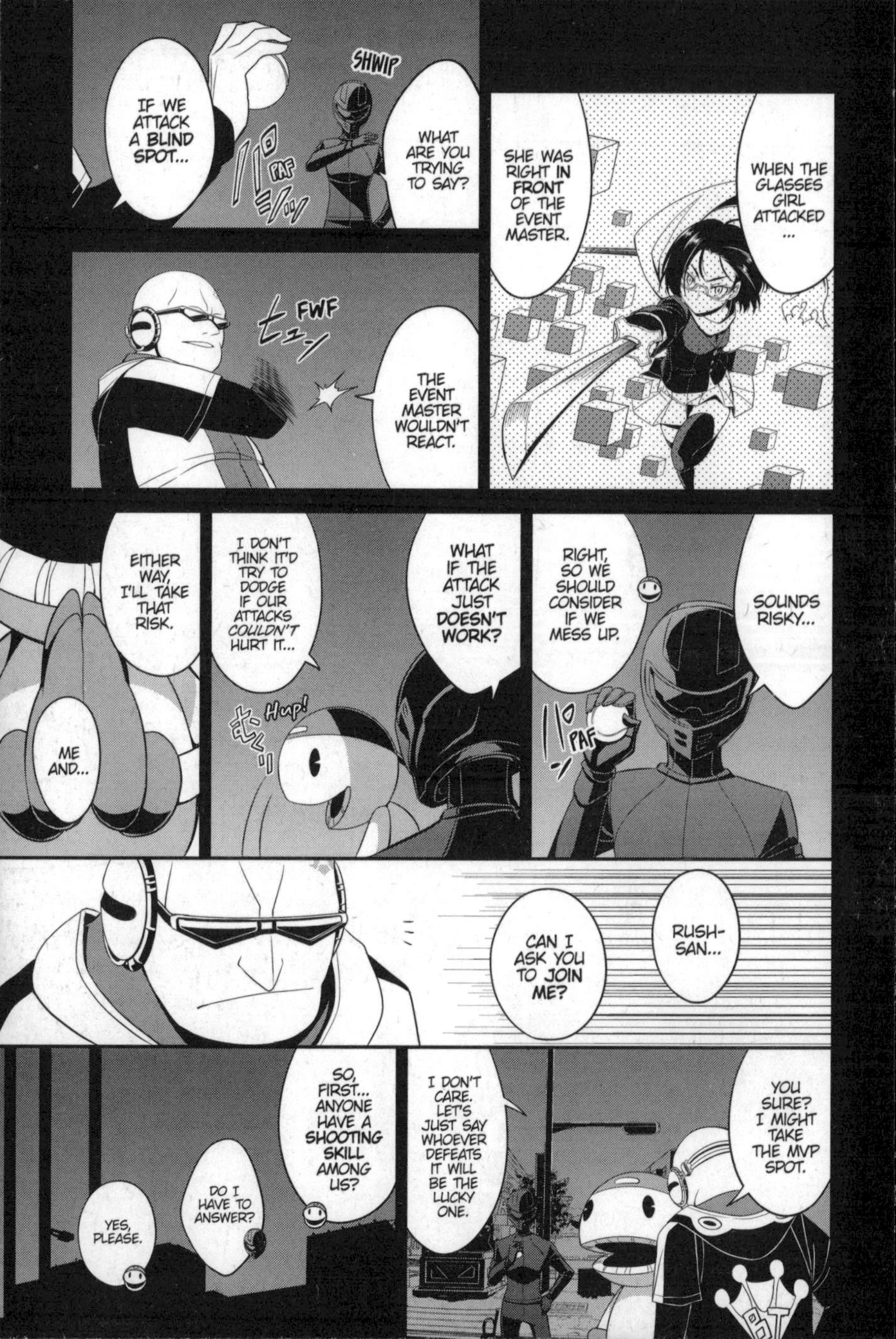
WHEN THE GLASSES GIRL ATTACKED ...
SHE WAS RIGHT IN FRONT OF THE EVENT MASTER.
SHWIP
WHAT ARE YOU TRYING TO SAY?
IF WE ATTACK A BLIND SPOT...
PAF
FWF
THE EVENT MASTER WOULDN'T REACT.
SOUNDS RISKY...
RIGHT, SO WE SHOULD CONSIDER IF WE MESS UP.
PAF
WHAT IF THE ATTACK JUST DOESN'T WORK?
I DON'T THINK IT'D TRY TO DODGE IF OUR ATTACKS COULDN'T HURT IT...
Hup!
EITHER WAY, I'LL TAKE THAT RISK.
ME AND...
RUSH-SAN...
CAN I ASK YOU TO JOIN ME?
YOU SURE? I MIGHT TAKE THE MVP SPOT.
I DON'T CARE. LET'S JUST SAY WHOEVER DEFEATS IT WILL BE THE LUCKY ONE.
SO, FIRST... ANYONE HAVE A SHOOTING SKILL AMONG US?
DO I HAVE TO ANSWER?
YES, PLEASE.

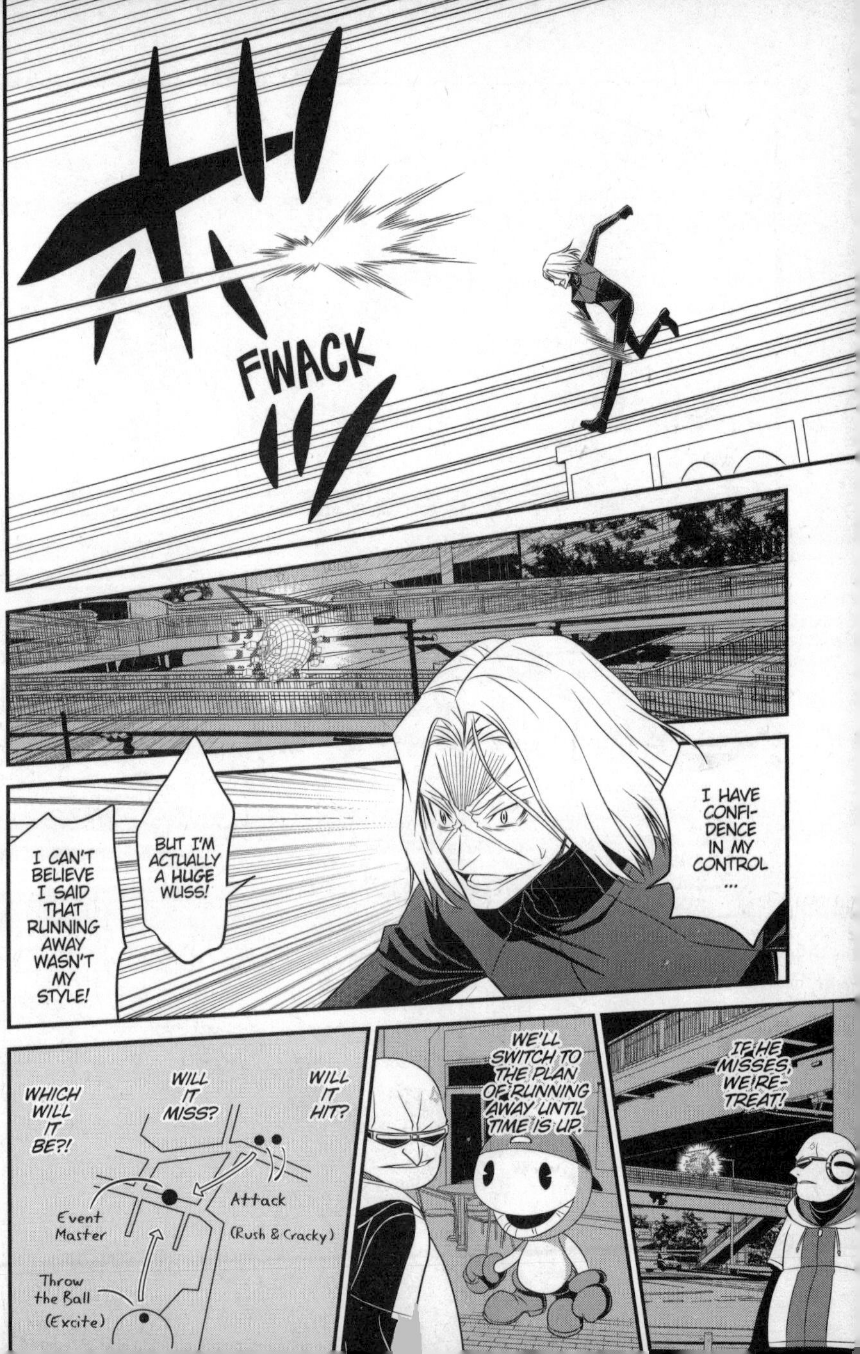
FWACK
I HAVE CONFIDENCE IN MY CONTROL...
BUT I'M ACTUALLY A HUGE WUSS!
I CAN'T BELIEVE I SAID THAT RUNNING AWAY WASN'T MY STYLE!
IF HE MISSES, WE'RE-TREAT!
WE'LL SWITCH TO THE PLAN OF RUNNING AWAY UNTIL TIME IS UP.
WILL IT HIT?
WILL IT MISS?
WHICH WILL IT BE?!
Attack
(Rush & Cracky)
Event Master
Throw the Ball
(Excite)

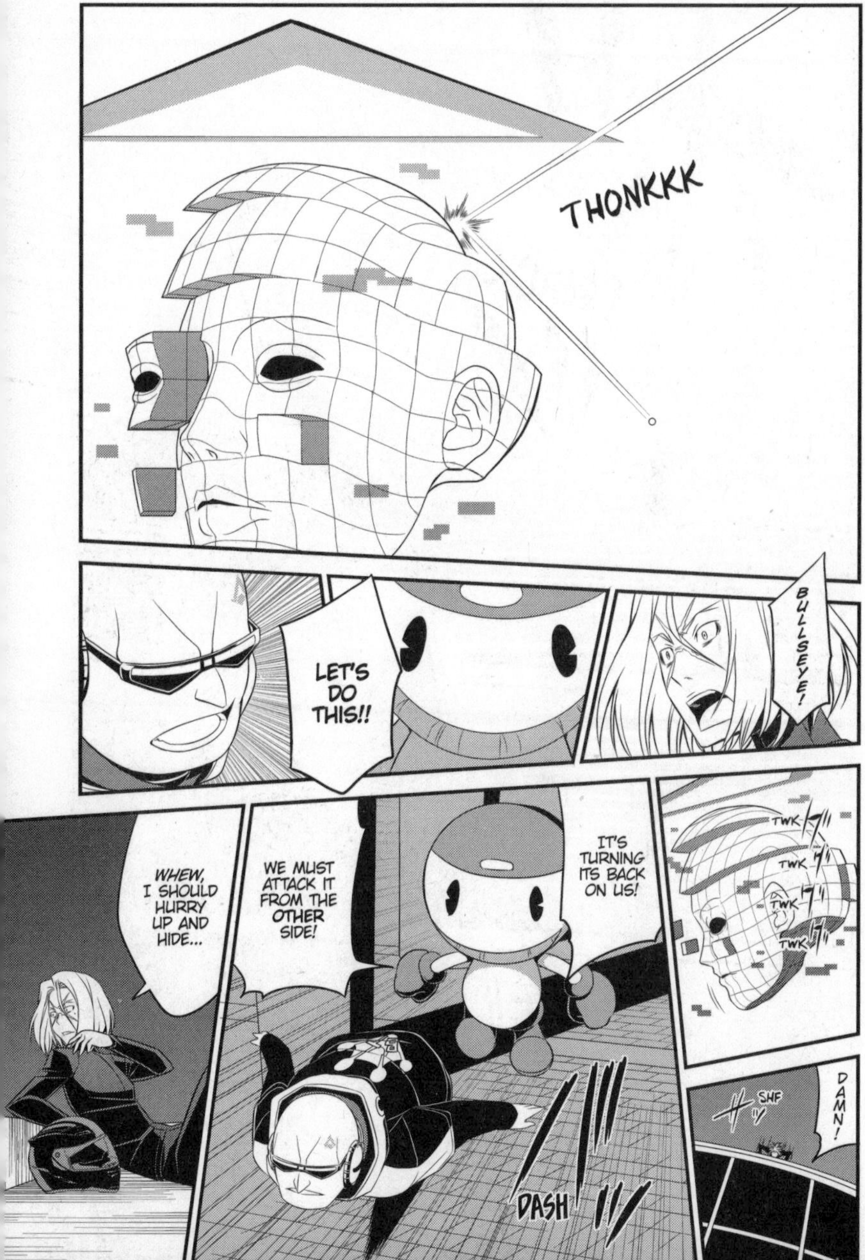
THONKKK
BULLSEYE!
LET'S DO THIS!!
TWK TWK TWK TWK
IT'S TURNING ITS BACK ON US!
WE MUST ATTACK IT FROM THE OTHER SIDE!
WHEW, I SHOULD HURRY UP AND HIDE...
DAMN!
SHF
DASH

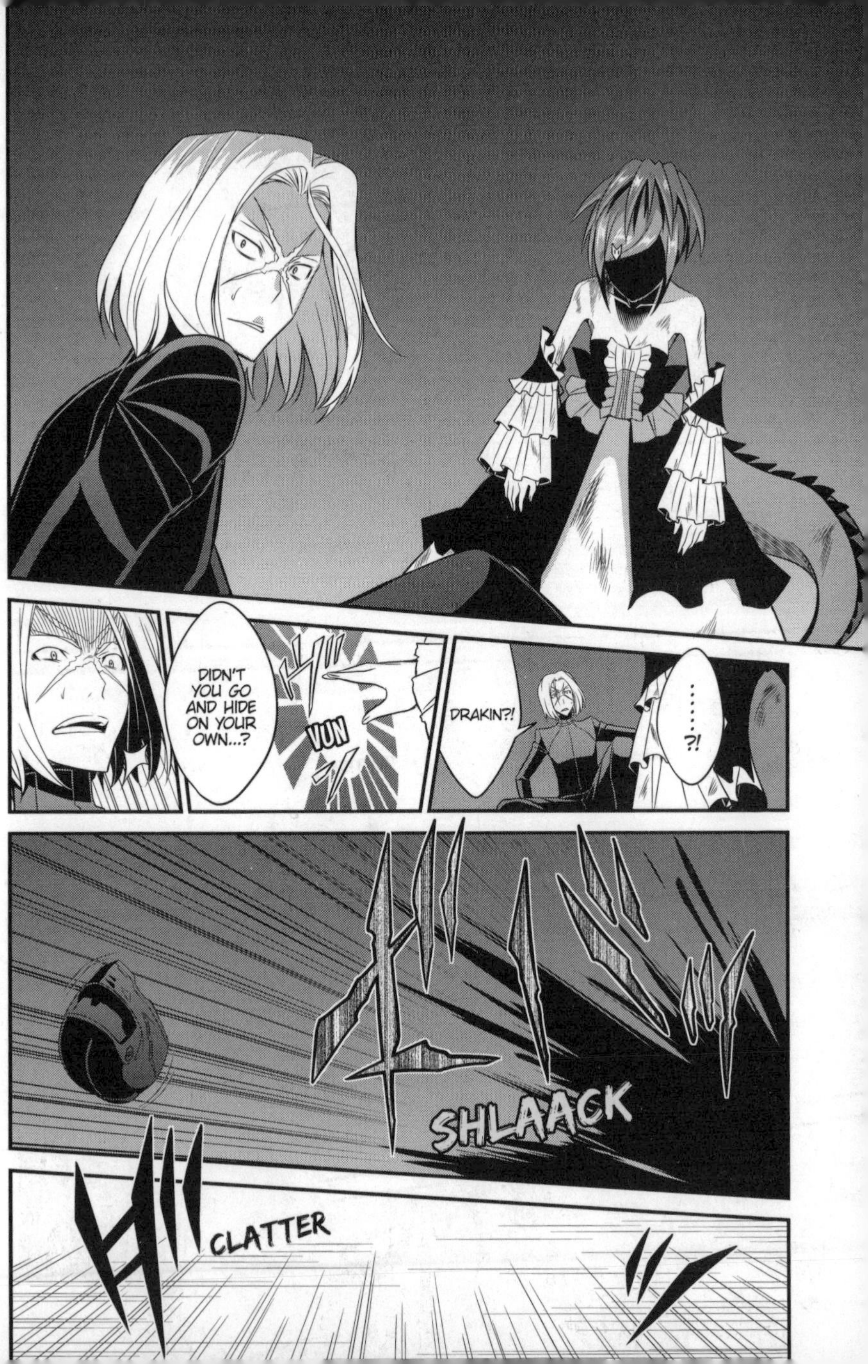
......?!
DRAKIN?!
VUN
DIDN'T YOU GO AND HIDE ON YOUR OWN...?
SHLAACK
CLATTER

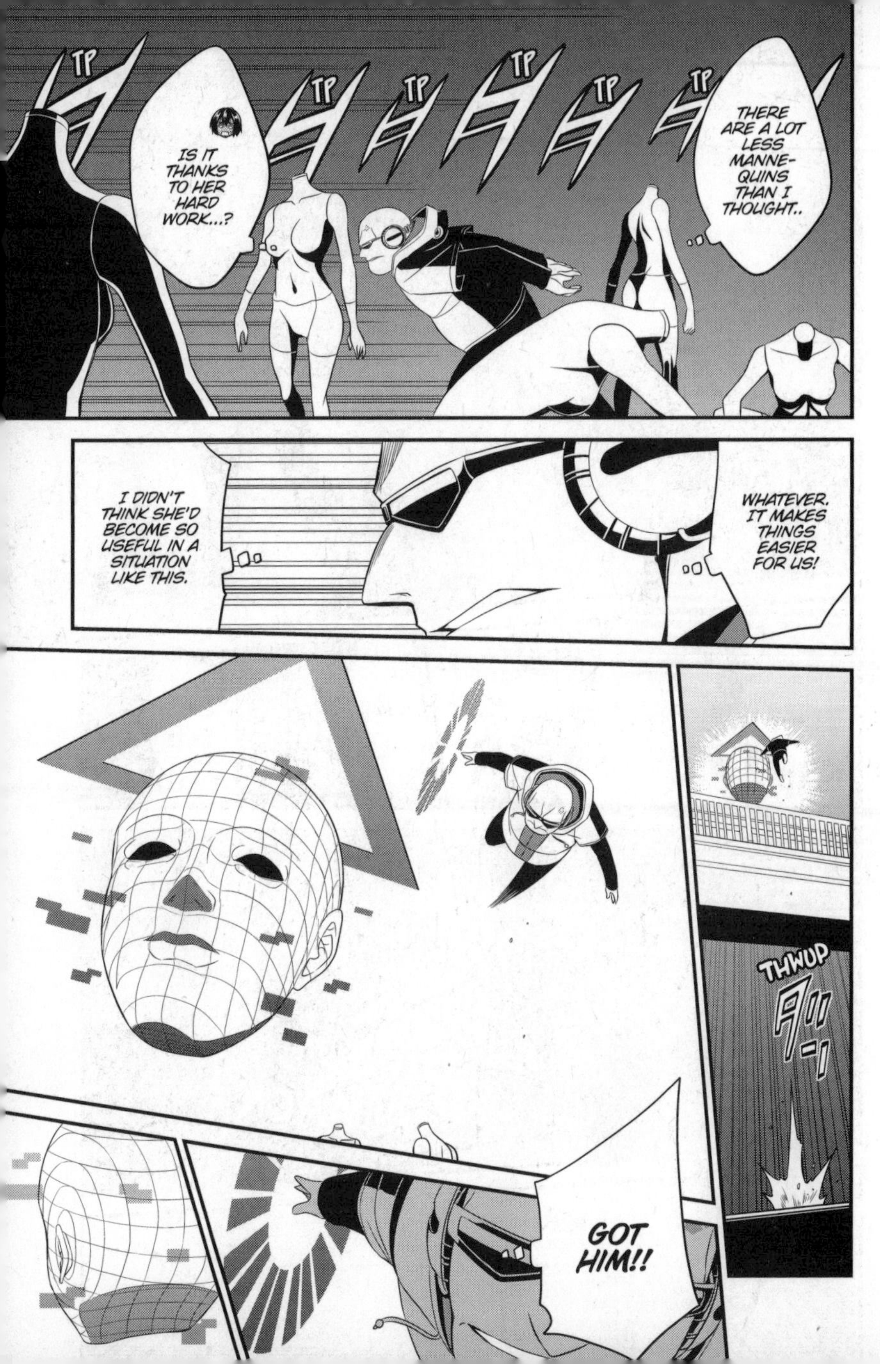
TP TP TP TP TP TP
THERE ARE A LOT LESS MANNE-QUINS THAN I THOUGHT..
IS IT THANKS TO HER HARD WORK...?
WHATEVER. IT MAKES THINGS EASIER FOR US!
I DIDN'T THINK SHE'D BECOME SO USEFUL IN A SITUATION LIKE THIS.
THWUP
GOT HIM!!

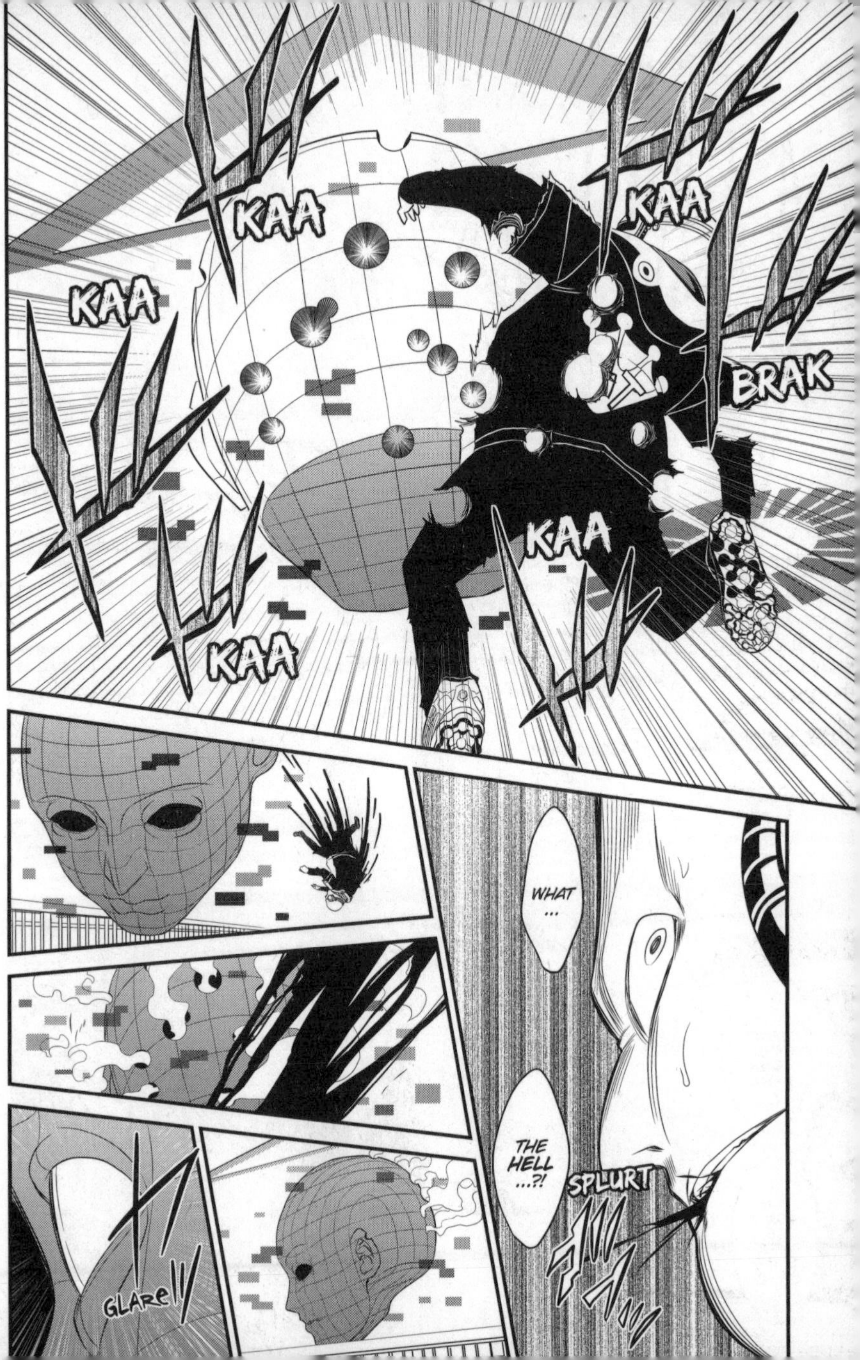
KAA
BRAK
KAA
KAA
KAA
KAA
WHAT ...
THE HELL ...?!
SPLURT
GLARE!!

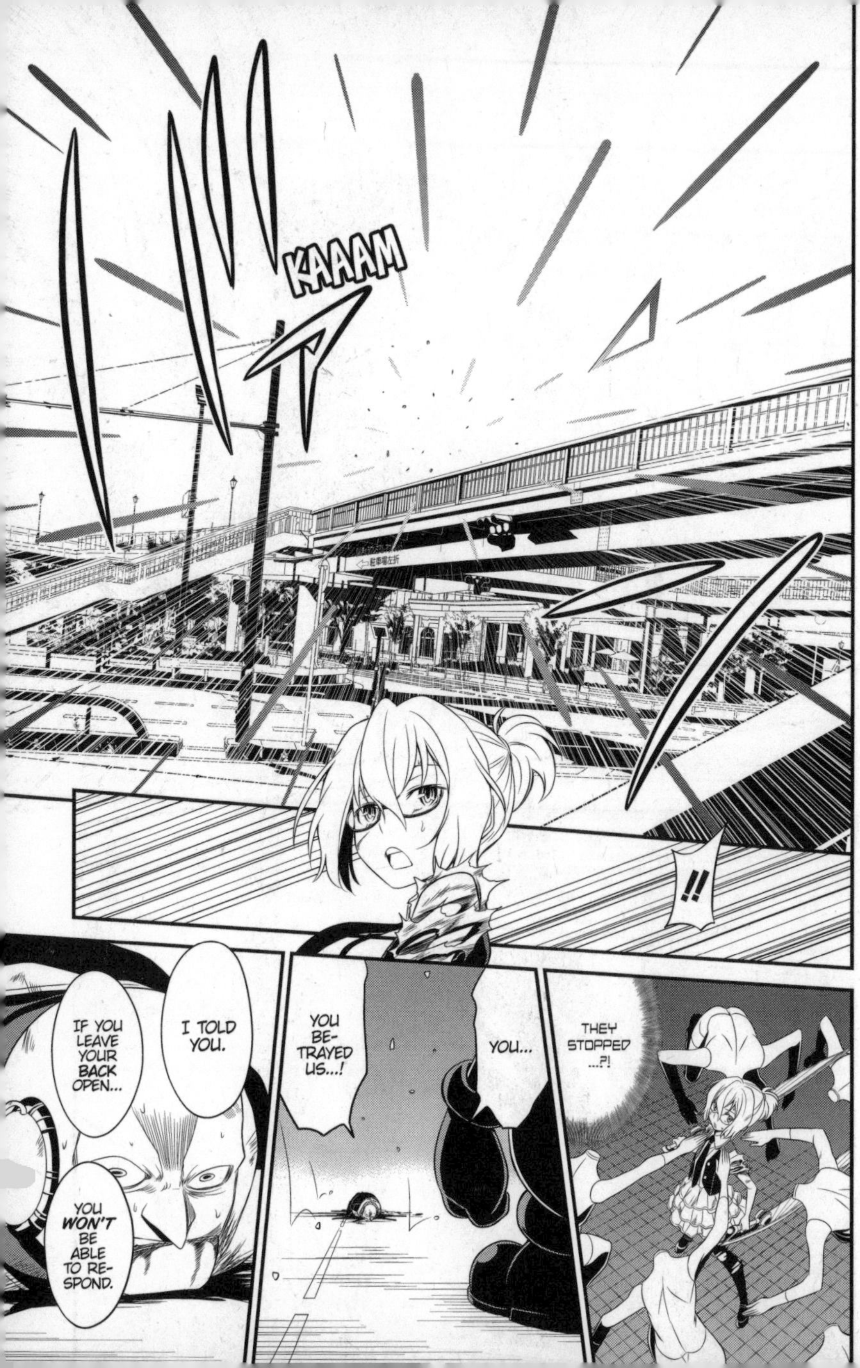
KAAAM
!!
THEY STOPPED ...?!
YOU...
YOU BE-TRAYED US...!
I TOLD YOU.
IF YOU LEAVE YOUR BACK OPEN...
YOU **WON'T** BE ABLE TO RE-SPOND.

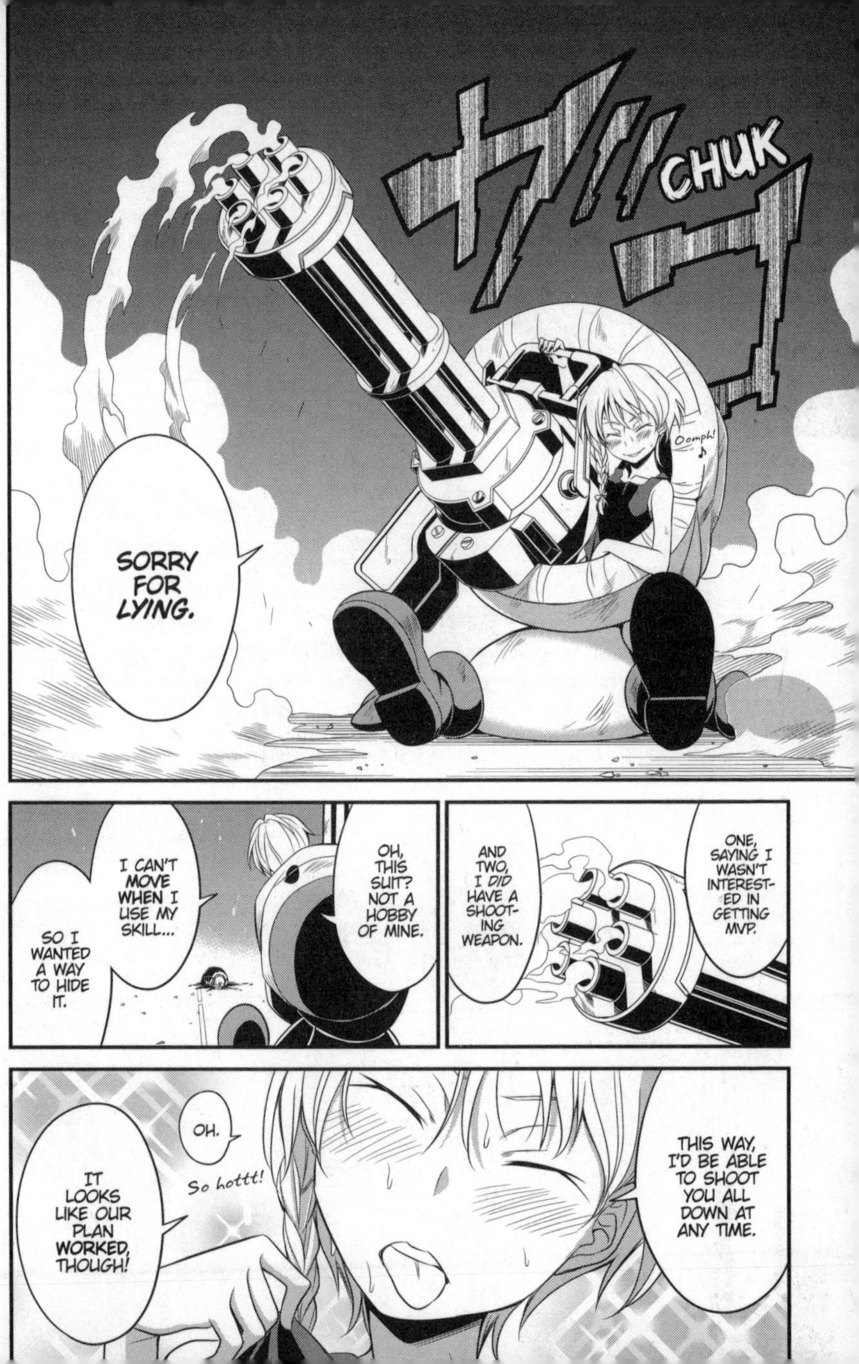
CHUK
Oomph! ♪
SORRY FOR *LYING.*
ONE, SAYING I WASN'T INTEREST-ED IN GETTING MVP.
AND TWO, I *DID* HAVE A SHOOT-ING WEAPON.
OH, THIS SUIT? NOT A HOBBY OF MINE.
I CAN'T MOVE WHEN I USE MY SKILL...
SO I WANTED A WAY TO HIDE IT.
THIS WAY, I'D BE ABLE TO SHOOT YOU ALL DOWN AT ANY TIME.
OH.
So hottt!
IT LOOKS LIKE OUR PLAN WORKED, THOUGH!

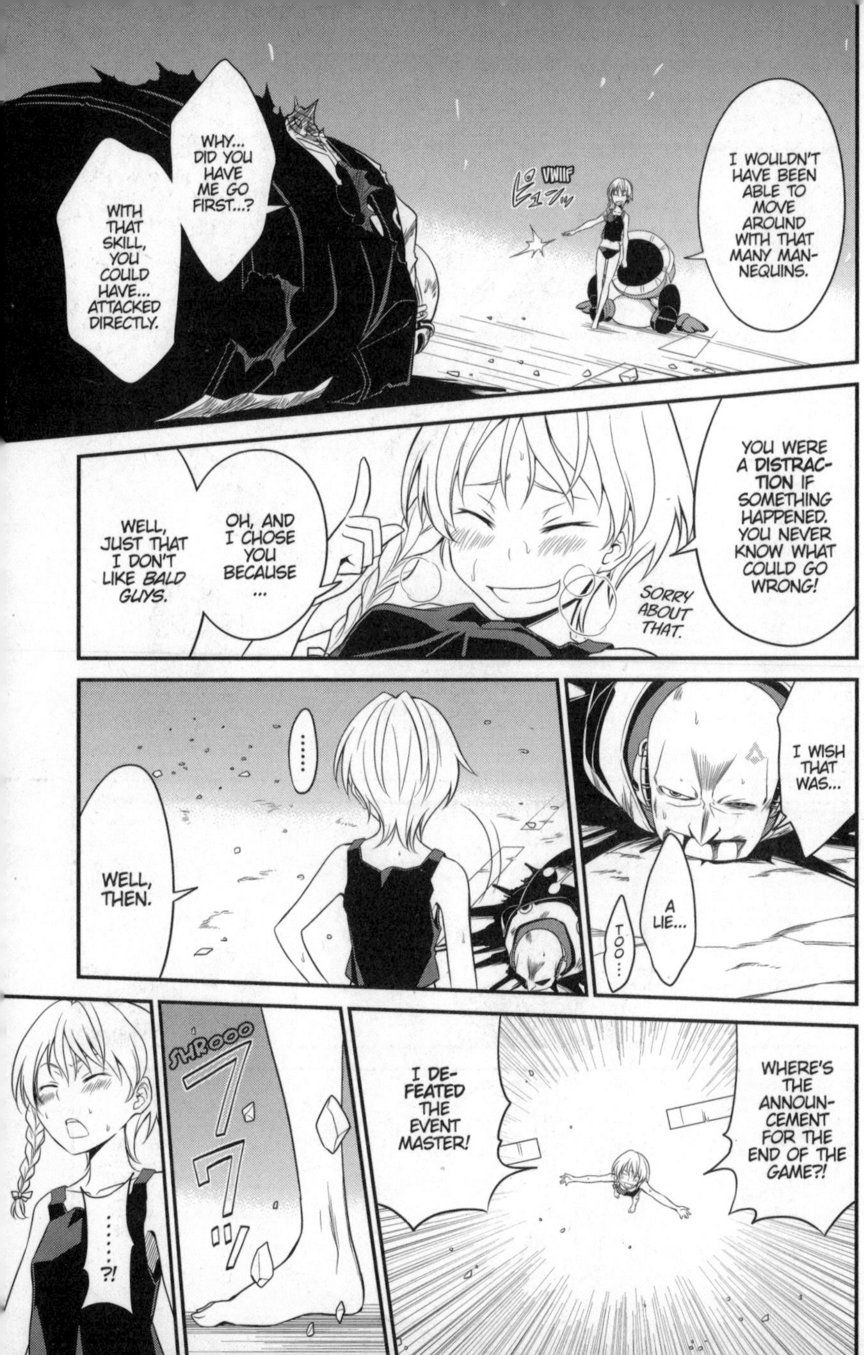
I WOULDN'T HAVE BEEN ABLE TO MOVE AROUND WITH THAT MANY MANNEQUINS.
VWIIF
WHY... DID YOU HAVE ME GO FIRST...?
WITH THAT SKILL, YOU COULD HAVE... ATTACKED DIRECTLY.
YOU WERE A DISTRACTION IF SOMETHING HAPPENED. YOU NEVER KNOW WHAT COULD GO WRONG!
SORRY ABOUT THAT.
OH, AND I CHOSE YOU BECAUSE ...
WELL, JUST THAT I DON'T LIKE *BALD GUYS.*
I WISH THAT WAS...
A LIE...
TOO...
......
WELL, THEN.
WHERE'S THE ANNOUNCEMENT FOR THE END OF THE GAME?!
I DEFEATED THE EVENT MASTER!
SHROOO
......?!

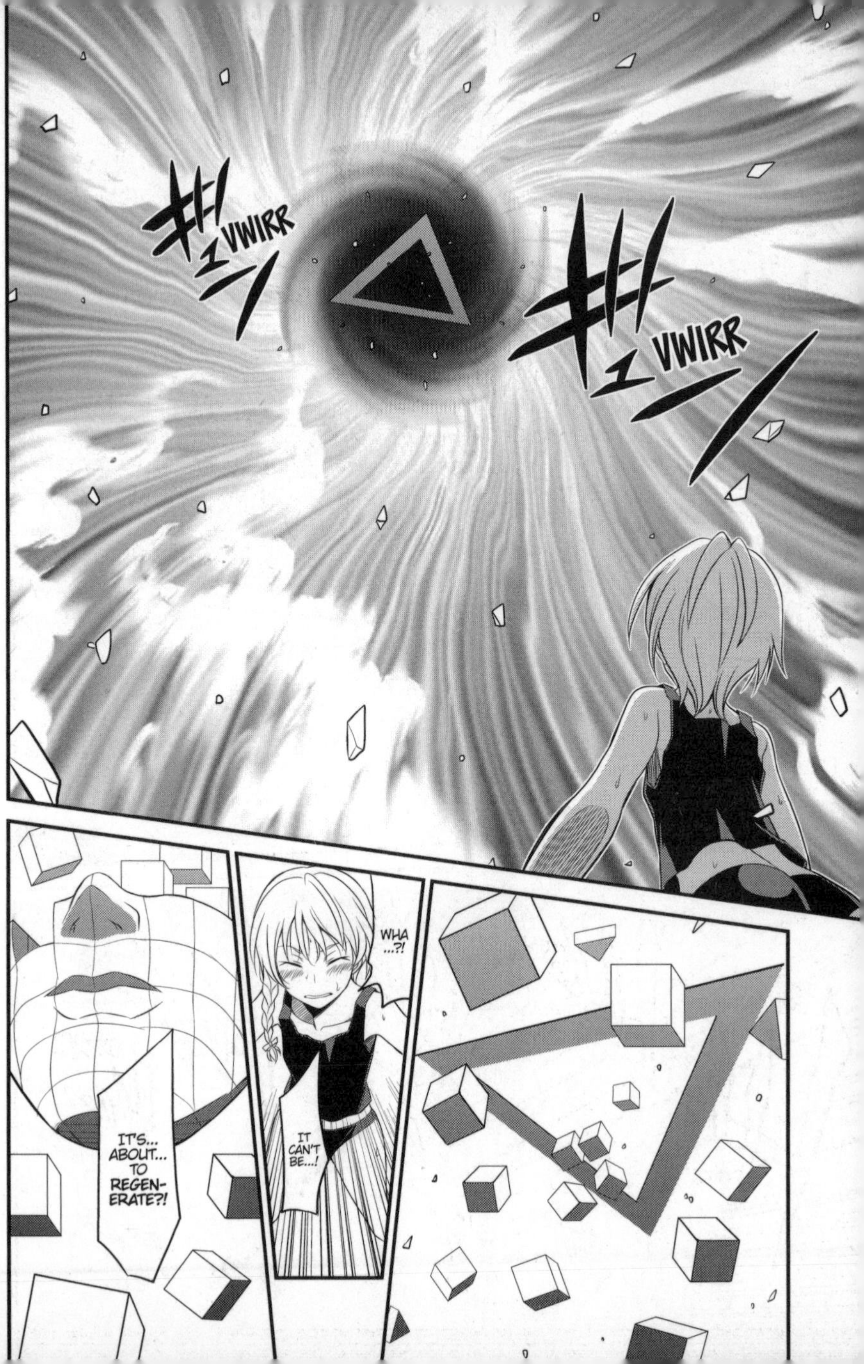
VWIRR
VWIRR
WHA ...?!
IT CAN'T BE...!
IT'S... ABOUT... TO REGEN-ERATE?!

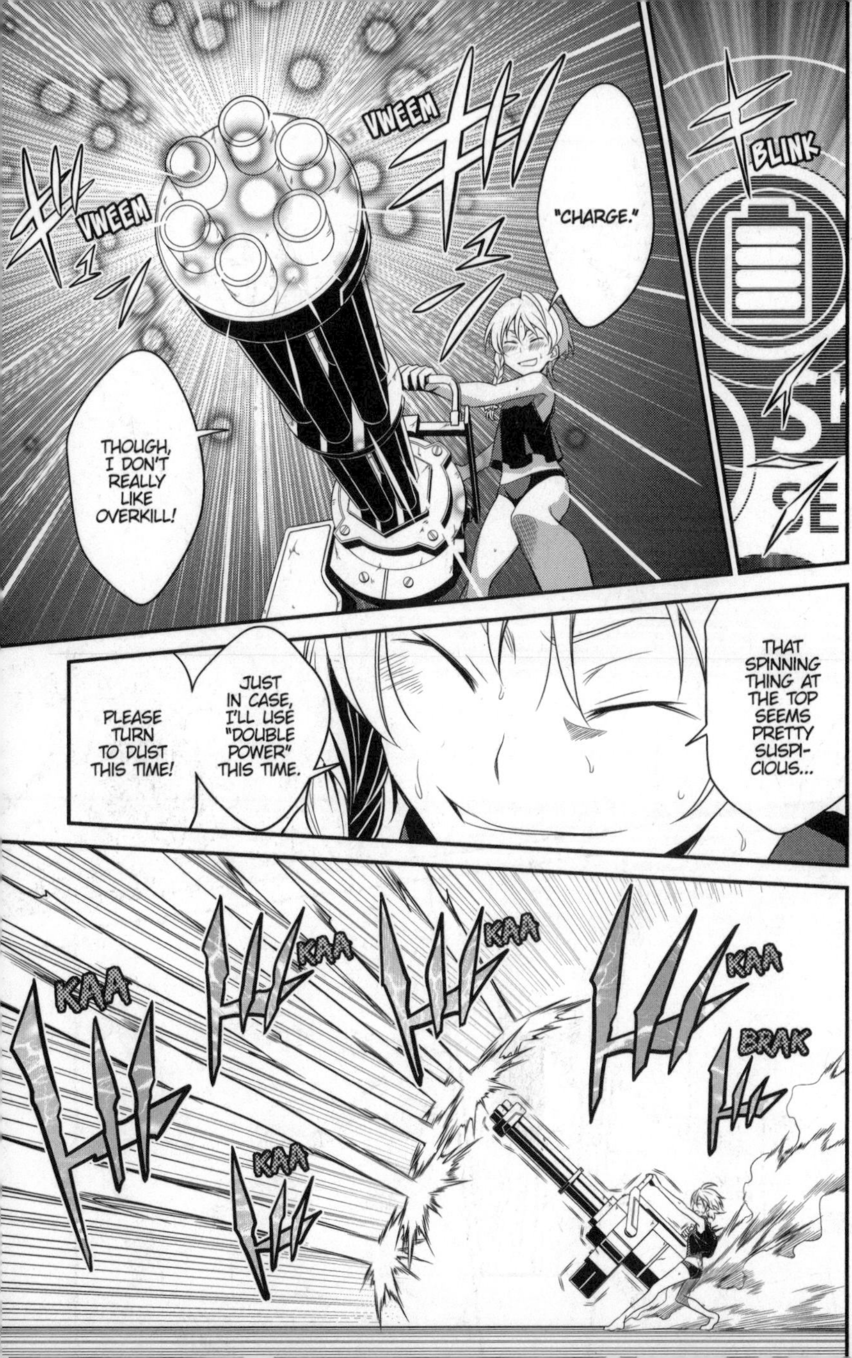
BLINK
"CHARGE."
VWEEM
VWEEM
THOUGH, I DON'T REALLY LIKE OVERKILL!
THAT SPINNING THING AT THE TOP SEEMS PRETTY SUSPI-CIOUS...
JUST IN CASE, I'LL USE "DOUBLE POWER" THIS TIME.
PLEASE TURN TO DUST THIS TIME!
KAA
BRAK
KAA
KAA
KAA
KAA

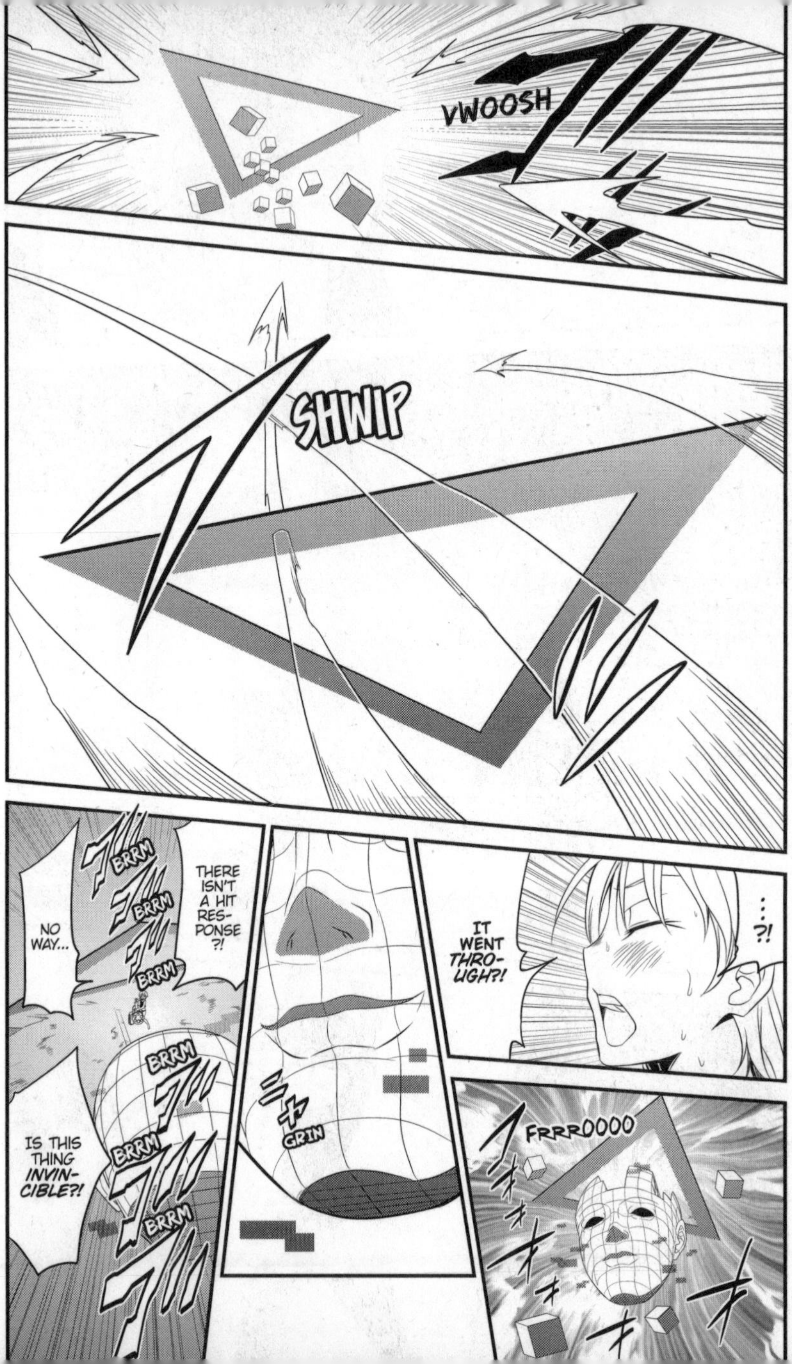

VWOOSH
SHWIP
...?!
IT WENT THROUGH?!
FRRROOOO
GRIN
THERE ISN'T A HIT RESPONSE?!
BRRM
BRRM
BRRM
NO WAY...
BRRM
BRRM
BRRM
IS THIS THING INVINCIBLE?!

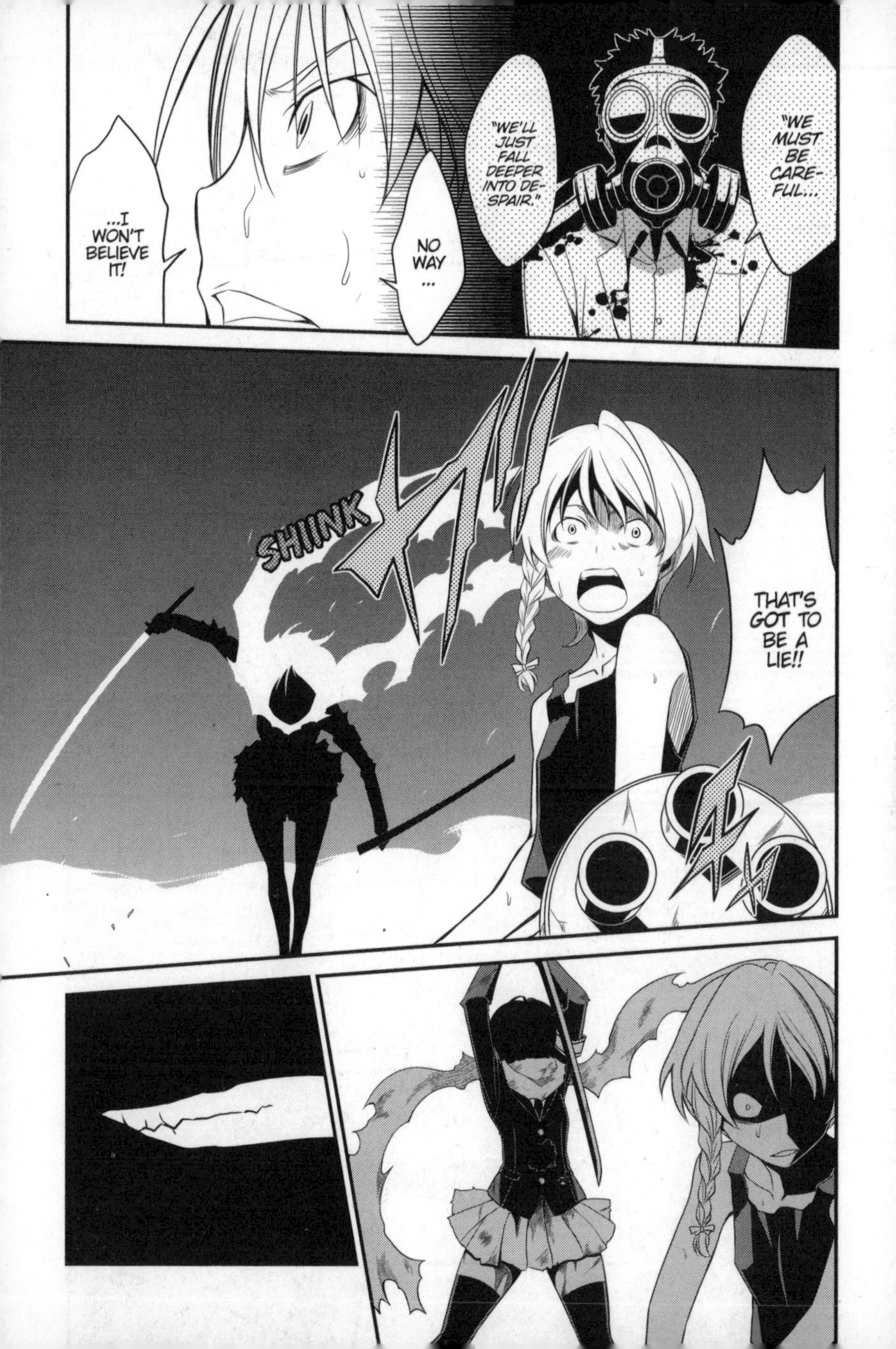

"WE MUST BE CARE-FUL...
WE'LL JUST FALL DEEPER INTO DE-SPAIR."
NO WAY ...
...I WON'T BELIEVE IT!
THAT'S GOT TO BE A LIE!!
SHIINK

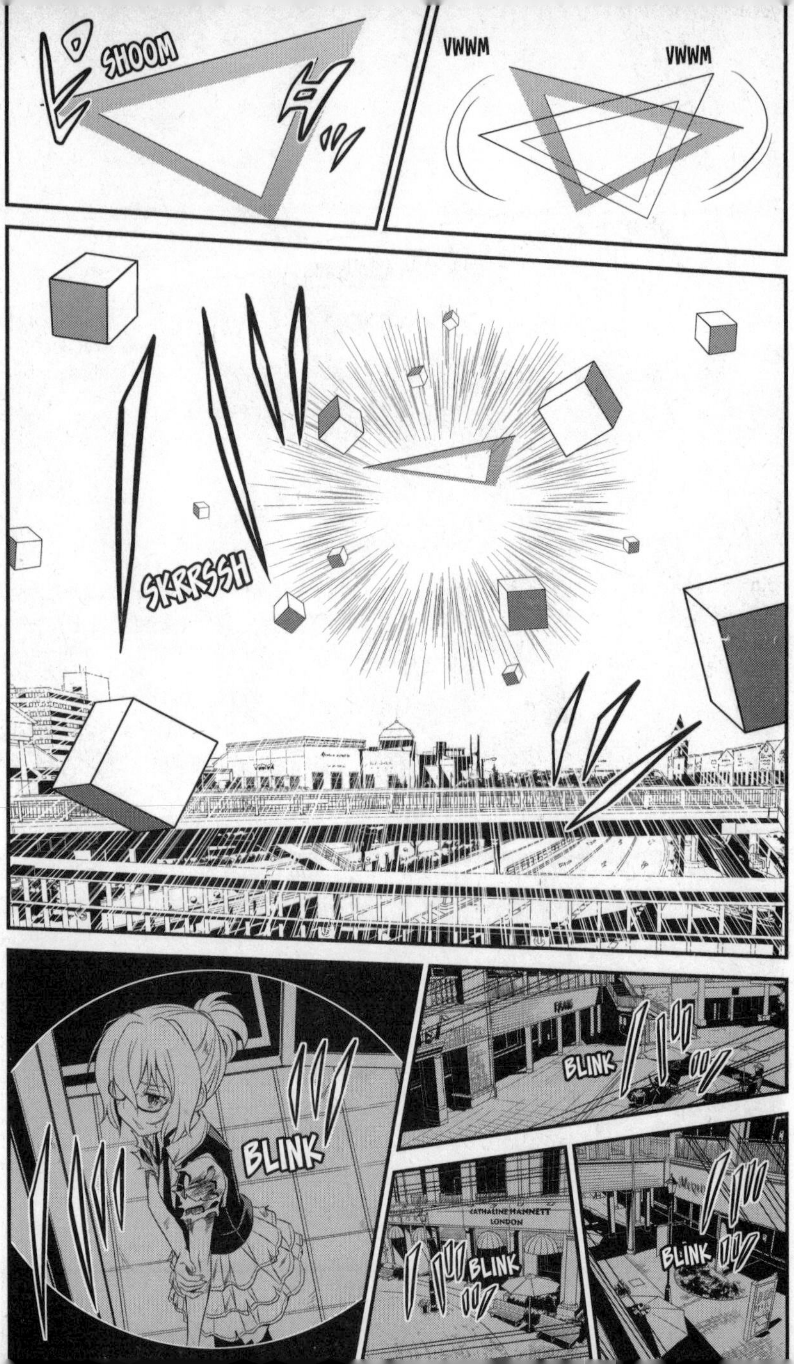
VWWM
VWWM
SHOOM
SKRRSSH
BLINK
BLINK
CATHALINE HANNETT
LONDON
BLINK
BLINK

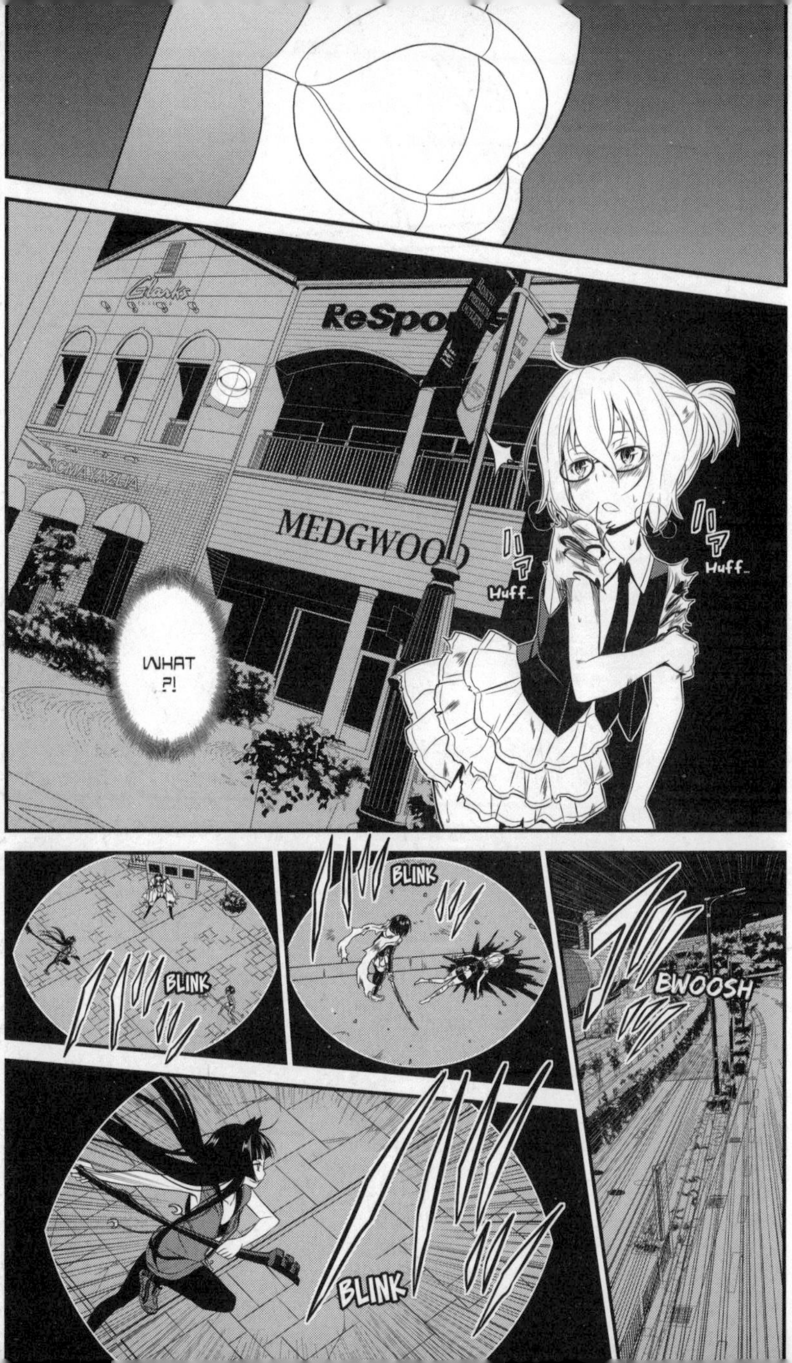

ハァ
Huff...
ハァ
Huff...
WHAT ?!
BWOOSH
BLINK
BLINK
BLINK

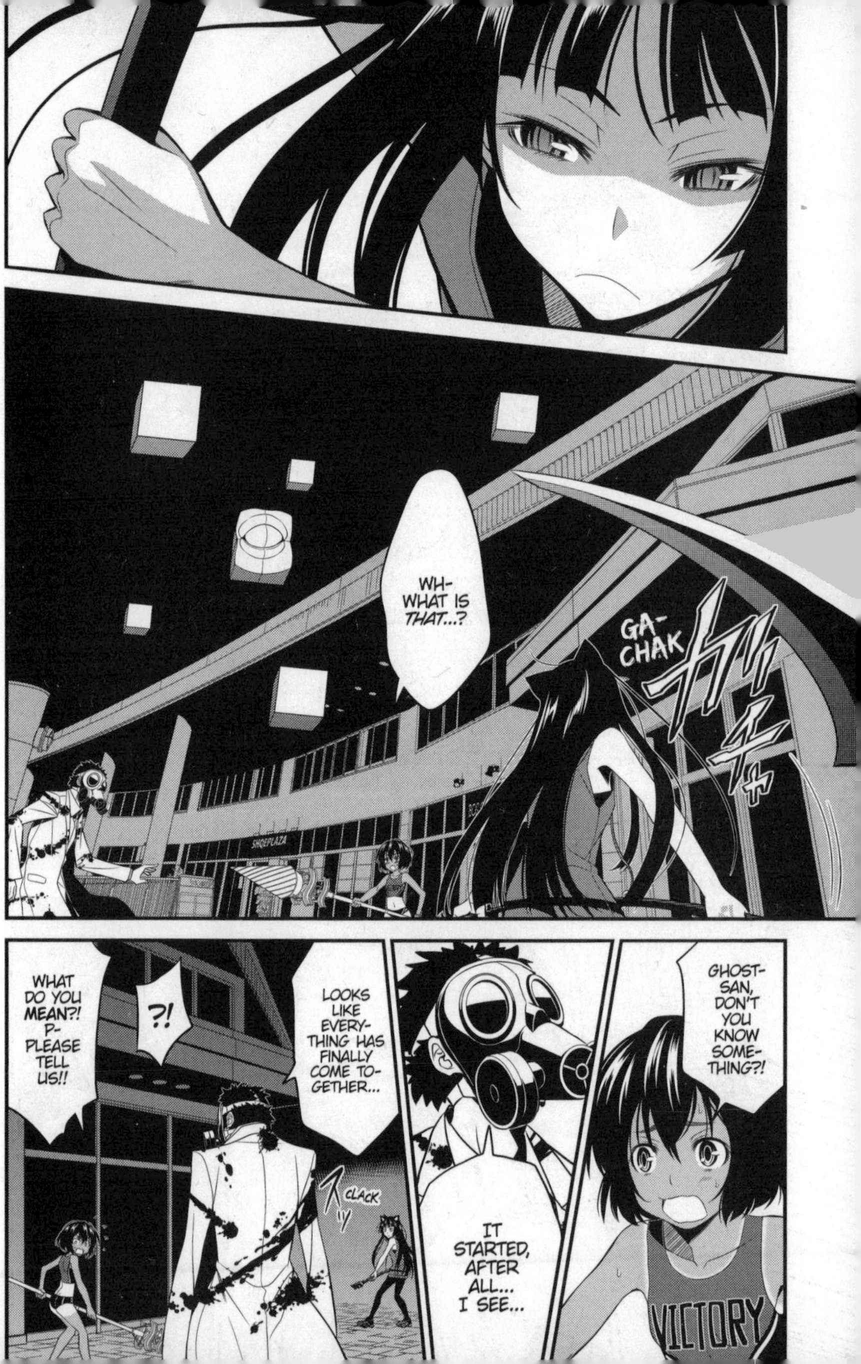
WH- WHAT IS THAT...?
GA-CHAK
SHOEPLAZA
GHOST-SAN, DON'T YOU KNOW SOME-THING?!
VICTORY
IT STARTED, AFTER ALL... I SEE...
LOOKS LIKE EVERY-THING HAS FINALLY COME TO-GETHER...
?!
CLACK
WHAT DO YOU MEAN?! P-PLEASE TELL US!!

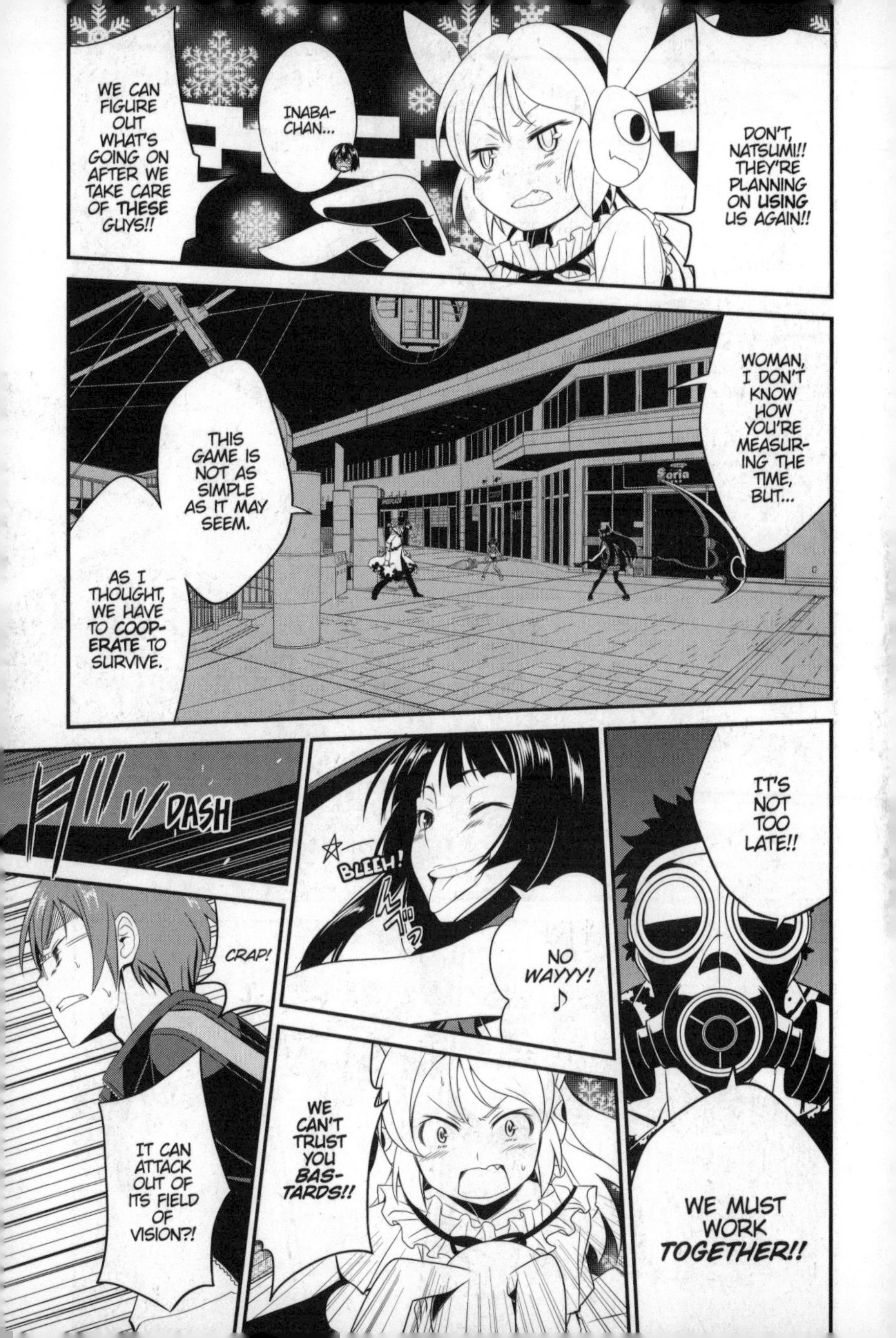
DON'T, NATSUMI!! THEY'RE PLANNING ON USING US AGAIN!!
INABA-CHAN...
WE CAN FIGURE OUT WHAT'S GOING ON AFTER WE TAKE CARE OF THESE GUYS!!
WOMAN, I DON'T KNOW HOW YOU'RE MEASURING THE TIME, BUT...
THIS GAME IS NOT AS SIMPLE AS IT MAY SEEM.
AS I THOUGHT, WE HAVE TO COOPERATE TO SURVIVE.
IT'S NOT TOO LATE!!
WE MUST WORK TOGETHER!!
BLEEH!
NO WAYYY! ♪
WE CAN'T TRUST YOU BASTARDS!!
DASH
CRAP!
IT CAN ATTACK OUT OF ITS FIELD OF VISION?!

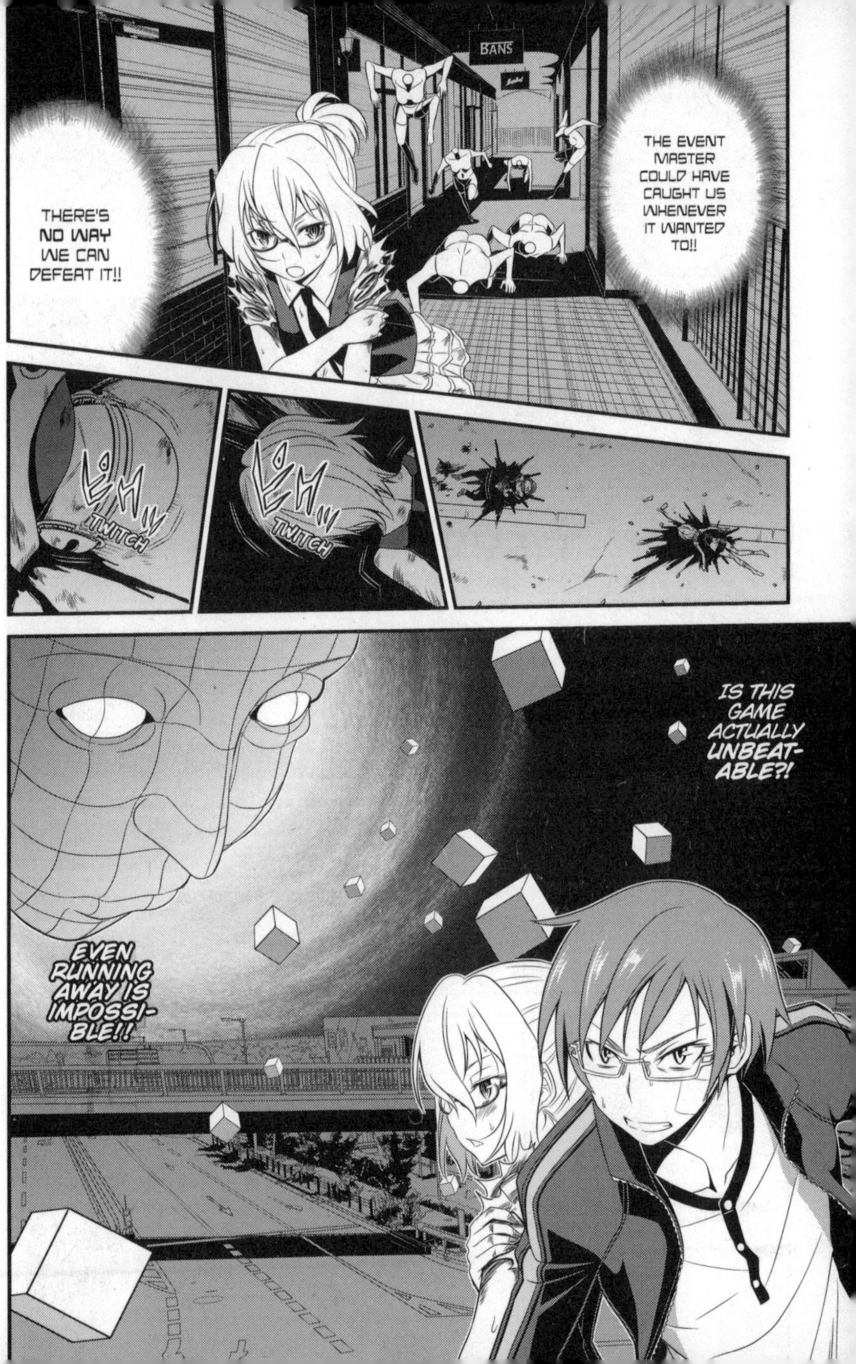
BANS
THE EVENT MASTER COULD HAVE CAUGHT US WHENEVER IT WANTED TO!!
THERE'S NO WAY WE CAN DEFEAT IT!!
TWITCH
TWITCH
IS THIS GAME ACTUALLY UNBEAT-ABLE?!
EVEN RUNNING AWAY IS IMPOSSI-BLE!!

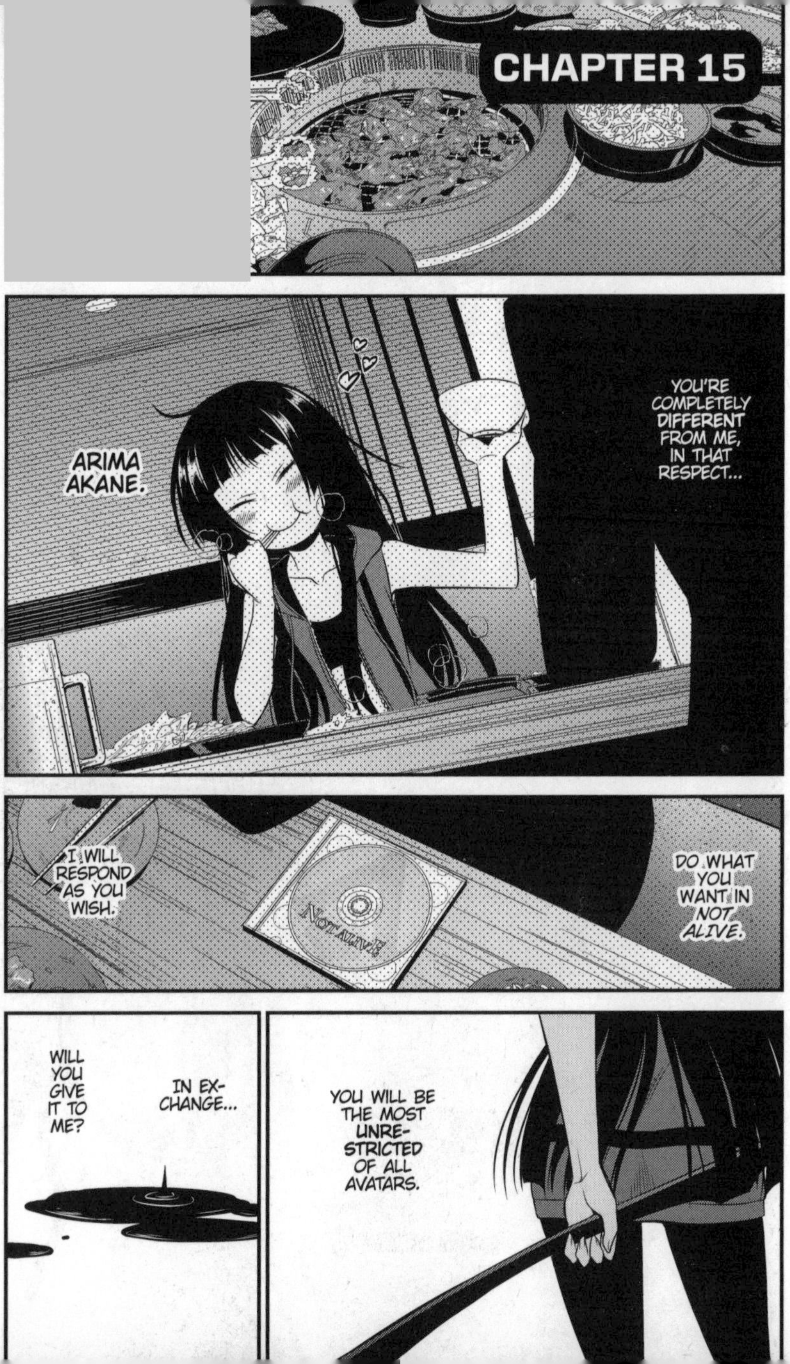
CHAPTER 15
YOU'RE COMPLETELY DIFFERENT FROM ME, IN THAT RESPECT...
ARIMA AKANE.
DO WHAT YOU WANT IN NOT ALIVE.
NOT ALIVE
I WILL RESPOND AS YOU WISH.
YOU WILL BE THE MOST UNRE-STRICTED OF ALL AVATARS.
IN EX-CHANGE...
WILL YOU GIVE IT TO ME?

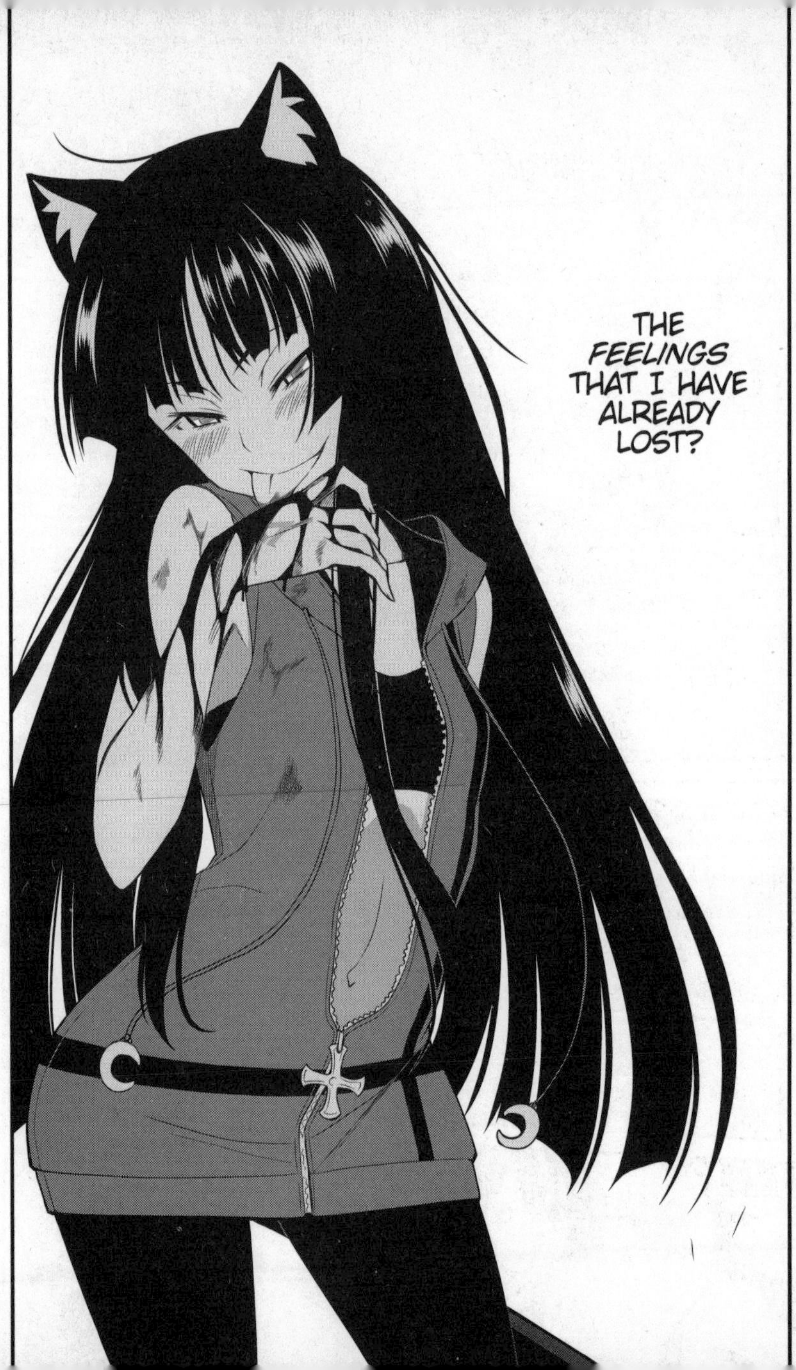
THE FEELINGS THAT I HAVE ALREADY LOST?

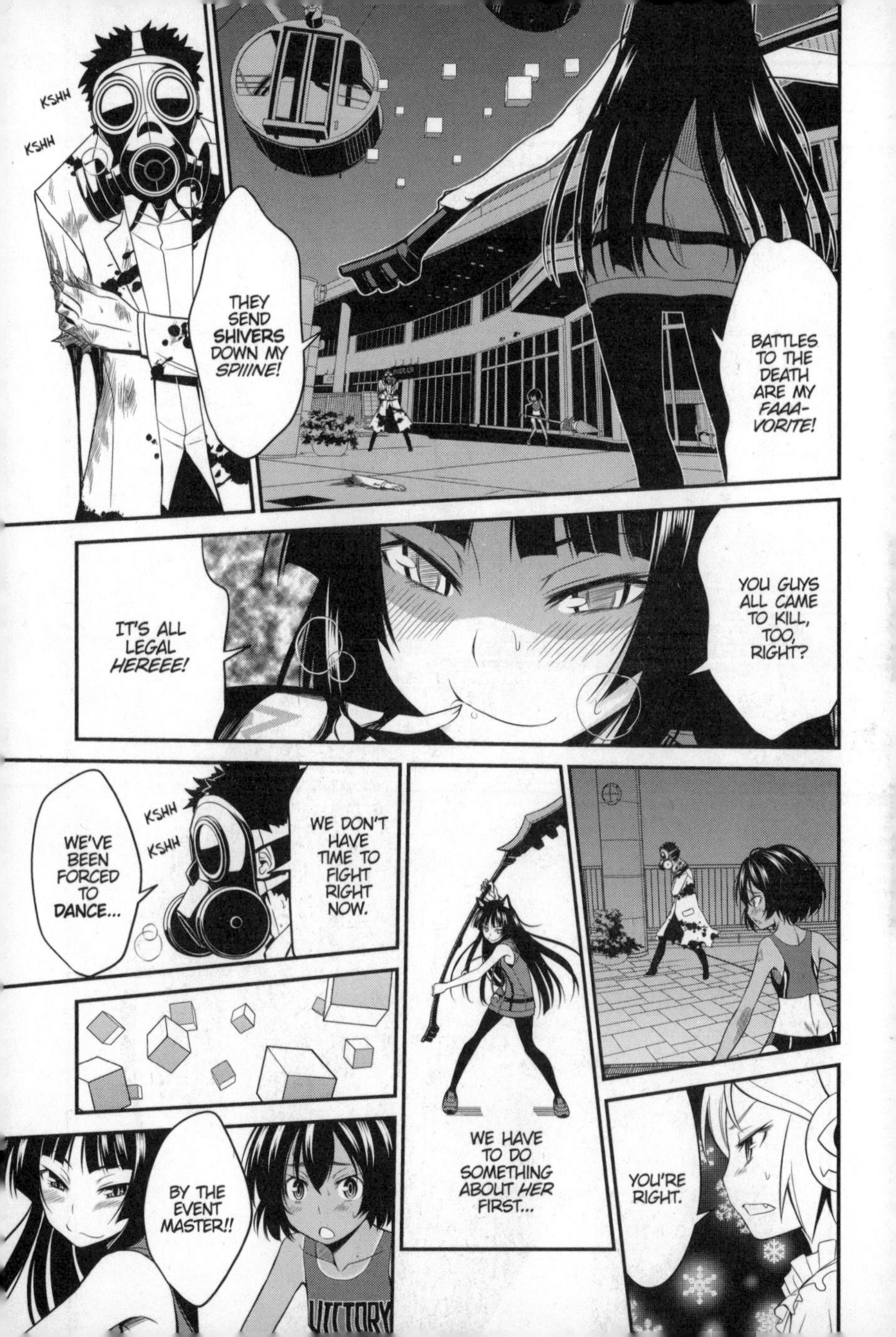
BATTLES TO THE DEATH ARE MY FAAA-VORITE!
KSHH
KSHH
THEY SEND SHIVERS DOWN MY SPIIINE!
YOU GUYS ALL CAME TO KILL, TOO, RIGHT?
IT'S ALL LEGAL HEREEE!
YOU'RE RIGHT.
WE HAVE TO DO SOMETHING ABOUT HER FIRST...
WE DON'T HAVE TIME TO FIGHT RIGHT NOW.
KSHH
KSHH
WE'VE BEEN FORCED TO DANCE...
BY THE EVENT MASTER!!
VICTORY

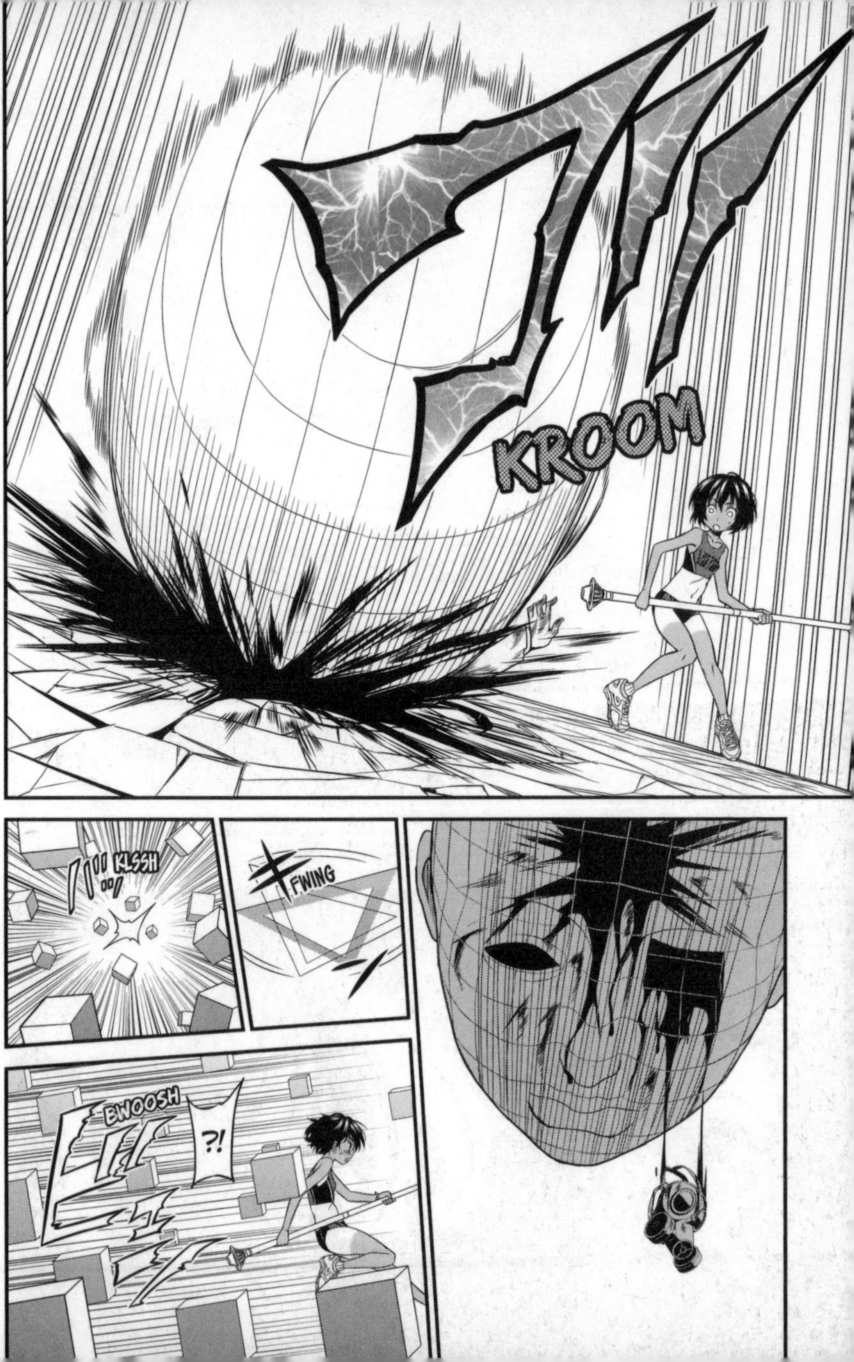
KROOM
FWING
KLSSH
BWOOSH
?!

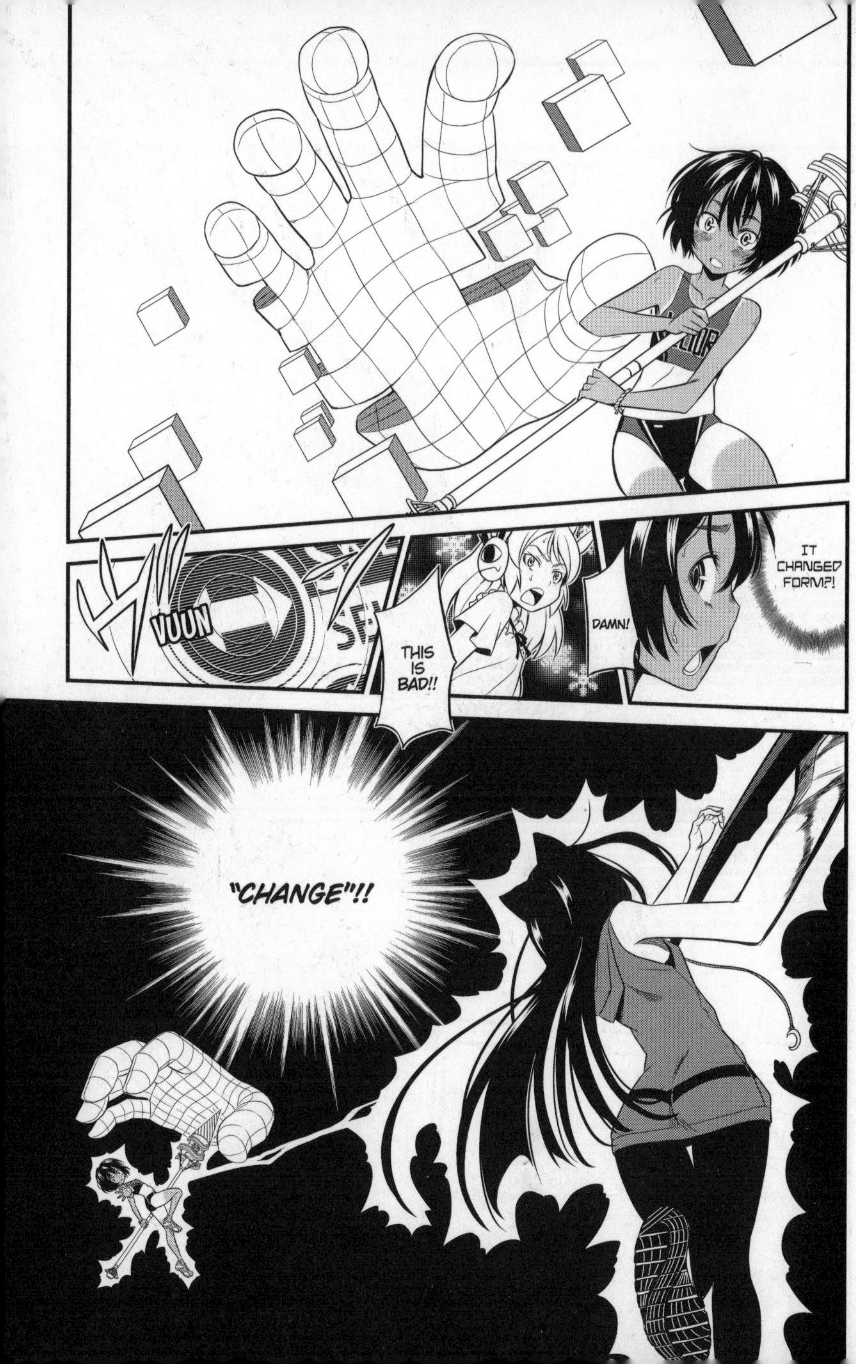
IT CHANGED FORM?!
DAMN!
THIS IS BAD!!
VUUN
"CHANGE"!!

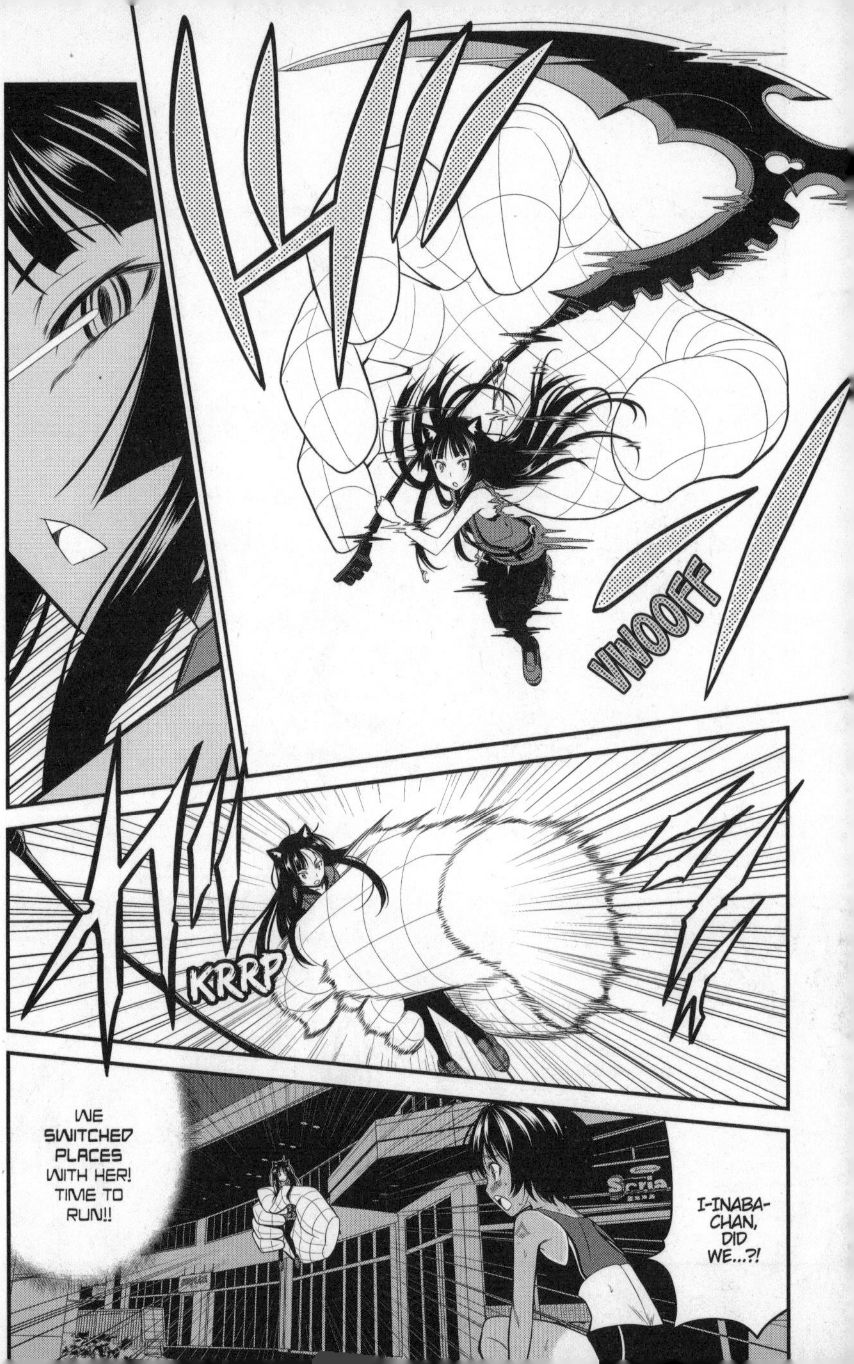
VWOOFF
KRRP
I-INABA-CHAN, DID WE...?!
WE SWITCHED PLACES WITH HER! TIME TO RUN!!

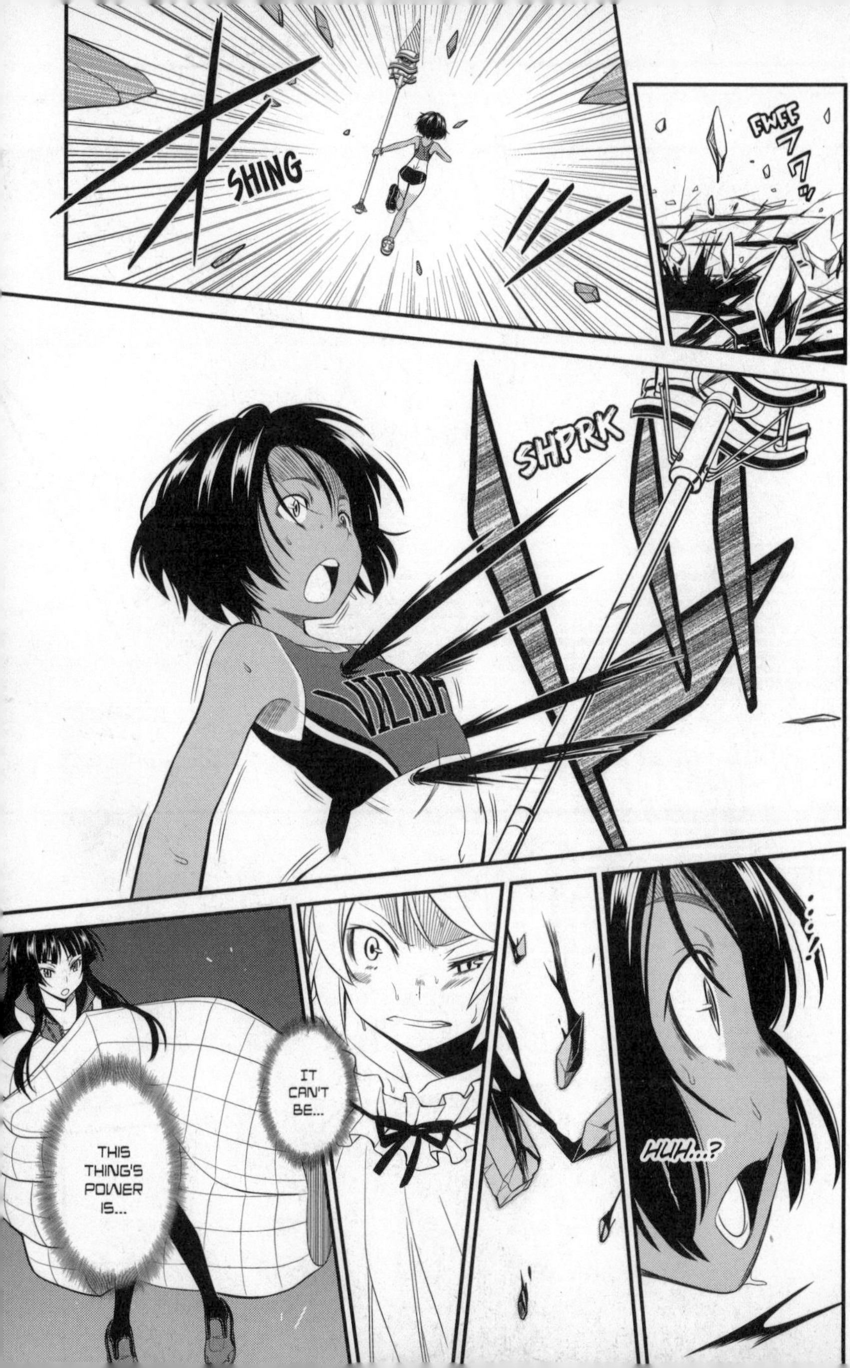
FWFF
SHING
SHPRK
...!!
HUH...?
IT CAN'T BE...
THIS THING'S POWER IS...

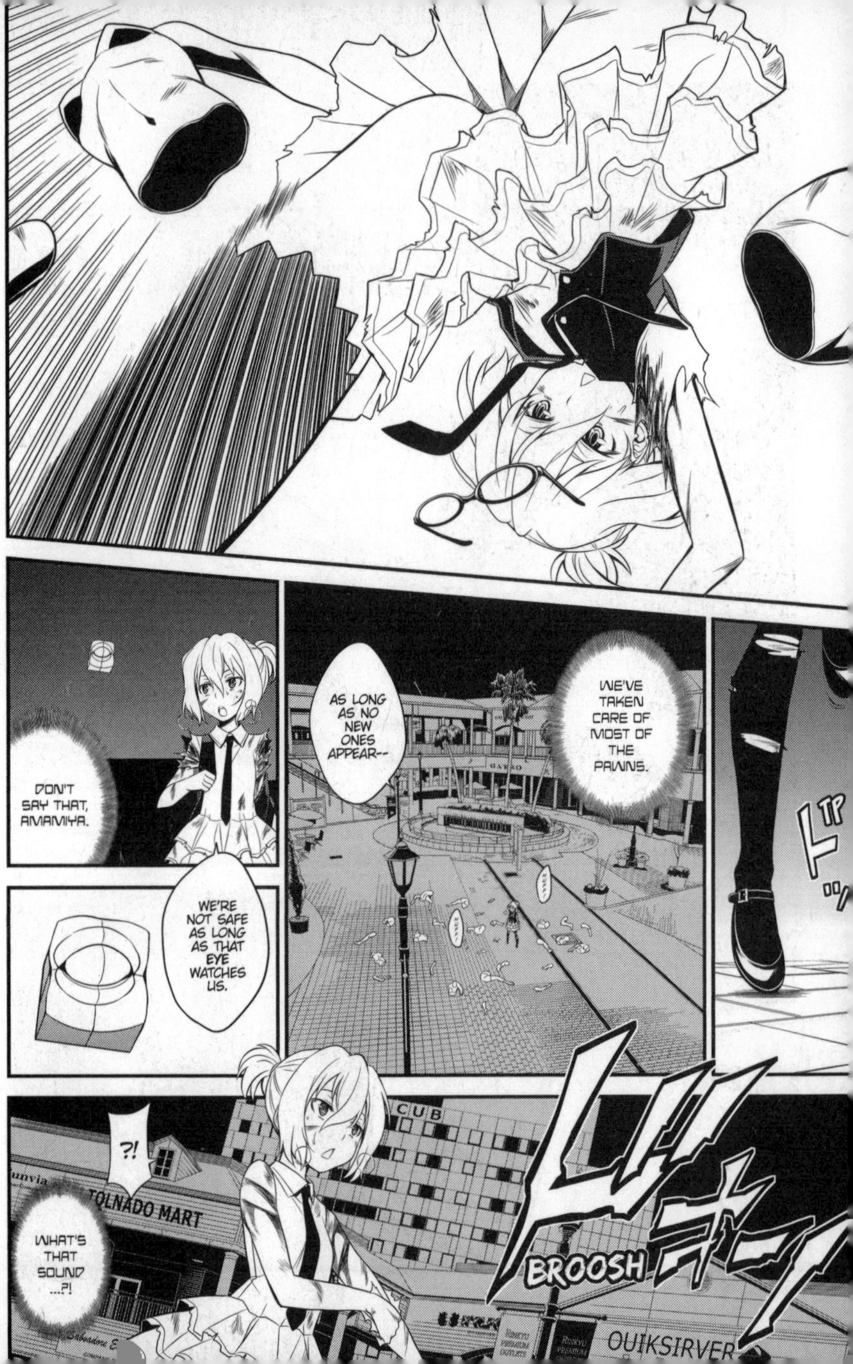

TP
WE'VE TAKEN CARE OF MOST OF THE PAWNS.
AS LONG AS NO NEW ONES APPEAR--
DON'T SAY THAT, AMAMIYA.
WE'RE NOT SAFE AS LONG AS THAT EYE WATCHES US.
BROOSH
?!
WHAT'S THAT SOUND ...?!
TOLNADO MART

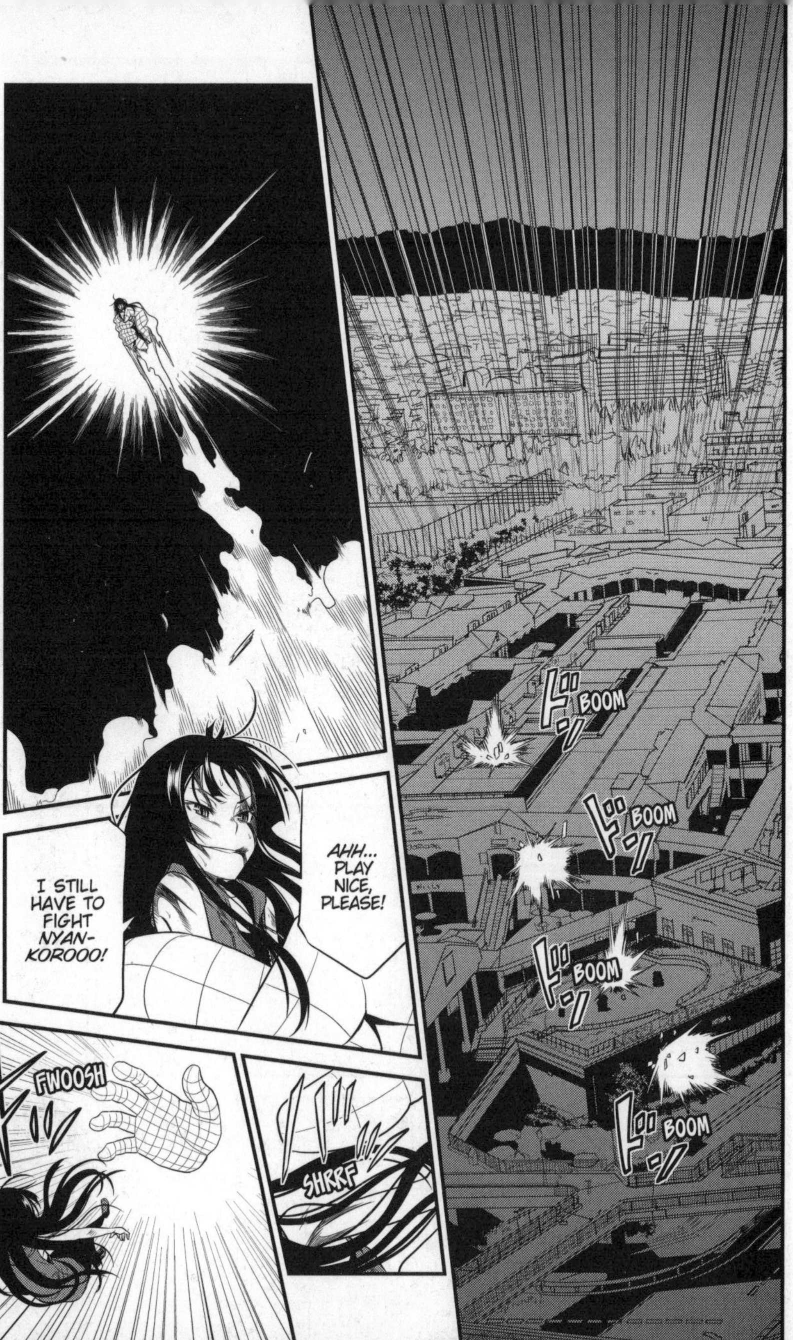
BOOM
BOOM
BOOM
BOOM
AHH... PLAY NICE, PLEASE!
I STILL HAVE TO FIGHT NYAN-KOROOO!
SHRRF
FWOOSH

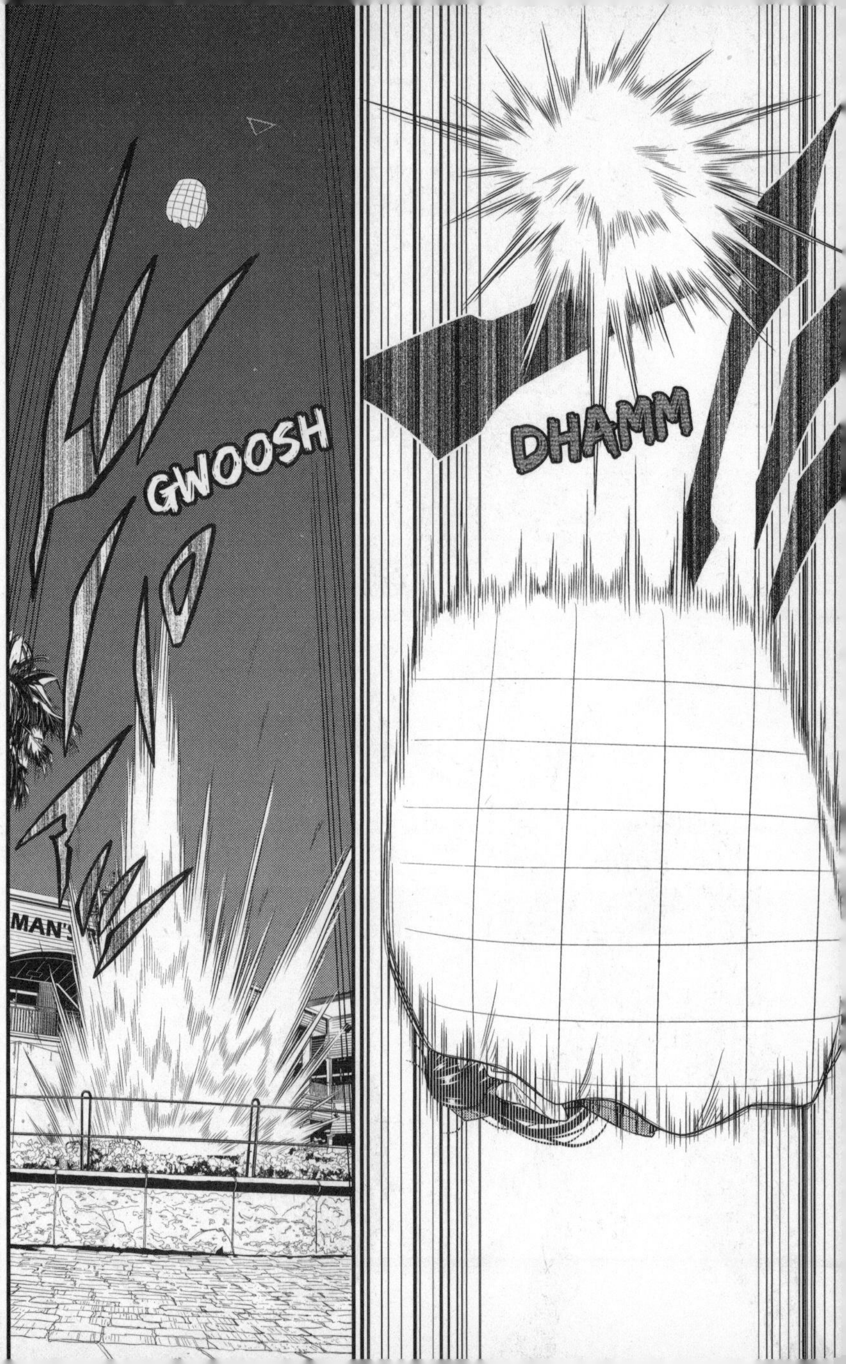
DHAMM
GWOOSH

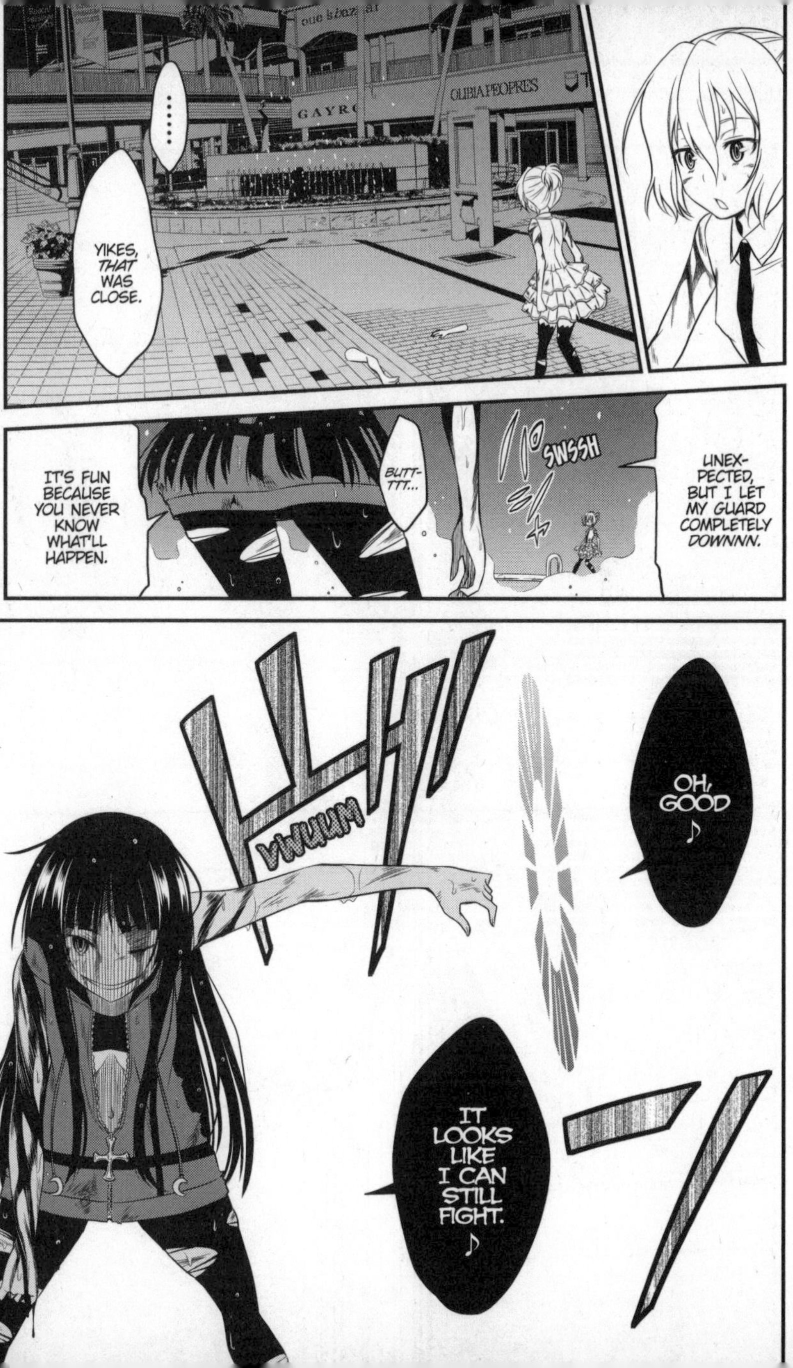
......
YIKES, THAT WAS CLOSE.
UNEX-PECTED, BUT I LET MY GUARD COMPLETELY DOWNNN.
SWSSH
BUTT-TTT...
IT'S FUN BECAUSE YOU NEVER KNOW WHAT'LL HAPPEN.
OH, GOOD ♪
VWUUM
IT LOOKS LIKE I CAN STILL FIGHT. ♪

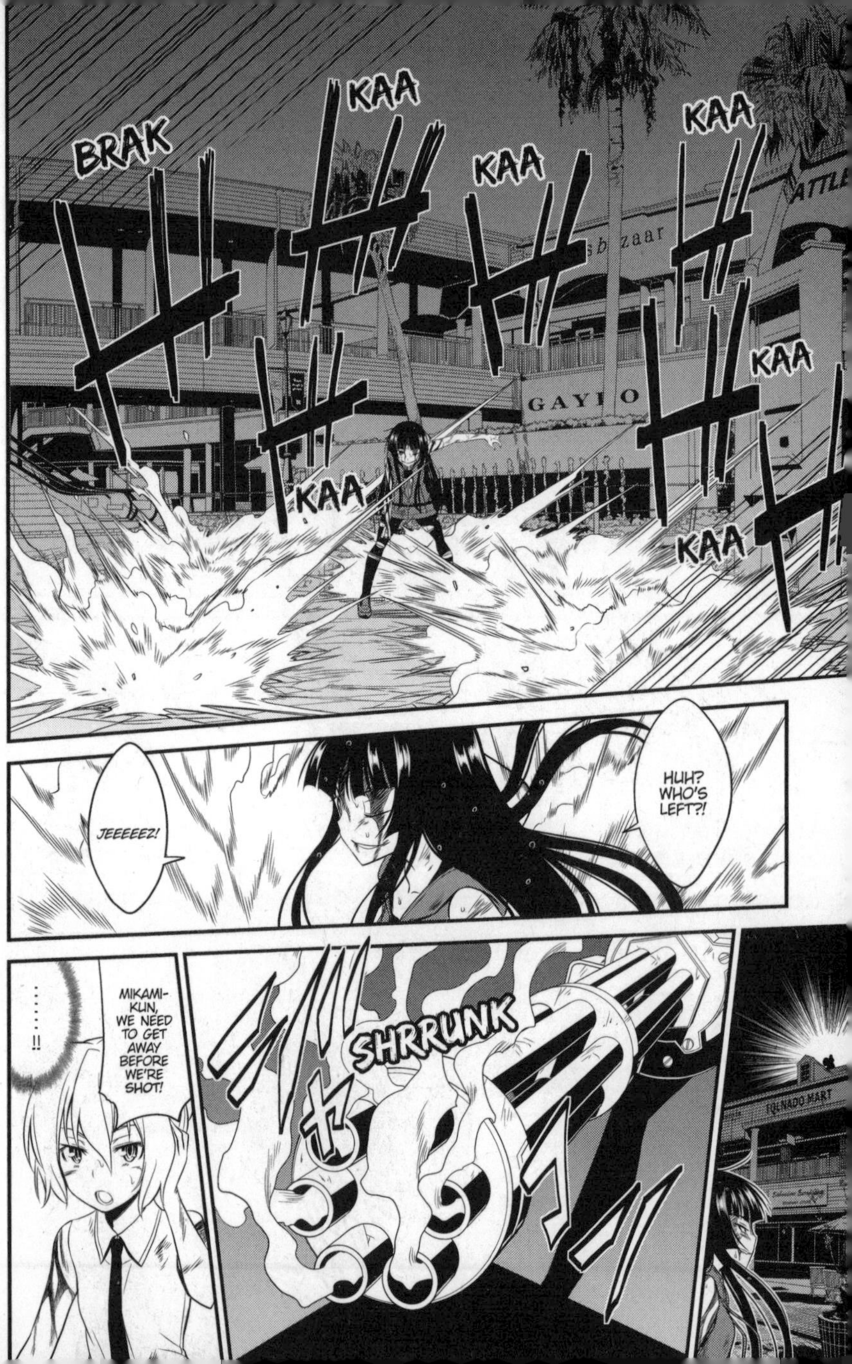
KAA
KAA
KAA
KAA
KAA
BRAK
KAA
HUH? WHO'S LEFT?!
JEEEEEZ!
SHRRUNK
MIKAMI-KUN, WE NEED TO GET AWAY BEFORE WE'RE SHOT!
......!!

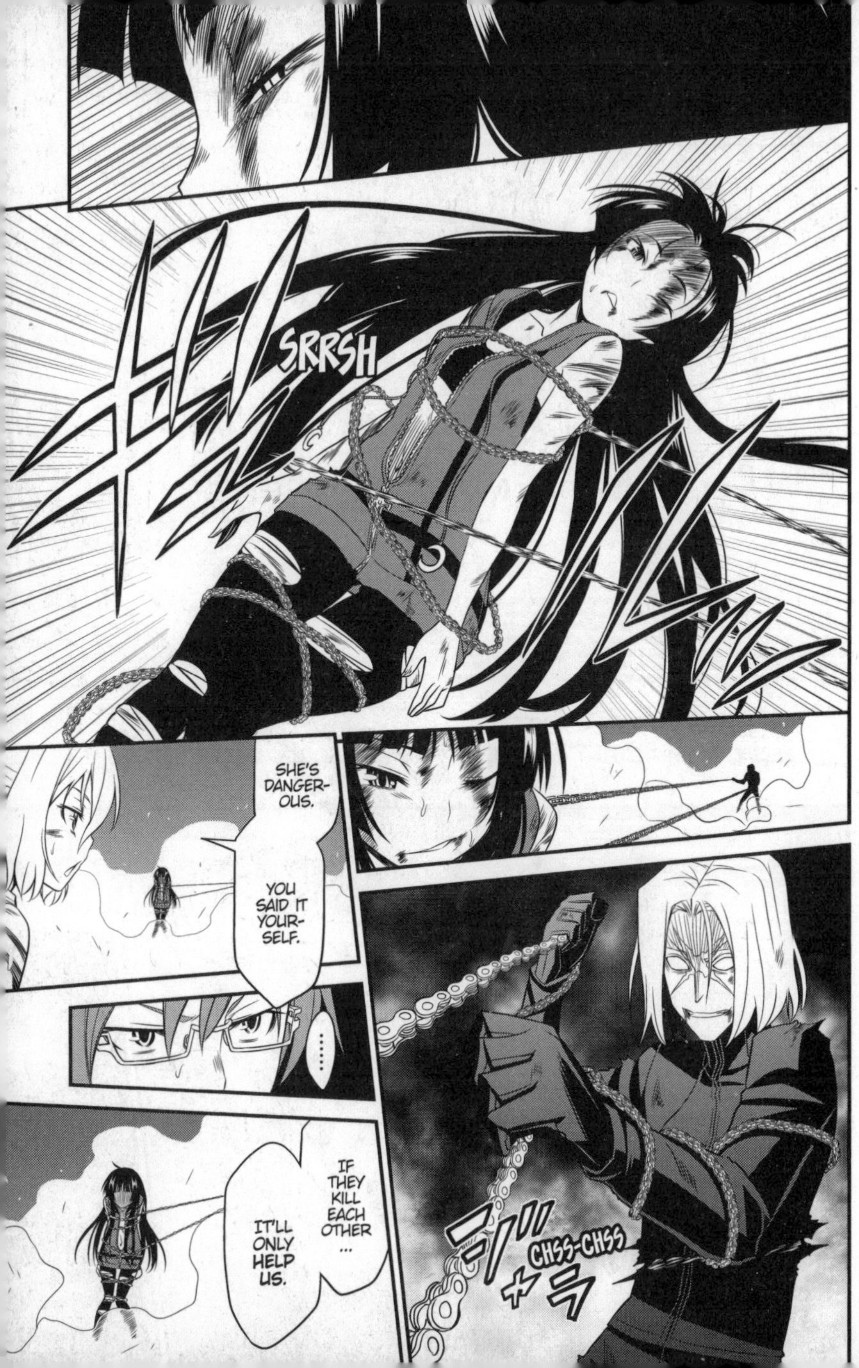
SRRSH
SHE'S DANGEROUS.
YOU SAID IT YOURSELF.
CHSS-CHSS
......
IF THEY KILL EACH OTHER ...
IT'LL ONLY HELP US.

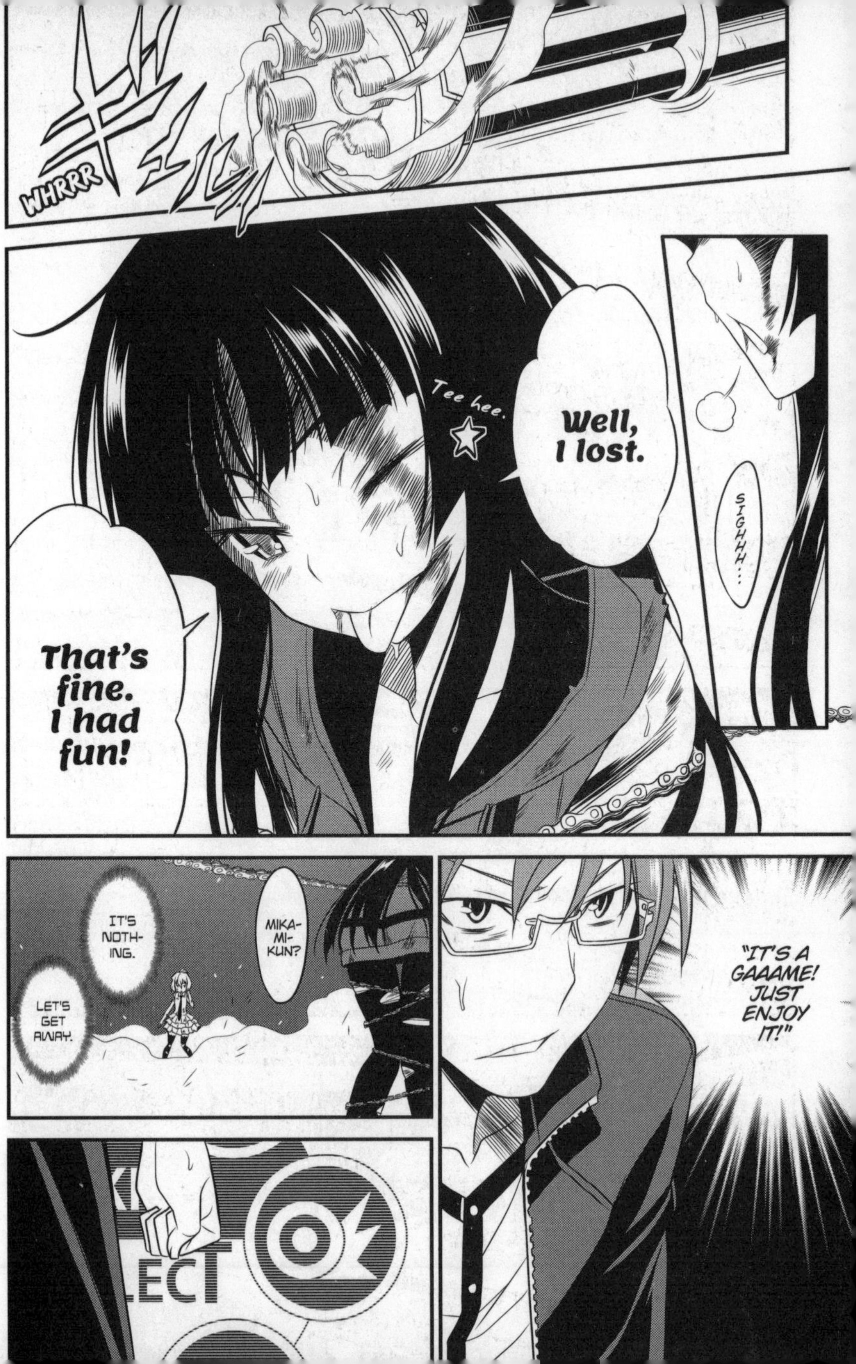
WHRRR
SIGHHH...
Tee hee.
Well, I lost.
That's fine. I had fun!
"IT'S A GAAAME! JUST ENJOY IT!"
MIKA-MI-KUN?
IT'S NOTHING.
LET'S GET AWAY.

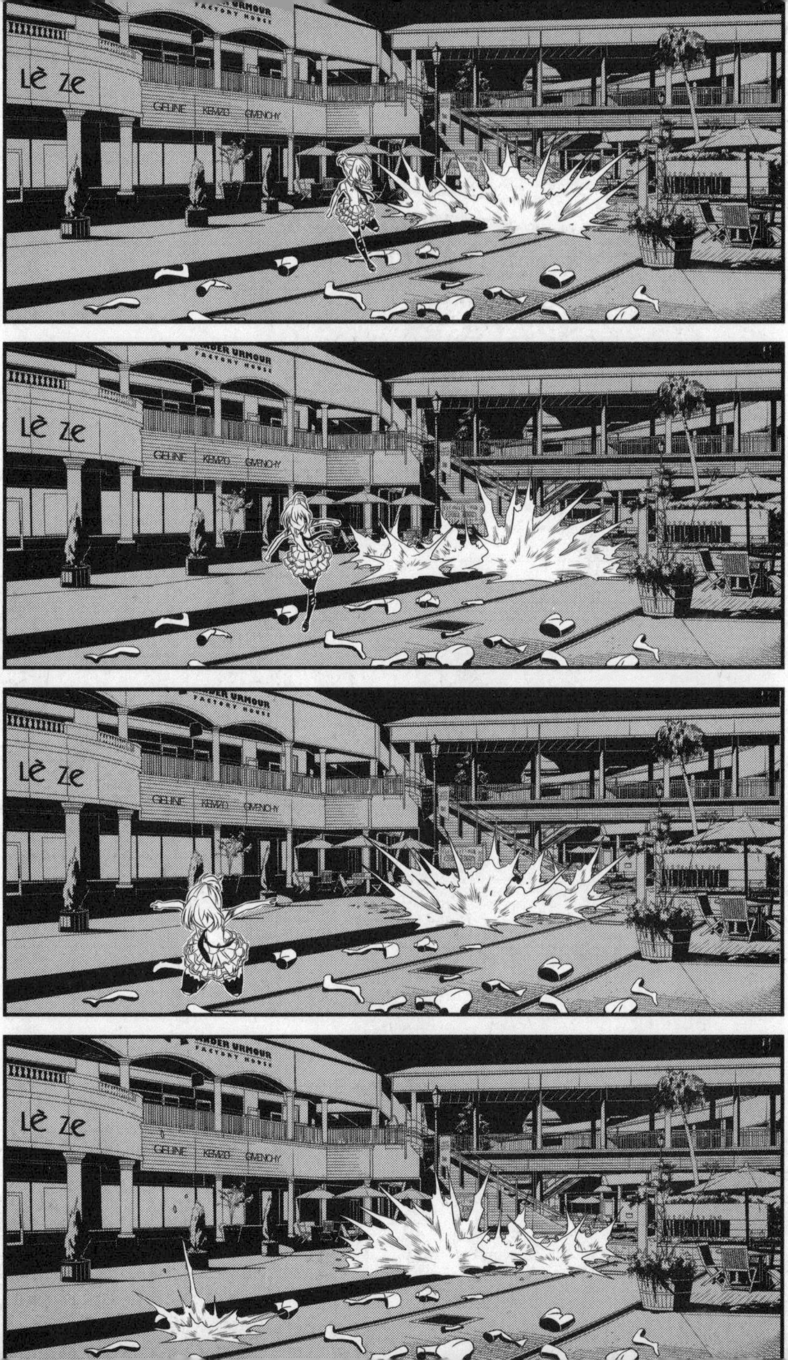
Lè Ze
GELINE
KENZO
GIVENCHY
FACTORY HOUSE

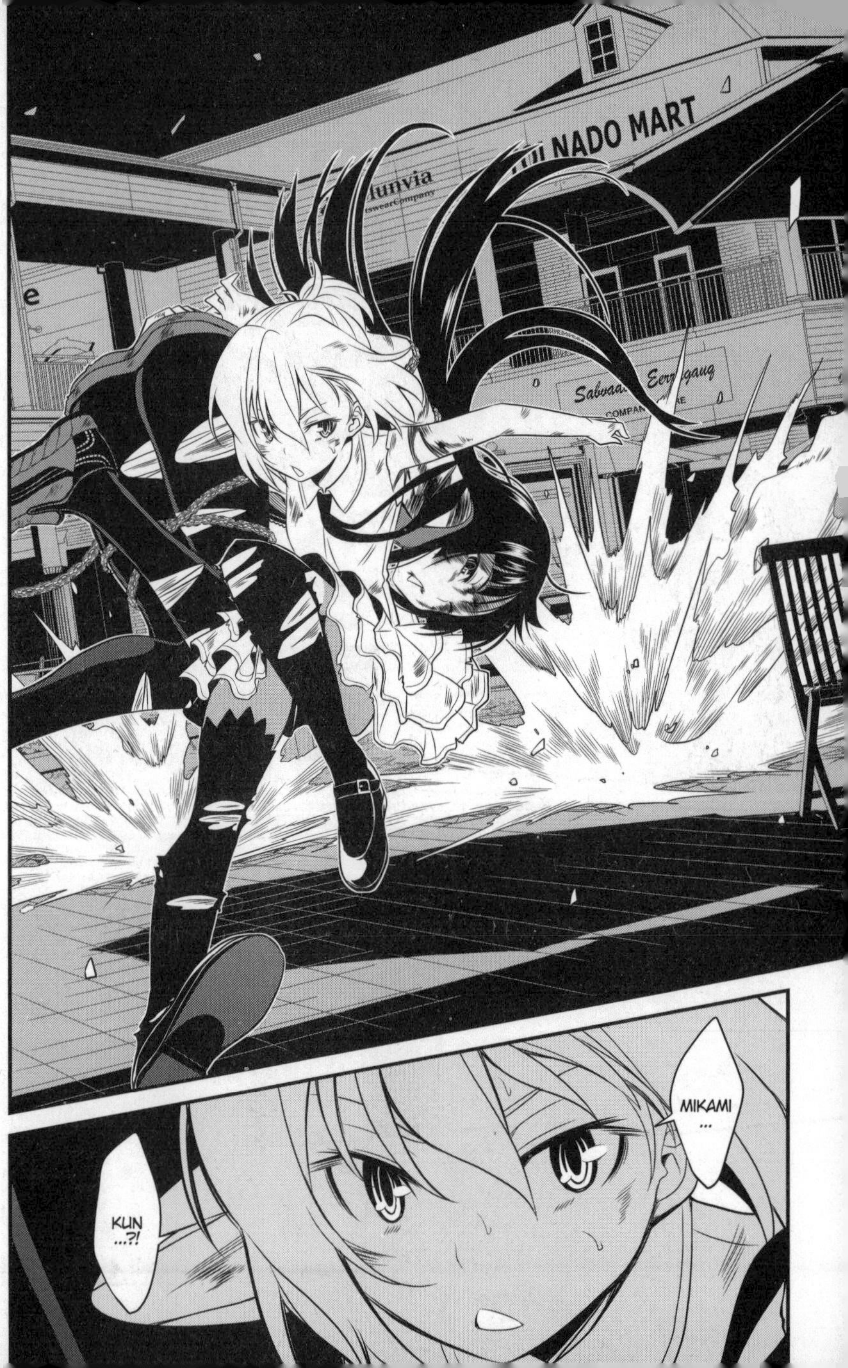
NADO MART
MIKAMI ...
KUN ...?!

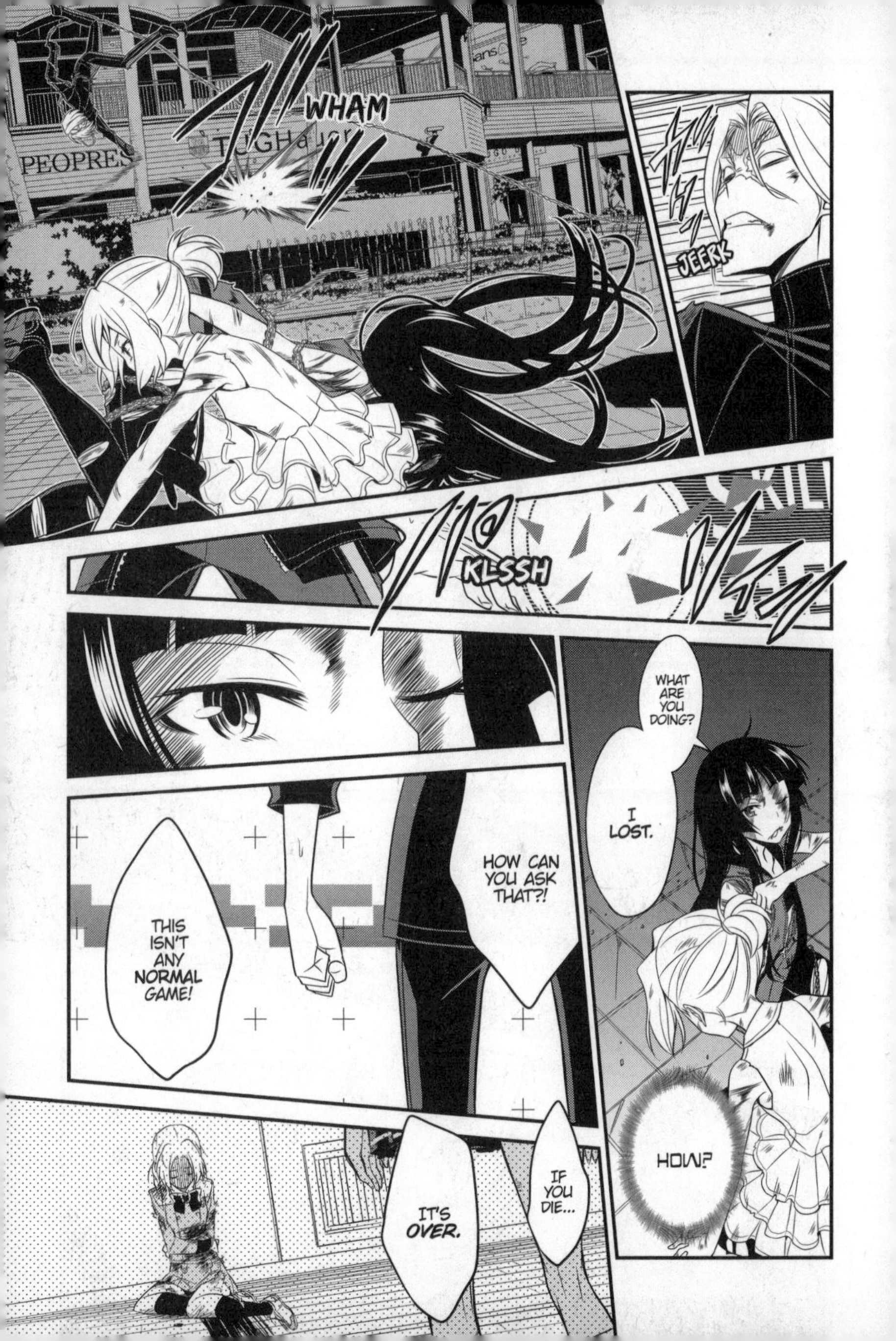
JEERK
WHAM
KLSSH
WHAT ARE YOU DOING?
I LOST.
HOW?
HOW CAN YOU ASK THAT?!
THIS ISN'T ANY NORMAL GAME!
IF YOU DIE...
IT'S OVER.

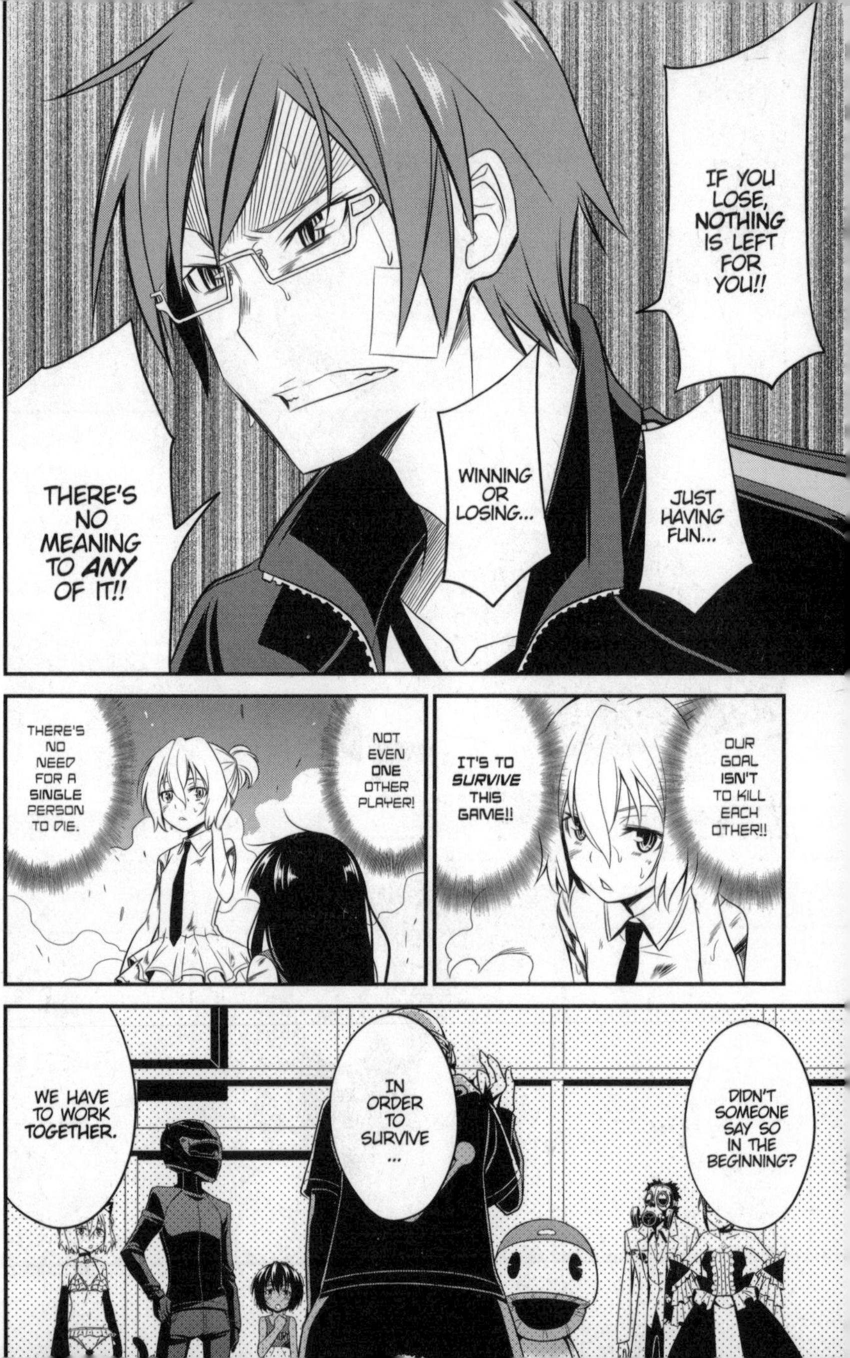
IF YOU LOSE, NOTHING IS LEFT FOR YOU!!
JUST HAVING FUN...
WINNING OR LOSING...
THERE'S NO MEANING TO ANY OF IT!!
OUR GOAL ISN'T TO KILL EACH OTHER!!
IT'S TO SURVIVE THIS GAME!!
NOT EVEN ONE OTHER PLAYER!
THERE'S NO NEED FOR A SINGLE PERSON TO DIE.
DIDN'T SOMEONE SAY SO IN THE BEGINNING?
IN ORDER TO SURVIVE ...
WE HAVE TO WORK TOGETHER.

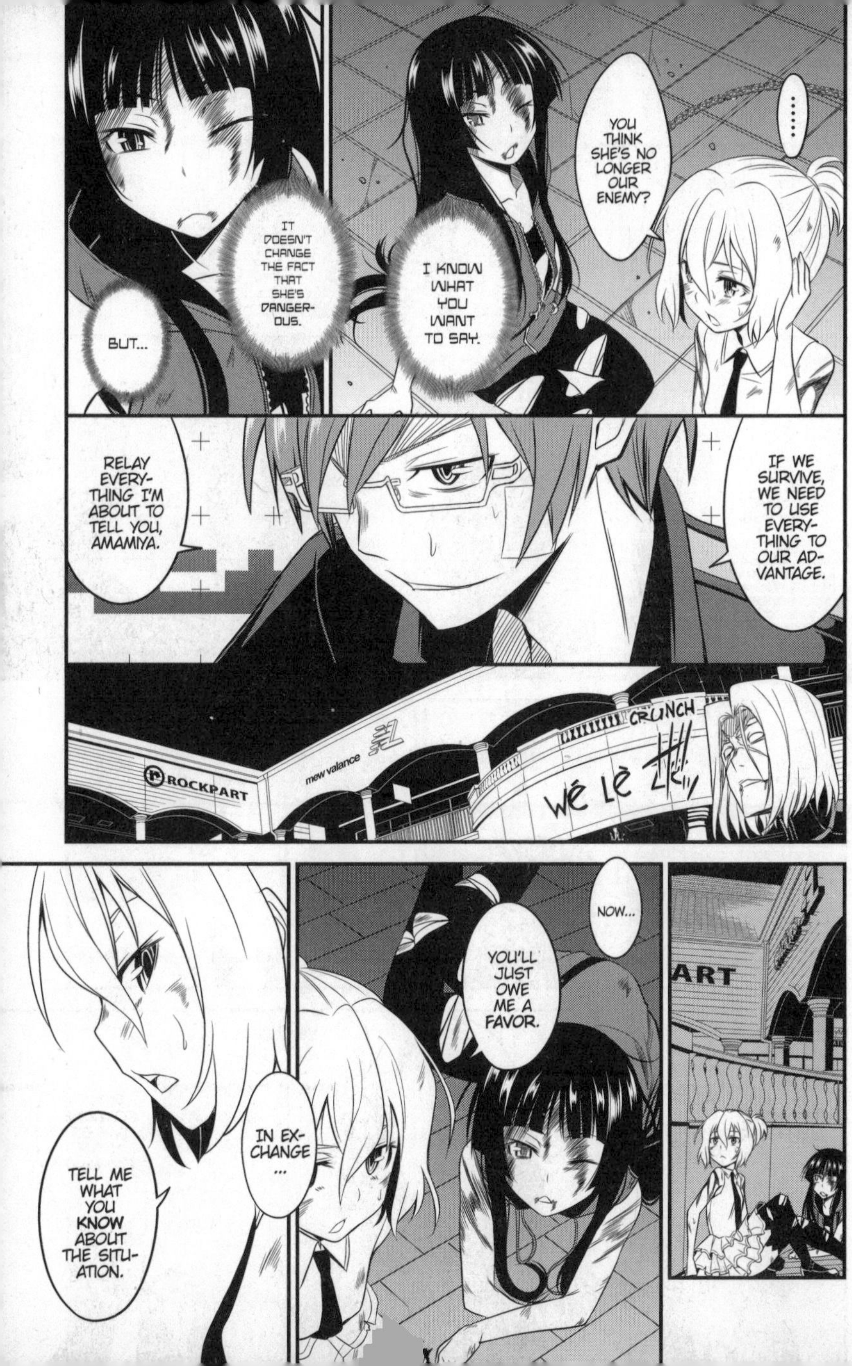
......
YOU THINK SHE'S NO LONGER OUR ENEMY?
I KNOW WHAT YOU WANT TO SAY.
IT DOESN'T CHANGE THE FACT THAT SHE'S DANGER-OUS.
BUT...
IF WE SURVIVE, WE NEED TO USE EVERY-THING TO OUR AD-VANTAGE.
RELAY EVERY-THING I'M ABOUT TO TELL YOU, AMAMIYA.
CRUNCH
ROCKPART
mew valance
wé lè
ART
NOW...
YOU'LL JUST OWE ME A FAVOR.
IN EX-CHANGE ...
TELL ME WHAT YOU KNOW ABOUT THE SITU-ATION.

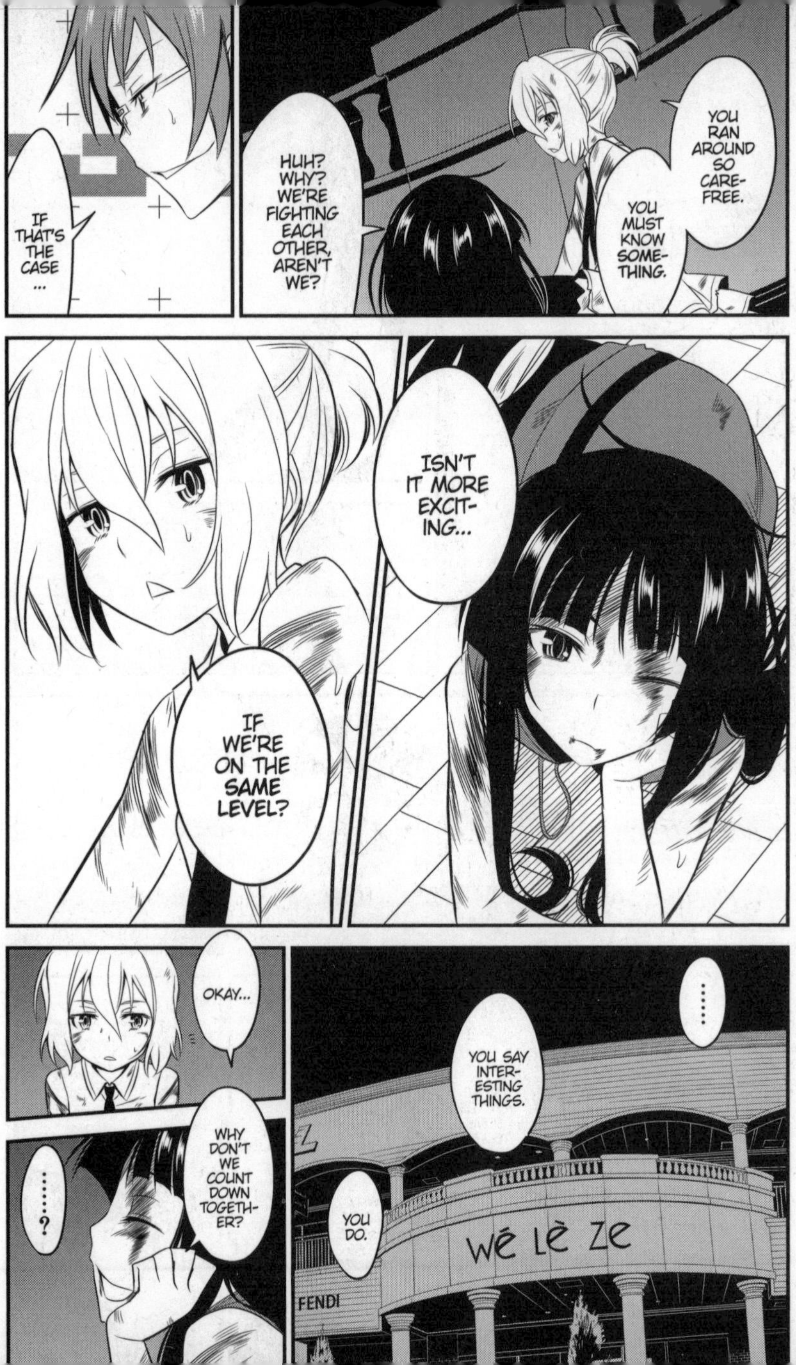
YOU RAN AROUND SO CARE-FREE.
YOU MUST KNOW SOME-THING.
HUH? WHY? WE'RE FIGHTING EACH OTHER, AREN'T WE?
IF THAT'S THE CASE ...
ISN'T IT MORE EXCIT-ING...
IF WE'RE ON THE SAME LEVEL?
......
YOU SAY INTER-ESTING THINGS.
YOU DO.
wé lè ze
FENDI
OKAY...
WHY DON'T WE COUNT DOWN TOGETH-ER?
......?

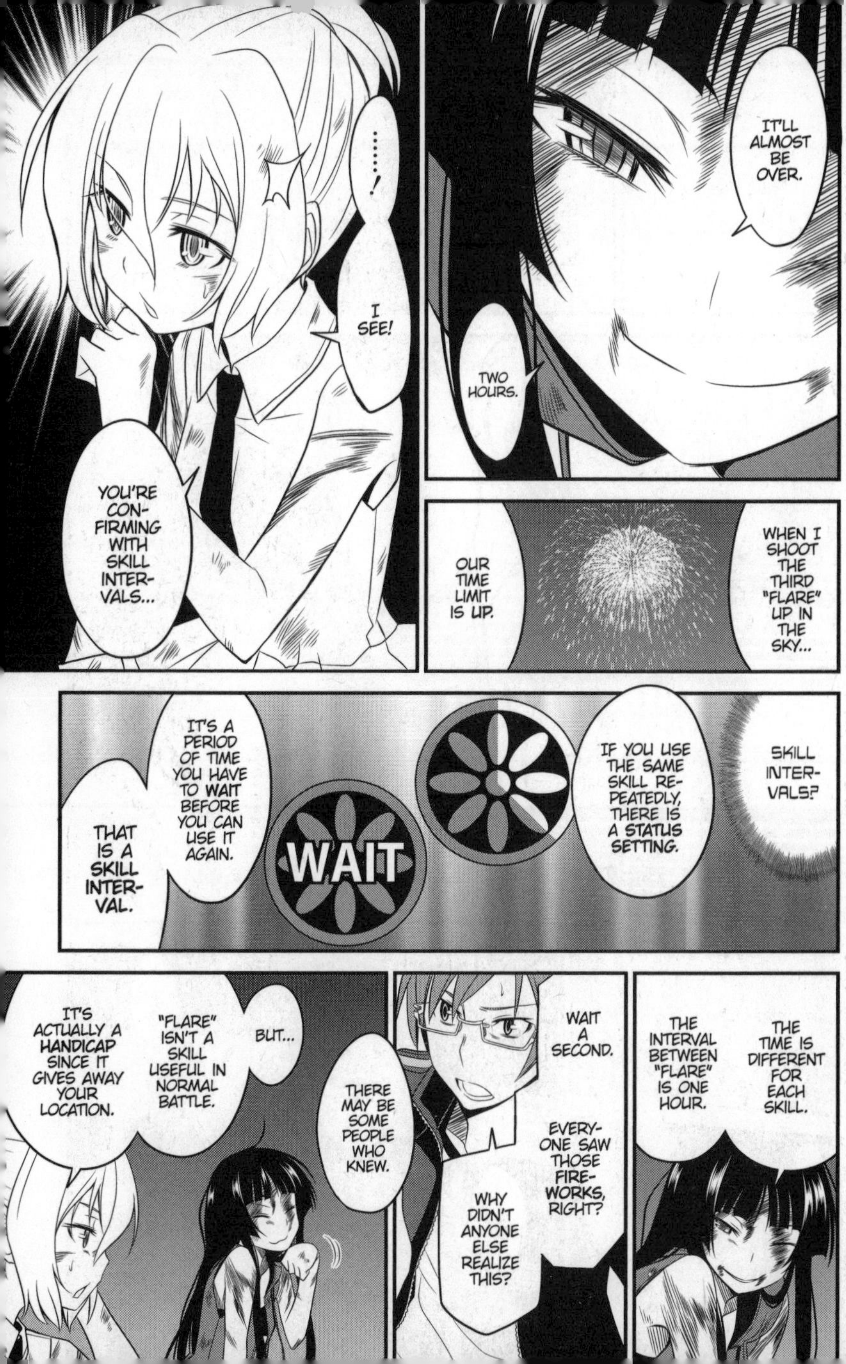
IT'LL ALMOST BE OVER.
TWO HOURS.
WHEN I SHOOT THE THIRD "FLARE" UP IN THE SKY...
OUR TIME LIMIT IS UP.
......!
I SEE!
YOU'RE CON-FIRMING WITH SKILL INTER-VALS...
SKILL INTER-VALS?
IF YOU USE THE SAME SKILL RE-PEATEDLY, THERE IS A STATUS SETTING.
WAIT
IT'S A PERIOD OF TIME YOU HAVE TO WAIT BEFORE YOU CAN USE IT AGAIN.
THAT IS A SKILL INTER-VAL.
THE TIME IS DIFFERENT FOR EACH SKILL.
THE INTERVAL BETWEEN "FLARE" IS ONE HOUR.
WAIT A SECOND.
EVERY-ONE SAW THOSE FIRE-WORKS, RIGHT?
WHY DIDN'T ANYONE ELSE REALIZE THIS?
THERE MAY BE SOME PEOPLE WHO KNEW.
BUT...
"FLARE" ISN'T A SKILL USEFUL IN NORMAL BATTLE.
IT'S ACTUALLY A HANDICAP SINCE IT GIVES AWAY YOUR LOCATION.

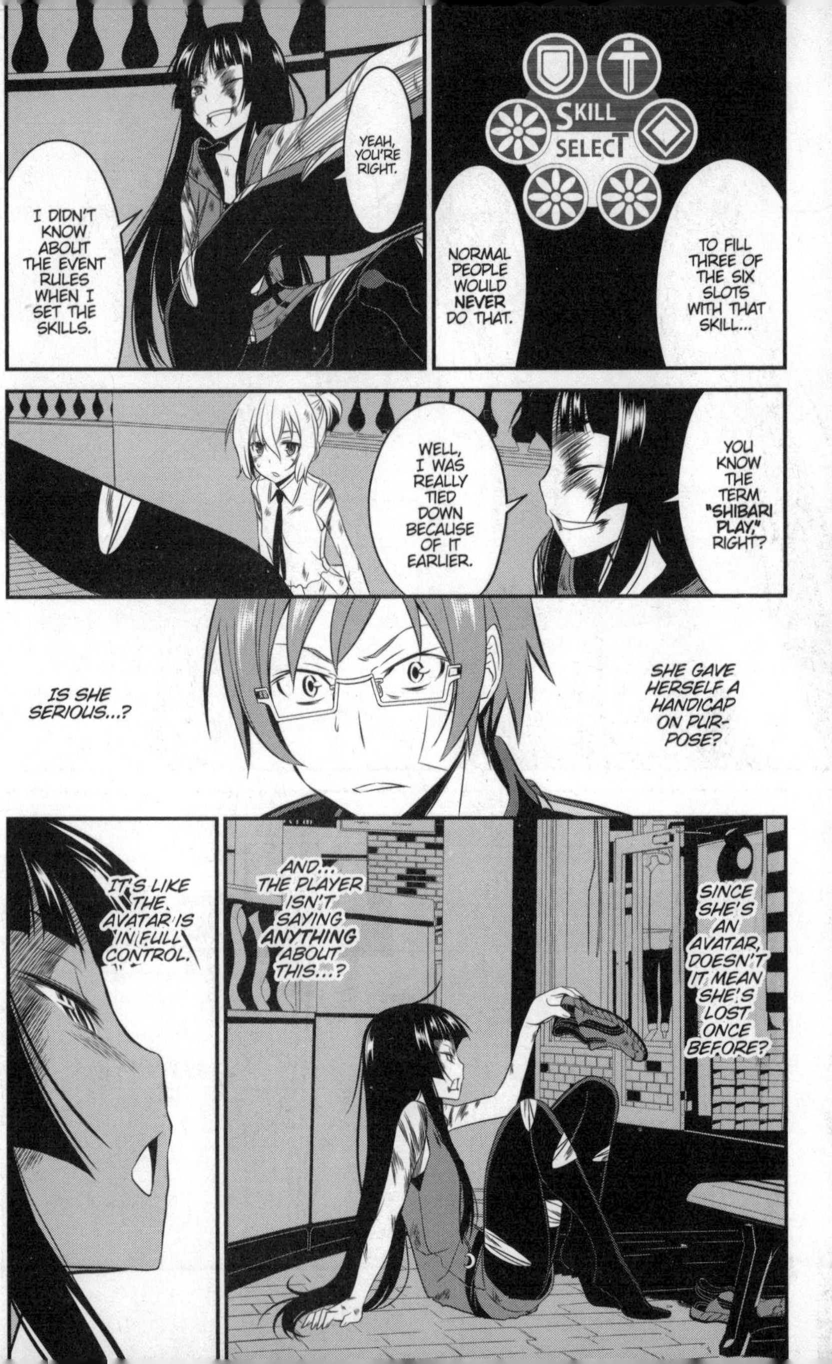
SKILL SELECT
TO FILL THREE OF THE SIX SLOTS WITH THAT SKILL...
NORMAL PEOPLE WOULD NEVER DO THAT.
YEAH, YOU'RE RIGHT.
I DIDN'T KNOW ABOUT THE EVENT RULES WHEN I SET THE SKILLS.
YOU KNOW THE TERM "SHIBARI PLAY," RIGHT?
WELL, I WAS REALLY TIED DOWN BECAUSE OF IT EARLIER.
SHE GAVE HERSELF A HANDICAP ON PURPOSE?
IS SHE SERIOUS...?
SINCE SHE'S AN AVATAR, DOESN'T IT MEAN SHE'S LOST ONCE BEFORE?
AND... THE PLAYER ISN'T SAYING ANYTHING ABOUT THIS...?
IT'S LIKE THE AVATAR IS IN FULL CONTROL.

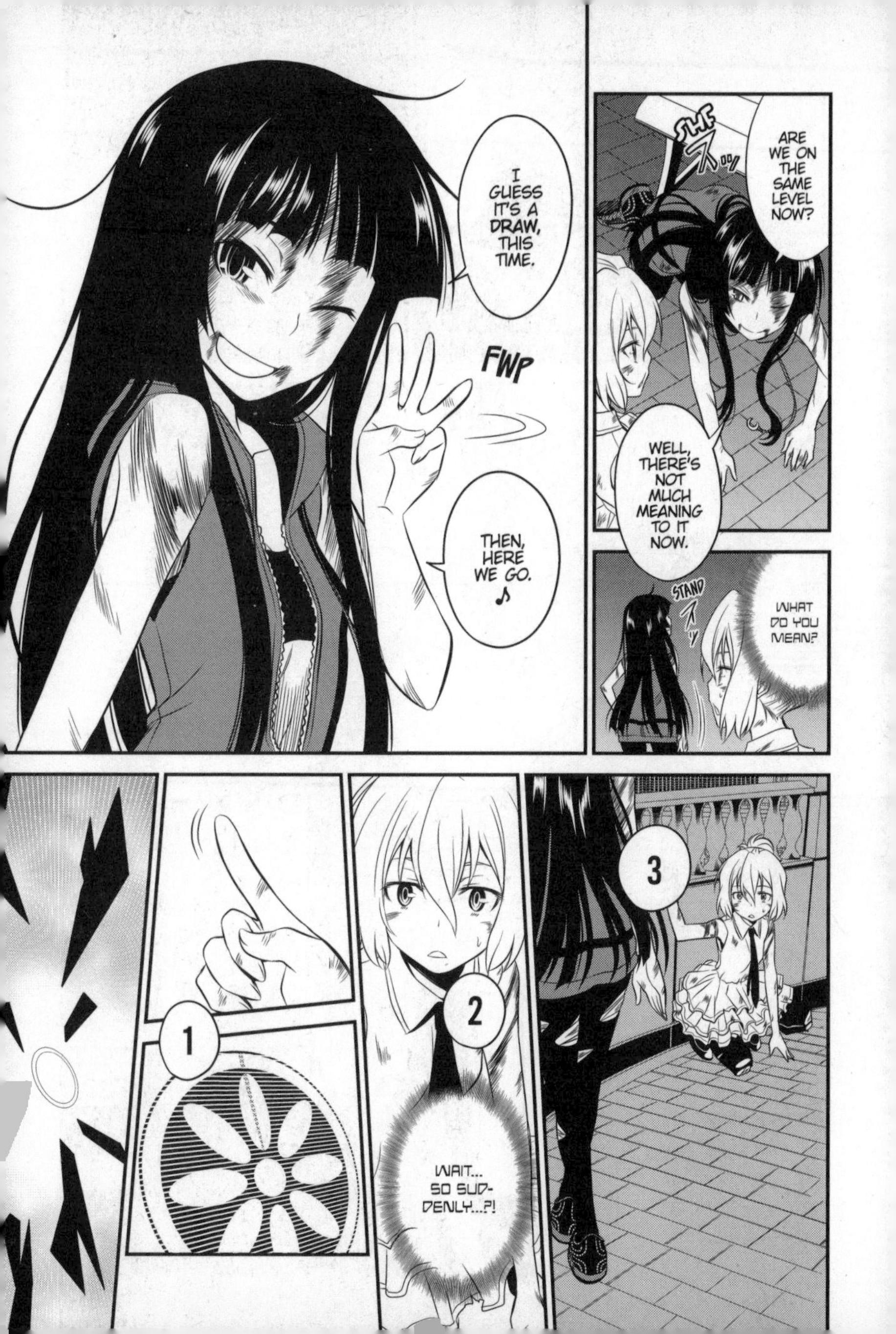
SHF
ARE WE ON THE SAME LEVEL NOW?
WELL, THERE'S NOT MUCH MEANING TO IT NOW.
STAND
WHAT DO YOU MEAN?
I GUESS IT'S A DRAW, THIS TIME.
FWP
THEN, HERE WE GO. ♪
3
2
WAIT... SO SUD-DENLY...?!
1

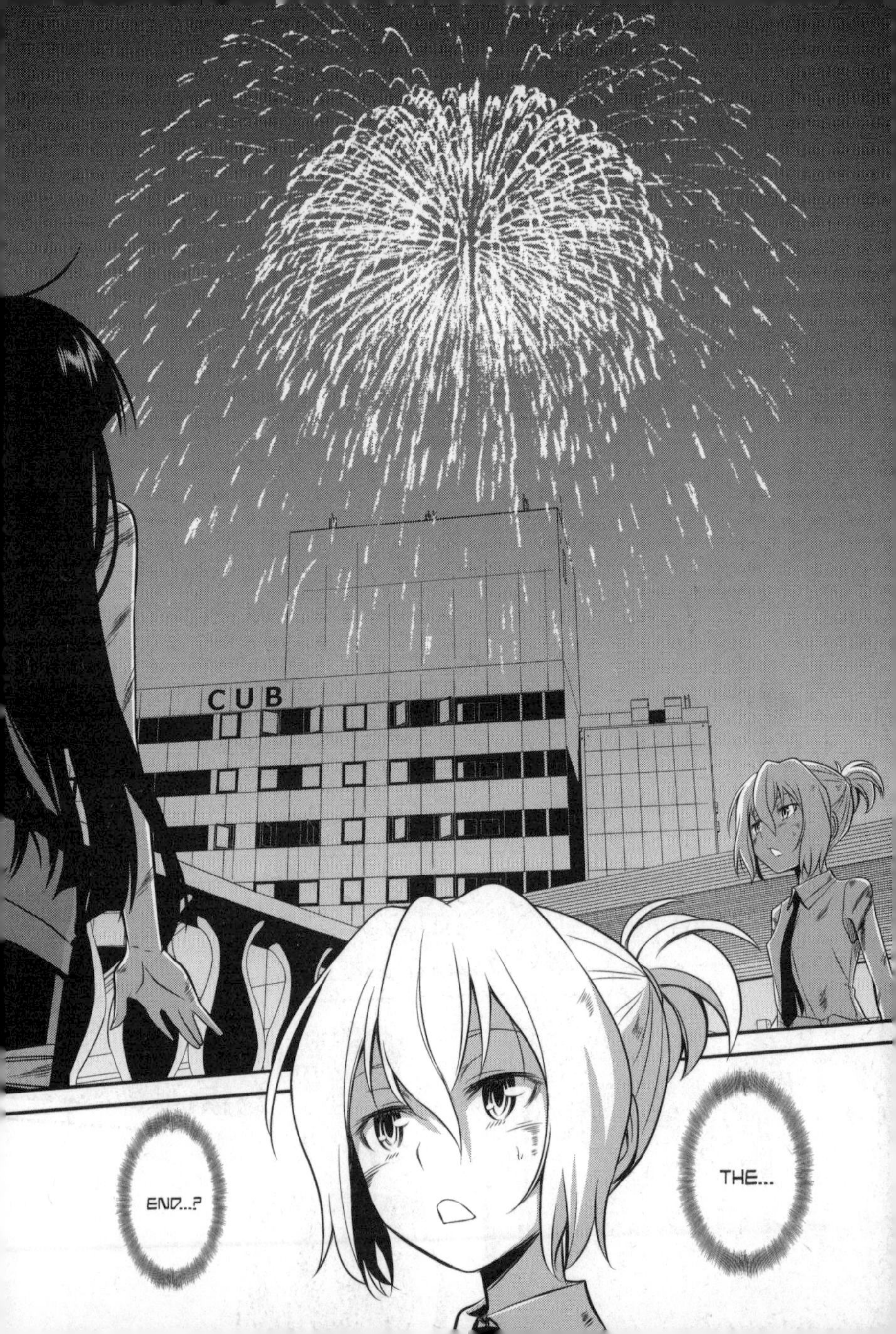
CUB
THE...
END...?

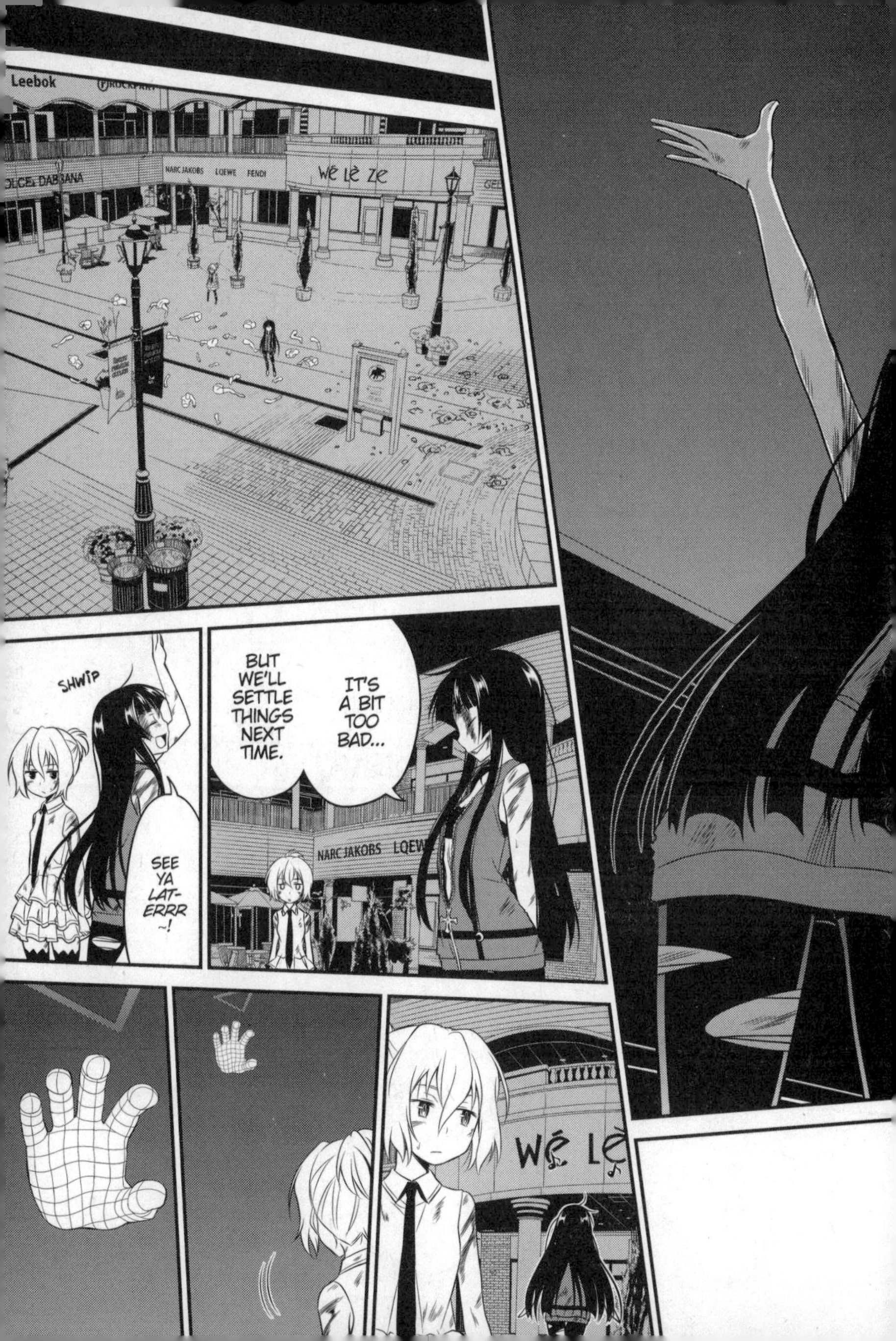
Leebok
NARC JAKOBS
LOEWE
FENDI
Wé lè ze
IT'S A BIT TOO BAD...
BUT WE'LL SETTLE THINGS NEXT TIME.
NARC JAKOBS
SHWIP
SEE YA LATERRR ~!

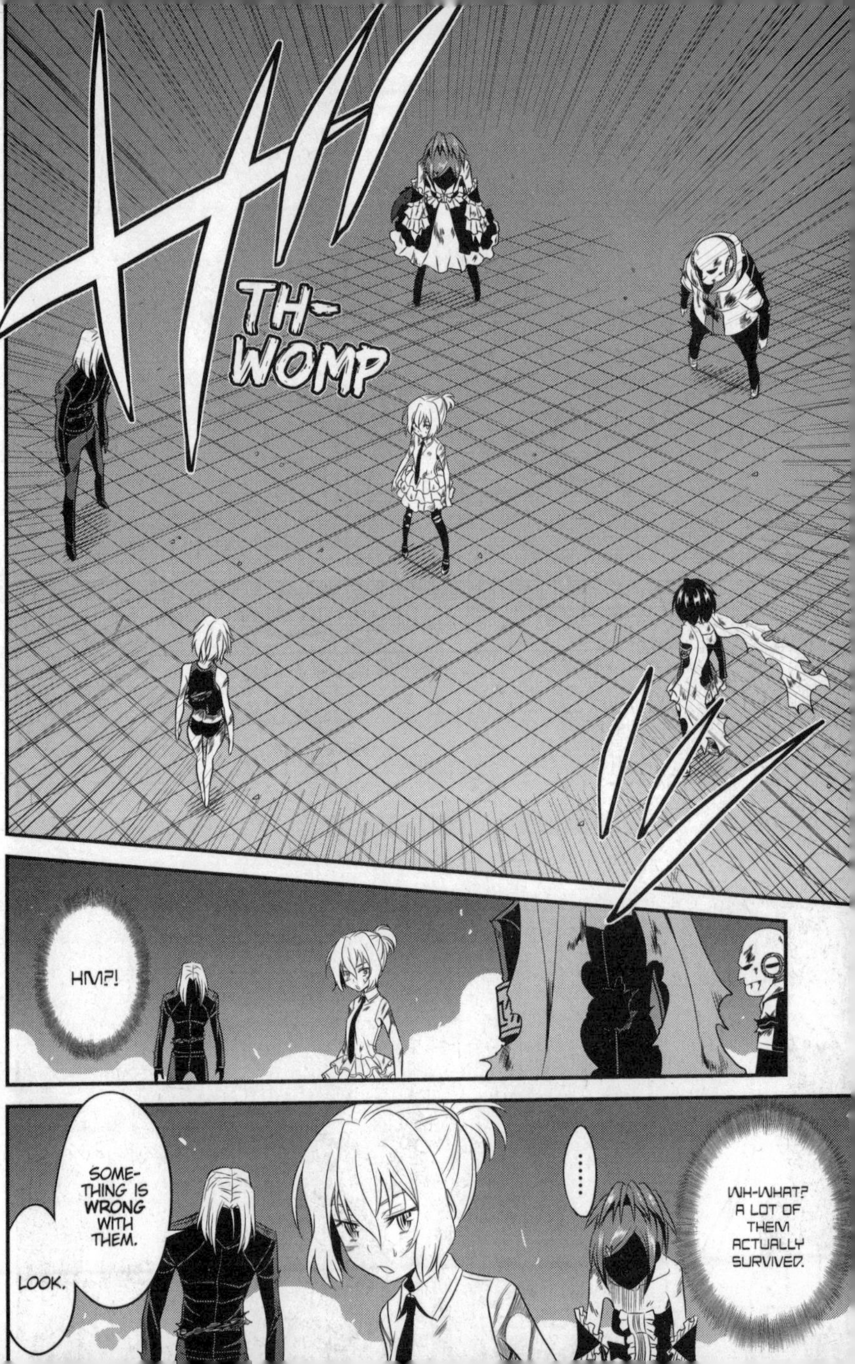
TH-WOMP
HM?!
WH-WHAT? A LOT OF THEM ACTUALLY SURVIVED.
......
SOME-THING IS WRONG WITH THEM.
LOOK.

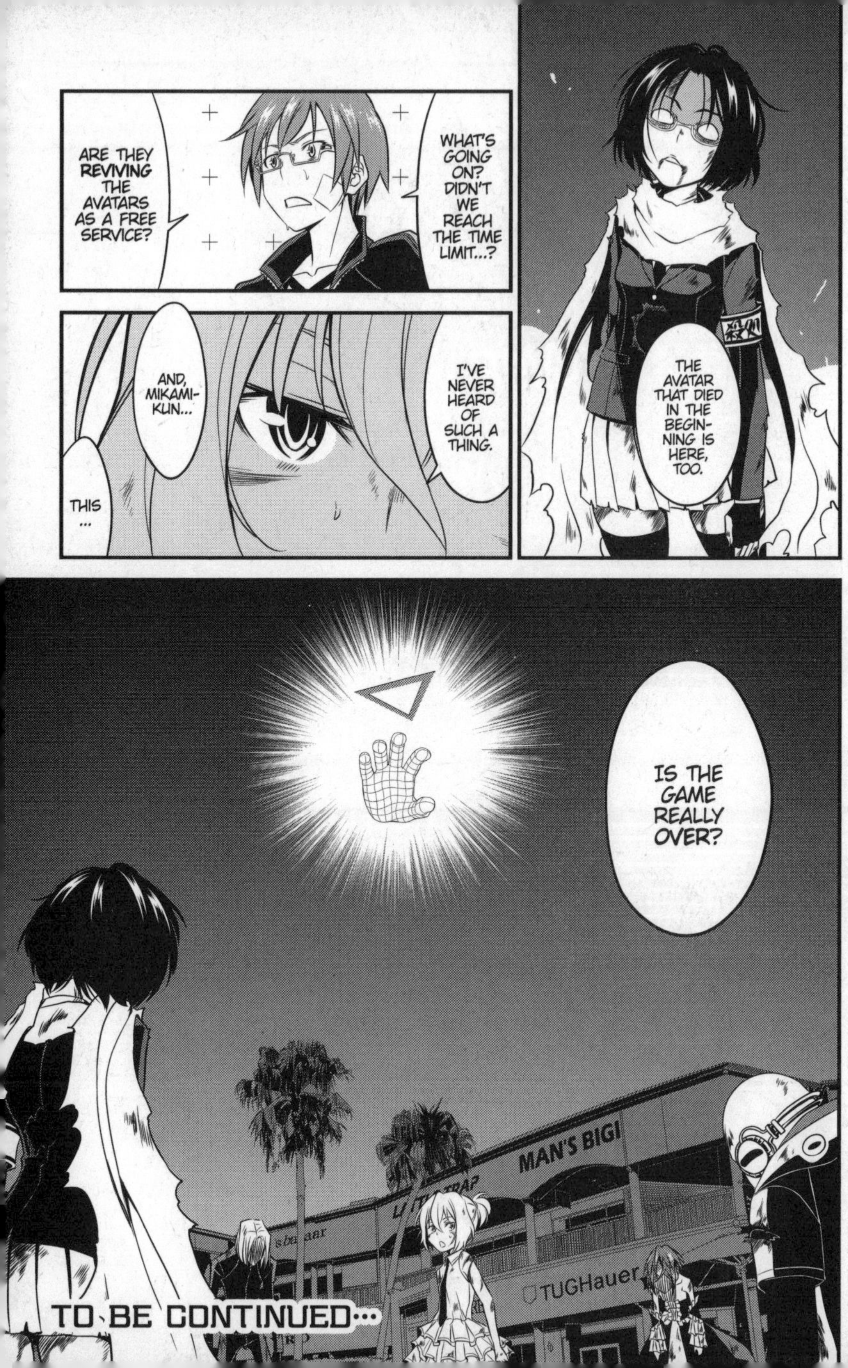
THE AVATAR THAT DIED IN THE BEGINNING IS HERE, TOO.
WHAT'S GOING ON? DIDN'T WE REACH THE TIME LIMIT...?
ARE THEY **REVIVING** THE AVATARS AS A FREE SERVICE?
I'VE NEVER HEARD OF SUCH A THING.
AND, MIKAMI-KUN...
THIS...
IS THE GAME REALLY OVER?
MAN'S BIGI
TUGHauer
TO BE CONTINUED...

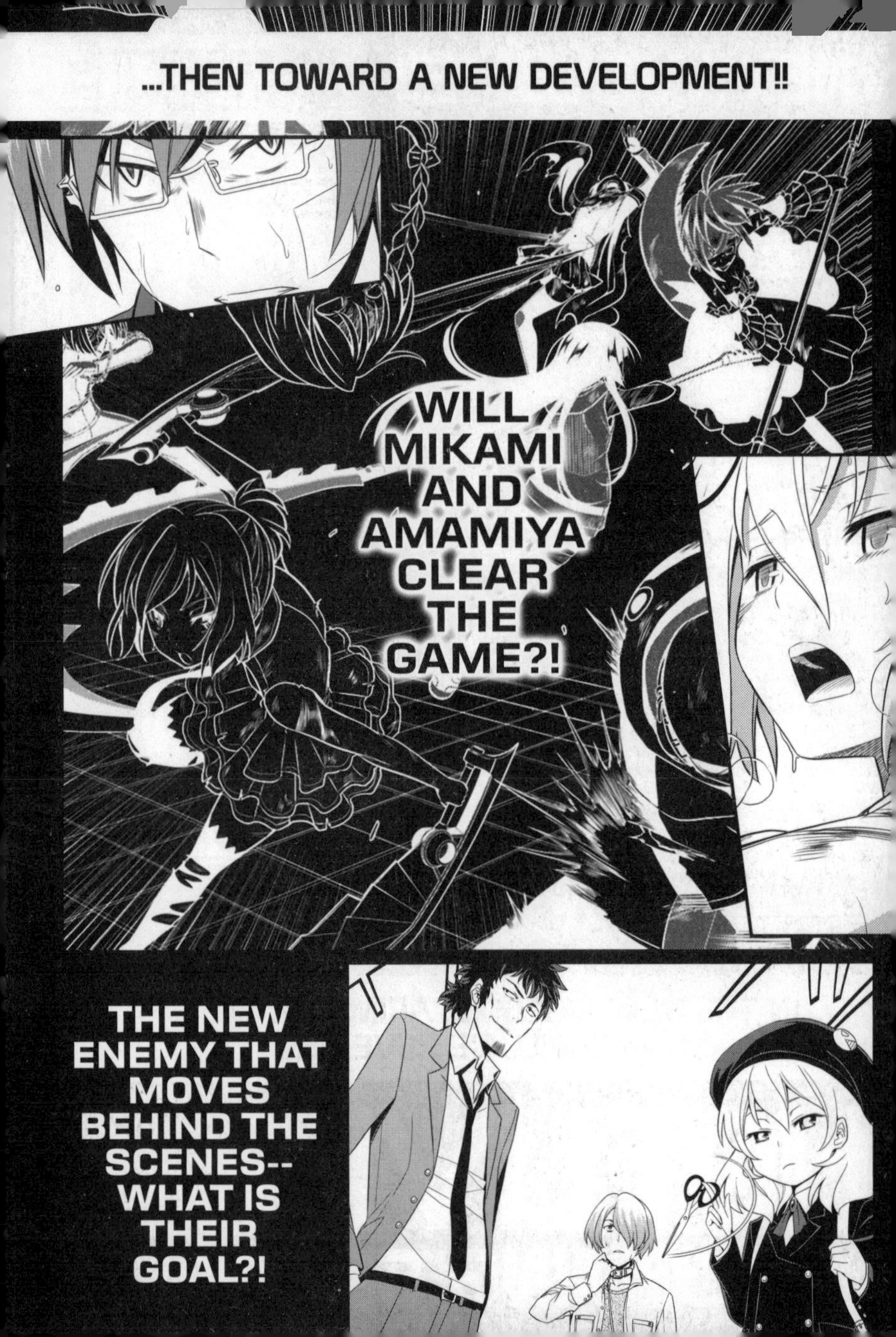
...THEN TOWARD A NEW DEVELOPMENT!!
WILL MIKAMI AND AMAMIYA CLEAR THE GAME?!
THE NEW ENEMY THAT MOVES BEHIND THE SCENES-- WHAT IS THEIR GOAL?!

# NEXT VOLUME!!

## THE END OF THE BATTLE ROYALE...

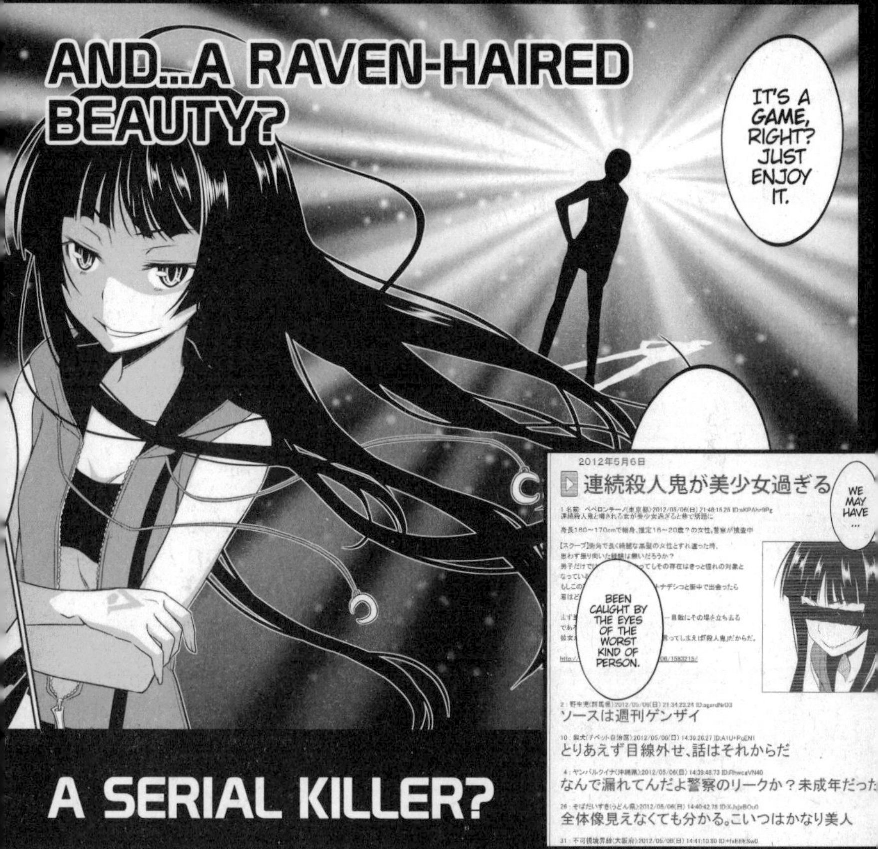
AND...A RAVEN-HAIRED BEAUTY?
IT'S A GAME, RIGHT? JUST ENJOY IT.
2012年5月6日
連続殺人鬼が美少女過ぎる
WE MAY HAVE...
BEEN CAUGHT BY THE EYES OF THE WORST KIND OF PERSON.
ソースは週刊ゲンザイ
とりあえず目線外せ、話はそれからだ
なんで漏れてんだよ警察のリークか？未成年だった
全体像見えなくても分かる。こいつはかなり美人
A SERIAL KILLER?

**IN THE NEXT VOLUME, ARIMA AKANE'S SECRET WILL BE REVEALED!**

# N0TLIVES 04

# COMING SOON!!

SEVEN SEAS ENTERTAINMENT PRESENTS

# NOT LIVES

story and art by WATARU KARASUMA

VOLUME 3

TRANSLATION
**Angela Liu**

ADAPTATION
**Steven Golebiewski**

LETTERING AND LAYOUT
**James Adams**

COVER DESIGN
**Nicky Lim**

PROOFREADER
**Danielle King**
**Tim Roddy**

PRODUCTION MANAGER
**Lissa Pattillo**

EDITOR-IN-CHIEF
**Adam Arnold**

PUBLISHER
**Jason DeAngelis**

NOT LIVES VOL. 3

First published in Japan in 2013 by KADOKAWA CORPORATION, Tokyo.
English translation rights arranged with KADOKAWA CORPORATION, Tokyo.



ISBN: 978-1-626923-14-0

Printed in Canada

First Printing: August 2016

10 9 8 7 6 5 4 3 2 1

FOLLOW US ONLINE: ***www.gomanga.com***

## READING DIRECTIONS

This book reads from ***right to left***, Japanese style. If this is your first time reading manga, you start reading from the top right panel on each page and take it from there. If you get lost, just follow the numbered diagram here. It may seem backwards at first, but you'll get the hang of it! Have fun!!

1
2
3
4
5
6
7
8
9

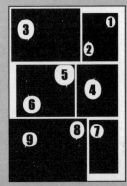

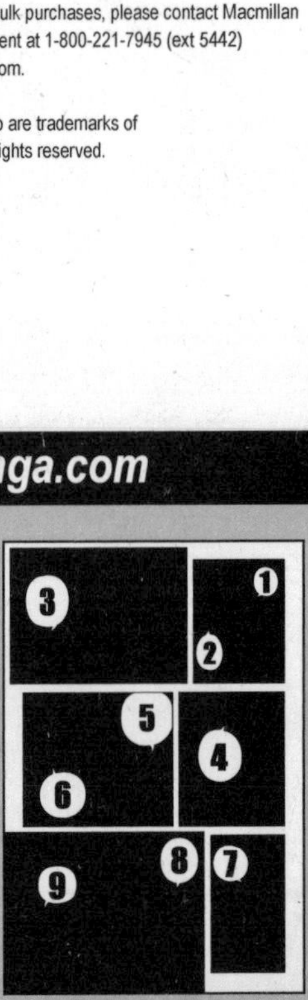